Dearest Jean

MANCHESTER
1824

Manchester University Press

Dearest Jean

Rose Macaulay's letters to a cousin

MARTIN FERGUSON SMITH

Manchester
University Press

The right of Martin Ferguson Smith to be identified as the author of this work has been asserted by him in accordance with the Copyright, Designs and Patents Act 1988.

Published by Manchester University Press
Altrincham Street, Manchester M1 7JA, UK
www.manchesteruniversitypress.co.uk

British Library Cataloguing-in-Publication Data is available

ISBN 978 1 5261 2300 8 *paperback*

First published by Manchester University Press in hardback 2011

This edition first published 2017

Printed by Lightning Source

Contents

List of illustrations

Editor's preface

'Take my camel, dear,' said my aunt Dot, as she climbed down from this animal on her return from High Mass.

Few twentieth-century novels have more memorable opening words than *The Towers of Trebizond*, published in 1956. The last of Rose Macaulay's books, it was a literary sensation at the time, making headlines like 'Mad Camel Plays a Big Part in Unusual Book', proving a big hit with members of the British Royal Family, receiving much critical acclaim, and winning a major book-prize. Half a century after the author's death, it continues to be read and enjoyed, but much of her other work is comparatively neglected, and the fiftieth anniversary of her death (30 October 2008) passed virtually unnoticed.

This neglect is undeserved. Rose was one of the most versatile, influential, and successful writers of the first half of the twentieth century, admired for her powers of observation, description, and imagination, and for her cleverness, wisdom, satire, and wit. In a writing career that spanned fifty years, she produced twenty-three novels, six volumes of essays and criticism, five volumes (one published posthumously) of travel and history, two of poetry, and an anthology. She wrote many hundreds of articles and reviews for newspapers and magazines and made numerous contributions to BBC radio programmes.

As a thinker and writer, she was not only of her time but also in some ways ahead of it. A notable example of this is her portrayal of men and women in her novels. Many of her characters do not conform to conventional types of masculinity and femininity. Although not a feminist, she firmly believes in the common humanity and basic similarity of men and women. Like Daphne Sandomir, a character in her anti-war novel published in the middle of the Great War, 'she didn't draw distinctions, beyond the necessary ones, between women and men; she took women as human beings, not as life-producing organisms; she took men as human beings, not as destroying-machines' (*Non-Combatants and Others* 268). Her belief that women and men are essentially alike is reflected in the frequent assignment of male names to females and vice versa and in the use of names that are gender-neutral. Although her novels are novels, not sociological treatises, her rejection of sexual stereotyping in her explorations of human relationships is of great interest and importance and is one of the many reasons why she deserves much more attention than she receives today.

In addition to the writings Rose produced for publication, she wrote numerous letters. These were almost always penned rapidly, often on trains, in a hand that was not easily legible even at the best of times. As one would expect, they are not literary masterpieces, but what they lack in craftsmanship and polish they make up for in freshness, vitality, variety, candour, and humour. In them we can 'hear' Rose 'talking' as she might in an actual conversation face to face or on the telephone.

The present collection of letters, previously unpublished and unknown, nicely complements and supplements the two collections of letters published soon after Rose's death in 1958 by her third cousin Constance Babington Smith. These are the letters she wrote to Hamilton Johnson, an Anglican priest in Boston, Massachusetts, in the last eight years of her life, and to her sister Jeanie Macaulay between 1926 and 1958. The 'new' letters, written to Jean Smith, a first cousin ten years her junior, span a longer period (1913–1958) than those in the published collections, and more than half of them were written between 1919 and 1926, a very important period in Rose's life and career and one not covered in any other collection of her letters, published or (to the best of my knowledge) unpublished. The later letters in the new collection are valuable too, for in many years no letters to Jeanie survive, and in any case what Rose wrote to Jean was usually very different from what she wrote to her sister.

Babington Smith's publication of Rose's letters aroused considerable controversy at the time, both within the family and outside it. Rose had wanted all private letters, with the sole exception of those she exchanged with Gilbert Murray, destroyed. There is no doubt at all that she would have been implacably opposed to their preservation and publication. The controversy about the publication of the letters to Father Johnson was particularly intense, given that they were addressed to a priest, to whom the writer was disclosing, as to a confessor, matters that troubled her conscience, notably the secret love-affair she had had with Gerald O'Donovan, a married man and former Roman Catholic priest, for 24 years, from 1918 until his death in 1942. Under the headline 'Did this priest betray this woman?', *The Daily Mail* reported the outraged reaction of some of Rose's friends, including that of Rebecca West: 'It made me want to vomit. That this could happen to my dear Rose and against her known wishes fills me with infinite disgust.' Another who disapproved was E.M. Forster. But other friends, including Raymond Mortimer in *The Sunday Times* and Harold Nicolson in *The Observer*, welcomed publication.

What Babington Smith did was brave, and yet she exercised considerable restraint in her editing of Rose's letters – necessarily so, because so many people mentioned in them were still alive to be hurt and perhaps even to sue for libel. So she made many omissions. In the case of the letters to Father Johnson, we shall have to wait until 12 June 2012 to read the censored passages. But no embargo was placed on the original letters to Jeanie Macaulay, and looking up the passages deemed unsuitable for publication in 1964 can be rather entertaining. For example, when, on the subject of *The Towers of Trebizond*, Rose mentions that Princess Margaret 'kept reading bits of it aloud to her companions', the editor felt obliged to suppress the following words: 'especially she liked the bits about adultery'. The cuts in the published letters to Jeanie are much more numerous and extensive than those in the letters to Father Johnson, involving not only anything that 'might cause embarrassment to living persons' but also passages that were judged to be repetitious or trivial; indeed a significant number of letters, including 14 of the first 24 preserved, are omitted in their entirety.

The present collection comprises all the surviving letters from Rose to Jean Smith, and each letter is printed without any cuts at all. So long after Rose's death, it is unlikely that publication of anything she has written will cause any embarrassment. As for repetitions and trivialities, which certainly exist, it seems best to preserve them not only to show that Rose can be repetitious and trivial (sometimes annoyingly, often attractively), but also because they reflect the conversational character of her letter-writing and illuminate her character. Suppression of them would have altered the balance and flavour of individual letters and of the whole collection.

Rose's biographers make little or no mention of Jean Smith, but, as the letters reveal, the two were deeply attached to one another and were particularly close until the late 1920s. Unlike sister Jeanie, cousin Jean was an intellectual, who had a university education, was private secretary to the famous Greek scholar Gilbert Murray after the First World War, and wrote poetry, and their shared literary and intellectual interests are reflected in the letters. Rose communicates news of her own writings, finished, current, and projected, and her frank opinions of other writers and their works. Some of the revelations and comments are surprising. For example: she confesses to 'a gross fraud' that involved making her sister Margaret review some books under her (Rose's) signature (*L*41); commenting on Storm Jameson's first novel, she is under the misapprehension that the author is a man (*L*4: 'I daresay he's been crossed in love, or beaten by a woman in some excoriation'); Raymond Mortimer, who was to become one of her dearest friends, is described, admittedly in a letter written before they had met, as 'a bumptious and offensive youth' (*L*32); as for George Bernard Shaw, 'what an old silly [he] was in many ways, and *how* untruthful' (*L*103).

Many of the leading writers of the day make appearances, ranging from the substantial to the fleeting, in the 'new' letters. They include J.D. Beresford, John Betjeman, Amber Blanco-White (Reeves), Edmund Blunden, Elizabeth Bowen, G.K. Chesterton, Clemence Dane, Walter de la Mare, Lawrence Durrell, T.S. Eliot, E.M. Forster, John Galsworthy, Douglas Goldring, Robert Graves, Graham Greene, A.P. Herbert, Katharine Hinkson (Tynan), Pamela Hinkson, Aldous Huxley, Sheila Kaye-Smith, Robert and Sylvia Lynd, A.A. Milne, Nancy Mitford, Henry Newbolt, Robert Nichols, Ezra Pound, Naomi Royde-Smith,

Edward Shanks, the Sitwells, J.C. Squire, Freya Stark, G.B. Stern, Edward Thomas, Helen Waddell, Evelyn Waugh, H.G. Wells, Rebecca West, Romer Wilson, Humbert Wolfe, Virginia Woolf, and Francis Brett Young.

The letters describe and discuss a great number and variety of people, events, topics, opinions, and places. As one would expect in correspondence with a first cousin, there is much talk of family. This can be amusing as well as vivid, like the report of the quick-fire cross-examination of Rose's sister Eleanor by their aunt Frances Conybeare (*L*16) and the description of a family gathering in Scotland attended also by 'the absurd Mr Impey', who contributed to 'a lovely comedy' (*L*54). Rose is sometimes critical of relations, but the overall impression is of her keen interest in family members and of her affection for them. The same is true of her attitude to her numerous friends.

In June 1927 Rose confided in Jean about her affair with Gerald O'Donovan, entrusting her with a secret that Jean was to keep faithfully. She mentions him in several letters, without giving any indication that he is anything more than a very good friend, until, writing in February 1942, just after Gerald has been diagnosed with incurable cancer and given only a few months to live, she admits to 'a queer dazed feeling – a sudden precipice yawning across a road that has run for nearly 25 years' (*L*78).

Rose, who had spent part of her childhood in Italy, quite often went abroad during her adult life. She describes to Jean visits not only to Italy but also to France, Switzerland, Mallorca, Spain, Portugal, Cyprus, and Turkey. Of special interest are her letters from Geneva, where she was attending the Second Assembly of the League of Nations in September 1921 (*L*26), and from Trebizond in June 1954 (*L*98). She had a particular love of Italy and the Italians. Her admitted dislike of Indians (*L*75) and Turks (*L*98, 100) seems rather harsh, given that she never went to India and visited Turkey only briefly and did not speak the language. The fact is that she had her contradictions and, while usually broadminded and open, could be narrow-minded and prejudiced. This less attractive side of her is manifested also in the hostility she showed after 1950, when she returned to being a communicant member of the Anglican Church, to Roman Catholicism or at least to a dogmatic brand of it that she regarded as unenlightened. Jean, who had become a Roman Catholic in 1933, was to be on the receiving end of criticism.

In the letters to Jean there is a marked contrast between the earnest treatment of religion in the late ones and the more light-hearted approach, taken in the earlier ones, of one who once described herself as 'a High Church agnostic'. *L*21 (2 August 1920), in which she reports a discussion, at one of Naomi Royde-Smith's soirées, of the relationship between Christianity and civilisation, is particularly entertaining. One of those who spoke up strongly for Christianity was G.K. Chesterton, who 'enjoyed himself hugely, and broke the springs of the settee on which we had arranged he was not to sit. . . . He is really rather a darling. And it's so nice when people are so sure of what they believe.' When Rose adds that 'the Anglican Fellowship hadn't a notion what it believed', one cannot help thinking that her comment has a remarkably modern (early twenty-first century) ring to it.

Items of daily news on which Rose comments range from events in the Second World War to the extraordinary case of John Wakeford, who in 1921 was accused, under the Clergy Discipline Act, of immoral conduct (*L*24). Another mystery discussed by Rose is that of who had fathered the illegitimate daughter of Jean's and her friend Madeleine Symons, a much-respected trade unionist and social reformer (*L*65). In 1926, not long after a national newspaper had published a false report of her marriage (*L*57), Madeleine's trade-union career was terminated by pregnancy and motherhood. The identity of the father, a married man and prominent public figure, is revealed, apparently for the first time, in the present volume.

Rose's surviving letters to Jean certainly do not comprise all those she wrote, but there is no way of knowing how many are lost. The number is likely be considerable, given that we have virtually nothing prior to 1919, and nothing at all from 1922, 1931–1932, 1934, 1936, 1939–1941, 1945, and 1948–1949. At the same time it is probable that the volume of correspondence between the two did diminish after the late 1920s, partly because their relationship, although still very affectionate, was less close than before, partly because from 1940 onwards Jean, like Rose, had a flat in London, so that it was easy for them to meet or communicate by telephone. Likewise, both were working in London throughout 1917–1918, and during Jean's undergraduate years in Cambridge, 1911–1915, she was frequently seeing Rose, who was living just a few miles away.

Only two letters from Jean to Rose survive. They are preserved because Jean typed them and retained carbon copies. They are included in the present collection (*L*102, 107) together with one letter from Rose to Jean's brother Jim (*L*100).

Appendix I contains three letters, previously unpublished and unknown, written by Rose's parents in the early days and weeks of her life.

I conclude by expressing two hopes. The first is that Rose's ghost, now over fifty years old, will forgive her first cousin, once removed, for making public these letters she wrote to his aunt. It is his belief that they are of interest and value, and that, although they reveal some prejudices, overhasty judgements, and egoism (features that add to their interest), the picture they present of both writer and addressee is a favourable one. He only met Rose on one occasion, when he was aged 14, but he now feels that he knows her rather well, and with growth of knowledge has come growth of affection. The second hope is that the publication of the letters may help to encourage a renewal of interest in her and her books.

M.F.S.
Isle of Foula, Shetland Islands
June 2010

Editor's preface to the paperback edition

When it first appeared in 2011, *Dearest Jean* was given a favourable reception, and this edition, issued in good time for the sixtieth anniversary of Rose Macaulay's death (30 October 2018), contains no substantial changes, but the opportunity has been taken to make some minor corrections and updates and to augment the list of books about the author (p. 282).

In 2011 the fifty-year embargo on access to Rose's letters to Father Hamilton Johnson was still in force (p. viii). The letters had been published in bowdlerised form by Constance Babington Smith in 1961–1962, and naturally I was keen to read the passages that were deemed unsuitable for publication soon after Rose's death. Indeed, such was my keenness that I booked my place at the front of any queue to see the letters in the Wren Library of Trinity College, Cambridge, more than eighteen months in advance of their release on 12 June 2012. Anticipating that the project would be more enjoyable and productive if it were a collaborative one, I invited Rose's biographer Sarah LeFanu to join me, and luckily she agreed. So, when the Wren Library opened to readers that day, the two of us were waiting at the door, wondering in particular what frank revelations about Rose's long-running affair with her married lover, Gerald O'Donovan, might be awaiting us.

Our first day's work was interrupted for four and half hours by a bomb alert. While bombs fell on London during the Second World War, Rose worked as a volunteer ambulance driver; her flat was destroyed by a bomb; and her first post-war novel, *The World My Wilderness*, is partly set in the bombed-out area around St Paul's Cathedral. Given that she had a mischievous streak and would have been horrified at the idea of her letters to Father Johnson being read by anyone other than their addressee, it was tempting to believe that her ghost was behind the hoax. Speculation that research on a deceased wartime writer can provoke an incident that requires the attention of the emergency services was given added credibility during the week that followed. On 14 June Sarah and I were joined in Cambridge by Lara Feigel, seeking material for her book *The Love-charm of Bombs: Restless Lives in the Second World War* (London: Bloomsbury, 2013), about Rose, Graham Greene, and three other writers who lived and worked in wartime London. On 19 June her and John Sutherland's new book *Stephen*

Spender: New Selected Journals, 1939–1995 was launched at a meeting in the Senate House of the University of London. From 1941 Spender was employed as an auxiliary fireman. The book launch itself proceeded smoothly, but the reception that immediately followed it was interrupted by a fire alarm, and the guests were evacuated to a courtyard, where, with typical British sang-froid, they continued partying as if nothing untoward had happened.

The story of what emerged from our reading of the unexpurgated letters to Hamilton Johnson has been entertainingly recounted by Sarah LeFanu in *Dreaming of Rose: A Biographer's Journal* (Bristol: SilverWood, 2013) 197–214, and a brief account will suffice here.

Although we made some unexpected discoveries, none of them were explosive or incendiary. Most of the omissions were made by Constance Babington Smith to avoid giving possible offence to living people. The most remarkable one is of all mention of Father Harry Whiteman, priest in charge of Grosvenor Chapel, Mayfair (see *L*95 n.8, p. 222). Rose was devoted to him and frequently refers to him in glowing terms. He played an important part in her spiritual life from early 1951, when she returned to active and enthusiastic membership of the Church of England. When editing her letters to Jean Smith, I was puzzled as to why, although he lived until 1981, his last appearance in *Crockford's Clerical Directory* is in the 1954–1955 edition. The answer, revealed by the letters to Father Johnson, is that he lost his faith and left the priesthood. He gave the news to Rose in a letter he wrote to her in mid-November 1954, and it is undoubtedly this to which Rose alludes at the end of *L*101 to Jean (p. 239), when she writes:

> I have had to-day rather a body-blow, metaphorically speaking, and feel slightly dazed. But it's all rather private.

Previously I conjectured that she had received bad news about the marriage of Gerald O'Donovan's son, Dermod, and his wife, Muriel. The conjecture seemed plausible, and in fact in the same letter to Father Johnson that reveals the sensational news of Father Whiteman (3 December 1954; ERM 12.169) there is also mention of concern about Muriel; but 'new' passages of the letters to Father Johnson show that worry about Muriel and Dermod's marital problems had been ongoing for several months. The systematic suppression of the references to Father Whiteman, made at his insistence, affects many letters and passages. It is ironic that, having done so much to restore Rose's faith in the Church, he lost it himself.

Hamilton Johnson too did some censorship of Rose's letters to him. There are four places where he used a pen to squiggle out a passage he must have regarded as particularly sensitive. Where he has done this in the letter of 9 January 1951 (ERM 12.9), one can decipher enough traces of some of the deleted text to get the gist of the passage and see that Rose is, in Sarah LeFanu's words, 'giving him no biography-changing revelation', but 'talking about the state of her soul'. At a fairly early stage of the correspondence she put him in the picture about her affair with Gerald O'Donovan, but she does not do this in the preserved letters. She may have done it in her letter of 27 November 1950 (ERM 12.4). This letter is incomplete, and was incomplete when Constance Babington Smith received it from Father Johnson. In her letter of 15 December 1950 (ERM 12.6) Rose thanks him for being so wise and understanding and for not having been surprised at her confession. She continues:

> I might have known that, of course. But when I wrote that rather difficult letter, I wasn't sure.

If she does not mean the missing section of her letter of 27 November 1950, she must be referring to another letter, which Father Johnson destroyed in its entirety. It is indeed possible that he destroyed several letters.

The uncensored letters to Father Johnson are more informative and interesting than the published ones, but, censored or uncensored, the collection is unlikely to be much to the taste of many readers, partly because of the frequent discussion of liturgical matters, partly because of the smugness with which the Anglican position is propounded and defended. Only in the late letters in *Dearest Jean* are Rose's ardent Anglicanism and her distaste for Roman Catholicism manifested, and there her remarks have the added interest of being addressed to a Roman Catholic.

Most readers of Rose Macaulay's letters are likely to agree with A.N. Wilson that the ones she wrote to Jean Smith are her best.

M.F.S.
Isle of Foula, Shetland
November 2016

Acknowledgements

I am very grateful to my cousin Veronica Babington Smith for her kind permission to publish the letters from Rose Macaulay to Jean Smith and to make use of other material of which she owned the copyright, and it is a matter of great regret and sadness for me that she did not live to see the publication of this book. I am equally grateful to my elder brother, Colin Ferguson Smith, Jean's surviving executor, not only for permission to publish the two surviving letters from Jean to Rose but also for passing the whole collection of correspondence to me and encouraging me to publish it. I received similar encouragement from the late Rosemary Smith, the widow of Jean's brother James ('Jim') Stewart Smith. She and Jim did some preliminary sorting of the letters during the years when they had custody of them after Jean's death in 1979. I am further indebted to Rosemary for passing to me notebooks and other papers of Jean and for writing, at my request, a brief biographical sketch of her. My first cousin Anne Saint Pierre kindly lent me Jean's two commonplace books (Introd. II.3) and has been generous with information.

The most extensive and important archive of letters and other papers by or about Rose Macaulay and her family is in the Wren Library of Trinity College, Cambridge, and I thank David McKitterick (Librarian) and his colleagues for their extraordinary helpfulness and hospitality.

Letters of Gilbert Murray and his wife, Lady Mary, are quoted by kind permission of Alexander Murray. The main collection of Murray's papers is in the Bodleian Library, Oxford, and these are cited in the form 'GM 90.124' (box 90, folio 124). Naomi Royde-Smith's diaries and letters are quoted by kind permission of the Society of Authors.

For supplying copies of letters of Rose Macaulay in their possession I thank the following: Nancy Nichols (letter of 26 October [1926] to Sylvia Lynd, her grandmother); Ana Vicente (letters to Luiz and Susan Marques, her parents); John Rylands University Library, University of Manchester (letters to Katharine Tynan Hinkson, cited as KTH 1/656/1–13); Morris Library, South Illinois University, Carbondale (letter of 13 April 1954 to Lawrence Durrell, collection no. 42); King's College Library, Cambridge (letters to E.M. Forster, John Maynard Keynes, Rosamond Lehmann, and J.T. Sheppard); The Henry W.

and Albert A. Berg Collection of English and American Literature, The New York Public Library Collection, Astor, Lenox and Tilden Foundations (letters to Humbert Wolfe).

For information about Gerald and Beryl O'Donovan and their family, as well as about Rose Macaulay, I owe much to Mary Anne O'Donovan and Muriel Thomas.

I have received generous assistance from many other sources. The libraries to which I am particularly indebted include Cambridge University Library (CUL), The Bodleian Library, Oxford, and Durham University Library. I owe special gratitude to Marjolein Wytzes and Neil Hudson of CUL, to Colin Harris, Lucy McCann, Emma Mathieson, and Christine Mason in the Bodleian, and to Judith Walton in Durham. I thank also: The British Library; National Archives, Kew; The London Library; Dr Williams's Library, London; Lambeth Palace Library; The National Library of Scotland; The Theatre Museum, Covent Garden; Glasgow University Archives Services; Bryn Mawr College, Pennsylvania; University of Wales, Cardiff; Queen Mary, University of London; Institute of Education, University of London; University of Reading, Special Collections; Marion E Wade Center, Wheaton College; Special Collections, Paley Library, Temple University, Philadelphia; Harry Ransom Humanities Research Center, University of Texas; the archivists of Downing, Emmanuel, Girton, Gonville and Caius, King's, Newnham, St John's, and Trinity Colleges of Cambridge University and of Balliol, Corpus Christi, Merton, Oriel, St John's, Somerville, and University Colleges of Oxford University; Cheltenham Ladies' College; Downe House School; Eton College; The Godolphin School, Salisbury; Lancing College; Malvern College; Repton School; Rugby School; Winchester College; Cambridge Archives Service; Penrith Library; British Federation of Women Graduates; English Association; Hawthornden Trust; Lincoln's Inn Library; Foreign and Commonwealth Office, London; Toynbee Hall, London; Society of Jesus, British Province; Westminster Diocesan Archives; British Medical Association; Royal Society of General Practitioners; Royal College of Nursing; Society for Psychical Research; Royal Agricultural Society of England; Radcliffe Meteorological Station, Oxford.

I wish also to thank the following individuals for their help and encouragement: Jane Abram, the late Roger Absalom, Pauline Adams, Neil Aiken, Sally Alexander, Michele Allan, Alan Argent, Helen Babington Smith, Bede Bailey, George Baker, Nicola Beauman, Aidan Bellenger, Jill Benton, Meg Beresford, Valerie and Michael Berkson, Jerome Bertram, Bonnie Blackburn, Ian Blakemore, Philip Bolam, Mike Bott, the late James Brabazon, Kate Bradley, David Braund, Tony Brown, Anthony Bryer, David Butterfield, Emily Cain, Niall Campbell, Dori Chamoun, Cecilia and Jeremy Chance, Victoria Chance, Anne and William Charlton, Val Considine, Margaret Copley (Tabor), the late Peter Copley, Michael Cotsell, Stuart Curran, Celia Denney, Cynthia Dove, Sally

Dowding, Katherine Duncan-Jones, Richard Duncan-Jones, Anne and Peter Duncumb, Margaret Duppa-Miller, David Fairer, Dermot Fenlon, Nicholas Fenn, Karen and Michael Fillingham, John Foot, Helen Forshaw, John Fraser, Simon Gaine, David Gill, the late John Gillum, Mary Rose Gillum, Michael Goater, John Gribben, Christopher Vorley Harris, Leofranc Holford-Strevens, the late Michael Houghton, David Howell, David Huntingford, Gerard Irvine, Joanna Jamieson, Simon Jenkins, Simon Johnson, Ted Kenney, Ursula King, Sarah LeFanu, Peter Lewis, Jack Lynch, Daniel McCarthy, Rohan McCullough, Brian Mastin, Kyi Kyi May, Joanna Matthews, Randle Meinertzhagen, Hans Mooij, Daw Tin Tin Myaing, Gwen Paton, Fiona Pritchard, Jane Redmond, Hugh Reid, Barbara Reynolds, Susan Reynolds, the late Peter Rossiter, Michael Royde Smith, Bonnie Kime Scott, Dominic Serra, John Sharp, Michael Sharratt, Michael Sherborne, Caroline Ferguson Smith, Ciara Barrett Smith, James Macaulay Smith, Jane Stuart Smith, Lucinda Ferguson Smith, Judith and William Stancomb, Sylvia Stoddart, Christopher Stray, Tom Taaffe, Hilde Thomas, Anne Thomson, Mary Totton, Peter van de Kamp, Ana Vicente, Angiola Volpi, Benedicta Ward, Justin Watkins, Hugh Whitemore, Deborah Wilkes.

Of those listed in the preceding paragraph, four have given me so much help on so many occasions that they almost qualify for the title 'research assistants'. They are: David Butterfield (Christ's College, Cambridge); Sister Helen Forshaw (Society of the Holy Child Jesus, Oxford); Lucinda Smith, my daughter; and Anne Thomson (Archivist of Newnham College, Cambridge). I am deeply grateful to them, and also to Jill Benton (Pitzer College, Claremont, California), who has been a mine of information about Naomi Royde-Smith, to Ana Vicente (Estoril, Portugal) for her generous interest and support, and to Sally Dowding, to whom this book is dedicated in profound appreciation of her unfailing encouragement of my research in many fields over many years.

Chronology

1878
1 April: George Campbell Macaulay is appointed assistant master at Rugby School.
10 October: George is elected Fellow of Trinity College, Cambridge, but remains in Rugby.
19 December: George marries Grace Mary Conybeare.

1880
23 March: George's and Grace's first child, Margaret Campbell Macaulay, is born in Rugby.

1881
1 August: Emilie Rose Macaulay is born at 11 Hillmorton Road, Rugby.
18 September: Rose is baptised in the Church of England.

1882
25 July: Jean ('Jeanie') Babington Macaulay is born in Rugby.

1883
3 September: Aulay Ferguson Macaulay is born in Rugby.

1884
22 November: William ('Will') John Conybeare Macaulay is born in Rugby.

1887
15 June: Eleanor Grace Macaulay is born in Rugby.
15 September: Macaulay family leaves Rugby.
20 October: Macaulay family leaves England.
26 October: Macaulay family arrives in Varazze, near Genoa, and agrees terms for the tenancy of a flat.

1888
9 October: Gertrude Mary Macaulay is born in Varazze.

1891

29 April: Macaulay family moves to Villa Levante (called Villa Macolai or Villa Inglese by the locals) in Varazze.

18 September: Jean Isabel Smith, the fourth (second surviving) child of Charles ('Charlie') Smith and Anne ('Nannie') Smith, *née* Macaulay, is born in Putney, London.

1892

17 April: Gertrude Macaulay dies in Varazze, aged 3½. Soon afterwards, Rose makes her first acquaintance with Venice.

1893

1 May: Uncle Harry (Henry William Macaulay) dies of fever in Muang Phrai, Siam, aged 36.

1894

July: Macaulay family returns to England.

13 August: Macaulay family takes 3 Clarendon Villas, Park Town, Oxford.

18 September: Rose becomes a pupil at Oxford High School for Girls.

1895

20 November: Rose is confirmed in the Church of England.

1896

September: Macaulay family moves to Thule, 350 Banbury Road, Summertown, Oxford.

1898

December: Rose's poem 'The Sea' is printed in *The Oxford High School Magazine* – her first publication.

1899

29 July: Rose leaves school.

1900

October: Rose enters Somerville College, Oxford, to read Modern History.

1901

September: George takes up appointment as Professor of English at University College of Wales, Aberystwyth.

5 December: Macaulay family moves into Ty-issa (Tŷ Isaf), between Llanfarian and Llanilar, near Aberystwyth.

1903

June: Rose leaves Somerville College with an aegrotat.

1905

March–April: Rose and Margaret in Italy with Uncles Willie and Kenneth.

27 May: Rose's rhymed 'Alphabet of Novelists' is printed in *Saturday Westminster Gazette*.

6 December: George is appointed Lecturer in English, Cambridge.

1906

24 April: George takes up his duties in Cambridge.

2 June: Macaulays agree to buy Southernwood, Great Shelford, near Cambridge, for £1,800.

7 July: Rose hears that John Murray will publish her first novel, provisionally entitled *The Aftermath*, provided that she lets in 'a gleam of light' at the end to relieve the gloom.

28 July: Macaulays gain possession of Southernwood.

3 October: Macaulays leave Ty-issa.

6 October: Macaulays move into Southernwood.

7 December: *Abbots Verney*.

1907

April: Rose and Margaret in Venice with Uncles Willie and Kenneth.

5 November: *The Furnace*.

1908

April: Rose on bicycling holiday in Italy with her father, Uncle Willie, and Margaret.

1909

11 February: Aulay is murdered in the North-West Frontier Province of India, aged 25.

13 February: News of Aulay's death reaches his family.

5 March: *The Secret River*.

1910

June: First meeting between Rose and Jean Smith and the start of their friendship.

15 October: Gerald O'Donovan marries Beryl Verschoyle.

1911

18 January: *The Valley Captives*.

15 May: Rose's first *recorded* meeting with Naomi Royde-Smith.

September: Macaulays sell their house in Varazze.

7 October: Jean goes up to Newnham College, Cambridge.

1912

8 February: *Views and Vagabonds.*

4–22 April: Rose and her father take a Hellenic cruise.

Late July: Rose wins first prize of £600, with *The Lee Shore*, in Hodder and Stoughton's £1,000 competition for the best novel.

August: Rose stays with Sir John Ross and family in co. Tyrone.

13 September: Eleanor goes to teach in India.

18 October: *The Lee Shore* is published.

1913

21 June: Margaret is ordained deaconess.

Before end of year: Rose acquires her first London flat, 19 Southampton Buildings, off Chancery Lane.

1914

2 March: *The Making of a Bigot.*

5 March: Margaret's novel, *The Sentence Absolute*, is published.

1 April: *The Two Blind Countries*, dedicated to Jean, is published.

30 June: Rose's flat-warming party, with Rupert Brooke, Walter de la Mare, and Naomi Royde-Smith among the guests.

17 July–25 September: Rose and her father visit Will in Canada.

4 August: Britain declares war on Germany.

1915

23 April: Rupert Brooke dies, aged 27.

Spring or summer. Rose gives up her London flat.

June: Rose takes part-time work in Red Cross auxiliary hospital at Mount Blow, Great Shelford.

14 June: Jean leaves Cambridge.

6 July: George dies, aged 62.

1916

Early in the year: Rose begins work as a land-girl, while continuing at Mount Blow.

February: Jean becomes a temporary civil servant, working in the Ministry of Munitions.

30 August: *Non-Combatants and Others.*

4–7 December: Rose and her mother move to Hedgerley End, Beaconsfield.

1917

8 January: Rose begins work as a clerk in the War Office.

1918

24 June: Rose becomes secretary to Walter Seton, Political Secretary to the Department of Propaganda, Ministry of Information. She and Gerald O'Donovan had probably met and fallen in love before this.

22 July: Southernwood is sold.

5 September: Rose is transferred to the Department of Propaganda in Enemy Countries at Crewe House, where she works on Italian affairs.

3 October: Will is wounded at Le Catelet, France.

11 November: Armistice between the Allies and Germany. A few days later, Rose leaves Crewe House and is re-employed by the Ministry of Information.

December: Ministry of Information is wound up. Rose is soon transferred to the Foreign Office and continues to work on Italian affairs.

1919

Late March: *What Not* is published.

End of April/beginning of May: Rose resigns from the Civil Service and is soon taken ill.

July: Rose at Kirnan, Argyllshire.

21 July: Jean becomes private secretary to Gilbert Murray at Boars Hill, near Oxford.

October: *Three Days*.

1920

Late May: *Potterism*.

1921

April: Rose visits Varazze with Margaret.

20 May: *Dangerous Ages*.

September: Rose attends the Second Assembly of the League of Nations in Geneva.

Before the end of the year: Rose takes a flat at 63 Edgware Road.

1922

January: Jean leaves the employment of Gilbert Murray.

February: *Dangerous Ages* wins Rose the Femina-Vie Heureuse Prize of 1,000 francs.

14 April: Likely date of Rose's last confession for almost thirty years.

30 October: *Mystery at Geneva*.

1923

July: Jean appointed secretary to R.W. Chapman at Clarendon Press, Oxford.
25 October: *Told by an Idiot.*

1924

Mid-November: *Orphan Island.*

1925

January: Rose takes flat 2, St Andrews Mansions, Dorset Street, London W1.
April: Rose visits Mallorca with Margaret and Jeanie, and afterwards meets up with Gerald in France.
5 May: Grace dies, aged 69.
July: Rose at Kirnan.
August: Rose in Switzerland as a Lunn tour lecturer; afterwards in France with Gerald.
29 October: *A Casual Commentary.*

1926

1 February: Hedgerley End is vacated and sold.
27 February: Rose's dinner-party with Virginia and Leonard Woolf among the guests.
Between May and December: Rose moves from flat 2 to flat 10, St Andrews Mansions.
July: Jean leaves Clarendon Press.
August: Rose in France with Gerald.
September: Margaret finds a house, Heathlands, in Petersfield.
Late October: *Crewe Train.* Rose's friendship with Naomi Royde-Smith under strain.
November: *Catchwords and Claptrap.*

1927

April: *The Augustan Books of English Poetry: Rose Macaulay.*
June: Rose tells Jean about her affair with Gerald, shortly before Jean enters Fairacres, an Anglican convent in Oxford.
July: Rose in Switzerland with Margaret.
August: Rose in France and Italy with Gerald.
December: Jean leaves Fairacres.

1928

2 February: Jean's *Shepherd of Souls*, dedicated to Rose, appears.
Late March: *Keeping up Appearances.*
April/May or September: Jean joins the staff of Downe House School.

1929
3 May: Unfavourable report on Rose's heart.
August: Margaret moves from Petersfield to Liss.
December–February 1930: Rose travels in USA with Margaret and Will.

1930
Spring: Rose falls on her head and suffers concussion.
Late summer: Rose moves to flat 7, Luxborough House, Northumberland (later, Luxborough) Street.
22 September: *Staying with Relations*.

1931
May: *Some Religious Elements in English Literature*.
July or December: Jean leaves Downe House School.

1932
Late summer or early autumn: Jean is admitted to a nursing home and stays there for several months.
14 October: *They Were Defeated*.

1933
20 June: Uncle Kenneth (K.A. Macaulay) dies, aged 77.
September: Jean becomes a Roman Catholic.

1934
January: *Milton*.
23 February: Jean's father, Rose's Uncle Charlie (C.S. Smith) dies, aged 75.
Early July: *Going Abroad*.
October: *The Minor Pleasures of Life*.

1935
Summer: Jean in hospital for several months.
October: *Personal Pleasures*.

1936
Autumn: Jean in USA.
11 March: *The Times* reports the settlement, in the plaintiff's favour, of a libel action brought by Lord de Clifford against Rose and *The Spectator*.
June: Rose becomes a sponsor of the Peace Pledge Union.
28 November: Uncle Willie (W.H. Macaulay) dies, aged 83.

1937

February: *I Would Be Private.*
Autumn: Jean visits her brother Jim in Nigeria, returning in March 1938.
15 December: Uncle Regi (R.H. Macaulay) dies, aged 79.

1938

March: *The Writings of E.M. Forster.* Rose resigns as sponsor of the Peace Pledge
  Union.
August–September: Rose motors in France and Italy with Gerald.
November: *All in a Maze.*

1939

March: Rose registers as a volunteer ambulance driver in London.
26 June: Rose's bad driving causes a car crash near Alston, Cumberland; Gerald
  is injured.
18 July: Rose (under the name of Emily Macaulay) appears at Penrith Police
  Court on a charge of driving without due care and attention. She is fined and
  has her licence endorsed.
3 September: Britain declares war on Germany.
Autumn–summer 1940: Jean in Clent, working in support of Polish refugees.

1940

June: *And No Man's Wit.*
Summer 1940: Jean goes to London to work for the Catholic War Refugees'
  Spiritual Welfare Committee; she takes a flat in Ashley Court, close to
  Westminster Cathedral.

1941

1 March: Margaret Macaulay dies, aged 60.
18 April: Mary O'Donovan, Gerald's younger daughter, dies, aged 23.
10–11 May: Luxborough House is bombed, and Rose's flat destroyed.
13 May: Rose discovers the loss of her flat and its contents. She soon rents a
  bedsit at 35 Manchester Street.
June, second week: Rose moves into 20 Hinde House, Hinde Street, her last
  London flat.

1942

23 February: Gerald has an operation after the discovery of colorectal cancer.
26 July: Gerald dies, aged 71.
September: *Life Among the English.*

1943

6 March–7 May. Rose in Portugal.

Late August: Rose in hospital.

Autumn: Jean works for the Red Cross Library in Oxford until 25 November, when her mother is taken ill.

1945

8 May: Germany surrenders.

16 November: Will Macaulay dies in Alberta, Canada, aged 60.

1946

September: *They Went to Portugal.*

1947

5 July–11 September. Rose travels alone by car in Spain and Portugal.

1949

April: *Fabled Shore.*

1950

January: Rose in hospital.

May: *The World My Wilderness.*

August: Rose visits Italy, including Varazze, with Dermod and Muriel O'Donovan.

29 August: Rose receives the first letter from Fr Hamilton Johnson and soon returns to active membership of the Church of England.

3 November: Jean's mother, Rose's Aunt Nannie (A.G. Smith), dies, aged 89.

1951

7 June: Rose receives honorary degree of LittD (Doctor of Letters) from Cambridge University.

1952

March–autumn: Rose has recurrent attacks of brucellosis.

5 August: Eleanor dies at Ranchi, India, aged 65.

1953

29 January: Aunt Mary (M.F. Macaulay) dies, aged 85.

16 May–1 July: Rose visits Cyprus, Lebanon, Syria, and Israel.

2 July: Fire-damage in Rose's sitting-room.

7 December: *Pleasure of Ruins.*

1954

27 February: Rose disturbs burglars in her flat.

2 June–6 July: Rose visits Turkey, including Trebizond.

1955

9 March: Rose becomes the first woman to be elected to the Council of the Royal Literary Fund.

1956

3 September: *The Towers of Trebizond.*

15 November: Dinner-party for Princess Margaret to meet Rose.

1957

February: *The Towers of Trebizond* wins Rose the James Tait Black Prize for the best novel of 1956.

6–30 May: Rose visits Venice.

20 May: Gilbert Murray dies, aged 91. Afterwards Jean is asked to sort his papers and to co-edit *Gilbert Murray: An Unfinished Autobiography*, published 1960.

1958

1 January: Announcement of Rose's appointment as DBE.

11 February: Investiture at Buckingham Palace.

18 February: Rose is a guest at private dinner-party hosted by The Queen and The Duke of Edinburgh at Buckingham Palace.

20 March: Rose falls and is in hospital until late April.

27 August–12 September: Rose accompanies a cruise to the Aegean and Black Sea, including Trebizond.

30 October: Rose dies from heart attack, aged 77.

3 November: Funeral service at Golders Green Crematorium.

6 November: Requiem Mass at Grosvenor Chapel.

13 November: Memorial service at St Paul's, Knightsbridge.

1961

October: Jean's first visit to Sicily in the steps of John Henry Newman.

23 October: *Letters to a Friend.*

1962

May: Jean has hospital treatment for depression.

15 October: *Last Letters to a Friend.*

1963

July: Jean moves from London to Oxford.

1964

6 April: *Letters to a Sister.*

May: Jean's second visit to Sicily in the steps of J.H. Newman.

1968

6 April: Beryl O'Donovan, Gerald's widow, dies, aged 81.

1973

26 January: Jeanie Macaulay dies, aged 90.

1979

7 July: Jean dies in Malvern, Worcestershire, aged 87.

1990

6 March: English Heritage blue plaque, honouring Rose, unveiled on exterior wall of Hinde House by A.N. Wilson.

1 November: *They Went to Portugal Too.*

Abbreviations

Bensen	Alice R. Bensen, *Rose Macaulay* (New York, 1969)
Bibliog.	Bibliography
CBS	Constance Babington Smith, *Rose Macaulay* (London, 1972)
Crawford	Alice Crawford, *Paradise Pursued: The Novels of Rose Macaulay* (Cranbury, NJ, 1995)
DNB	*Dictionary of National Biography*
Emery	Jane Emery, *Rose Macaulay: A Writer's Life* (London, 1991)
ERM	Emilie Rose Macaulay. When 'ERM' is followed by a number (as in 'ERM 4.209'), the reference is to the Rose Macaulay archive in the Library of Trinity College, Cambridge
Introd.	Introduction
L	*Letter(s)* in the present collection (e.g. *L3* = *Letter 3*)
LeFanu	Sarah LeFanu, *Rose Macaulay* (London, 2003)
LF	*Letters to a Friend from Rose Macaulay 1950–1952*, ed. Constance Babington Smith (London, 1961)
LLF	*Last Letters to a Friend from Rose Macaulay 1952–1958*, ed. Constance Babington Smith (London, 1962)
LS	*Letters to a Sister from Rose Macaulay*, ed. Constance Babington Smith (London, 1964)
ODNB	*Oxford Dictionary of National Biography*
SWG	*Saturday Westminster Gazette*
TLS	*The Times Literary Supplement*

1. Jean Smith in a punt on the Cam, 1912

2. Rose Macaulay (second from right) and her dog, Thomas, with her parents and her sisters Jeanie (centre) and Margaret (right), Southernwood, Great Shelford, 1913/1914

3. Gerald O'Donovan, Northrepps Cottage, near Cromer, 1915

4. Grace Macaulay in her donkey-chaise, Great Shelford, 1916

5. Jean Smith (back right) with her parents and five brothers, Cross Bank, Clent, 1921. Brothers (L–R): Henry, Tom, Regie, Bill (standing), Jim. Dorothy, Jean's elder sister, is absent

6. St Andrews Mansions, Dorset Street, London W1. Rose Macaulay rented a ground-floor flat there, 1925-1930, occupying first no. 2, off the left side of the courtyard, then no. 10, whose windows can be seen on the far side of the courtyard

7. Madeleine Symons, c. 1924

8. Jimmy Mallon, Warden of Toynbee Hall, London, c. 1925-1930

9. Naomi Royde-Smith, c. 1926

10. Rose Macaulay, late 1920s

11. K.A. Macaulay (Uncle Kenneth) at the door of Walton House, Clent, 1929

12. W.H. Macaulay (Uncle Willie): portrait by Roger Fry, 1930. In a letter to Kenneth Clark from King's on 2 May 1930, Fry describes his subject as 'a very noble handsome old don', but adds: 'It's just a year or two too late to do him because he's never been to a good dentist, which makes his mouth a terrible problem. I wish I could get him a good plate, but it's rather too ticklish a question to urge.'

13. R.H. Macaulay (Uncle Regi[e])

14. M.F. Macaulay (Aunt Mary)

15. Grosvenor Chapel, South Audley Street, Mayfair: Rose Macaulay's favourite seat by the door (Letter 95 n. 8)

16. Rose Macaulay with Fr James Dunlop Crichton of Pershore, doyen of English Roman Catholic liturgists, after he had officiated at the marriage of Jean Smith's brother Jim to Rosemary Hughes, 24 September 1955

17. Jean Smith pretending to fish, c. 1955

MAYFAIR 1938.

2 ST. ANDREWS MANSIONS,
DORSET STREET, W.1

Aug. 1st
1925

My dearest Jean

The meats are lovely, &
quite the correct idea for Andrew—
thirty. A lot. I got home this
morning at 8, after not a bad
train night, & plunged into a hot bath,
& immediately everyone came singing
at the door — the postman, the porter, &
I don't know who else — so I had to
leap in & out of the water like a
porpoise: — the one drawback, this, of

18. Rose Macaulay's letter of 1 August 1925 to Jean Smith, beginning and end

Introduction

ROSE MACAULAY: THE FIRST HALF OF HER LIFE

This section deals with Rose's life down to April 1919, the date of the first preserved letter (as opposed to note or message of greetings) to Jean. The continuation of the story is supplied by the letters and the commentary on them.

1 The daughter who was not a boy (1881–1894)

Nothing could have gone better than our affairs today, except that Grace has not got the boy she wished for, and was a good deal depressed by her disappointment. (Appendix 1, Letter 1)

Emilie Rose Macaulay was born in Rugby, Warwickshire, on 1 August 1881, at 11 Hillmorton Road, a few doors from the house (no. 5) in which Rupert Brooke was born six years later. She was the second eldest of the seven children of George Campbell Macaulay, an assistant master at Rugby School, and Grace Mary Macaulay, *née* Conybeare. Grace wanted to be the mother of boys and was disappointed when each of her first three children (Margaret, Rose, and Jeanie) was a girl. She was delighted when two boys (Aulay and Will) followed, but then came two more girls, of whom the younger, Gertrude, died before her fourth birthday and the elder, Eleanor, was not loved by her mother and was excluded from family activities and holidays.

Grace's treatment of Eleanor, and George's readiness to condone it, was shameful, and her behaviour not only towards Eleanor but also towards her other children, who were very conscious of her strong partialities and prejudices, may help to explain why none of them married, and why they were eager to leave home as soon as they could.

Nevertheless Grace had her virtues as well as her faults. She communicated to her children her enthusiasm for reading, and she allowed them considerable freedom when it came to play. That freedom was increased when the family went to live abroad. Grace's health, not assisted by the bearing of five children in five years, was causing so much anxiety by the summer of 1887 that she and George decided to leave Rugby for a warmer climate. They chose Italy and, taking the whole family, including their sixth child, four-month-old Eleanor, left England for Genoa in October. The move was a bold one: apart from the adventure of a new life in a foreign country, George would no longer have his schoolmaster's salary and no accommodation had been secured in advance. It was only after arrival in Genoa that the Macaulays found a flat in Varazze, a small seaside town, west of the city, in which they turned out to be the only foreign residents.

Varazze was to be their home for seven years, and a very happy home it was for the children, except for poor Eleanor, despite the death of Gertrude from meningitis in April 1892. The children's education was provided mainly by their parents. George took them for most subjects, including mathematics, Latin, and Italian, Grace for reading, writing, and dictation; she also taught the three eldest girls needlework, and gave all the children religious instruction. Both parents did much story-telling and reading aloud. Rose's own reading, most of it done outside lessons, was prodigious. It included tales of adventure and romance and, when she was eight, Tennyson, then Shelley, Browning, and Swinburne. Lessons usually occupied the greater part of the morning. When they were over, there was ample time for recreation, including walking in the hills, riding, and, at appropriate seasons, bathing and boating. The five eldest children had great fun, often acting out in their play the stories they had read of (for example) castaways and pirates, as well as following their own imaginations. This good life became even better from the spring of 1891, when the Macaulays moved from their flat in the town centre to the Villa Levante, bought with the help of money given by Grace's mother. As 'Levante' suggests, the property was on the eastern side of the town, so close to the sea that the waves would sometimes invade the garden and basement. To the locals, who treated the children with much kindness, the house was the Villa Inglese or Villa Macolai. Rose always looked back on the Varazze years as time spent in paradise. Italy and bathing were to be lasting passions, and the whole experience of life in Varazze had a profound influence upon her and her writing. For one thing, her belief in equal opportunities for the sexes is particularly understandable in one who between the ages of six and nearly thirteen was brought up in an environment far removed from the restrictive conventions of Victorian society in England. Although she was conscious of her gender and would have preferred to be a boy (not surprisingly, given that her mother had wanted that too), 'the five', girls and boys, were educated together and enjoyed the same freedoms. But a big change was to come about in the summer of 1894, abruptly terminating Rose's dream of becoming a man and joining the navy.

Varazze had benefited Grace's health and suited her in other ways too. George, however, had been less happy, and not only because, in the summer of 1890, he was seriously ill with typhoid and pneumonia. Although he had continued with his scholarly research and writing, completing a highly competent translation of Herodotus, with notes and indexes, published in two volumes by Macmillan in 1890, and producing, among other things, a *Graduated German Reading Book* (1888), it was a handicap not to have regular access to a major library, as he implies when he refers, at the end of the preface to his *Herodotus*, to the time 'when the British Museum was within my reach'. A return to England was desirable for the sake of his work. It was also desirable for the education of the children, the eldest of whom, Margaret, was now fourteen.

2 *Growing wings (1894–1903)*

Given that George was a former scholar and fellow of Trinity College, Cambridge, the Macaulays might have been expected to move to Cambridge, but Grace could not abide the thought of being in close proximity to her elder brother, Edward Conybeare, and his wife, Frances.[1] So they decided on Oxford. George had access to the Bodleian Library for his research on the fourteenth-century poet John Gower, whose works he was to edit in four volumes for the Clarendon Press (1899–1902), although it was in Cambridge University Library that he struck gold on 5 April 1895, when he discovered the manuscript that is the only surviving copy (incomplete) of Gower's *Speculum hominis* or *Mirour de l'omme*. In the words of Douglas Gray in *ODNB*, 'the Macaulay edition laid the foundation for serious study' of the poet. It also did much for George's career. As well as being good for his research, Oxford had excellent schools for the children. Margaret, Rose, and Jeanie were enrolled at Oxford High School for Girls (Rose under the name of 'Emily'), Aulay and Will as day-pupils at the Oxford Preparatory School, now the Dragon School. Aulay went on to Clifton College in 1897, Will to Marlborough the following year.

The Macaulays took up residence in Oxford in mid-August 1894. Their first home there was about a mile from the city centre at 3 Clarendon Villas, Park Town, off Banbury Road. After two years they moved further out, to Thule, 350 Banbury Road, Summertown. It was reckoned that the house was appropriately named in view of its remoter location. Although 'the five' at first continued to live and play together, life in suburban Oxford was much changed from life in Varazze: the girls were no longer being taught with the boys; school education was very different from home education; and both in school and out of it the children were exposed to social conventions and pressures unknown to them before.

Rose's headmistress, Lucy Soulsby, considered moral training more important than academic education, her stated aim being to produce 'a race of leisured girls'

---

[1] In an unpublished letter (in the editor's possession) of 28 January 1940 to Graham Greene's wife, Vivien, Rose writes unflatteringly of Edward Conybeare: 'my uncle, who was rather mad, was many years since vicar of Barrington, but he turned Roman Catholic so had to move into Cambridge instead, where he lived in the shadow of the cathedral [Our Lady and the English Martyrs Catholic Church] but couldn't be a priest because of his wife, though she would have been rather glad if he had put her away and been one. He was most peculiar.' He may have had his eccentricities, but his *Diary*, held by Cambridge Archives Service (R84/075) and covering 1854–1860 and 1862–1925, is a remarkable record.

and so 'to make fine women who will be fine wives and fine mothers'. In the great debate of 1895–1896, as to whether Oxford should award degrees to women (it was decided that it should not), she raised her voice in opposition, being convinced that women should not have the same kind of education as men. After the years in Varazze, the atmosphere at Oxford High School must have made Rose feel like a fish out of water, and adjustment to it must have been made more difficult by the Macaulays' retention of the Villa Macolai and their return there from time to time, including for the whole of the spring term in 1897. As a pupil, Rose was shy and subdued and not particularly outstanding either academically or in any other way, although in her last year she won a prize, offered by the school-magazine, with a four-stanza poem entitled 'The Sea'. Her best subject was history, in which she gained a distinction in the Higher Certificate Examination just before she left school in the summer of 1899.

Rose was qualified for a university education, but at this stage her parents could not afford to meet its costs: George had not had a regular salary for twelve years, and, although Grace's mother, Eliza Conybeare, who had already been generous to the family, was to leave Grace a substantial sum of money when she died, she lived until January 1903. But in 1900 Rose's godfather and uncle Regi Macaulay (*L*6 n. 2), a wealthy bachelor who was always generous with his money, offered to pay her fees at Somerville College, and in October she embarked on a three-year course in Modern History. Although her family was still living in Oxford during her first year, she resided in college.

Somerville was one of two women's residential colleges in Oxford that began life in 1879. The other, Lady Margaret Hall, was Anglican, but Somerville was non-denominational, and its atmosphere of greater religious, social, and cultural diversity was one that Rose was likely to find more congenial and stimulating.[2] Although her three years at Somerville were to have a disappointing conclusion, she benefited greatly from them. Rose Macaulay the university student was much less shy and reticent than Emily Macaulay the schoolgirl, although she remained somewhat diffident and was considered eccentric, not least in respect of her eating habits or rather her disinclination to eat. She participated in debates, speaking so quickly that it was sometimes difficult to follow what she was saying. She formed good friendships with fellow-students, including the future Roman archaeologist and historian Margerie Venables Taylor, the future headmistress Olive Willis (*L*15 n. 1), and the future Principal of Somerville Helen Darbishire (*L*5 n. 11). She enjoyed playing hockey and messing about on the river. As for her studies, she particularly loved seventeenth-century history, in which she chose to specialise. That period was to remain her favourite, and she was to make brilliant use of her knowledge of it in her historical novel *They Were Defeated* (1932).

---

[2] The Society of Home Students, the forerunner of St Anne's College, was also established in 1879, but its students were accommodated in lodgings.

Although women were not eligible for Oxford degrees until 1920, they were classed just like the men in the examinations. When the time came for Rose to take her finals in the early summer of 1903, the expectation must have been that she would perform well. In the event, she did not perform at all. According to her sister Jeanie, she had had a bout of influenza and did not feel well enough to tackle the papers, but Olive Willis (admittedly no longer at Somerville in 1903) thought that the real problem, or at least the main one, was Rose's 'dislike of formal questions and answers when there seemed so much more to say on every subject'. Whatever the true explanation may be, Rose was granted an aegrotat, indicating that the examiners believed that illness had prevented her from achieving the respectable result of which she was capable. Although an aegrotat was not a failure, and Rose seems to have been outwardly cheerful in her last days at Somerville, it would be surprising if she had not felt keen disappointment at the outcome. She chose to appear in the Somerville going-down pageant as a caterpillar, a symbol of immaturity. Her own picture of herself is not out of harmony with that sketched by Olive Willis: 'She looked like an unfledged bird, a young eaglet perhaps, but in that thin defenceless form, it wasn't easy to realize future development. In the almost unintelligible torrent of words, it wasn't possible to recognize a master of language.'[3]

In September 1901, when Rose was about to begin her second year at Somerville, George Macaulay took up the post of Professor of English at the University College of Wales, Aberystwyth. He needed the salary that went with it, and no doubt was appointed largely on the basis of his edition of Gower, the second and third volumes of which appeared in 1901. In early December the family moved into Ty-issa (Tŷ Isaf, 'Lower House'), a substantial, four-storeyed house four miles south-east of Aberystwyth, between Llanfarian and Llanilar. The situation is attractive, with a thickly wooded ridge rising steeply behind the house and meadows sloping down to the River Ystwyth in front. There was a lawn suitable for tennis and croquet, and the surrounding countryside was delightful for walking and cycling.

3 *The valley captive (1903–1906)*

After Rose left Somerville, Ty-issa became her home all the year round. She was not blind to its attractions, but was restless. Indeed she felt like a prisoner. One reason for this was the isolated rural location: life in the Cardiganshire countryside was very quiet and dull compared with life in Oxford, and intellectually much less stimulating. Another aspect of Rose's 'imprisonment' was the attitude of her mother, who wanted her three eldest daughters at home and expected

---

[3] Quoted by Anne Ridler, *Olive Willis and Downe House: An Adventure in Education* (London, 1967) 53.

them to stay there until they had found husbands. For the sons, of course, it was different: Aulay, who had gone on from Clifton to the Royal Military Academy at Woolwich in 1900, sailed to India with the Royal Engineers in February 1904; and Will, who had gone to an agricultural college in Suffolk at the end of February 1903, decided to farm in Canada and left in early April 1906.

The first adult sister to make her escape was Jeanie: in January 1905 she embarked on a nursing course at Guy's Hospital, London.[4] There was to be no early escape for Margaret or Rose, but there were interludes of freedom. A notable such interlude was a holiday in Italy with their bachelor uncles Willie and Kenneth Macaulay in March–April 1905. It took them to Rome, Naples, and Como. Rose also sought and found freedom in writing. Soon after she returned to Wales from Italy, she began work on her first novel, *Abbots Verney*, largely set in Rome. It was published by John Murray in December 1906 and given a generally favourable reception by the critics. While Rose was writing it, her father was appointed Lecturer in English at Cambridge. He took up the post in April 1906, although his family remained at Ty-issa until early October. His appointment to the Cambridge lectureship was good news not only for him but also for Rose: Cambridge offered much that Aberystwyth did not, one of its many advantages being its proximity to London. While living in Wales, Rose not only wrote *Abbots Verney* but also started contributing to *Saturday Westminster Gazette*. The earliest contribution of hers found by the present writer is a rhymed 'Alphabet of Novelists' in the issue of 27 May 1905.

4 *The secret river (1906–1914)*

In the summer of 1906 the Macaulays bought Southernwood, an attractive house in two acres of grounds in the village of Great Shelford, four miles south of Cambridge.[5] Built in 1898, it has four reception rooms and seven bedrooms. In the late summer of 1907 the Macaulays acquired the substantial piece of land, now a public recreation area, which extends southwards from the western boundary of Southernwood to the River Cam or Granta. The following summer Willie Macaulay gave the family a fine boathouse, and it was here that Rose wrote part of her third novel, *The Secret River* (1909). A corner of the boathouse appears in the photograph of the foliage-canopied river used as the frontispiece of the novel, with the caption: 'The slumbrous afternoon was on the slow green river, like the burden of a dream'. One of those with whom Rose went swimming and boating was Rupert Brooke, an undergraduate at King's College, Cambridge, in 1906–1909, and it is difficult to believe that the hero of *The Secret River*, the

---

[4] For a brief summary of Jeanie's long career as a nurse, see *L*13 n. 1.

[5] Cephas Luther Edwards, the first owner, who sold the property to the Macaulays, was an unusual man (and not only in name), being a commercial traveller with an interest in Greek philosophy. His three sons were to have distinguished careers as scientists.

young poet Michael Travis, is not based, in part, on Rupert, although the character is also modelled on Rose herself. After graduation, Rupert lived in nearby Grantchester, and his friendship with Rose, six years his senior, continued, but the two were never anything more than affectionate friends.

Rose's second novel, *The Furnace*, had been published in November 1907 – fittingly enough, in view of the title, on Guy Fawkes Day. It was set entirely in Italy, in Naples and Varazze. During the writing of it Rose and Margaret made another visit to Italy with their uncles Willie and Kenneth. This time (April 1907) their destination was Venice, from where Rose wrote, on a postcard to her brother Will in Canada: 'We are having a splendid time here. Our gondolier let us gondol ourselves the other day, its [*sic*] quite easy. I should be a gondolier if I was a man' (ERM 15.112). In April 1908 the two sisters were back in Italy on a bicycling holiday with Uncle Willie and their father.[6] Places visited included Varazze, Savona, Spezia, Lerici, Massa, San Gimignano, Siena, and Florence.

If another trip in the spring of 1909 was contemplated, the plan was abandoned, for on 13 February that year, three weeks before the publication of *The Secret River*, a tragic piece of news reached the family at Southernwood. It was that Aulay, who was due to come home on leave in the spring after five years' service with the Royal Engineers in the North-West Frontier Province of India, had been murdered two days earlier in the Miranzai Valley. The motive for the murder was robbery: Aulay was cycling along a road, when he was attacked by three or four local men, who knew that he was delivering wages to labourers working on a new road. He was bound, blindfolded, led away from the road, and shot through the heart. Despite many messages of sympathy from relatives and friends and abundant testimony to the great respect and affection in which he was held by all who worked with him in India, the family was almost inconsolable. Grace had lost her favourite child. Edward Conybeare, visiting Southernwood on 21 March, found her 'utterly stricken' and George 'quenched'. As for Rose, on 10 May Edward describes her as 'sadly broken'. For several months she was unable to write much; and her next novel, *The Valley Captives*, was her darkest, born out of the anguish and anger generated by Aulay's untimely death. The writing of it was a necessary act of catharsis that helped her to come to terms with the loss of her brother.

Writing to Jean in 1927 about the unhappiness of their mutual friend Madeleine Symons, Rose wishes she would write something, because 'it keeps one's thoughts . . . employed'. She goes on to say: 'Life is a queer, wry business, and she's got to a bad place in it, but she'll get through it of course. She's so much pluck. No religion, of course, which is unlucky' (L68). After the death of Aulay, Rose used religion as well as writing to help her recover. Hitherto she had been a church goer through custom and duty as much as through conviction. Now

---

[6] Emery 110 misdates the trip in the summer of 1909.

she began to take her church going more seriously, to attend retreats, to go to confession, and to undertake various church duties such as teaching in Sunday school. She particularly liked the High Church services in nearby Sawston and the sermons of Father Philip Waggett (*L*69 n. 4) in Cambridge.

Another development that helped the process of healing was the increasing frequency with which she visited London, where she went to the theatre and socialised with people in the literary world. She was often in the company of Rupert Brooke, 'who walked about the streets without a map, often with a plaid rug over his shoulders, as if he was Tennyson, which seemed to me a very good idea and gave him prestige, and people turned to look at him as he strolled through Soho with his golden hair and his rug, and I was proud to be with him'.[7] The most important contact Rose made in London before the First World War was Naomi Royde-Smith, editor of the 'Problems and Prizes' section, and from 1912 literary editor, of *Saturday Westminster Gazette*, to which she had been submitting contributions, usually poems, for several years. The two first met not later than May 1911, but perhaps as early as 1910. Naomi introduced Rose to many literary friends and acquaintances of hers, including Walter de la Mare. The warm friendship between Rose and Naomi and the circumstances in which it cooled are discussed in *L*4 n. 8 and 57 n. 10.

Rose's frequent escapes to London, which became easier before the end of 1913, when Regi Macaulay's generosity enabled her to take a small flat in Southampton Buildings, off Chancery Lane, were precious to her and helped to make life in the family home at Great Shelford more bearable for her. Margaret, to their mother's consternation, had announced in March 1911 that she was going to join, as a postulant, a community of deaconesses in East London (*L*7 n. 2), and in September 1912 Eleanor, after education in boarding schools followed by two years of teacher-training, sailed for India, where she was to spend the rest of her life as a teacher and missionary (*L*12 n. 4; 16 n. 6). With Will farming in Canada and Jeanie nursing, Rose was now the only daughter or son still living at home. It was a state of affairs that was to continue until Grace Macaulay's death in 1925.

After the interruption caused by her grief for Aulay, Rose recovered her earlier productivity as a writer. *The Valley Captives* (January 1911) was followed by two novels, her fifth and sixth, in 1912. *Views and Vagabonds* (February 1912) is significant as her first attempt at satire. Concerned with what the publisher's reader called 'the fashionable cult for socialism and "the poor"', it pokes gentle fun at the Fabian ideas championed by Rupert Brooke. *The Lee Shore*, begun before *Views and Vagabonds*, but finished later, brought her not only critical praise but also fame and serious money, for at the end of July 1912 it was announced

---

[7] 'Coming to London – XIII' (Bibliog. I.7), 32.

that it had won her the first prize of £600 in Hodder and Stoughton's fiction competition. It was published in October.

In the spring of 1912 and again in the summer of 1914 Rose travelled abroad with her father. In 1912 they took a Hellenic cruise. The trip and the short story that Rose wrote after it are described in *L*110 n. 9. The 1914 holiday took Rose across the Atlantic for the first time. She and George visited Will in Canada. They had an eventful time. A few days after they had arrived aboard the SS *Megantic* (the vessel in which, two years earlier, the murderer Dr Crippen and his mistress, Ethel le Neve, had been escorted back to England after his arrest), the First World War broke out. On the return voyage they sailed in the Cunard Line's SS *Laconia*, the funnels and superstructure of which had been repainted to disguise its identity and nationality, for fear of attacks by German U-boats.[8] But this was not the only excitement Rose and George experienced: during their stay with Will, they took a walk along a railway line and were in a narrow cutting when they realised that a train was approaching; they had to run for their lives, and made it to safety only just in time.

Rose's father was her favourite parent, and she was his favourite daughter. Temperamentally, the two were much akin. She admired his logical mind, learning, and scholarly achievements, and she looked up to him as a model of integrity and as a source of sound advice. He admired her ability and success as a writer. Despite their very special bond of love and the delight they took in one another's company and conversation, there were sometimes tensions and disagreements between them. A notable disagreement occurred in the summer of 1910, when Rupert Brooke invited Rose to accompany him on a trip in a horse-drawn caravan. Rose, aged 28 or 29 at the time, wanted to accept the invitation, but reluctantly declined after her father had expressed strong disapproval. She answered back in *Views and Vagabonds*: 'One understands that it is rather *outré* to travel alone with a cousin of the opposite sex in a van, even with the most fraternal feelings. Whoever lays down the law on these and similar principles of conduct would appear to have laid that one quite firmly. Of course the sensible plan is tranquilly to ignore the law, if one wishes to do so; the best people always do that with laws' (191).

This was not the only time she used her fiction to express or imply criticism of her parents. It is noteworthy that all three of the novels she dedicated to them contain flawed characters apparently based on the dedicatees. The novels are *The Secret River* (1909) and *Dangerous Ages* (1921),[9] dedicated to her mother, and *The Valley Captives* (1911), dedicated to her father. The central theme of *The Valley Captives* is the bullying of a Welsh boy (Tudor Vallon) by his stepbrother (Phil Bodger), and the failure of Tudor's aesthete father (Oliver Vallon) to

---

[8] The *Laconia* was sunk by a U-boat on 25 February 1917.

[9] See *L*2 n. 1.

protect him. The exceptional bitterness of the novel probably reflects not only Rose's state of mind after the death of Aulay but also her unhappy experience as a 'valley captive' in mid-Wales and her disapproval of her father's failure to protect Eleanor from mistreatment by her mother.

March and April 1914 saw the publication of Rose's seventh novel, *The Making of a Bigot*, and her first volume of poems, *The Two Blind Countries*, praised by Walter de la Mare.[10] In the same week that her new novel appeared her sister Margaret's one and only novel, *The Sentence Absolute*, dedicated to their mother, was published too.

5 War and love (1914–1919)

On 30 June 1914, just over a fortnight before Rose and her father sailed for Canada, she gave a party in her London flat. The guests included Naomi Royde-Smith, Walter de la Mare, Iolo Aneurin Williams, Rupert Brooke, and Frank Sidgwick, publisher of *The Two Blind Countries*. No doubt Rose hoped and expected that she would continue to have the flat as a refuge from home-life and as a base for enjoyment of London's literary and cultural scene for years to come, but fate decreed otherwise. She retained it until at least mid-March 1915,[11] but not for much longer.

The year 1915 was an unhappy one for her. Her general horror of war was accompanied by deep concern about Will, who was serving with the King's Royal Rifle Corps. He was to come through the conflict, but by no means unscathed (L3 n. 22). The death of Rupert Brooke, at the age of 27, on 23 April was a heavy blow, but less severe than a second death that soon followed. On 6 July George Macaulay died a few days after suffering a paralysing stroke. Of his five surviving children, only Margaret and Jeanie attended his funeral, the latter having rushed home from France, where she was serving with the French Red Cross. Eleanor was teaching in India and Will was soldiering in the Balkans. Rose was at home in Great Shelford, but, like Grace, was apparently too distressed to appear at the funeral, although she may have absented herself on the ground that she needed to stay with her mother during the service. Henceforth Grace's demands on Rose's attention were naturally greater than before, and for a while it was less easy for Rose to escape to London. That was not only because her mother was now a widow and often in poor health but also because shortly before George's death she (Rose) had started working part-time at Mount Blow, a Red Cross auxiliary hospital in Great Shelford, where she carried out menial duties like washing floors with a distaste that was matched only by her incompetence.

Early in 1916 she took on a second part-time job, working as a land-girl on a

---

[10] Unsigned review in *TLS*, 9 April 1914, 174.
[11] Edward Conybeare, *Diary*, 16 March 1915.

local farm. In a letter of 4 March 1916 to Katharine Tynan, she writes: 'I wish I could write poetry in these days: I somehow can't. The war seems to have killed all that; I can only just struggle with prose. I am trying to get through with a novel, in moments snatched from nursing in a V[oluntary] A[id] D[etachment] hospital and working on the land for 3d an hour.'[12] The work on the land, which Rose much preferred to the work in the hospital, inspired a group of pieces in her second collection of poetry, *Three Days* (1919), while her experiences in the VAD hospital left their mark on the novel she mentioned to Katharine Tynan. The novel, *Non-Combatants and Others*, dedicated 'To my brother and other combatants', appeared in August 1916. It is the only book of Rose's to have been published during the Great War. Among novels written about the war and during it, it is unusual for its focus on those at home, including those who have returned from the Front, for its recognition of the psychological damage caused by war, and for its whole anti-war message. Unsurprisingly, the book did not receive a warm reception in 1916: it was considered lacking in patriotism and was also criticised for being 'episodic'. In several respects it was a book ahead of its time.

Four months after George's death Grace decided to leave Great Shelford 'for sake of R[ose]' (Edward Conybeare's Diary, 22 November 1915). Certainly Rose wanted to live nearer London, but there will have been other considerations too: Southernwood was now far too large for the family; a house nearer London would be more accessible to Margaret, who was continuing to work in the East End, having been ordained deaconess in 1913; and Grace probably liked the idea of living further away from her brother and sister-in-law. Just over a year was to pass before the move was made, in early December 1916, to Beaconsfield, Buckinghamshire. The house, Hedgerley End, Hedgerley Lane, has four main bedrooms on the first floor, and two further rooms, evidently intended for servants, on the floor above under the roof.[13] It now has about half an acre of garden, but in the Macaulays' time the grounds were much more extensive. This was to be Grace's home until her death in May 1925, and it was to be Rose's home or main home for most of that time, although she often spent part of the week in London and during the last three or four years of her mother's life had a flat there.

In the middle and later years of the First World War many university-educated women were recruited to work in government departments. Jean Smith had been so recruited early in 1916. In January 1917 Rose followed suit. The move was to have a profound effect on her life, for it brought her into contact with a man with whom she fell deeply in love. But this did not happen immediately.

---

[12] KTH 1/656/3.

[13] Emery (158–159, 161, 179) and LeFanu (115) err in placing the house in the village of Hedgerley, south-east of Beaconsfield. Now called Hedgerley End House, it is in Beaconsfield old town itself, on the south-east side of it.

Her first post was that of an administrative clerk in the War Office, where she was involved with applications for exemption from military service. While so employed, and indeed throughout the twenty-eight months of her employment as a civil servant, she was commuting between Beaconsfield and London. According to Edward Conybeare (*Diary*, 8 January 1917), she was spending ten hours a day in the office and three hours a day travelling.

It is not known exactly when Rose left the War Office, nor is it known exactly when she first met Gerald O'Donovan. According to her biographers, she was transferred early in 1918 to the Italian section of the Department of Propaganda in Enemy Countries, and it was then that she met Gerald, whom they call 'the head' of that section. The Department was established under the directorship of Lord Northcliffe in February 1918, and in March became part of the new Ministry of Information, although it reported direct to the War Cabinet. Its home was Crewe House (now the Royal Embassy of Saudi Arabia) in Charles Street, Mayfair. Rose did indeed go to Crewe House, where Gerald was Secretary (not 'head') of the Italian Committee, in 1918, and the two did indeed fall in love that year, but a letter of 19 November 1918 from G. Gale Thomas, Assistant Director of Finance, Ministry of Information, to the Secretary of H.M. Treasury reveals that she went to Crewe House as late as 5 September 1918, and that her previous post, to which she was appointed on 24 June 1918 at a salary of £2 15s a week, was as shorthand-typist-secretary to Dr Walter Seton in the Foreign Department of the Ministry of Information.[14] Seton (Secretary of University College, London, from 1903 until his death in 1927) was Political Secretary to the Ministry, with responsibility for propaganda in the Balkans. In the light of the 'new' evidence, the question of how and when Rose and Gerald met requires reconsideration. Despite the obvious relationship between Seton's department and the Department of Propaganda at Crewe House, it seems unlikely that Rose first met Gerald after she became Seton's secretary. Why? Because Gerald was in Italy all through July 1918 (*L*16 n. 11), and, given that Rose's novel *What Not*, in which her feelings for him are clearly reflected (*L*3 n. 4), was ready for publication in November 1918 (*L*3 n. 17), a first meeting in August or early September would have allowed little or no time for her experience of falling in love to be written into the book before it went to the printers and binders. One possibility is that Rose worked for Gerald at Crewe House before as well as after she was Seton's secretary; in this connection, it is to be noted that the commencement of her work with Seton coincided with Gerald's departure for Italy.

Gerald O'Donovan, previously Jeremiah Donovan, was ten years older than Rose and probably aged 46 when they first met. He was born in Kilkeel, situated 'where the Mountains of Mourne sweep down to the sea' in Co. Down, Ireland, on 15 July 1871. He trained for the Roman Catholic priesthood and was

---

[14] National Archives Box T1 12276, file 3541/1919.

ordained on 23 June 1895. From 1896 he was parish administrator at Loughrea, Co. Galway. He was an enlightened and popular priest, energetic not only in performing his pastoral duties but also in campaigning for better living conditions for his parishioners and in promoting social welfare, education, and Irish culture.[15] Until 1903 he had the support of a sympathetic bishop, John Healey, but in that year Healey was succeeded by Thomas O'Dea, who was unsympathetic and obstructive. The following year Fr Jeremiah resigned as parish administrator and left Loughrea, disgusted with the attitude not just of his bishop but also of the Roman Catholic Church in Ireland, especially with regard to education. For the next four years he divided his time between London and Dublin. In May 1908 he resigned from the priesthood and in March 1910 became sub-warden of Toynbee Hall, the university settlement opened in 1884 to promote social welfare and education in East London. By now he was calling himself Gerald O'Donovan. Presumably he wanted a new name, now that he was embarking on a new life. He may also have wished to avoid any possible confusion with the militant Irish Republican Jeremiah O'Donovan Rossa (1831–1915).

On 15 October 1910 Gerald married a woman fifteen years his junior, Beryl Verschoyle, whose father, a retired colonel, belonged to a northern Irish Protestant family. On their marriage certificate Gerald's entry under 'Rank or profession' is 'of independent means', but in fact she was the one of independent means, while he had virtually no money. She had been partly brought up in Italy and was accustomed to living in comfortable circumstances and surroundings. Not surprisingly, the austerity of Toynbee Hall and the dirt and smells of the surrounding area did not suit her. In June 1911 Gerald resigned his post, and he and Beryl moved to west London.

Gerald and Beryl had become engaged just five days after first meeting. He was attracted by her good looks and girlish gaiety. She was bowled over by the attention of an older man whom she found 'charming' and 'exceedingly brilliant intellectually'.[16] But it turned out that they had few interests in common, apart from the welfare of their three children, Brigid (born 14 December 1911), Dermod (born 16 June 1913), and Mary (born 8 April 1918). Beryl was fluent in Italian, but was not well-read in English literature or a good conversationalist. She did not satisfy Gerald intellectually, and it is not entirely surprising that, after seven or eight years with a wife who bored him, he was attracted to a lively woman who was well able to discuss matters that interested him, being

---

[15] An account of his life and career, especially detailed on his life in Ireland, is given by John F. Ryan, 'Gerald O'Donovan: Priest, Novelist, and Irish Revivalist', *Journal of the Galway Archaeological and Historical Society* 48 (1996) 1–47.

[16] Beryl O'Donovan, *Locusts Food* 75, 78. The page numbers are those of the typescript of the unpublished memoir. I am grateful to Mary Anne O'Donovan for kindly giving me a copy and allowing me to make use of it. It makes no mention of Rose.

extremely well-read and, like him, a writer. Many of the things that attracted him to Rose were the same as those that attracted her to him. They evidently found themselves very much on the same wavelength. So far as writing is concerned, she had been much the more productive of the two: before they met, she had published eight novels and a volume of poetry, whereas he was the author of just two novels, *Father Ralph* (1913) and *Waiting* (1914), both based on his unhappy experience of the Roman Catholic Church in Ireland. He was to publish four more novels in the three years 1920–1922, then nothing more in the remaining twenty years of his life. His last novel, *The Holy Tree*, set in rural Ireland, is the story of a woman who does not love her husband and falls passionately in love with another man. A few weeks after Gerald's death, Rose wrote to Rosamond Lehmann: 'To me his real book, the one I love, is *The Holy Tree*, that he wrote in 1922, for me. In that he puts his whole philosophy of love, through the medium of Irish peasants – all the things he used to say to me about love and life, all he felt about me, all we both knew.'[17]

During the Great War Gerald had a variety of posts before he went to Crewe House in 1918. At the outbreak of war he and Beryl were living near Cromer in Norfolk (Fig. 3). From May to October 1915 he served as a first lieutenant in the Army Service Corps in Hull. In 1916 he was employed in the Ministry of Munitions, and in 1917 by the Glasgow publishers William Collins, who had just opened a London office. In each position he exhibited a tendency, inimical to his prospects of continuing employment, to take a firm stand on matters of principle, even if this involved disagreement with his superiors. It was the same tendency that had manifested itself when he was a priest in Ireland; and it manifested itself again in the summer of 1918, when, on a mission to Italy as a representative of the Italian Committee at Crewe House, he ruffled many feathers and was accused of exceeding his authority both diplomatically and financially (*L*16 n. 11). In the letter to Rosamond Lehmann quoted above, Rose says that 'he would have made a good statesman'. One begs to differ.

Despite some disagreement with Collins in 1917, Gerald retained influence with the firm, and he used it to persuade them to publish, on terms favourable to Rose, the first novel she wrote after the war, *Potterism* (*L*15). Henceforth all her novels were published by them. Much more important than Gerald's advice about the publishing of novels was his influence on the writing of them. Undoubtedly this was considerable, although it is impossible to quantify it.

If the love story in *What Not* at all accurately reflects Rose's own experience, she and Gerald agonised much about what to do after they fell in love. The options would have ranged from Gerald quitting his marriage to severance of

---

[17] Letter, dated 20 August [1942], in King's College Library, Cambridge. The quotations of the letter in Emery 186–187 and LeFanu 141 are inaccurate. *ODNB*, in its article on Gerald, says that *The Holy Tree* is 'dedicated to Rose Macaulay', but there is no such dedication.

all contact between him and Rose. What actually emerged was an intermediate 'solution'. Gerald remained with Beryl and their children, to whom Rose was presented as a very good friend. She often visited the O'Donovans' home. But she and Gerald had many other opportunities for seeing one another: during the first half of the 1920s they often went to lunches and evening parties together; sometimes Gerald was a guest at Hedgerley End; when Rose again acquired a flat in London, he will often have come there; and they even managed to share holidays at home and abroad. Whether Beryl was fully aware of the real nature of the relationship between the two is not known. Even if she thought that the friendship was platonic, it is difficult to believe that she was entirely comfortable about her husband going off on holiday with Rose. But the arrangement meant that she still had a husband, and her children a loving father. For Gerald the main advantages of continuing to live with his wife were his children and, thanks to Beryl's money, a comfortable home life. What about Rose? Her adultery certainly troubled her conscience until the end of her life, but her involvement with a married man protected her from marriage, which she certainly did not want, and, while satisfying her need for a man's love, enabled her to maintain her independence. She expressed her point of view in a newspaper article, in which she discussed the pros and cons of marriage: 'Some men and women might well prefer to live alone, meeting their beloved only when it suits them, thus retaining both that measure of freedom (small though any human freedom is) enjoyed by the solitary and the delicate bloom on the fruit of love which is said to be brushed off by continual contact'.[18]

---

[18] 'People Who Should Not Marry', *The Daily Mail*, 26 October 1929, 10.

II   JEAN SMITH

1 The Consul's daughter (1891–1911)

Jean Isabel Smith was born on 18 September 1891 at 173 Upper Richmond Road, Putney, in south-west London, not far from Riverbank, the spacious Georgian home of her paternal grandmother, Susan Parker Smith, daughter of the judge and vice-chancellor Sir James Parker and widow of the mathematician Archibald Smith. Jean was the fourth of nine children of Charles ('Charlie') Stewart Smith and his wife, Anne ('Nannie') Georgiana, a younger sister of Rose's father, George Macaulay. The first four children were girls, but the first girl died the day she was born and the third before her first birthday. After the girls came five boys. The family responsibilities Jean had as she grew up, as an elder sister to five brothers, were all the greater because of frequent family separations and travel. She took these responsibilities very seriously, and she continued to take them seriously throughout her life. She was devoted to her parents, her sister, and her brothers, and deeply and affectionately interested in the wider family as well. In *L*103 Rose writes: 'You must now (I hope) be enjoying a relaxing peace, having sped an inexperienced brother and an erratic niece so efficiently across the seas. What *would* they all do without you?' In particular, since, like Rose, she never married, she assumed chief responsibility for the care of her widowed and elderly mother (*L*85 n. 1; 93 n. 15).

The news of Jean's birth was telegraphed to Charlie in Poona (Pune). He was visiting India from Zanzibar, where he was British Consul. He had been appointed to that post in 1889 after retirement from the Royal Navy. He was no stranger to the area, having served in it as a naval officer, employed in the interception of Arab dhows carrying off African slaves. Although he remained in East Africa until May 1893, it was judged too dangerous for Jean to go there, and with good reason: the coastal regions were malarial, and in August 1890 Charlie's and Nannie's daughters Dorothy and Frances, aged two and a half years and eleven months respectively, had succumbed to the disease. Dorothy recovered after falling dangerously ill, but Frances died.

In January 1894 Charlie took up his appointment as British Consul in Bilbao, which was to be his and his family's home for six years. Jean was two when she arrived in Spain and eight when she left. She and Dorothy acquired three brothers (Tom, Regie, and Bill) in Bilbao and two more (Jim and Henry) in Odessa, to which the family moved in the summer of 1900 after Charlie had been promoted to Consul-General there. At this time Odessa, chief port on the Black Sea and the fourth-largest city of Imperial Russia, had a population of around 450,000, about a third of whom were Jews. The post was an important one, involving responsibility for eleven (later, thirteen) consular districts in southern Russia. Charlie was to hold it until 1913 and witness momentous events that included the Russo-Japanese War of 1904–1905, the mutiny of sailors aboard the Russian warship *Potemkin* anchored off Odessa (28 June 1905), the rioting and massacre that immediately followed the mutiny, and several pogroms.

Odessa, with its mixed population, broad streets, busy harbours, bitter winters, short springs, and long summers, made a deep impression on Jean and her siblings, as did the long journeys they made between it and England. These journeys were made sometimes by sea, but more often by train. Even the rail journey took three days, via Warsaw, Berlin, and the Hook of Holland.

Until 1904 Jean was educated in Odessa, as in Bilbao, by a governess. But on 15 September 1904, three days before her thirteenth birthday, she went as a boarder to the Godolphin School, Salisbury, which her sister, Dorothy, had entered a year earlier. Established under the will of Elizabeth Godolphin in 1726, the school (Cornish motto: 'Frank and loyal thou art') began life near the Cathedral in 1784 and, after several relocations, moved in 1891 to its present site, where it flourished under its inspiring headmistress, Mary Alice Douglas. Like Dorothy, Jean was in School House. Her all-round achievements are chronicled in the pages of *The Godolphin School Magazine* (*GSM*). She performed well not only academically but also in sport, especially cricket and lacrosse, and in other extra-curricular activities. In her last year (1909–1910) she was Head Girl, secretary of the Debating Society, and editor of *GSM*. Her successor in the last post was Dorothy L. Sayers, who gives a lively and mostly favourable picture of her time at the Godolphin in the letters she wrote to her parents and mentions Jean several times.[19] Sayers's experiences at the Godolphin are strongly reflected also in her unfinished novel *Cat O'Mary*.[20] It was in *GSM* that poems by Jean first appeared in print. Paying tribute to her when she left, Mary Douglas said: 'She loved the School with all her heart.' Jean's own assessment, communicated to her mother at the time and recalled by her in later life with wry amusement, was that, in fulfilling her responsibilities as Head Girl, she had probably done the best of her life's work. Although that was not true, it seems that she was more confident and happy during her Godolphin schooldays than she was to be in much of her adult life.

In 1905, after Jean's first year at the Godolphin, her parents took the lease of Cross Bank, a house in the Worcestershire village of Clent, mid-way between

---

[19] See Barbara Reynolds (ed.), *The Letters of Dorothy L. Sayers. 1899–1936: The Making of a Detective Novelist* (London, 1995) 15–64; M.F. Smith, '"Golliwog", Wolley-Dods, Wollaston, and Others: Some Contemporaries of Dorothy L. Sayers at the Godolphin School, Salisbury', *Proceedings of the Dorothy L. Sayers Society 34th Annual Convention* (Hurstpierpoint, 2010) 85–106.

[20] See Barbara Reynolds (ed.), *Dorothy L. Sayers, Child and Woman of Her Time* (Cambridge, 2002).

Stourbridge and Bromsgrove. A base in England was badly needed: several children were, or would soon be, at boarding school, and it was impracticable for them to make the long journey to Odessa in the shorter holidays. Moreover, the serious disturbances in Odessa in 1905 meant that it was safer for the children to be in England. The house, small for a family of nine, was retained for over 45 years, until after Nannie's death in December 1950. Clent was already well known to the Smiths, because Nannie's brother Kenneth Macaulay had lived there for fifteen years. Kenneth was a hospitable bachelor, and his home, Walton House, whose outbuildings and garden were a children's paradise (*L*87), had been enjoyed by the holidaying Smiths just as much as it had been by the holidaying Macaulays. The close proximity of Cross Bank to Walton House was not only pleasant and convenient but also comforting, given that Charlie was in Odessa for eleven months out of twelve each year, and that Dorothy, after she had left school, was sometimes left in charge of the household during school holidays, while her mother and the two youngest children joined her father in Russia.

In June 1910, during her last term at the Godolphin, Jean, who had applied to read Classics at Newnham College, Cambridge, took the University's Previous Examination, often known as 'Littlego', and gained Class I in both parts. It is very likely that, when she went to Cambridge to sit her papers, she stayed with the Macaulays in Great Shelford. Anyhow, according to her own account, her friendship with Rose began at this time.[21]

2 Cambridge (1911–1915)

Jean's entry into Cambridge was postponed for a year. From the early autumn of 1910 until July 1911 she was in Odessa, giving secretarial assistance to her father and helping to mind and tutor her youngest brother, Henry, who was yet to follow the older children to boarding school in England. Her parents were by no means wealthy, and the cost of rearing and educating seven children had put a considerable strain on their finances. The cost of Jean's studies in Cambridge would have been an additional burden, had her uncle and godfather Regi Macaulay not come to the rescue and paid for her university education, just as he had for Rose's.

'Jeanie Smith came up to Newnham, having lost her luggage in flood.' So reports Edward Conybeare, *Diary*, on 7 October 1911. During her four years at Newnham Jean was quite often entertained by Edward and his wife, Frances, to Sunday lunch or tea. But she was a still more frequent visitor to the Macaulays' house in Great Shelford. Her friendship with Rose blossomed, and Rose introduced her to friends of hers, including Rupert Brooke. Poetry was one of the interests Jean and Rose shared. *L*1, written in January 1913, contains Rose's

---

[21] Letter from Jean to Constance Babington Smith, 5 February 1973 (ERM 4.209).

comments on the draft of a poem Jean has composed. Given that Rose, who was ten years senior to Jean, had been to some extent her mentor and was a well-known writer, it is not at all remarkable that, when Jean's volume of poetry, *Shepherd of Souls*, was published in 1928, she dedicated it to Rose. What *is* remarkable is that Rose dedicated her first collection of poetry, *The Two Blind Countries*, to Jean. The volume was published in the early spring of 1914, when Jean was 22 and still an undergraduate.

Jean's poetic output was never to be large, but there is no doubting the quality of it, even at this early stage. During her time at Newnham she had poems printed not only in the College magazine, *Thersites*, but also in *The Cambridge Review*, Aelfrida Tillyard's *Cambridge Poets 1900–1913: An Anthology* (Cambridge, 1913), the South African magazine *Woman's Outlook*, and *The 'Golden Hynde'* (London, 1914). One of her poems from this period, 'Compensation', begins: 'From Trumpington to Shelford | The road runs straight and high'. This is the road she took on her bicycle when visiting Rose and her family. Her friendship with Rose was the most important one to her during her years in Cambridge, and it was a friendship that was to endure until Rose's death.

Several of Jean's contemporaries at Newnham also became lifelong friends. They included Dorothy Garrod, destined for a distinguished career as an archaeologist and prehistorian (*L*28 n. 1), 'Bice' Burton-Brown (*L*8 n. 4), who became headmistress of Prior's Field, Godalming, and Madeleine Symons, whose first career, as a trade unionist, was to be terminated by the birth of an illegitimate daughter (*L*63, 65, 68).

Jean's four years at Newnham were happy ones. As at school, she threw herself wholeheartedly into extra-curricular activities, including sport. She was a member of the College cricket team and co-founder and captain of the Lacrosse Club. But her academic performance, at least as measured by examination results, was undistinguished. Her First-Class results in the Previous Examination must have created an expectation of excellent performances in the Tripos (Honours) Examinations as well. But in the Classical Tripos Part 1 in 1914 she was placed in the Second Class, Division Two, and in the Medieval and Modern Languages (English) Tripos in 1915 she was placed in the Third Class. The reasons for these disappointing performances are not known, but one may conjecture that they included the same combination of diffidence and perfectionism that largely explains why the quantity of her literary output in later life was to be so small – out of all proportion to its fine quality. Whether she was at all impeded, as she was to be later on, by physical illness or bouts of depression, is not recorded. One of her English teachers in her final year was her uncle George Macaulay, Rose's father. Towards the end of her life she recalled that the students found his lectures 'rather dry and dull'.[22]

---

[22] Letter to H.F. Smith, 25 October 1972.

3 Munitions and sugar (1916–1919)

From February 1916 until September 1918 Jean worked as a clerk in the Labour Regulation Department of the Ministry of Munitions. The Department's offices were in Whitehall Gardens, London SW1, off the east side of Whitehall and very close to Downing Street and the River Thames. One of Jean's published poems is entitled 'Whitehall Gardens, Floodtide'. She was fortunate to work under James Cruickshank Smith, a Classics and English scholar, who took a friendly interest in her and an admiring interest in her poetry (*L*78 n. 11). In September 1918 she was transferred to the Royal Commission on the Sugar Supply at 3 Grosvenor Gardens, SW1, where her work as a statistical officer inspired another of her poems, 'Statistics' (*L*18 n. 1). While working as a civil servant, she recorded in a notebook, which she entitled *Interdepartmental*, incidents and conversations, often of an amusing character, that she witnessed in the office, on the pavements and buses of London, and in other locations. The entries are both entertaining and instructive. Several other notebooks of hers are preserved, including two best described as commonplace books, into which she copied passages of prose and verse that interested her for religious, philosophical, and other reasons. The first book was begun about 1909, when she was still at school, and the last entries in the second one were made a few years before her death in 1979. The extracts are remarkable for their wide range of authors, languages (English, Latin, Greek, German, French, Spanish, and Italian), form, and content.

From the autumn of 1916 Jean shared a flat in Bloomsbury with Madeleine Symons (*L*2 n. 1). Madeleine, four years her junior, had read Economics at Newnham in 1913–1916. An only child of wealthy parents, she was working for the Women's Trade Union League. Jean was sometimes a weekend guest at the Symonses' large (ten-bedroomed) Georgian house, Hadley Lodge, twelve miles north of London, near Barnet and Potters Bar. One Sunday evening (1 October 1916) she, Madeleine, and a friend (identified only as 'D.', but almost certainly Dorothy Garrod) witnessed the shooting-down of a Zeppelin airship, which crashed in flames into Oakmere Park, Potters Bar. She gives a dramatic and detailed account of the event in *Interdepartmental*—of how they saw the Zeppelin being picked up by searchlights, catching fire, diving and roaring in flames, and breaking up before hitting the ground. She describes too the excitement and celebrations of local people and Londoners who came to view the site of the crash. She, Madeleine, and D. did not join in the celebrations or head for Oakmere Park. Instead, 'D. was sobbing by me *de profundis* for the dying', and then 'we ate biscuits, and went to read ourselves to sleep, hearing more guns and seeing searchlights'.

Jean was a profoundly religious person, who, although she possessed a good sense of humour and had an infectious laugh, was essentially serious-minded in her attitude to life. On her, as on so many other thoughtful and sensitive people, the horrific slaughter and destruction of the Great War made a deep and lasting impression. All human suffering appalled her, and she was extremely concerned about those of her brothers who were old enough to be in the services. The eldest, Tom (*L*60 n. 11), was an officer in the Royal Navy, serving in destroyers off the east coast of England and later in the Mediterranean. Regie went to France with the Artists' Rifles in 1915 and became a second lieutenant in the Queen's (Royal West Surrey) Regiment in 1916. Bill (*L*53 n. 2) joined the Gloucestershire Regiment in 1916, starting as a lieutenant and ending the war as acting colonel. All three survived the war, although only Tom came through unscathed. Regie and Bill, fighting on the Western Front, were wounded (Bill three times), and Regie was reported 'missing, believed killed'; two months passed before news was received that he was not dead, but had been taken prisoner. With Charlie Smith serving as Consul-General in Barcelona, Dorothy working in her father's office there, and Nannie too spending much time in Barcelona, Jean was often the senior member of the family in England, and, if her mother was away, it was her responsibility to meet and look after Tom, Regie, and Bill when they returned home, and to see them off at the end of their leave. It was also her responsibility to look after her two youngest brothers, Jim and Henry, who were boarders at Marlborough College and Shrewsbury School respectively. Jean's care for her brothers was admirable, but it is not unlikely that the stresses and strains of her wartime experiences exacerbated, if they did not precipitate, her tendency to suffer bouts of depression through much of her adult life. As Rose showed in *Non-Combatants and Others*, war can be very hard on those who stay at home as well as on those who go off to fight.

When the Armistice between the Allies and Germany came into force at 11.00 on 11.11.1918, Jean was in her office at the Sugar Commission. Preserved are a short note she wrote on a small sheet of the Commission's headed paper, with entries timed at 11.10 and 11.25, and a much longer account, occupying two sides of a quarto sheet, completed at 12.15. The description of the events–the firing of guns, the running, the blowing of bugles by policemen on bicycles, the laughing, the playing of a barrel-organ, and the cheering – is interspersed with biblical quotations: 'Praise the Lord, O Jerusalem . . .' (Psalms 147.12), 'The morning stars sang together . . .' (Job 38.7), 'Thou, O Lord, art in the midst of us . . .' (Jeremiah 14.9). Despite the celebrations, 'London is', she writes, 'nearer tears than it can let anyone see'.

Early in 1919 Jean left the Sugar Commission, and between 15 March and 12 May travelled in Spain and Mallorca (*L*3 n. 18) with Regie. In June Charlie left his post in Barcelona and retired from the consular service. That same month Jean accepted the offer of a new job.

4 *Helicon and the Isis (1919–1926)*

The job, which Jean started on 21 July 1919, was that of private secretary to Gilbert Murray at Boars Hill, just south of Oxford. To Jean, classicist and poet, the opportunity must have seemed extraordinarily enticing and exciting. Murray, Regius Professor of Greek in the University of Oxford since 1908, was one of the most distinguished Greek scholars of the day. Moreover, he was well known outside the field of Greek scholarship, both for his English translations of Greek plays, which were widely read and performed, and for his involvement in political matters, especially as a prominent figure in moves towards the establishment of the League of Nations. As for Boars Hill, to which the Murrays moved from the city of Oxford only a few days before Jean took up her duties in their house, Yatscombe, it had, during her time there, so much poetic talent among its population of about five hundred that it was sometimes known as Helicon or Parnassus.

Who were the poets? Heading the list was Robert Bridges, the Poet Laureate, closely followed by John Masefield, who was to succeed Bridges as Poet Laureate in 1930. (A.E. Housman, writing from Cambridge to congratulate Masefield on his appointment, quipped: 'In sporting circles here they are asking the question: if Boar's Hill get it three times, do they keep it?')[23] Then there were three young poets–Edmund Blunden (*L*22 and n. 3 there) and Robert Graves (*L*13 and n. 2 there; *L*17 and n. 7 there), who started courses in Oxford in the autumn of 1919 after their war service, and Robert Nichols (*L*20 and n. 6 there), who arrived in 1920. None of them stayed long, but all were there for part of the time when Jean was working for Murray. She certainly met Bridges and Masefield, and it would be surprising if she did not encounter Graves and his wife, 'pretty Nancy Nicholson in knickerbockers' (*L*13), not only because they lived in a cottage at the bottom of the Masefields' garden but also and above all because they kept the Boars Hill Shop for the six months of its unprofitable existence (*L*13 n. 2). The Graveses used to undercharge their poorer customers and, to compensate, overcharge their richer ones, which presumably means that, if ever Jean went shopping for the Murrays, she was overcharged. It is a pity that her letters describing her time on Boars Hill do not survive.

Another resident, who, although not a poet, is bound to have interested her, was Sir Arthur Evans, former Keeper of the Ashmolean Museum, Oxford, and world-famous for his excavations of the Bronze Age 'Minoan' palace at Knossos in Crete. He incorporated Minoan architectural and artistic features in his rambling house.

Jean remained Murray's secretary until early in 1922, living first in lodgings (*L*10), then, from September 1920, at Yatscombe. It would be nice to be able to report that her time on Helicon was one of uninterrupted fulfilment and happiness, but in fact it was marred by illness. She underwent major surgery in the spring of 1920 – surgery that had more than purely physical consequences, for it

---

[23] Letter of 11 May 1930, in Archie Burnett, *The Letters of A.E. Housman* (Oxford, 2007) II 184–185.

meant that she could never have a child (*L*19 and n. 1 there). Perhaps she would not have married and wanted children in any case, but the psychological impact of the operation is likely to have been considerable. After a summer of convalescence, she returned to Boars Hill, but she was unwell again, or still unwell, in May 1921 (*L*25), and it was illness that caused her to resign as Murray's secretary. Although one cannot be sure, one suspects that some of her illnesses in the 1920s already had a psychosomatic character, as some of her illnesses in later life did.

Any psychological or psychosomatic problems Jean experienced at this stage may well have been exacerbated by contact with Murray's wife, Lady Mary, a daughter of George James Howard, ninth Earl of Carlisle. Lady Mary was essentially a very kind, generous, and unselfish person, who did much good during her life – for refugees, for example. But she was also a formidable woman, who could come across as domineering, tactless, and insensitive. It did not help that she had no real sense of humour. In contrast, Murray seemed the embodiment of reasonableness and sensitivity and had a very keen sense of humour. When Mary Midgley became his secretary more than twenty years after Jean, she was warned that she 'would soon find out why Murray had never managed to keep any of his secretaries for long'. The reason was of course Lady Mary, of whose character and behaviour Midgley gives a vivid description. She explains: 'The thing that made my work most difficult, . . . and that put most strain on my digestion, was her passion for interrupting things. She would come in at any time in the middle of whatever was going on and tell me to drive down into Oxford *at once* with a list of complicated commissions, each of which was liable to involve a long message to the tradespeople involved. While she explained these she interrupted herself constantly by thinking of new ones, and ended by hurrying me off, calling out, "And don't forget, lunch is early!"'[24] Jean was a tidy and orderly person, who had spent the previous three years working in government offices. If she was treated by Lady Mary in much the same way as Mary Midgley and Murray's other secretaries were, she would certainly have found the strain considerable, perhaps intolerable. Nevertheless she remained on affectionate terms with the Murrays until the end of their lives.[25] Rose was to become a friend of Murray, but had little contact with his wife.

After leaving Boars Hill early in 1922, Jean took more than a year off. The aim, presumably, was to recover her physical health and if, as is likely, she had been suffering from depression as well, to rid herself of that. It may be significant that

[24] *The Owl of Minerva: A Memoir* (Abingdon and New York, 2005) 144–146.

[25] The present writer was taken by Jean to have tea at Yatscombe at the end of August 1956. Neither he nor his aunt saw Lady Mary, who was in bed gravely ill and died two or three days later, on 2 September. Aged sixteen, he was apprehensive about meeting Murray, but fears that the great man might expose imperfections in a schoolboy's knowledge of Greek irregular verbs soon evaporated. He was gentle and charming.

there is a gap in Rose's surviving letters to her between 15 September 1921 and 9 March 1923. It should not be supposed that the correspondence ceased during this period, but perhaps Jean's low spirits explain why she did not keep the letters. Family records reveal that she travelled in France and Spain with her father in the spring of 1922, saw the Passion Play at Oberammergau with Regie in July, and went on to spend time with the family of her Ministry of Munitions boss, J.C. Smith, in Scotland. She was abroad between February and May 1923, first in Paris, then in Rome (*L*28 and n. 1 there).

By the summer of 1923 she must have been feeling stronger and more confident. She applied for a Research Fellowship at Newnham College. The application was unsuccessful, but in July she was appointed secretary to Robert Chapman, Secretary to the Delegates of the Clarendon Press in Oxford (*L*29 and n. 1 there). She took up the post in the autumn. Almost immediately she was off sick (*L*30), but if the illness was connected at all with worries about her new job, she overcame her nerves. She stayed with the Press until July 1926, and her three years there seem to have been generally happy ones. She left not because she disliked the work, but because a new life was calling her, and she needed to prepare herself for it.

5 *Canterbury or Rome? (1926–1938)*

During her years in Oxford Jean's active practice of Anglicanism had brought her into contact with the Cowley Fathers, as the members of the Society of St John the Evangelist are often called (*L*27 n. 2), particularly with the Rev. Lucius Cary, whom Rose had encountered in London before and during the Great War. Cary was Father Director of Fairacres, the Oxford home of the Community of the Sisters of the Love of God, a contemplative Anglican order founded by one of the Cowley Fathers (*L*61 n. 7). In the summer of 1926 Jean announced her intention of joining the Community as a postulant. Rose's reaction to the news is contained in *L*59, Gilbert Murray's similar one in n. 3 there. It is clear from Murray's letter to her that, in explaining her decision to become a nun, Jean used the image of passing though a door into a garden. We shall see that she was to use the same image a few years later, when she made another important decision.

Jean entered Fairacres in late June 1927. She had spent much of the winter in Exmouth, helping her parents look after her sister Dorothy's children, while Dorothy joined her husband in India. In February and March she had been in Spain and Mallorca with her father. Shortly before she disappeared behind the walls of the convent, Rose confided in her about her affair with Gerald O'Donovan and asked for her prayers (*L*61 and n. 1 there). Once a member of the Community, Jean was rarely permitted to write letters, although she was able to receive them, but Rose received favourable news of her from Jean's brother Henry in mid-September (*L*66), and from Jean herself in early November (*L*68).

But all was not well. In December she left Fairacres. Why? The explanation given to and accepted by her family was that the regime, which included physical tasks (kitchen work, cleaning, laundry, gardening, etc.) and rising for devotions during the night as well as early in the morning, was too demanding for her. There is no reason to query the truth of this. But was it the whole truth? Or was part of the problem that she had developed doubts about whether she had found the right door into the spiritual garden she craved to enter?

While she was in Fairacres, her collection of poems, *Shepherd of Souls*, was being printed, with the dedicatee, Rose, looking after its progress through the press. Published by Oxford University Press on 2 February 1928, it contained thirty-three pieces, including some that had appeared in print before. Her poems received a warm reception from the critics. *The Observer*, 26 February 1928, declared that 'Hers is a quiet, naturally gentle Muse, but with a core of real intelligence and genuine feeling. Whether her subject be "Shepherd of Souls", or "The Dustcart", or "Scythes", she envelops it with a slow, clear light that elucidates small but abiding lovelinesses. She has genuine technical ability, vision; and a sort of holy calm sets a lingering seal on all she writes.' The critic in *The Daily News*, 13 June 1928, wrote: '"The Requiem Mass", in its governed and gracious pity, has a power and dignity that make it one of the great poems about death.' The glowing comments of Charles Williams and Naomi Royde-Smith are quoted in *L*61 n. 4 and 70 n. 3.

A few months after abandoning her intention of becoming an Anglican nun, Jean joined the teaching staff of Downe House, the girls' boarding school at Cold Ash, Thatcham, near Newbury. The school's headmistress and founder was Rose's friend Olive Willis, a senior contemporary of hers at Somerville (I.2 above), and Rose may have suggested Jean to Olive, or Olive to Jean, although Olive and Jean already knew one another (*L*46). Olive was an unorthodox but brilliant headmistress, who, while maintaining discipline, kept rules to a minimum, allowed the girls a good deal of freedom, and did as much as possible to make their time at Downe House interesting and enjoyable. How many headmistresses nowadays would announce at breakfast that, since it was such a fine summer's day, there would be no classes at all and everyone was to take a sandwich lunch and go off to explore the countryside? And how many, on noticing three bored girls moping about on a wet Saturday afternoon, would invite them to her study and enchant them with her reading of Robert Browning? These and other incidents are related by Mary Midgley, who was a pupil at Downe House from 1932 to 1937 and taught there briefly during the Second World War.[26]

It is not known whether Jean went to Downe House at the beginning of the Summer Term 1928 or in September. Nor is it certain exactly when she left, but

---

[26] *The Owl of Minerva* 54–75, 134–135. The full story of Olive and her school is told by Anne Ridler, *Olive Willis and Downe House: An Adventure in Education* (London, 1967).

she remained until at least the end of the Summer Term 1931 and perhaps until the end of the Autumn Term. She taught Latin and perhaps some Greek too. The pages of the school-magazine reveal that she was president of the Downe House Philosophical Society. Among her papers are the notes she made for a talk she gave it on the nature of poetry, together with the manuscripts or typescripts of several poems she wrote at Cold Ash. The reason for her departure from Downe House is not recorded, but was almost certainly her poor health, which necessitated several months of treatment in a nursing home in 1932 and early in 1933 (*L*73 n. 1).

The health problems Jean experienced around this time were aggravated by her worries over religion. Whether or not it is the case that she came out of the Anglican convent partly because she already had doubts about remaining in the Anglican Church, Lady Mary Murray was saying in the early spring of 1929 that she would not be surprised if Jean became a Roman Catholic (*L*71 n. 1). According to Jean's sister-in-law Rosemary Smith, an event that had a significant influence on her was the decision of a friend. In the years she was working in Oxford before entering Fairacres, her church-going had brought her into contact and friendship with Charis and Herbert Thomas and their three children, described by Rosemary as 'a gifted and warm-hearted family reflecting Anglo-Catholic faith and practice at its most attractive'. Charis was the daughter of the artist and bibliophile Lionel Muirhead, a lifelong friend of Robert Bridges. On 7 March 1931 Charis and her twelve-year-old daughter, Bridget Mary, were received into the Roman Catholic Church. Charis's move triggered or intensified a conflict in Jean's mind and conscience. She experienced severe insomnia and was brought to the verge of a nervous breakdown.

The nature of Jean's mental conflict at this time is clear enough. On the one hand, there was her loyalty to the Church in which she had been brought up and confirmed, and to which as an adult she had hitherto given her devoted allegiance; and there was also her love and respect for her elderly parents, who were devout Anglicans and certain to be upset if she transferred her allegiance from Canterbury to Rome. On the other hand, she yearned to find her true spiritual home and had come to believe more and more firmly that she would find it in the Roman Catholic Church. She became a Roman Catholic in September 1933. Her parents took the painful news better than she had feared and wished her well. Her father died in February 1934. A few months later Nannie learned from her son Jim that he was following in his sister's footsteps, but she again responded with dignity and affection. In his privately printed memoir Jim reports Jean as telling him that 'she felt as if, while an Anglican, she had been looking at a garden through a window, and that upon becoming a Catholic had escaped out of doors into the garden itself.[27] She had used the same image before entering Fairacres, but this time had found the right door.

[27] J.S. Smith, *The Last Time* (1974) 110.

In November 1934, immediately after Jim's reception into the Roman Catholic Church, he and Jean spent a blissfully happy fortnight together in Rome. They had hoped that an introduction they had been given to a Vatican official might possibly lead to their being included in a general audience with Pope Pius XI. But they were to have a surprise. On returning to their hotel one evening, they found a message informing them that the Holy Father would receive them in a *private* audience the next day. Jim, taller and broader than most Italians, had difficulty in hiring suitable attire at short notice and went to the Vatican 'dressed like a waiter' in a tailcoat that was 'rather tight and shiny'. During the next twenty years he was to do much good work in support of Catholic organisations in Nigeria, where he was serving in the colonial administration, and in 1953 the Vatican recognised his services by appointing him a Knight Commander of the Order of Saint Gregory the Great. As for Jean, the Catholic Church was to remain a central part of her life until she died. One of her early actions after her conversion was to give the Dominicans of Blackfriars, Oxford, an item that had been bought by her father in northern Spain during the period when he was Consul in Bilbao (1894–1900). The item was a Dominican Gradual, a precious liturgical manu-script written about 1260. The binders of the Clarendon Press made some repairs to it in 1925, at which time Jean was an employee of the Press, but she probably did not become its owner until the death of her father in 1934. She presented it to the Dominicans not later than the summer of 1936.[28]

Although Jean's admission to the Catholic Church ended her conflict of con-science, it did not rid her of the intermittent attacks of deep depression to which she was prone. These were to continue to plague her for almost another thirty years. In the summer of 1935 she was in hospital for several months, perhaps for treatment of a psychosomatic illness (*L*74 n. 6). After she left Downe House in 1931, at the age of about forty, she never again had regular, paid employment. But life was certainly not spent in unrelieved gloom. In the autumn of 1936 she crossed the Atlantic for the first time, to visit her brother Bill, his American wife, and three small children in Massachusetts, and in the autumn and winter of 1937–1938 she spent several months with Jim in Nigeria.

6 *War, duty, and darkness (1939–1960)*

When war broke out in September 1939, Jean's base was still Cross Bank. Her mother was approaching eighty and relied on Jean, more than on anyone else, for care and companionship. Jean's sister, Dorothy, who lived in Surrey, was a busy wife and mother, and four of their five brothers were overseas – Bill in the USA, Regie in Southern Rhodesia, Jim in Nigeria, Henry in India. Jean spent the winter of 1939–1940 at home, working for the relief of Polish refugees. Then, in

---

[28] See Walter Gumbley, OP, 'The Blackfriars Codex', *Blackfriars* 17, 197 (August 1936) 611–614.

the summer of 1940, she went to London to assist the work of the Catholic War Refugees Spiritual Welfare Committee, established in May by Cardinal Arthur Hinsley, Archbishop of Westminster, and Peter Emmanuel Amigo, Archbishop of Southwark, in order to bring religious and moral assistance, as well as social and material support, to war refugees. It was then that she acquired a flat, 39 Ashley Court, Morpeth Terrace, practically next door to Westminster Cathedral – very convenient both for her work and for the practice of her religion. She was to continue to have a flat in Ashley Court until 1963, but soon moved to no. 21 and later (1956) to no. 6. In 1940 her friend Rosalind Toynbee, daughter of Gilbert and Mary Murray, acquired a flat (no. 30) in the same building. She too had become a Roman Catholic in 1933.

In 1941–1942 Jean was dividing her time between London and Clent, between care for refugees and care for her mother. She was in London in May 1941, when Rose lost her flat and its contents in the Blitz, and in the following days and weeks did what she could to help her (*L*78 n. 2). Some time in 1943 she let 21 Ashley Court. After several months with her mother in Clent, she went in September to work in the Red Cross Library in Oxford. She was there until late November, when she had to rush home after hearing that her mother had been taken ill (*L*85 n. 1). Although Nannie lived for another seven years, she required more care than before, and Jean provided most of this. After the war she took back her London flat and got away there for much-needed breaks. She managed holidays in Scotland (1945), Portugal (1947), and Ireland (1949), but her movements and activities were somewhat restricted until after Nannie's death on 3 November 1950 (*L*93 n. 15). The following year Cross Bank was sold, and she was then free to resume her own life in London.

Henceforth she and Rose had more opportunities to meet, but they did not take advantage of them as much as one might have expected. Their relations continued to be affectionate, but were put under some strain by their differences over religion. Now that Rose had returned to being a practising Anglican, she became increasingly annoyed about what she saw as the self-righteousness of many Roman Catholics and their contempt for Anglicans and Christians of other denominations (*L*106). Although she excluded Jean, Jim, and his wife, Rosemary, from their number, she nevertheless found it irritating that Jean and Jim did not join in the prayers at Anglican baptisms and funerals (*L*104 and n. 1 there). On at least one occasion Rose's irritation with what she regarded as Jean's narrow-mindedness in religion spread to irritation, expressed in a letter to her sister Jeanie, with 'her didactic ways' and her fondness for relating stories about her and her siblings' childhood (*L*109 n. 2). Jean was well aware of Rose's irritation about her practice of Roman Catholicism and undoubtedly found it painful. But their last meeting, a few days before Rose died, was harmonious and, in Jean's words, 'the best time I had had with her for years' (*L*111 n. 7).

In the spring of 1952 Jean made a second visit to her brother Bill and his family in the USA (*L*95), spending time in New York as well as in Massachusetts. Three or four months after her return, her elder sister Dorothy died (9 August), at the age of 64, followed only seven months later by Dorothy's husband, Sid (4 March 1953). Jean was very fond of Dorothy's children, as of all her nieces and nephews, and in January 1954 visited Italy, Sicily, and Malta with her sister's younger daughter, Helen (*L*97).

While Rose was staying in Venice in May 1957, the death occurred of Gilbert Murray. Although he was 91, she was much saddened by the passing of a great man who had been a friend of hers for many years and particularly since 1941, the year her flat was bombed (*L*79 n. 15). Jean communicated the news by letter, and in her reply Rose pays a warm tribute to him and his many-sided achievements, praising his scholarship, kindness, and humanity, and commenting that 'a great tree has fallen' (*L*105). To Jean too his death was a heavy loss. Ever since she had worked for him in 1919–1922, she had enjoyed an affectionate friendship with him and Lady Mary. In view of her triple status as former secretary, classicist, and friend, it is not surprising that she was invited both to sort Murray's papers and to edit, in collaboration with Rosalind's ex-husband, the historian Arnold Toynbee, the proposed memoir of his life. The memoir, *Gilbert Murray: An Unfinished Autobiography, with Contributions from His Friends*, consists of an autobiographical fragment, two examples of Murray's skill at translating English prose and verse into Greek, an introduction by E.R. Dodds, and chapters by Jean, Arnold Toynbee, Isobel Henderson, Sybil Thorndike, Salvador de Madariaga, and Bertrand Russell.

Jean found both tasks a considerable strain. At the time she undertook them, she was passing through one of her dark, depressive phases, and her responsibilities tended to deepen her depression. In the circumstances, it is much to her credit that she did not give up. She made an excellent job of sorting the papers. Her work as editor was less successful, although the shortcomings of a book that is interesting, but rather scrappy, cannot all be laid at her door. Publication took place on 17 March 1960.

7 'Lead, kindly Light' (1961–1979)

Jean's family and friends hoped that, with the completion of her work on Murray's papers and the publication of *An Unfinished Autobiography*, she would feel liberated and confident. Instead, she continued to suffer from black depression, and in the spring of 1962, a few weeks after the death of her brother Bill (27 February), she was admitted to Powick Hospital near Worcester. The hospital, opened in 1852 as Worcester County Pauper and Lunatic Asylum, was a grim-looking place, which achieved notoriety for the treatment, between 1952 and 1972, of hundreds of patients with psychedelic psychotherapy – a controversial method involving the use of LSD. Fortunately, Jean was given not LSD but electroconvulsive therapy (ECT), and this was very beneficial. In the last few years of her life she lost her memory for recent events, but for about ten years, until she was in her early eighties, she enjoyed happy normality.

After her three years of work on Gilbert Murray, she turned her attention to something very different. She became deeply interested in the Mediterranean travels of John Henry Newman in 1832–1833 and, in particular, in the nature of his experience during and after his dangerous illness in Sicily in May 1833. On visits to Sicily in October 1961 and May 1964, she traced Newman's journey and tracked down descendants of the family who had cared for him while he was ill and his life was in the balance. She hoped to publish the results of her researches, but, now well into her seventies and with her physical and mental powers declining, she did not manage to convert her notes and drafts into a finished piece of writing. However, after her death, Rosemary Smith completed the work and published an article under Jean's name: 'Newman and Sicily', *The Downside Review* 107 (1989) 155–182. Rosemary justly remarks of Jean: 'As a classical scholar . . . and a convert to the Roman Catholic Church from a deeply-held Anglicanism, she had a double affinity with her subject' (180 n. 1).

In 1963 Jean disposed of her London flat and moved to Oxford, where she occupied a flat at 3 Crick Road, a house rented by her dear friend Polly Porter, an eminent crystallographer and Honorary Research Fellow of Somerville College. In 1973 she and Polly moved to flats in the newly opened Wyndham House, Plantation Road, and in 1976 to flats in Ritchie Court, 380 Banbury Road, close to where Rose and her family had lived in 1896–1901. Ritchie Court too was a new development, and a major attraction of it was the promised provision of a nursing wing, but, because of a shortage of funds, this never materialised, and so, when Jean's mind failed more and more, the care and supervision she needed were not there. Early in 1979 the situation had become impossible. After a stay of several weeks in Pershore Cottage Hospital, near the home of Jim and Rosemary, she was cared for in the Court House Nursing Home, Malvern, where, two months later, she died on 7 July 1979, aged 87.

THE LETTERS

Editorial note

In general, the way in which the letters were written has been faithfully preserved, but, for the sake of clarity, some minor alterations have been made. Dates of letters are presented in a full and standardised form, e.g. 27 April 1919 for 27.4.19. Titles of books, periodicals, and newspapers are italicised, while those of articles and individual poems are placed in quotation marks. Also italicised are words that were underlined for emphasis. Single quotation marks are used, except where one quotation appears inside another. Ampersands and abbreviations like 'cd' and 'wd' have been converted to 'and', 'could', and 'would'.

Square brackets are used to indicate an editorial supplement, e.g. [January 1913] at the head of *L*1, *The Times* [*Literary Supplement*] at the end of *L*11.

Angled brackets are used to indicate repair of a mistake, misspelling, or omission, e.g. 18 January 195<4> at the head of *L*97 (where Rose wrote '1953'), Mos<le>y in *L*85 (where she has 'Mosely'), and <time> (obliterated by an ink blot) in *L*90.

Usually Rose's punctuation has been retained, but a problem concerns her frequent use of dashes, or what look like them. Sometimes a dash is clearly the punctuation intended, but quite often it is employed, presumably for the sake of speed, where a full stop or comma is required, and in these cases the 'correct' punctuation has been substituted. Inevitably there are some borderline cases, where it was difficult to decide what to do.

Another peculiarity of Rose's punctuation is that she frequently asks a question without using a question mark. This peculiarity has been retained, for it occurs when she has little or no doubt that the answer to the question is 'yes', so that her words, although put in an interrogative form, are virtually equivalent to a statement. An example, from *L*6, is: 'I love "Harlequin", don't you'.

1

[January 1913][1]

I like this most awfully – the sound and the colour and the atmosphere and the idea and all about it; thank you so much for letting me see it. I like the Greek sound for the frogs' noise better than the 'fluting' – *is* it soft?[2] Well, perhaps sometimes – but only a rare frog here and there, I should say. Do you know, you've got just the atmosphere of the Greek countryside – odd, isn't it.[3]

Do you really want me to criticize? I don't quite see why I should, but I will if you like. I don't care for cockney rhymes such as corn and dawn – in fact, I don't think you can possibly have them. Why not 'day unborn', or even 'morn', if you must have corn – no, I should hate 'morn' – I always do – but there must be a way out. I don't *much* like 'wresting heavy toll' – again I should think there must be a way out, even keeping the rhyme, which you should, because the 4th line is so particularly nice. But perhaps you don't mind toll – I don't really, only I don't positively like it, as I do most of it. What does 'speak ye well' mean? Is he addressing his fellow-peasants? And is it good to have this and then the sudden turn to Hecate? – perhaps it's all right, though. I rather like the sudden shortening of that line. But really I love it all – I think I'd like a copy to keep rather, only I've no time to make one to-day, being frantically rushed with wedding-arrangements and visitors etc. etc. *What* a time. We'll see you to-morrow, shan't we. I love the melon and the hen![4]

R.

1 This note, the earliest surviving communication from Rose to Jean, carries no address or date, but is to be assigned to January 1913, when Jean, aged 21, was in her second year at Cambridge, and Rose was living in her parents' house, Southernwood, Great Shelford. It may be assumed that Rose was writing from there to Jean at Clough Hall, Newnham College. The note contains her comments on a poem Jean has composed. The poem has the title (not given by Rose) 'Trivia', the Latin name of Hecate as 'goddess of the crossroads'. Among Jean's papers are two manuscripts of the poem: one is the version she sent to Rose, the other the revised version. She notes that the poem was composed in June 1912, revised during the winter of 1912–1913, and published in the second and last issue of *The 'Golden Hynde'* (London, June 1914) 47–49. That issue was edited by Beatrix Oliver and Marjorie Napier, and other contributors include Hilaire Belloc and John Buchan. 'Trivia' was first published anonymously in the Newnham College magazine *Thersites* 33 (11 November 1913).

Since the poem was revised during the winter of 1912–1913, Rose's note must be similarly dated. What makes more precise dating possible is her mention of 'being frantically rushed with wedding-arrangements and visitors etc. etc.'. Her cousin the Rev. Donald Macaulay and her Great Shelford friend Gladys Fanshawe were married in Great Shelford on 21 January 1913. Rose was bridesmaid. When Rose mentions seeing Jean 'tomorrow', she may well mean at the wedding, in which case the note was written on 20 January. Given that Jean too was a cousin of the bridegroom, one would certainly expect her to have attended.

2 'The Greek sound' is *brekekekex koax koax* (Aristophanes, *Frogs* 209–210 etc.). In her original version Jean had 'Frogs are fluting soft and well'. In the light of Rose's criticism, she substituted 'Little frogs sit sentinel'.

3 Unlike Rose, who had been on a Hellenic cruise with her father in April 1912 (*L*110

n. 9), Jean had not visited Greece, although she had sailed through the Aegean en route from Odessa to Antwerp in July 1911.

4 The last four lines of the third stanza are: 'Where the city-buyers come | Armed with crooked wit, | All to cheat poor husbandmen | Of a melon or a hen.'

2

With love for Xmas from Hedgerley Lane.[1]

1 The message, written on a postcard, is unsigned. The year has not come out in the postmark, but it must be 1916, 1917, or 1918, because the card is addressed (with the request 'Please forward') to 'Miss J.I. Smith, 14a Knollys Road, Compton Street, W.C.'. This is the address, although not the entirely correct one, of the flat Jean shared with Madeleine Symons while working as a civil servant from 1916 until early 1919. The Compton Street of the address is now part of Tavistock Place. 'Knollys Road' is an error for 'Knollys House', a block of flats that stood on the north side of Compton Street (numbered 39–41), near its junction with Judd Street. The flat, described by Jean's mother as 'a nice little place' with 'a good kind of charwoman who cooks the breakfast, and does the morning work, and washes up the supper things', is likely to have been chosen because of its close proximity to the offices of the Women's Trade Union League at 34 Mecklenburgh Square, where Madeleine worked. It seems, from a letter written by Jean's mother, that Madeleine's parents were paying the rent or most of it.

The postcard carries a photograph (Fig. 4) of Grace Macaulay, wearing coat and hat, sitting in a basketwork donkey-chaise and holding the reins. She had acquired the donkey, named Felicity, and chaise in the spring or early summer of 1916. The photograph was taken in Great Shelford, from which Grace and Rose moved to Beaconsfield in early December 1916, and it is most likely that it was used to convey greetings for Christmas 1916.

Jean attached the card to the page facing the dedicatory inscription in her copy of Rose's novel *Dangerous Ages* (1921). She had a good reason for doing this, for Rose's dedication reads: 'To my mother driving gaily through the adventurous middle years'. Emery 94, after pointing out that 'the verb has a double meaning, literal and metaphoric', claims that the literal image is untrue because Grace never managed to drive a car competently. But she did drive a donkey-chaise, and that is what Rose has in mind, as is confirmed by the mention of one in the book (20) and the portrayal of one on the dust cover. Grace derived much pleasure from hers. What gave her no pleasure at all was the realisation that her character and behaviour had contributed much to Rose's unfavourable depiction of Mrs Hilary in the novel.

3

Hedgerley End
Beaconsfield
27 April 1919

Dearest Jean

Thank you for yours <of > 19th.[1] I don't know if this will catch you before you leave[2] or not, but it doesn't matter.

Mother and I chuckled over Aunt Mary[3] and the things I oughtn't to know about.[4] It is lovely – no-one else has implied ever before, among all the things they've said about me, that I am risqué! She is a wonderful aunt.

I'm glad you like it, and glad you like Kitty. *The Athenaeum* pleased her by saying that they hoped this was going to be the type of the political and business woman of the future.[5] And *The New Statesman*[6] pleased *me* by saying that my love story was 'impressive and affecting' – I am proud of my love story, you see: it didn't come so easy or so naturally to me as the rest, so I like to see it approved. Some, however, complained that it was out of key with the rest. The reviews have entertained me a good deal. And I can't make out, after reading so many opinions on the subject, whether I approve of the Ministry of Brains or am entirely against it. *The Manchester Guardian*[7] was afraid I had 'occasional lapses' when I believed in it – *Punch*[8] says I have a 'furtive admiration for it underneath my gibing'. J.C. Squire[9] says I understand both sides. E.M. Forster, in the *Daily Herald*,[10] thinks I was bitterly and rightly opposed to such interference. And they mostly think I merely meant a joke.[11] But the dear old Master of Peterhouse[12] wrote (such a charming letter) to say that the hope for the future of the world lay with its Chesters! And all the time of course I do believe in it, if only the public were civilised enough to fall in with it. It's a tract against individual selfishness, not, as most people think, against state interference.

I'm afraid I'm probably giving up the Peace Conference book. By the time it was finished, it would be too much a portion and parcel of the dreadful past – besides, can't manage it without having been in it myself – not really satisfactorily. I may do it – but I think probably not.[13]

Do you know, a dreadful thing has occurred, which I hope Constable[14] won't ever hear of. A man I met at the Squires[15] the other night, who had just been reading *What Not*, told me that in the copy he read, which came from Mudie's,[16] he was puzzled by finding two pages in it numbered the same, and one was about a lawyer and a shorthand man coming out from a screen and convicting Mr Percy Jenkins of blackmail! Obviously in some cases the work of plucking out the pages was ineffectively done. This man, who knew nothing of the history of it, had been bewildered, and asked me for an explanation. I hope it isn't so in many cases, and that Mr Bottomley won't get hold of one.[17]

Majorca must be very near heaven. I wish I could see it. I'll remember the C'an

Pentinado at Sóller – I don't know what 4.50 pesetas is, but I suppose it's cheap, and anyhow it sounds worth it. It's *snowing* here to-day – it always is when I write to you and think of sun and juniper and lemon flowers. But I'll go there one day, and you shall come and tell me about pesetas etc., and it shall be May or June, and we'll slip off the lava rocks into blue water and spend the day there, shall we? I want to hear lots more about it.[18]

By the way, I'm chucking my job. I'm ashamed to sit there any more, cementing friendship with Italy – look at the results! As a matter of fact, the job is petering out and getting too thin, and I'm bored. I've quite enjoyed the office lately, in a room to myself, and a good man at the head of the section who doesn't interfere, but is pleasant to talk to.[19] I was told it is foolish to go (by the establishment Branch), as a departmental rise for me had just been sanctioned – but honestly I don't think it was going to develope [*sic*] into a job I permanently wanted to do – so when I was told of a job going on *The Daily News* I applied for it, and after some dallying got it. Quite a subordinate and behind-the-scenes job, but still an opening. I think it partly consists in answering letters from the public, who write and ask things about Acts of Parliament etc – and have to be satisfied with something or they might stop taking in the paper. And other jobs, but don't know what yet exactly. I begin on Monday week.[20]

I got Mr O'Donovan to write me a lovely testimonial, which I can't conceivably live up to – if ever you want a testimonial, get an Irishman to do one for you – the weak point is that they'll soon find out it was mostly blarney, I fear. However, I am amused by the prospect of the job at present. *The D[aily] N[ews]* is a good little nag on the whole. Aunt Mary will be still more worried about me, I fear, because it's cocoa, and free church, and so on. (By the way, I hope she agrees with *The New Witness*[21] about *What Not*, which says 'the Church comes well out of this lively piece of writing', or something. I want Constable's to extract that remark by itself and advertise it in *The Church Times*.)

Goodbye: it will be nice to see you again. My love to Aunt Nannie and Uncle Charlie, please. Also Aunt Mary, if there.

Will is just going to have the operation to join up the severed nerves in his shoulder. He's at Woolwich now – the Royal Herbert – the last place on earth, he says.[22] He and I saw Charlie Chaplin yesterday afternoon – I hadn't seen him before, he is frightfully funny – you laugh all the time.

Mother sends a lot of love – so do I.

Rose.

1 Rose has written 'for 19th'.
2 Jean's wartime job as a civil servant in London had come to an end, and in March she had gone out to Barcelona, where her father, the British Consul-General there, was about to retire. She stayed in Spain until mid-May.
3 Mary Macaulay, sister of Rose's father and Jean's mother. Although Rose calls her 'a

wonderful aunt' just below and was good about visiting her towards the end of her life, when Mary was mentally as well as physically ill (*L*89–91, 93–94), she considered her eccentric and difficult (*L*23).

4 Rose's ninth and latest novel, *What Not: A Prophetic Comedy*, a satire on bureaucracy inspired by her experience of life in government offices, includes a love-story that involves Kitty Grammont, an employee in the Ministry of Brains, and Nicholas Chester, the Minister. The account of the affair and of Kitty's feelings undoubtedly owes much to her own affair with Gerald O'Donovan.

5 See *The Athenaeum*, 11 April 1919, 173–174. The reviewer, not identified there, was Katherine Mansfield, whose second husband, John Middleton Murry, had just become the periodical's editor.

6 12 April 1919, 49.

7 4 April 1919, 5. The review, by 'A.M.', is for the most part very favourable, but criticises the love-story and comments: 'An awful thought crosses our mind that Miss Macaulay has moments of lapse when she too believes in the farcical endeavour of the Minister of Brains.'

8 23 April 1919, 331. The reviewer's exact words are: 'The odd thing is that under all her gibing the author seems to have a queer furtive admiration for her precious Ministry of Brains.'

9 Journalist, critic, and poet, Squire had been literary editor of *The New Statesman* since 1913 and was its acting editor in 1917–1919. In the autumn of 1919 he was to become founder-editor of *The London Mercury* (*L*9, 11). His very favourable review of *What Not* is in *Land and Water*, 17 April 1919, 27.

10 19 April 1919, 2. Forster had become literary editor of the paper after his return from India in January 1919. His review of *What Not* is highly favourable. He calls it an 'admirable satire' and 'a remarkable book, for it is both amusing and profound'. Rose admired his novels and was influenced by them. The two became personal friends. In *L*75 she shares with Jean some of the thoughts she has had while preparing her critical study of his work, *The Writings of E.M. Forster* (1938).

11 It may be noted that Rose herself, in a letter to Katharine Tynan, had written of *What Not*: 'it deals less with people than with departmental politics, and is really meant more for a joke than earnest'. The letter (KTH 1/656/13) is dated 22 March 1918. At that time the novel was still far from finished, and it is doubtful if Rose had fallen in love with Gerald O'Donovan (see Introd. I.5); so it is possible that she had not yet thought of introducing the love-story.

12 The political historian Sir Adolphus William Ward. Already aged 81, he was to remain Master of Peterhouse, Cambridge, until he died in 1924.

13 In September 1921 Rose was to attend the Second Assembly of the League of Nations in Geneva (*L*26) – an experience that contributed much to her novel *Mystery at Geneva*. It is interesting to learn from the present passage that she had already been thinking of writing a book, presumably a novel, featuring a post-war international conference.

14 The publisher of *What Not*.

15 Jack Squire and his wife, Harriet, who was also a writer, lived in Chiswick. See *L*23 n. 10.

16 A lending library founded by Charles Edward Mudie in 1842.

17 Publication of *What Not* was delayed from November 1918 until March 1919. The reason is explained by Regi Macaulay in a letter (in the present editor's possession) written from his London home to his sister Mary on 6 March 1919: 'Rose was here yesterday. Her new book *What Not* is coming out now. It was kept back ever so long because at the last moment a libel was detected in it and two pages had to be rewritten. The book was bound already so two pages had to be picked out by girls. I can't help thinking that they will sometimes have picked out the wrong pages and the libel may yet come to light. Rose would have liked to leave it and have the fun of a libel action and trust to pay the cost out of the increased sale of the book but the publishers were against it.' How right Regi was in foreseeing a problem to do with the page-picking! The leaf that had to be picked out and replaced is the one that carries pp. 207–208. Some copies of the book contain a sheet bearing a note in which Rose explains that the delay came about because 'a slight alteration in the text was essential, to safeguard it against one of the laws of the realm'. The reason Rose hoped Horatio Bottomley would not get hold of a copy containing the libel is presumably the fear that he would publicise it in his weekly *John Bull*. Bottomley's switchback career as a journalist, financier, and politician was at this stage going well. In 1918 he had been discharged from bankruptcy and re-elected a Member of Parliament. The situation was to change in 1922, when he was convicted of fraud, sent to prison, and expelled from the House of Commons. On the interest he and *John Bull* took in the sensational Wakeford case in 1921, see *L*24.

18 Rose was to visit Mallorca and stay in 'Jean's' inn in Sóller in April 1925, but not with her: her companions were to be her sisters Margaret and Jeanie (*L*47). The inn, established in 1880 and situated close by Sóller's railway station, is still in business (under the name Hotel El Guia) and still retains much of the character that appealed to Jean and Rose. Jean had the company of her brother Regie and a dog called Jock. One of her notebooks contains a detailed and often poetic description of the inn (in which they spent the nights of 10–12 April), Sóller, and the surrounding area. She was to return to Mallorca in April 1922 and again early in 1927 (*L*60), on both occasions with her father.

19 On Rose's employment as a temporary civil servant in 1917–1918, see Introd. I.5. After the Armistice with Germany (11 November 1918) the Department of Propaganda at Crewe House, which she joined, or perhaps rejoined, from the Foreign Department of the Ministry of Information on 5 September 1918, was very quickly wound up. It ceased to exist on 31 December, but many of its staff left its employment within days. Most, including Gerald O'Donovan, left the civil service, but some, including Rose, were redeployed inside it. A letter of 19 November 1918, from G. Gale Thomas, Assistant Director of Finance, Ministry of Information, to the Secretary of H.M. Treasury (National Archives Box T1 12276, file 3541/1919), reveals that she was re-employed by the Ministry of Information after she left Crewe House, but this cannot have been for more than a few weeks, for the Ministry itself was wound up, and its building, the Howard Hotel in Norfolk Street, just off the Strand, vacated, before the end of December 1918. Rose's letter to Jean shows that she continued to work on Italian affairs, and she will have done this in the News Department of the

Foreign Office, which took over from Crewe House the work of propaganda in Italy (National Archives, INF 4/1B). 'The head of the section' was Lieutenant-Colonel Charles Henry Alexander. An excellent linguist, with an Italian wife, he had been Chief Commissioner of Propaganda in Italy, but was recalled to England soon after the war to take charge of the Italian Section of the News Department of the Foreign Office (National Archives T 12469; FO 395/301; INF 4/1B). The News Department was housed in Norfolk Street, as the Ministry of Information had been, but in a different building. On Crewe House, see also *L*16 n. 11.

20 5 May 1919. If Rose ever began this job, she left it within a few days, for on 12 May Edward Conybeare wrote in his diary: 'Sad card from GMM [Rose's mother] of Will with abscess and Rose broken down.' There has been speculation about the cause or causes of her breakdown (CBS 93; LeFanu 139). That it was connected with her relationship with Gerald is possible, but unproven. Anyhow, she was soon on the road to recovery, as her next letter to Jean shows.

21 11 April 1919, 488: 'The Church of England comes out quite well in this lively piece of writing'.

22 Rose's surviving brother, who had been a captain in the King's Royal Rifle Corps and had won the Military Cross, had been wounded at Le Catelet in north-east France on 3 October 1918. He lost his left lung and the use of his left arm. The operation to reconnect the severed nerves in his shoulder did not take place until 1 October (*L*9). It had little, if any, beneficial effect, but he continued to lead a physically active life on the farm he had acquired in Alberta before the war.

4

Hedgerley End
Beaconsfield
17 June [1919]

Dearest Jean

Thanks much for *The Pot*[1] and your letter, and mother's love and thanks for hers, and come whenever you can and will. (For choice not a Thursday night, as with Will at home and Margaret there's not much room then – Will's coming this week to stay on.)

I'm not sure that I *liked The Pot* – it interested me – but something in its attitude worried me – not its attitude towards the things he oughtn't to know about, but towards life in general and women in particular.[2] He hates them too much to be truthful or really observant, I think – or *are* the women at the Northern Universities like that? Athenais is the only decent one, and she hates and despises all the rest. However, I daresay he's been crossed in love, or beaten by a woman in some excoriation, and if so time may cure him. I daresay the people would belong to the 1917 if they could afford the subscription, but I doubt if they could.[3] (Did you know that Mr Duncan-Jones belongs – because of being Democratic, doubtless, not because of disliking marriage ceremonies. He is rumoured, in fact, to dislike their annulment.[4] I meet him there when I lunch with Molly Hamilton,[5] and as he was a great friend of her divorced husband[6] it is a little awkward).

Yes, I was poisoned afresh by the fate of our Heart.[7] Not to be even 'unconsciously funny' was too depressing – we might have hoped for that even if we missed admiration for our beauty – I'll ask N[aomi][8] if she read it carefully, when I next see her.

I'm kept from being indolent on this rest-cure[9] by the whole press having apparently taken into its head at once that I should like to write articles for it. *The Daily Telegraph* now wants two for later on on some woman's subject – at first I thought this meant Cooking or Clothes, but it seems what they want is Women in the State, Country, Church, Industry, Education, Fiction, or anywhere else. What shall I choose? I think it would be rather fun to hold forth on Women in Modern Fiction – (e.g. *The Pot Boils* and similar works) – or Women as Clergymen?? Too controversial, perhaps. Or How Women Vote, or Why does a woman look old sooner than a man? The field is wide.[10] And I love the *Telegraph*, because it asks me to name my own terms and then falls in with them. Wish I'd said more. Meanwhile I babble for *The Star* and [*Daily*] *Chronicle* and *Everyman* etc. I babbled for *The Star* on Outside the Albert Hall at the L[eague] of N[ations] meeting – about the literature that was being sold, and the people – it was all quite true and some of it rather personal, and they may not take it.[11] You see I was there very early, and then discovered I couldn't get a ticket, they were all gone, and the kind doorkeeper said if anyone gave him back one he'd save it for me, and so I waited till someone actually gave up a beautiful loggia ticket, and I saw and heard beautifully. I felt I had to go, whether rest-curing or not. I was interested to hear the account of an eye-witness of the Voice, which said few things I could understand, (except that they were meant for rudeness) and I couldn't unfortunately see the ejection, only its reflection in the fascinated gaze of those who could.[12] Yes, I liked Lord R[obert] immensely. But who, oh *who* is Dr Irvine?[13] And did they know he was like that when they asked him to speak? I suppose not. Or had he, possibly, been dining too well? He certainly was the Star Turn of the Piece.

Much love, and do come.

R.

1 *The Pot Boils* (London, 1919), the first novel of Margaret Storm Jameson.

2 In taking 'M. Storm Jameson' to be a man, Rose makes the same mistake as some reviewers of the early novels of 'R. Macaulay'. In her autobiography, *Journey From the North* I (London, 1969) 160–162, Jameson vividly describes the Thursday-evening gatherings of 'friends and protégés, and protégés of friends' hosted by Naomi Royde-Smith at 44 Princes Gardens (see n. 8 below), and mentions Rose's kindness to her

on her first evening. For her description of Rose and Arnold Bennett at one of the soirées, see *L*18 n. 5.

3 The 1917 Club was at 4 Gerrard Street, close to Leicester Square. Although its birth coincided with the revolution in Russia and some of its members were Marxists, it was far from being a Marxist club. Ramsay MacDonald was its first president, and its membership represented a wide range of radical political opinions, mostly Labour and Liberal. Moreover, it soon came to be favoured by many whose interests were much more cultural, literary, and artistic than political. There is a useful note on it, with many bibliographical references, by John Saville in J.M. Bellamy and J. Saville (eds), *Dictionary of Labour Biography* 5 (London, 1979) 100–102. Rose calls it 'rather a low hole' (*L*23) and contrasts it with 'our respectable club' (*L*10), and other writers attest to its dinginess and scruffiness, to the poor quality of the food, and to the sordidness of its surroundings, Gerrard Street being a favourite haunt of prostitutes and pimps: see, for example, Douglas Goldring, *The Nineteen-Twenties* (London, 1944) 145–152. But it was certainly a place to meet many 'progressive' people who mattered. It features in the next novel Rose was to publish, *Potterism* (41, 89–91).

4 Arthur Duncan-Jones, an Anglo-Catholic, was at this time Vicar of St Mary's Church, Primrose Hill, London. He was to be appointed Dean of Chichester in 1929. Educated at Gonville and Caius College, Cambridge, he married Caroline ('Caia') Roberts, one of the two daughters of Ernest Stewart Roberts, the Master. From 1912, when Ernest died, his widow, Mary Roberts, their other daughter, Margaret ('Gonvillia'), and Mary's sister, Maggie Harper, were neighbours and friends of the Macaulays in Great Shelford. Duncan-Jones is mentioned also in *L*21, 24. His life and career are described by S.C. Carpenter, *Duncan-Jones of Chichester* (London, 1956).

5 Mary Agnes Hamilton was a cultured woman of many interests and talents. She wrote books on ancient Greece and Rome and novels, but was best known as a Labour politician and economist. One of those whose biography she wrote was Ramsay MacDonald. She was MP for Blackburn in 1929–1931. She writes warmly of Rose in her autobiographical book *Remembering My Good Friends* (London, 1944) 138–139.

6 Charles Joseph Hamilton, an exact contemporary of Arthur Duncan-Jones at Caius College, Cambridge, took holy orders, but devoted most of his working life to the study and teaching of economics. In 1901 he was appointed Lecturer in Political and Commercial Science at University College, Cardiff, and it was there that he met Molly, who was Assistant Lecturer in History, in 1904–1905. Their marriage was short-lived, and she did not like to talk about it. He became Professor of Economics first in Calcutta, then in Patna.

7 The reference seems to be to a joint composition of Rose and Jean (or possibly a piece of Jean's in which Rose had taken a close interest), probably submitted to *SWG*, of which Naomi Royde-Smith (see next note) was literary editor.

8 Naomi Royde-Smith had worked for *SWG* for about eight years before becoming its literary editor in 1912. In that post, which she held until 1922, she exerted consider-able influence on the literary scene in Britain, since *SWG* was the nursery in which many new writers budded and flowered. She and Rose, whose contributions, from 1905 onward, had often been published on Naomi's 'Problems and Prizes' page in *SWG*, first met between 1910 and 1912, according to Rose, who confesses that she

'was dazzled, for she was amusing and interesting and brilliant, and had beauty, and almost more charm than anyone else' ('Coming to London – XIII' (Bibliog. I.7), 32). The first mention of Rose in Naomi's diaries seems to be in the entry for 15 May 1911: 'E.R. Macaulay to lunch'. In the diaries for the following years numerous meetings are mentioned. Naomi introduced Rose to friends of hers, including Walter de la Mare. The friendship between the two women was close through the First World War and for several years after it. From late 1919 to 1921 Rose sometimes lodged during the week in Naomi's top-floor flat at 44 Princes Gardens, and assisted her in organising Thursday-evening gatherings there for refreshments and discussion (see *L*12, 15, 21, 23). (Rose's biographers refer to her as joint-hostess. Naturally she did act as that to some extent when she was lodging at no. 44, but essentially the Thursday soirées were Naomi's show: she had been holding them since well before the First World War; the venue was always her home; and probably she alone paid for the coffee, chocolates, and cigarettes that were provided.) The friendship was less close and warm from 1926 (*L*57 n. 10). After leaving *SWG*, Naomi became a prolific writer. Her output included, as well as many novels, several biographies and plays. On 15 December 1926 she married the American-born Jewish actor Ernest Giannello Milton. She was 51, he 36. Both became Roman Catholics in 1942.

9 See *L*3 n. 20.

10 At this time *The Daily Telegraph* had 'A Page for Women' on Saturdays. It seems that Rose made only one contribution to it between June and December 1919. Her article, in the issue of 5 July 1919, 14, is entitled: 'Woman; What Is She? Some Popular Fallacies'. The chief fallacy she seeks to combat is 'that women resemble each other'. She protests that people often speak or write 'as if woman was a kind of separate species, like the beetle, not merely the feminine half of humanity'. The theme is one to which she was to return later: see, for example, *Crewe Train* (1926) 198–199 and a review of John Newsom, *The Education of Girls* (London, 1948) in *TLS*, 17 April 1948, 216.

11 *The Star* printed Rose's article in its issue of 17 June 1919, 2. The meeting took place in the evening of Friday, 13 June, with Viscount Grey of Fallodon, former Foreign Secretary, in the chair.

12 Lord Robert Cecil had had much to do with the drafting of the League of Nations Covenant and was to be President of the League of Nations Union from 1923 to 1945. It was his speech that was interrupted by the 'Voice'. The exchange between it and the speaker is reported in *The Star*, 14 June 1919, 3. The heckler vehemently opposed Lord Robert's desire to see Germany admitted to the League 'sooner rather than later' and, before being ejected by eight stewards, told him he was 'a bloody traitor'.

13 Alexander Irvine, born in Antrim town, Northern Ireland, one of twelve children of a cobbler, was a coal-miner and soldier, among other things, before emigrating to the USA, where he received a university education, was ordained, and began writing as well as preaching. During the First World War he served as a chaplain in the British Army. He was a passionate campaigner for the League of Nations.

5

Beaconsfield.
30 June 1919

Dearest Jean

Here is *Father Ralph*,[1] which keep till everyone has read it who would like to – I noted it in the hall after you had gone. It was marvellous that you caught that train; Will told us yours came in about the same time as his.

I'm very glad about the rooms, and the lunch, and everything.[2] G[ilbert] M[urray] has an article this morning in *The D[aily] News* – rather nice, he always is.[3] I shall come all right, if you'll have me, next term.[4] If you can't put me up I'll stay in Somerville.

Do you remember the Roberts' and Miss Harper, at Shelford? Rather fun, they are. Miss H. has taken a house at Headington from Sept: – I'll let you know where later, and she could be rather pleased if you went there ever.[5]

Cross Bank sounds rather strenuous – but I hope the housemaid has begun to function by now. I wonder if Uncle Charlie and Aunt Nannie turned up all right.[6] I think you ought to have gone to Walton House[7] – anyhow for meals. If we'd known it would be like that we would have made you stay on here and sleep in my bed with me or something, or made up another bed in the tiny room out of mother's, it would have been quite easy and I wish we had. However, I hope all is well now.

How lovely about Regie's[8] novel: do you see it as it goes on? I should love to read it – do steal it for me sometime when he's off the scenes.

I'm perishing with cold – and thanking heaven I'm not with that Broads party, sailing in an open boat! I hope the poor darlings won't all get pneumonia.

I went up to town on Saturday afternoon, to get some ideas on Rejoicings – I got a desperate appeal on Friday from Mr Thorogood, of *The Star*, for an article on the subject, exhorting me to 'stifle any natural cynicism on the gruesome subject, find something out of the wreck to be cheerful about, and then, please, be cheerful about it'.[9] So I had to try. I *hope* the result isn't cynical – I did my best not to make it so.

But who could rejoice truly and wholesomely this weather? Will and I had to play tennis hard all yesterday to keep warm; everytime we stopped we cooled down and couldn't bear it. The back nets are a great success, and the patches resist all attacks.

Goodbye my dear; have a nice holiday till the 21st, and I hope it will be jolly and entertaining after that; I expect it will, rather. How's the Hammond?[10] If I meet Helen Darbishire or any other Oxford people at the Somerville meeting this Saturday may I tell them you are going to Oxford.[11] I believe H.D. knows the Murrays rather well. My love. Rose.

We've got the geyser in. It goes off, and the flames leap round the bathroom, and we all scream, and Will plunges his hand in among them to turn off the gas.[12] This happens whenever it is windy. A queer and unreliable geyser – but still, a geyser. Like the Peace, as I have been observing in *The Star*.

1 The first and best-known novel of Gerald O'Donovan.
2 Jean, who was to start work as Gilbert Murray's private secretary on 21 July, had found lodgings about a mile from the Murrays' house, Yatscombe, at Boars Hill. Probably it had been arranged for her to have lunch at Yatscombe.
3 'Freedom's Instrument: What the League of Nations Can Do', *The Daily News*, 30 June 1919, 10.
4 For Rose's visit in late October, see *L*10.
5 On Mary Roberts and Maggie Harper, see *L*4 n. 4. The house on Headington Hill, on the east side of Oxford, was to be the home not only of Maggie, but also, until 1921, of Mary and her daughter, Margaret. When Mary wrote a memoir of her own life, *Sherborne, Oxford and Cambridge: Recollections of Mrs Ernest Stewart Roberts* (London, 1934), she asked Rose to write an introduction. Rose rather reluctantly agreed to do this, and then, to Mary's disappointment, insisted on the deletion of almost all the reminiscences of her and her family. Only the fighting between the two families' dogs escaped her censorship, and she forbade any mention of herself even in this story. The correspondence with Mary about her book (ERM 15.159–167) shows Rose to be paranoid about the defence of her privacy. In *L*101 she displays the same paranoia when she asks Jean, if she should talk to Gerard Irvine, not to say anything about her or her family.
6 Cross Bank, the Smiths' family home in Clent, had been let furnished since early 1917, but, with Charlie having just retired from the consular service, he and Nannie needed it back. Jean had been cleaning up after the tenants, in advance of her parents' return from Spain at the end of June.
7 The home of Uncle Kenneth (Macaulay), also in Clent. See *L*87 and n. 9 there.
8 A brother of Jean. It is not known if he completed his novel. Certainly it was not published.
9 'Rejoicings', counting ten blessings in addition to the Peace, was published in the evening of the day Rose wrote this letter: *The Star*, 30 June 1919, 2. Horace Thorogood, literary editor of *The Star* from 1915 to 1927 and afterwards on the staff of *The Evening Standard* for twenty years, established a deserved reputation for tastefully humorous journalism. A selection of his humorous articles, illustrated by David Low, was published under the title *Low & Terry* (London, 1934).
10 The reference is obscure.
11 Helen Darbishire, an exact contemporary of Rose at Somerville, took a first class in English in 1903. She returned to the College in 1908 as tutor and remained there until her retirement. She was Principal in 1931–1945. Her scholarly specialities were Wordsworth and Milton. 'The Somerville meeting' on Saturday 5 July 1919, was the AGM of the Somerville Students' Association. It was held in the Kensington home of one of the Committee members. Darbishire was not present, nor indeed was any other member of Somerville's SCR, because all were heavily involved in the College's move back into its own accommodation from its temporary quarters

in Oriel College during the war, when Somerville was converted into a military hospital.

12 The experiences with the Macaulays' geyser are echoed in the novel Rose was writing at this time: 'The rooms were jolly (only the new geyser exploded too often)' (*Potterism* 32–33).

6

Hedgerley End
Beaconsfield
2 August 1919

Dearest Jean

Thank you very much indeed for your letter, and for *The Birds*, which I hadn't yet got, and which, of course, I wanted. There is a lot of beauty in it – and more interest, I think. He's been going through a phase, I think – quite different from the one in which he wrote *The Lily of Malud* – I wonder what he'll emerge into next.[1] I love 'Harlequin', don't you.

Well, we're just back from Kirnan,[2] where we had a thoroughly nice time – Margaret sketched, Will fished hard with one hand, and I did what Will called 'walking the hills in an irresponsible manner' – and wrote. I had a lot of time for writing, really, and as I took a rest from reviewing and articles I could attack my new book. Of course now I'm home I find the other things all wanting to be done too, so there isn't so much time. It was fun there. Did you know the uncles are all turning religious? Presbyterianism is the form it's taking – that's the spirit of their Macaulay ancestors catching them when they set foot on their native heath[3] – they all troop off to kirk on Sunday morning, which interested us greatly – and sit there as quiet and devout as anything. (I gather Aunt Mary had been scrapping with them about it – she thinks it's schism or something – no, it can't be schism, because it's the established church of the country – but anyhow something one shouldn't do for some reason). Anyhow, there they sit, while a fiery and earnest young minister delivers an impassioned and emotional sermon – and they didn't turn a hair under it – except that Uncle Willie[4] fluttered the pages of his Bible about. I think it might make a good short story – the 3 agnostic men of the world caught by their ancestors' spirits and turned into Presbyterians – sabbatarians, too, (which Will said was hypocrisy, but I really think it goes deeper than that with them now – with Uncle Kenneth,[5] anyhow).

I'm glad it's being nice. Yes, isn't the Bodleian a good place. Do you see many people, besides the Murrays? I suppose no-one much is there till next term, really. Mother says she is going to write to Lady Markby about you – she was a Miss Taylor, of Weybridge,[6] and was always very nice to us at Oxford – I expect the Murrays know her.

Can you come for the 24th – that week-end? Till then the house is full of family, but Margaret goes on the 21st. Do try and do that. The one after that I shall be with the O'Donovans in Cornwall, and after that I gather you are having a holiday? If you can't do the 24th, what about a week-end in the 2nd half of September, or in October, or whenever it is that you go back to Oxford? But that is a long way off, so do the 24th if possible.

Of course you can't come for the day – it's *much* too far. And I'll come to Oxford next term, shall I? That will be great fun. We'll go and call on a few people, I think – Helen Darbishire at Somerville, and the Sidgwicks[7] – and go on the river if we can. Don't you love Oxford? There's no other place in the least like it, of course, really. Do you go to church, and if so where?

I'm bored with having to review a good book and a bad in the same article. I hate doing that, I think it insults the good one – I've a good mind to say it can't be done. I've not *touched* the Church article, dash it – thought I could at Kirnan, but was too busy with other things. Poems[8] coming out in September, now. Did I tell you, Mr Marsh has refused Mr Shanks' suggestion about putting me in *Georgian Poetry*. He said he wouldn't have any women at all[9] – he's as bad as Uncle Regie! Don't bother with *Fr Ralph*, bring it on 24th – no, wait till you get back to Clent – any time. My love – wish you were here.

R.

1 Rose is talking about poetry of J.C. Squire: *The Birds, and Other Poems* (London, 1919), and *The Lily of Malud, and Other Poems* (London, 1917).
2 An estate, leased by Regi Macaulay for over thirty years until his death in 1937, at Kilmichael Glassary near Lochgilphead in Argyllshire. The shooting and fishing were good, and Regi developed a fine garden (*L*57 n. 3). He used Kirnan not only for his own recreation but also for that of family, friends, and business-associates. Rose describes another visit to Kirnan in *L*53–54 and makes it, under the name Arshaig Lodge, the setting of chapters 11–16 of *The World My Wilderness* (1950). Regi, the youngest of the five Macaulay brothers, was educated at Eton and King's College, Cambridge (1878–1882). At King's he was a Scholar and obtained a first in the Classical Tripos. He was an outstanding athlete and association football player, who made a significant contribution to the Old Etonians' 1–0 defeat of Blackburn Rovers in the final of the Association Challenge Cup in 1882. In 1884 he joined Wallace & Co., East India Merchants of Bombay, and, after a period of training in London and Manchester, spent about twenty years in India. From 1890 to 1905 he was a partner in the firm, resident in Bombay. While he was there, he had the unusual experience of reading his own obituary. It appeared in *The Pioneer*, a widely read English-language paper published in Lucknow, on 19 March 1899. Six years after this exaggerated report of his demise, he transferred to Wallace & Co.'s sister company, Wallace Brothers, in which he was first a partner, then (from 1911) a director. From 1905 he was based in London, but made frequent visits to India, Burma, and Siam. The activities of the Wallace 'empire' were highly profitable, and Regi became a rich man. He

never married, and used his wealth mainly for the benefit of others. He was generous to members of his family (*L*90 n. 15), to friends, and to people in the neighbourhood of Kirnan, especially to the children. Among the institutions that benefited from his generosity was King's, Cambridge, which in its annual report for 1938 noted that he 'became through gifts made in his lifetime one of the principal benefactors of the College in recent times'.

3 The Macaulays were of course Scots, originating in Lewis in the Outer Hebrides. When Rose refers to 'the spirit of their Macaulay ancestors catching them when they set foot on their native heath', part of her thought may be that her uncles' great-grandfather the Rev. John Macaulay had been Church of Scotland minister at Inveraray, only twenty miles or so from Kirnan, in 1765–1775.

4 William Macaulay was educated at Winchester School, Durham University, and King's College, Cambridge, where he took a first in Mathematics in 1878. He was elected a Fellow of King's in 1879. In August–December of that year he and his brother Kenneth visited Canada, where Kenneth was thinking of farming. It is possible that the experience they gained of Canada and Canadian agriculture had some influence on the decision of Rose's brother Will to take up farming in Alberta in 1906. When Willie and Kenneth returned from their transatlantic travels, the former, after a few months with Chance Brothers (n. 5), spent four years with the Mountsorrel Granite Company, Leicestershire, very close indeed to Rothley Temple, a historic house with strong Macaulay connections, being, among other things, the birthplace of the historian, essayist, and poet Thomas Babington Macaulay. In 1884 Willie returned to Cambridge and devoted the rest of his working life to the service of King's, as Lecturer in Mathematics (from 1884), Second Bursar (1887–1902), sole Tutor (1902–1913), and Vice-Provost (1918–1924). He was also University Lecturer in Applied Mechanics. He continued to live in King's until 1933, when, after the death of Kenneth, he took over Walton House in Clent. On Willie's passion for riding and hunting, see *L*41 n. 4.

5 Kenneth Macaulay went on from Eton to King's College, London, where he distinguished himself in mathematics and the applied sciences. He spent his whole working life, a period of about forty years, with Chance Brothers, the famous glass-manufacturers, at Spon Lane, Smethwick, Birmingham. He started with the firm in 1877 at the invitation of (Sir) James Timmins Chance, who in 1845 had married Elizabeth ('Eliza') Ferguson, an elder sister of Kenneth's mother. He became a director in 1883. Like his brothers Willie and Regi, he remained a bachelor.

6 Lucy Taylor, daughter of John Edward Taylor of Weybridge, married William Markby in 1866. After distinguished service as a High Court judge in India, he was Reader in Indian Law at Oxford from 1879 to 1900. He and his wife lived in a house they built in Headington. After his death she published *Memoirs of Sir William Markby, KCIE, by His Wife* (1917). Rose's mother's family had had close connections with Weybridge: her great-uncle the Rev. Edward Joseph Rose had been rector there; and her grandmother Eliza Conybeare had lived there from shortly before the death of her husband, the Rev. William John Conybeare, in 1857 until her own death in 1903. Jean's family too had had links with Weybridge: Edward Rose's wife, Ellen, was a sister of Jean's paternal grandmother, Susan Emma Smith, *née* Parker, who moved to Weybridge not long after the death of her husband, Archibald.

7 Arthur and Charlotte Sidgwick and family. He and Rose's father were colleagues at Rugby School at the time she was born, in 1881. The following year Arthur, a fine Greek scholar, became a fellow of Corpus Christi College, Oxford, and the Macaulays no doubt saw much of the Sidgwicks when they were living in Oxford between 1894 and 1901. Rose's first collection of poems, *The Two Blind Countries* (1914), was published by Sidgwick & Jackson, the firm founded by Arthur's and Charlotte's elder son, Frank, described by Rose in Letter 54, after he had declined to publish Jean's poems, as 'a nice publisher, but stupid'. If, when Rose stayed with Jean at the end of October 1919, they did get to visit the Sidgwicks, they will have found Arthur in poor shape. In the last years of his life he suffered from an illness that severely affected his mental condition. He died on 25 September 1920.

8 Rose's second volume of poems, *Three Days*, was actually published in October 1919. She dedicated it to Naomi Royde-Smith.

9 Five volumes of *Georgian Poetry*, edited by Edward ('Eddie') Marsh, were published by Harold Monro's Poetry Bookshop in London between 1912 and 1922. Poets whose work appeared in the volumes of 1912, 1915, and 1917 included Rupert Brooke, W.H. Davies, Walter de la Mare, Robert Graves, D.H. Lawrence, John Masefield, and Siegfried Sassoon. On the critical reception of the 1919 volume, see *L14*. One of its contributors was female – Fredegond Shove. Vita Sackville-West contributed to the 1922 volume, but these two were the only women to have work included in *Georgian Poetry*. Marsh, a civil servant by profession, was a notable patron of painters as well as an encourager of poets. On Edward Shanks, a contributor to the 1919 and 1922 volumes of *Georgian Poetry*, see *L9* n. 1.

7

Hedgerley End
Beaconsfield
15 September 1919

Dearest Jean

Many happy returns of to-morrow.[1] Here's Margaret's *Deaconess*, in case you've not seen it, also the Chapbook for July – it's not good really, but there are a few nice things in it.[2] As to *The Deaconess*, as you probably know, it was written for propaganda purposes chiefly. Also here and there Margaret took some article by one of the other sisters from their magazine[3] (e.g. on Country Holidays) and didn't like to change the phraseology. So when you read things like 'a peep into God's beautiful world', and 'it was sweet to see the loving embraces between Alice (?)[4] and her mother', don't put them down to Margaret! It gives an interesting account of the life and work, I think.[5]

Well, it will be nice to see you this week-end. I hope you won't mind being mixed up with Tynan Hinksons, who will be staying at the Inn and coming in on Saturday afternoon and Sunday lunch. Mrs T.H. will amuse you; she is very ruddy and jolly, with a very fat Dublin brogue. She is bringing Pam and Pat, aged 19 and 20 or thereabouts.[6] I'm sorry they'll be here that Sunday, but they go away on Sunday afternoon, and you can help us amuse them. Come when you like on Saturday. I'm lunching in town and may have to be late rather, but mother'll be here. I'm glad you can do this week-end, as I shall be away for the next one, and the two after that may be full.

Will goes back to Woolwich on Wednesday, for his operation. He doesn't know when they'll operate, though. We've had nice holidays.

Uncle Willie was here last week-end. J.R. Brooke[7] came over (as usual) for tennis, and the combination was rather funny. Uncle W. is a wonderful man – knows so much that no-one else does, and so little that everyone else does.

I want to see *The Great Day* at Drury Lane, don't you?[8] Do you see anything at Oxford? But of course it's not been term-time yet. When you come, we'll arrange a date for me to go to you – what fun. We do want to see you – I wish it wasn't the Hinkson Sunday – there's such lots to hear. Will the Murrays give you a holiday for your birthday? Or a cake?

My love. R.

So sorry, I can't find *The Deaconess*, I'll give it to you when you come.

1 A mistake: Jean's birthday was on 18 September, not on the 16th.
2 On 1 May 1911 Margaret Macaulay joined as a postulant the Anglican East London Community of Deaconesses, founded in 1880 by Bishop Walsham How and based at All Saints House, Church Crescent, South Hackney, London E9. She was ordained by the Bishop of Stepney on 21 June 1913. Grace Macaulay, who could be very difficult, not least in relation to her four surviving daughters, reacted extremely badly to the news of Margaret's decision. Margaret, who was probably motivated partly by a desire to escape from her mother, communicated the news in a letter, not daring to do it face to face. Later Grace became reconciled to Margaret's choice of vocation and even expressed pride in her work. *The Deaconess*, by 'Sister Margaret', with a preface by A.F. Winnington-Ingram, Bishop of London, was published by the Faith Press (London, 1919).
3 *The Deaconess in East London.*
4 The query is Rose's. An Alice is mentioned in *The Deaconess* (59), but she does not seem to appear in the context mentioned by Rose. For the belief that 'real good has been done to soul as well as body by the peep into God's beautiful world' during a fortnight's holiday for poor city children in the country, see p. 93.
5 The book does indeed give a vivid and moving picture of the poverty and hardship experienced by many East Londoners at this time.
6 Katharine Tynan, a prolific author of poetry, novels, and other works, had been recently widowed. Her husband, Henry Albert Hinkson, died 11 January 1919. Her daughter, Pamela (born 29 November 1900) became a novelist, sometimes writing under the pseudonym of Peter Deane. Her best-known book is *The Ladies' Road* (London, 1932). Pat, the name given by family and friends to Giles Aylmer Hinkson, the younger of Katharine's surviving sons (born 7 February 1899), was for many years the Argentinian

correspondent of *The Times* and reported fearlessly throughout the Perón dictatorship. Katharine was born in Dublin 23 January 1859, not, as she believed for most of her life, in 1861, and so was 60 at the time of her visit to Beaconsfield and 22 years older than Rose. Friendly exchanges, including exchanges of publications, between the two began in the spring of 1913, when Katharine wrote to say how much she had enjoyed *The Lee Shore*, the book that won Rose first prize in Hodder and Stoughton's Novel Competition in the summer of 1912. Thirteen of Rose's letters to her, written between 6 May 1913 and 7 July 1930, are preserved in the Katharine Tynan archive in the John Rylands University Library, Manchester (KTH 1/656/1–13).

7 John Reeve Brooke was a first cousin of the poet Rupert Brooke. He was always known as 'Reeve' or 'J.R.' rather than as 'John', perhaps to distinguish him from his father, a barrister-at-law at Lincoln's Inn, who was also John Reeve Brooke. The family home was in Bushey, Hertfordshire, and it will have been from there that Reeve 'came over' to Beaconsfield for tennis. After serving as a Captain in the Royal Army Service Corps in 1914–1915, he had a series of senior civil-service posts during and after the First World War. He was a prominent member of a group of intellectuals who often met for lunch, usually on a Wednesday or Thursday. Sometimes the meeting-place was his top-floor apartment in 1 Mitre Court Buildings, Inner Temple, just off Fleet Street. Regulars at the lunches included Naomi Royde-Smith, Walter de la Mare, Molly Hamilton, and Rose. On 23 March 1920 (*L*18) he married Dorothy Lamb, a Newnham-educated classicist and archaeologist, who had worked in the Ministry of National Service (1916–1918) before moving to the Ministry of Food (1918–1920). He was Secretary to the Ministry of Transport from 1923 to 1927, then of the Central Electricity Board from 1927 to 1929. He was knighted in 1928. In 1929 he became a member, and in 1930 vice-chairman, of the Electricity Commission. He died in 1937. Two years later, Dorothy, who was for many years one of Rose's closest friends, married Sir Walter Nicholson, another career civil servant. On Dorothy's classical and archaeological career, see *L*51 n. 3.

8 A melodrama by Louis Napoleon Parker and George Robert Sims, with Sybil Thorndike playing the heroine, Clara Borstwick. The review in *The Times* (13 September 1919, 8) appears under the subtitle: 'LABOUR PLAY AT DRURY LANE. PEACE CONFERENCE "SENSATIONS"'. A silent film, based on the play and with the same title, was made in 1920. It is noteworthy only because the title-designer, aged just 21, was a certain Alfred Hitchcock.

8

Hedgerley End
Beaconsfield
25 September 1919

Dearest Jean

Here are documents re stove. Mother says, would you mind returning them sometime or other – no hurry. Ours glows still like banked fires, ardent yet suppressed. (I've done those reviews, by the way, and sent them in, but I daresay they won't appear just yet).

Thank you much for information about League of Nations. I was afraid that, like everything else just now, it wasn't wanting people. I'm advising her against the Journalism too, as various people, such as Naomi and Mr Randall,[1] both good judges, seem to think that, though it will doubtless be instructive, it will be no manner of use in helping people to get jobs, which is what she wants. Naomi jeered at the idea of any editor taking someone on because they had a University of London journalism diploma. I believe the only way for unknown people to make any way in journalism is to begin on provincial papers and get experience there. But I think she'd better, as she wants to write, just write in the home till she *can* write, which isn't quite yet.[2]

Are the railways going to strike?[3] If so, Bice[4] won't be able to come to-morrow, and I shan't be able to go to *The Wild Widow*.[5] We shall have to put that off to another night in that case, as I've got the box ticket! We're going to be 8 in a box, so we shall be nice and warm. I wish it was *The Great Day*, but *The Wild Widow* should be good too.

My poems are supposed to be out to-day, but I've not had them yet. You'll get one. I'm bored with them, many of them are so bad and all of them so ancient, I don't feel in the least interested in its fate. I want to write another, much better and more pleasing to me.

It was nice having you. Come again soon. Anytime. I'll come to you Oct: 25th, may I? At least, I think so.

My love. R

1 Alfred Randall, the son of a lamp-maker, was born and bred in London, and was employed as an insurance agent before moving into journalism. He worked for *The New Age*, a weekly that, despite its small circulation, won great respect and influence under Alfred Orage, its owner and editor from 1907 to 1922. Randall was a major contributor, writing articles on psychology and reviewing books and plays. A shy and temperamental man, he was a severe but well-informed and clever critic. The sardonic wit he often deployed in his writing is reflected in the pseudonym he adopted as a drama-critic who must often have induced a feeling of despair in those on the receiving end of his criticism – John Francis *Hope*. After Orage gave up *The New Age* in October 1922, Randall worked briefly and unhappily for *The Spectator*. He is described as having had a hungry and consumptive appearance. He did indeed suffer from pulmonary tuberculosis for many years – for fifteen years, according to his death certificate – and died from it and asthenia at his mother's house in Finchley on 6 July 1925, aged 43.

2 The young woman who has sought Rose's advice cannot be identified. She appears again in *L*14.

3 The answer is 'yes'. See *L*9.

4 Beatrice Burton-Brown was one of Jean's closest friends at Newnham, where she read Classics in 1910–1913. One may conjecture not only that she accompanied

Jean on some of her visits to Rose and her family in Great Shelford but also that she was immediately regarded with interest by them, because, like the Macaulays when Rose and her siblings were children, the Burton-Browns had spent several years in Italy when Bice was a child: they lived in Rome from 1896 until 1904, when she was between the ages of four and twelve. It was presumably during those years that she came to be given the Italian abbreviation of Beatrice. In 1914 she joined the staff of Prior's Field, Godalming, the avant-garde girls' school founded by Julia Huxley in 1902. Her mother, Ethel Ann Burton-Brown, was the headmistress (1906–1927), and Bice succeeded her in that post (1927–1952).

5 A play by Arthur Shirley and Ben Landeck, described by *The Times* as 'a drama of surprises'. It had opened at the Lyceum on 6 September.

9

This fragment occupies two sides of a sheet. At least one sheet is missing before it, and the end of the letter is missing too. Although the exact date of the letter cannot be determined, the reference to the national rail strike is helpful. It began on Friday 26 September 1919 and continued until Sunday 5 October. So, when Rose says that she stayed up in town 'most of last week', after bicycling half-way to London and completing the journey by Metropolitan, it is certain that she means the working week beginning Monday 29 September.

[London]

[Between 6 and 11 October 1919]

. . . *Mercury.* I heard about it from J.C. Squire the other day.

Naomi says Mr Shanks' head is 'terribly turned, poor lad' by his recent successes,[1] and predicts he will do something foolish in the *Mercury*. I think it promises well on the whole – though, of course, these things always do promise rather more than they ever perform. But J.C. Squire is so good and sound himself that it stands a good chance. I hear they are making a great stand against the newer schools of verse. Perhaps that is good.[2]

Anyhow, there's no precisely such monthly journal at present going, so I think it 'meets a long-felt want'.

I'm in town to-day. I stayed up most of last week, by the way; I bicycled half way and did the rest by Metropolitan, as it was before the amateur trains got going on the G.C.[3] Then I stayed at Uncle R[egi]'s (the club[4] being full) and let Mr Savile and his head clerk be shocked if they liked (because of course Uncle R. wasn't there).[5] I was up to get news of Will really and transmit it to Mother. They operated on Wednesday, and I saw him on Friday. The doctor said it was 'very satisfactory', which meant that they had been able to join up the nerves – that's all they can tell at present, of course. He's getting on all right in himself now he's recovered from the anaesthetic.

I have a letter from Jim asking me to tea. How nice of him! I'll go if . . .[6]

1 The justification for calling Edward Shanks a 'lad' is that he was aged only 27. The most notable of his 'recent successes' was winning the first Hawthornden Prize with *The Queen of China and Other Poems* on 10 July 1919. He was to remain with *The London Mercury* until 1922. Later (1928–1935) he was the chief leader-writer for *The Evening Standard*.

2 *The London Mercury*, a literary monthly, with Squire as editor and Shanks as assistant editor, was to begin publication in November 1919. For Rose's comments on the first issue, see *L*11.

3 Great Central Railway. The 'amateur trains' are those operated by military or civilian volunteers during the strike.

4 The University Club for Ladies, from which *L*10 was written. See n. 1 there.

5 P.B. Savile was secretary of Wallace Brothers & Co. Ltd, of which Regi Macaulay was a director. Probably Rose called at the company's offices, at 4 Crosby Square, off Bishopsgate, to collect the keys of her uncle's Hampstead house, 11 Eton Avenue, NW3. In a letter to Naomi Royde-Smith, written on 17 December [1937], a few days after Regi's death, Rose says: 'Yes, I remember that evening at Eton Avenue. Poor Mr Savile was there then – the tall thin one that lived with him – but he's gone deranged and lives in Devonshire now' (Naomi G. Royde-Smith Manuscript Collection, Temple University, Philadelphia).

6 Jean's brother Jim had just gone up to King's College, Cambridge, from Marlborough College, with an exhibition in Classics.

10

University Club for Ladies,[1]
4, George Street,
Hanover Square,
W.1
Monday [27 October 1919][2]

Dearest Jean

It was clever of you to send me to the garage.[3] I was the first in, and got the warmest corner. There about 15 of us packed in in the end – but all well-bred, which makes a difference at these times. (What would happen to anyone living on Boars or Foxcombe Hill[4] who was ill-bred? But perhaps they don't.) I sent my bicycle to Beac[on]s[field] and self to Paddington, and here I am, writing out reviews in a fair and legible hand in our respectable club – not the other one.[5] (Will things written at the other one suffer a taint, I wonder?)

Well my dear it was nice: nice seeing you and nice seeing the Murrays[6] and nice seeing the other people. I'm sorry to think of you bicycling down to Oxford this blustering and chilly afternoon. I suppose you are doing it now – I hope not in gossamer stockings. Mrs Trinder[7] was so kind to me, and took me to the garage and left her washing – what a dear! I'm glad you're with her.

I love you a lot, you and your poems too. Thanks for having me.

Rose.

1   The Club opened its doors in January 1887 at 31 New Bond Street. It moved to Maddox Street in 1894, to 32 George Street in 1899, and to 4 George Street in 1904. In 1921 it made a fourth move to 2 Audley Square and changed its name to the University Women's Club.

2   The letter can be dated on the basis of remarks in *L*8 and 11.

3   To shelter from the weather while awaiting the bus, run by Tommy Cotmore, from Old Boars Hill to Oxford. His garage was at Jarn Tree. See Margaret Aldiss (ed.), *A Boars Hill Anthology* (Oxford, 1998) 38. The morning bus left at 10 am, which explains why Jean, for whom Monday was a working day, could not see Rose off.

4   The Murrays' house was on Foxcombe Road, about a mile east of Old Boars Hill and a little south of Foxcombe Hill

5   The 1917 Club.

6   CBS 154 writes: 'Ever since childhood [Rose] had known and admired "Professor Murray" as a distinguished friend of her father's'. In a letter to Babington Smith of 5 February 1973 (ERM 4.209) Jean queried this report of a friendship between Murray and George Macaulay, pointing out that there seemed to be no surviving correspondence between the two, and that the Murrays were not living in Oxford when the Macaulays were there. Babington Smith replied (ERM 4.210) that her statement was 'based on repeated assertions' by Rose's sister Jeanie. Rose's present letter does not settle the matter, although, if she had not been introduced to the Murrays before, one might perhaps have expected her to say that it was 'nice *meeting*' them, rather than that it was 'nice *seeing*' them.

7   Trinder was (and still is) a not uncommon name in the Boars Hill area. Jean's landlady in Old Boars Hill is most likely to have been Florence, wife of Oliver Trinder, and the house is most likely to have been Ebor (later Southside, now Birch Cottage), Orchard Lane.

11

Gerrards Cross
3 November 1919

Dearest Jean

I'm waiting to see the dentist. Here's my room-money; if I didn't pay it I couldn't ever come again, you see.[1]

Your letter was refreshing. Mother and I were pleased by Mrs Durham and *Three Days*. I expect she'd been reading 'Spreading Manure', or 'Hoeing the Wheat'.[2] Quite right too: I *have* had a lot of trouble. I'm having a lot at the present moment, with a broken-off tooth, and 10 books of verse in my bag that I ought to be reviewing. Some aren't bad: Osbert Sitwell has some nice things – though I think his poems about non-combatants silly.[3] I've just waded through Mr Still's *Poems in Captivity* – so horrible they are! Just like this –

'What will the world be like after the war?
Will it be just the same as before?
Or shall we have built up a new humanity
Out of the ruins of old Christianity?

Shall we be kinder after the war,
To the pauper, the slave, the thief and the whore?' [4]

. . . And so on and so on. It is so bad I'm sending it back to Mr Lynd,[5] in case anyone else perhaps can find something kind to say about it – I saw one review which liked it, and there might be another, so I don't like just to leave it out, and I hate crabbing things wholly, it's so unkind. Talking of crabbing, have you seen *The Mercury*? Not very good, this number,[6] everyone seems to think, and I think I agree. And, though I think it is right to crab to some extent, I think it goes a little too far. Very nearly everything it reviews it condemns (except *Reynard the Fox*[7]). I was rather glad *Three Days* was just not in the month's poetry – I'm sure it wouldn't have escaped. I must say most of the verse it selected for review *was* pretty bad – but then why select it? I suppose they felt they had to do all that came into the month or something. The novels come off rather better, but not much. I don't think any of the original verse is good. The best things in it are, I think, the Editorial Notes, whose courage I admire, don't you – and Mr Lynd's thing on Walpole.[8] Robert Nichols's story[9] is very bad. So is Mr de la Mare's poem.[10] But I expect it will improve later on, and it has an attractive appearance.

I shall be interested to see if 'November' pleases the *Nation*. If not, try *The [New] Statesman* or *Westminster [Gazette]*.[11] Did you see *The Nation*'s dust-up with . . .[12]
. . . relieved about the Quakers![13]

I wonder how you spent Sunday? Socially, I hope? Oh yes, weren't you going to have someone? It was nice coming.

R.

(Mr de la Mare reviewed *Three Days* for *The Times* [*Literary Supplement*], but Mr Dalton didn't put it in last time, and perhaps won't this!)[14]

My cold's gone, thank you, and mother's very nearly.

1 The money is to reimburse Jean for the extra charge made by Jean's landlady.
2 Millicent Durham of Orchard Hill, Boars Hill. It seems, from what is said just below, that she remarked that Rose's recently published collection of poems showed that she had 'had a lot of trouble'. The pieces named by Rose are two of the five in the section of *Three Days* entitled 'On the Land, 1916' and strongly reflect the strenuousness and discomfort of some of the tasks she performed that year on farmland near Great Shelford.
3 Sitwell's *Argonaut and Juggernaut* (London, 1919), a collection of satirical poems, had been published on 30 October. For Edward Shanks's criticism of it, see *L*14.
4 John Still wrote *Poems in Captivity* (London and New York, 1919) while a POW in Turkey. Rose's quotation, evidently from memory, is by no means an exact one of lines from 'After the War' (pp. 76–77). What Still actually wrote was: 'What will the changes

be, after the war? | Nothing can ever be quite as before' (1–2); 'We can be friends to the growing humanity, | Built on the rocks of the old Christianity' (33–34); 'Can we be brotherly, after the war? | Kind to the broken, the wretched, the whore?' (13–14).

5 Robert Lynd, born in Belfast and an ardent proponent of Irish nationalism, was a journalist and a prolific essayist on a very wide range of topics. He joined *The Daily News* in 1908 and became its literary editor in 1912 – a post he occupied for over forty years (the paper became *The News Chronicle* in 1930). For over thirty years (from 1913) he contributed essays to *The New Statesman* under the pseudonym 'Y.Y.'. Rose was a friend of him and his wife, Sylvia, a novelist and poet.

6 *The London Mercury* 1, 1 (November 1919).

7 Poem by John Masefield (London, 1919).

8 Robert Lynd, 'Horace Walpole', on pp. 52–61.

9 'The Smile of the Sphinx', on pp. 16–33. On Robert Nichols, see *L*20 n. 6.

10 'Suppose . . .', on pp. 14–15.

11 Jean's poem, beginning 'And now November walks in the deep lanes . . .', was to be published under the title 'Caristia'. See *L*12.

12 Although the text breaks off here, there can be no doubt that the 'dust-up' was with J.C. Squire. In *Land and Water*, 9 October 1919, 31, Squire savagely reviewed George Bernard Shaw's *Heartbreak House, Great Catherine, and Playlets of the War* (London, 1919), claiming that 'a worse volume has never appeared under the name of a man of reputation, and seldom under any sort of name at all', and declaring that the author 'deserves to be tarred and feathered'. The review drew a sharp rebuke from 'A Wayfarer', author of 'A London Diary', in *The Nation*, 18 October 1919, 59, who described Squire's attack as an 'outrage on Mr. Shaw'. In its next issue (25 October 1919, 120) *The Nation* published a letter from Arnold Bennett, in defence of Squire, followed by a reply from 'Wayfarer'.

13 The lacuna before 'relieved' is sizeable. At least two sides, if not four, are missing. The end of the letter survives because Rose crammed it into the space at the top of the first side of the four-sided sheet that carries the first part of the letter.

14 Frederick Dalton had joined the editorial staff of *The Times* in 1893 and remained with the paper until his retirement in 1923. He was assistant editor of *TLS* from 1902 to 1923. De la Mare's (unsigned) review was printed not in *The Times*, but in *TLS*, 13 November 1919, 647. He mixes praise with criticism of some technical flaws that he attributes 'to her heedlessness or her earnestness'.

12

Hedgerley End
Beaconsfield
29 November 1919

Dearest Jean

I'm glad 'Caristia' has appeared so promptly.[1] It is a nice thing. Mother likes it. Naomi told me she'd written to you. By the way, you say nothing of your plan of possibly being in town for a day next week and coming in to 44 Princes

Gardens[2] on Thursday night – so I'm afraid you mean it's fallen through. If it *is* coming off, let me know, and I'll send particulars of how to get to us. It would be nice if you did, and if Jim came with you. Any time after dinner – about 9 or so. It *was* Dec: 4th you suggested, wasn't it? That Thursday would do nicely – in fact most Thursdays, (only not the 11th).

Come here any time in the vac. – but 1921[3] for choice, as the last week of the year is apt to be rather full of the family on its respective holidays, tho' I don't exactly know how long they last this time. But anyhow, now that there's Eleanor,[4] one more fills H[edgerley] E[nd]. But if you're in town during that time – i.e. the Xmas holidays – let me know, and we'll meet there.

I've been up at P[rinces] Gardens 3 days this week – it's a convenient place, and rather fun.

We got Wells' bright epitome of history when it came out, and it entertained and interested us.[5] I love him, he's so brave. Mine is the kind of brain that likes its history and science in these tabloid forms. I even admired the pictures, which everyone said were so bad. I think it's an enterprise worth making. I wondered what Professor Murray was doing to assist.[6]

I thought *The Times* [*Literary Supplement*] review of it quite futile – the reviewer seemed to want a few notes on Heaven thrown in or something![7] Really, one can't expect a history of heaven, as well as earth, even from H.G. Wells – though I've no doubt he would undertake it without any qualms if he saw fit.

What shall I write for *The Mercury*? J.C. Squire has asked me for 'prose or verse'. Which, I wonder, shall I try them with? At present I don't feel energy for either.[8] I'm wrestling with *Potterism* in odd moments, and even trying to get some more of it typed at intervals – and these other enterprises spend so much time and energy. I'm bad at the short story. I've got one in *Land and Water* this week – an old one left over from their Prize competition at Easter, that Ethel Colburn Mayne won – and mine is even worse than hers.[9] Its only bright spot is that it's adorned with the most appalling pictures – all the *L. and W.* things are. My young man of 24 looks in one picture like a fat major risen from the ranks, in the other like an imbecile poet. It's absurd of them to publish the story at all now, it was never any good and is now not even topical.

Rose omitted to sign this letter.

1 Jean's poem appeared in *SWG*, 22 November 1919, 7. It was republished, with a few alterations, in her *Shepherd of Souls* 40.
2 See *L*4 n. 8. Naomi Royde-Smith had taken up residence at 44 Princes Gardens in June 1919 and was to remain there until October 1923. She had known the house during the first decade of the twentieth century, when it was the home of Margaret Hamilton-Fellows, *née* Wills, the married elder sister of her close friend Kathleen Wills. Her occupation of a flat in it more than ten years after Kathleen's sister moved out is unlikely to be a matter of pure chance, but it is not clear what happened.

3 An error for 1920. The second paragraph of *L*13 shows that Jean remarked on it.

4 Rose's youngest surviving sister and her mother's least favourite child. Like Margaret and Jeanie, she decided to leave home, and in her case, unlike in their cases, Grace Macaulay did not oppose departure. That was in 1910, when she embarked on a teacher-training course. In 1912 she went to India to teach in Lahore. She was to work in India for forty years, until her sudden death there, from a heart attack, on 5 August 1952. From 1918 she was a missionary of the Society for the Propagation of the Gospel (*L*16 n. 6).

5 H.G. Wells, *The Outline of History, Being a Plain History of Life and Mankind*, the first of whose 24 parts, published at fortnightly intervals by Newnes of London, had just appeared.

6 Murray was one of four scholars whose 'advice and editorial help' is acknowledged on the title page, but Wells 'came to mistrust Murray's enthusiasm for fifth-century Athens, accusing him of creating a "city of demigods", glossing over slavery, and generally reading too many modern ideas into ancient times' (Duncan Wilson, *Gilbert Murray OM* (Oxford, 1987) 260). In the undated letter in which Wells asked Murray to help (GM 40.149), he described *The Outline of History* as 'the most exciting job I have ever done'.

7 See *TLS*, 27 November 1919, 693. The unnamed reviewer was Peter Chalmers Mitchell, secretary of the Zoological Society of London.

8 There is no contribution by Rose, in either prose or verse, in the early issues of *The London Mercury*.

9 Rose's story is 'Dennis Demobilised', *Land and Water*, 27 November 1919, 21–23. Ethel Colburn Mayne was joint winner of the Short Story Competition with 'The Man of the House', published in the issue of 12 June 1919, 17–19. She shared the prize with H.J. Jones, whose story, 'Five to One', appeared in the same issue, 20–22.

13

2 December [1919]

Dearest Jean

I'm sorry about the 4th – also that the 11th is no use. But if and when you are in town, come in some evening – any evening, almost – it needn't be a Thursday. You and Jim both. (The 10th is no use.) And Fridays aren't very good. Monday the 8th would do very well – or the following week, any night – (Thursday the 18th, if you're up then?). I'd love to meet Jim when he's in town, if he is willing. Shall we dine with Uncle R[egi] the same night, or won't the uncle be there? Or could Jim come and have tea at the club or something?

As to your coming to Beacs, you needn't, now I come to think of it, wait so long as till 1921, or even 1920, because if it isn't for a week-end, and why should it be if you're having holidays, there's sure to be room. It's Sundays that get so full, because of Jeanie[1] and Will and you never know when Will can come. No-one's Xmas holidays will begin till just before Xmas, when you won't be likely to want to come anyhow. So if you can manage a week-middle, do. Not including a Thursday (and on Wed: the 10th I shall be away in town). And I don't quite know what's happening the following week – Eleanor's got someone coming for one night, and Uncle K[enneth] is coming for another – it's all very involved, I'm afraid, and 1919, what's left of it, seems to consist mostly of days you *can't* come for – I'm so sorry! Perhaps 1920 would really be less trouble after all, if equally good for you. But propose anything you can manage, and I'll let you know if it suits.

I'm sure Robert Graves must be a dear, from *Fairies and Fusiliers*, which is charming. I like him the best of all those young soldier poets, I think. His wife I only know by hearsay as 'pretty Nancy Nicholson in knickerbockers'.[2]

I see *The Ladies' Field*, or one of those chatty publications which record the doings of society – I forget which – Naomi was fearfully pleased because she figured in it once – 'the clever and charming editress of the *Sat[urday] West[minster] Gazette]*', or something. (I haven't yet soared to those heights).[3]

I think what's the matter with Galsworthy is that he's a sentimentalist and has grown much soppier with middle age. *The Man of Property* and *The Country House* are really clever – *Saint's Progress*[4] mawkish and poor. Of course he's no glimmer of humour either, which must make it difficult for him. But he must be a rather lovable person.

I've just got £8 for a story.[5] Isn't it a lot! I'm going to get an evening dress!!! Wish you were here to help me choose it. All my real evening dresses – full evening – are pre-war, I'm ashamed to say. I've had them altered, but I really can't dine out in them any more.[6] Mother's been having flue. I'm on my way out to tea with G.B. Stern, to meet Clemence Dane, Sheila Kaye-Smith, and Rebecca West! Funny party.[7]

My love
R.

1 Sister of Rose and the next in the family after her, Jeanie was a nurse, trained at Guy's Hospital, London, and at the Royal Hampshire County Hospital, Winchester. In the First World War she and her lifelong friend and companion, Nancy Willetts, served in France with the French Red Cross; and in 1936–1939 she and Nancy worked in a South African mission hospital, the Jane Furse Memorial Hospital in the Northern Transvaal (now Northern Province). Otherwise she was employed as a district nurse, first in Deal, later in Romford. On her retirement in 1956, she was created MBE.

2 Evidently Jean had mentioned Robert Graves and his wife in her letter. They had married in January 1918 and come to live on Boars Hill in October 1919, when, after his demobilisation, he began reading English at St John's College, Oxford. They rented Dingle Cottage at the bottom of John and Constance Masefield's garden. They stayed on Boars Hill until 15 June 1921. Neither of them found it entirely to their liking, and a six-month experiment with running a shop was a failure. For Robert's own account, see his autobiographical *Goodbye to All That* (rev. ed., London, 1957) 257–261, 272–275. Nancy, the daughter of the artist William Newzam Prior

Nicholson and the sister of the artist Ben Nicholson, had artistic talent herself. A feminist, who 'ascribed all the wrong in the world to male domination and narrowness' (*Goodbye to All That* 256), she refused to call herself 'Mrs Graves', and the manner of her dress sometimes caused eyebrows to be raised, not least when, during the reception after her and Robert's marriage, she changed out of her wedding-dress into her land-girl's breeches and smock. She and Robert parted company in 1929. During the First World War Robert was an officer in the Royal Welch Fusiliers. *Fairies and Fusiliers*, his second volume of poems, was published in 1917.

3 After the parentheses about Naomi and herself, Rose has forgotten to tell Jean what had caught her eye in the magazine. If indeed the piece was in the *The Ladies Field*, a possible candidate, given that mention of Graves might have reminded her of another soldier-poet, is a laudatory review of John Still's *Poems in Captivity* (22 November 1919, 72), a work strongly criticised by her in *L*11.

4 This novel (Rose mistakenly has '*The*' before '*Saint's*') appeared in 1919, *The Man of Property* and *The Country House* in 1906 and 1907 respectively. John Galsworthy was a friend of Gilbert Murray, whose comments he had sometimes sought on drafts of his novels and plays.

5 Perhaps her story in *Land and Water* (*L*12).

6 Just over two years later Rose was to lose her evening dresses when her London flat was burgled (Edward Conybeare's diary, 28 February 1922).

7 It is not clear why Rose calls the party 'funny'. Perhaps it is mainly because all its members are women novelists. At 38, she was older than the other four, G.B. Stern being 29, Sheila Kaye-Smith 32, Clemence Dane 31, and Rebecca West almost 27. For G.B. Stern 1919 was the year in which she published *Children of No Man's Land* and married Geoffrey Lisle Holdsworth. She was to produce nearly 50 novels and much other work. Clemence Dane's third novel, *Legend*, had appeared in 1919. She became a prolific and versatile author, well known not only for her novels but also as a dramatist and screenwriter. Sheila Kaye-Smith, who was to write two books on Jane Austen in collaboration with G.B. Stern in the 1940s, produced novels that are notable for their carefully observed pictures of rural life. Her most recent novel was *Tamarisk Town* (1919). Rebecca West, a close friend of G.B. Stern, whom she called Tynx, was still involved with H.G. Wells, the father of her five-year-old son, Anthony. She had recently moved back to London from Leigh-on-Sea in Essex and had a flat in South Kensington. Her first novel, *The Return of the Soldier*, had been published in 1918. In *L*20 Rose calls her 'an inaccurate person, though clever'. On the accident Rebecca had in the garden of G.B. Stern's cottage in Cornwall in spring 1920, see *L*21 n. 14.

14

15 December [1919]

Dearest Jean

Thank you very much. It is very apt. I think I might use part of it 'These insidiously tempt us . . . out of doors' for my title page.[1] It is good. Of course I remember talking of *Potterism* in Hedgerley Lane. I'm nearly at the end of the book now – but it's an unholy jumble of irrelevant and incoherent odds and ends, I'm afraid – murders, manners and morals. I'm nearly sure it's bad.

I've spent a frantic Sunday reviewing Francis Brett Young,[2] who is good, *Wheels*,[3] which is mixed, Ezra Pound,[4] who is jolly when he's medieval and provençal and rather funny when he's classical and vulgar when he's 20th century – Richard Aldington,[5] who is better on War than on Desire, (but I wish these young soldiers would now stop writing about the nasty things they've seen at the front) and Gerald Cumberland,[6] who is silly. And reading 5 other poetry books too bad to mention – oh what people do write! I'm rather annoyed with the literary world just now, it does squabble so. Did you see Mr. Shanks' nasty little sneering notice of Osbert Sitwell in the *Mercury*[7] – and all because they'd been on the same Committee and quarrelled there. O.S. says he's going to get his own back again, and that he can be ruder than that if he tries – but I hope he won't – I hate these côterie quarrels. As to poor Mr Marsh, I think everyone is rather unkind to him about *Georgian Poetry*[8] – everyone, that is, but *The [New] Statesman* and *The [London] Mercury*. Did you see *The Athenaeum* and *The Nation* on him?[9] And *The Cambridge Magazine*. He's been compared to the Royal Academy, and to a literary sign-post pointing the wrong way.[10] Poor man, why shouldn't he make an anthology of the recent poems he prefers, if it pleases him? It makes a very nice collection, I think – of course with lots of bad things in it, but plenty of good ones too – and I think we should be grateful to all the anthologists, there's room for them all, even if we don't agree with their tastes. I'm glad 'Advent' is on.[11] You'll be able to finish it about 1940, perhaps, under the title of 'The Advents of a Busy Life' or something. It will be interesting to trace your progress from Advent to advent. The worst of it is that art is long and advent so short – so you can't get much of it done each year. You might publish it like Gilbert Cannan's *Nowell*,[12] in 12 parts – or like Wells' *History*.

Did you see that Mr Squire says Shaw's wife (on the cover of the above) is Maxim Gorky. But of course she's a wife – to me it's so apparent. Shaw, of course, is an obvious portrait.[13]

I wish we'd met longer and oftener last week. That poor little girl was in the way – a nice little girl too, and I had to keep fending off her compositions. I knew I should love to see them for two pins, and I do hate discouraging people. She's now retired to the country, having given up her hopes of getting a journalistic job for the present. Poor child – she doesn't know the waiting mobs of young men there are besieging newspaper offices for jobs and being turned away empty. Journalism is so frightfully pop<u>lar, naturally.[14]

I'm just going to hear J.C. Squire lecture on journalistic English – it ought to be rather nice.

By the way, *don't send me any Xmas present*. Please excuse my being in a train. My love. R.

1 The title-page of *Potterism*. There are five quotations on the page (vi) preceding the Contents, but they do not include the unidentified quotation supplied by Jean.

2 *Poems 1916–1918* (London, 1919). Rose's reviews of it and the four other volumes of poetry mentioned below are in *The Daily News*, 23 December 1919, 6.

3 *Wheels: A Fourth Cycle* (Oxford, 1919). *Wheels*, edited by Edith Sitwell, was an annual anthology of new poems, a modernistic counterpoise to Edward Marsh's *Georgian Poetry*, on which see *L*6 n. 9. Six volumes of *Wheels* appeared between 1916 and 1921. Edith and her brothers, Osbert and Sacheverell Sitwell, contributed poems to all of them, Aldous Huxley to all but the first. The volume reviewed by Rose includes seven poems by Wilfrid Owen, who had been killed a week before the armistice. See also *L*20 n. 6.

4 *Quia Pauper Amavi* (London, 1919).

5 *Images of War, a Book of Poems* (Westminster, London, 1919).

6 *Rosalys, and Other Poems by Gerald Cumberland* (London, 1919).

7 *The London Mercury* 1, 2 (December 1919) 206–207. The notice is of *Argonaut and Juggernaut* (London, 1919), on which Rose comments briefly in *L*11 (see n. 3 there). According to the reviewer, not identified in the journal, Sitwell 'cannot really play the revolutionary with gusto, so, as Queen Victoria said, "We are not amused"; and when he lapses into more ordinary forms and more connected statements he is revealed as an ordinary immature writer of verses'.

8 E[dward] M[arsh] (ed.), *Georgian Poetry, 1918–1919* (London, 1919).

9 *The Athenaeum*, 5 December 1919, 1283–1285; *The Nation*, 6 December 1919, 338, 340. The former review, by J. Middleton Murry, is of *Wheels: A Fourth Cycle* as well.

10 The review in *The Cambridge Magazine* 9, 9 (6 December 1919) 129–130 is headed 'Literary Signposts'. The reviewer calls the first *Georgian Poetry* 'a notable signpost' and continues: 'Since then many of us, guided at first by it, have gone eagerly ahead, searching, listening, looking, rewarded occasionally by exquisite discoveries. And now, at news of a newer signpost, a little further on the way we have gone, we look back hastily over our shoulders, and very likely sniff.'

11 Jean does not seem to have completed her 'Advent' project. There is no trace of it among her surviving papers.

12 A misspelling. The work is entitled *Noel: An Epic in Ten Cantos* (London, 1917–1918). It actually contains only four cantos. *Noel: An Epic in Seven Cantos* was to follow (London, 1922).

13 *The Outline of History*, Part 2: *The Making of Man*, published on 5 December 1919, has on the front cover (and also inside, opposite p. 48) a colour picture of two Neanderthaloid creatures defending their cave. The larger one, with a fierce expression, yellowy-orange hair and beard, and a club, does indeed bear a striking resemblance to George Bernard Shaw. The smaller one, standing behind the other and to the right of him and holding a stave, has orange hair but no beard, and there can be little doubt that Rose's identification is correct. She is commenting on remarks made by J.C. Squire in *The New Statesman*, 13 December 1919, 326, where he is writing under the pseudonym of Solomon Eagle.

14 This paragraph evidently refers to the young woman whose journalistic ambitions are discussed in *L*8.

15

[In a train between Beaconsfield and London]
5 January [1920]

Dearest Jean

I'm so sorry – the 17th week-end is full. Jeanie's coming, for her last Sunday before she goes to Deal (where she has a new district), and probably Will too. Can you manage the 24th–26th? Do if possible. I'm glad you'll be in town that week. Come to 44 Princes Gardens Thursday night, the 15th? *Do.* Olive Willis[1] is coming, and probably Christopher Cheshire[2] – and some other people as well, but I don't know who. Naomi would like to see you. And let's also meet somewhere else – and I'd like to meet Dorothy[3] too, if she's willing and has time, but perhaps she's none at all if she's shopping. What if you both had tea with me one day, at the Club or somewhere?

I never wrote to Dorothy – but I was awfully pleased and interested, all the same – it all sounds thoroughly satisfactory and suitable, doesn't it, though it seems a pity to have to live in India – but that is, after all, a question of individual taste. Please give her my love. I told you, didn't I, something about Dorothy Lamb and J.R. Brooke, in the past? Well, they've fixed themselves up now – just before Xmas they got engaged. I am awfully glad about it, it's not losing either of them in any sense, and they're both so alive, they'll make each other aliver still if possible. It's fun, as she observes. As to being in love – well, anyhow *he* is. And she too, really, only she's too unsentimental to spread herself much, even to herself, on that side of it. She just says it's all a lark.

I'm on my way up to town with my completed novel. Mr O'Donovan was here making Mr Beresford ask me for it (for Collins') – and wresting gilded terms out of them. Mr Beresford says I have the best unofficial agent he ever came across, and he wishes he had one like that! It's really rather a shame, and I shan't haggle for those terms.[4]

All my love
R.

1 A senior contemporary of Rose at Somerville, Olive Willis had co-founded Downe House School in Kent, in a house that had belonged to Charles Darwin, in 1907 and was its enlightened and inspiring headmistress for forty years. The school was to move in 1922 to its present site at Cold Ash, near Newbury. Jean was to teach there in 1928–1931 (Introd. II.5). In her diary Naomi Royde-Smith does not mention either Olive or Jean among those who came to 44 Princes Gardens on 15 January 1920, but that does not necessarily mean that they were not there.

2 At this time Warden of Liddon House and curate-in-charge of Grosvenor Chapel (*L*95 n. 8), as well as editor of *The Commonwealth*, a monthly periodical published by the Christian Social Union, Cheshire was one of the most prominent clergy in the diocese of London from 1914 until the mid-1950s. In the last years of his active life he

was Preacher at Lincoln's Inn and Chaplain to the Speaker of the House of Commons. He was the elder brother of Geoffrey Chevalier Cheshire, the distinguished jurist, and uncle of Group-Captain Leonard Cheshire, VC.

3 Jean's elder sister, who had become engaged to Sidney ('Sid') Gillum of the Bombay Company. The couple met at Kirnan (*L6* n. 2), where in November 1919 Dorothy had taken up a salaried post as housekeeper. Regi Macaulay, her uncle and employer, had mixed feelings when, after only three weeks, she left to prepare for her wedding. Dorothy and Sid began their married life in India, and their first child, Anne, was born in Bombay on 25 April 1921, but the climate did not suit mother and baby, who returned to England. Until 1927, when, after 28 years' service in India, Sid took up a post in London, he and Dorothy had little time together.

4 *Potterism* (1920) was the first of Rose's novels to be published by the Glasgow-based firm of William Collins, which was also to publish the thirteen other novels she was to write. Gerald O'Donovan, having been employed as editor in Collins' London office in 1917, was in a good position to twist the arm of the prolific novelist and essayist John Davys Beresford, literary adviser to Collins from 1918 to 1923, not least because in 1917 he had recommended acceptance of Beresford's psychoanalytic novel *God's Counterpoint* (1918) after it had been rejected by Cassell. The book sold better than any of Beresford's earlier works of fiction.

16

Hedgerley End
Beaconsfield
20 February 1920

Dearest Jean

Yes, come later than the 6th if it's better – not the 13th, I think – but any one after that. Either March 20th or 27th. Easter[1] is apt to be rather full of family – but the Sunday after would be all right – only that is rather late.

Margaret and Will enjoyed the wedding[2] – they said it all went so well and was so nice. Margaret said she didn't see either you or Jim half enough – partly because whenever she began to she was interrupted by the Walter Smiths.[3] We had Aunt Frances[4] here for a night this week, and she questioned Will minutely as to what everyone wore. Very creditably, he was able to produce the information that he believed Dorothy to have been clad in some sort of white – but he couldn't get much further.[5] You know her way of firing questions, one after the other, at you, but you don't have time to answer. As to Eleanor – 'Did you come across the Fletchers at all in Ranchi?'[6] Eleanor begins to explain about the Fletchers, but Aunt F. leaps in again 'And are you quite out of the jackal range?' E. begins on jackals, but is cut short by 'Do you feel you have a distinct flair for teaching native children?' which stumps her altogether, and she is still struggling with it when 'I suppose social cachet is as important for teaching out there as in England' does for her entirely. The Macaulay mind isn't quick enough to deal with things in this way. As to social cachet, I really think the poor old darling is a little mad on the point. According to her, Cambridge thinks of nothing else.

There's no hurry about sending *Full Circle*[7] or [*The*] *Mask*.[8] Bring them when you come. I'll give you *How They Did It* then too. It's not a good novel – but has points of interest to those who are familiar with their government departments. I found it extraordinarily difficult to review. I hate reviewing my friends' books.[9] It's so difficult to be quite judicial about them. I asked Uncle Regi what he thought about the corruptions in the Ministry of Munitions – he said the civil servants were, no doubt, dishonest – civil servants always were – but the Business men not – business men never were – which is so like Uncle Regi.[10] I really believe he thinks the Business men (the best sort) have the only real standard of honour that exists in the world – just because he's one, so happens to have come across it, just as, knowing men well and not women, he asserts that women are never honest. It seems rather egotistic. He ought to be too clever for it, really. In Mr O'Donovan's book, the Ministry of Munitions Business men are a terrible sort – it's all founded on things he came across when he worked there, so are the civil servants – but it's all touched with exaggeration. The part that interested me most was the Crewe House Committee part, because I knew all the people – Wickham Steed, Dr Seton-Watson, Sir Campbell Stuart, Mr Phillips etc. – but there isn't very much of that.[11]

I've just been reviewing such a jolly book of Serbian poetry translations – lovely stuff – you'd like it. I hate translations usually. I had, at the same time, two awful books of French verse translations – why they are always so stilted and dreadful, and why do people translate French verse at all? But you must read the Serbian one *Kossovo*.[12] And also *Limbo*, Aldous Huxley's book, which I did the other day – it's so jolly. I don't like his verse much – I hope he'll always stick to prose in future. I didn't quite like to tell him this in my review, though.[13] He's really frightfully funny, and clever and interesting too. A coming young man, I think – if only he'll avoid poetry, the snare of so many foolish young men who believe that it is their form of expression, nearly always so erroneously.

The Brooke–Lamb wedding was deferred till March. Dorothy wants to go out to Italy and get done there, on the q.t., to avoid what she calls the Family Funeral, which she doesn't feel she can bear. It would be rather cheating her mother,[14] I think, who loves such festivities. But she's not so unselfish as your Dorothy, and wouldn't think very much about that.

I've just finished the proofs of *Potterism*. The family has all been reading it, so I feel I know all its weak points by now. I got a lot of quotations for its title page – none exactly about sentimentalism, but some rather apt ones about other aspects of it. Now I'm frightfully interested in the careers of people in their middle forties – both married and not. Shall I wait till I get there, or do it while in the mood?[15]

No, Molly Hamilton has no sense of humour in her books – any amount in real life – really lots – it's one of those queer cases when people can't, or don't, get it onto paper. Lots of people can't, of course.

I suppose you're 'Miss Smith' now, aren't you?[16] I must remember that. By the way, I'm not Miss Macaulay – that's still Margaret's official title – she was here this morning when your letter came, and nearly claimed it. Not that it matters, if it saves you time. And of course M. is properly 'Sister Margaret' on envelopes, only it's not her legal title, only a courtesy one.

She had, by the way, an appalling journey home from Clent – I leave you to guess why![17] Aunt Nannie sent us a splendid slab of cake. How is Dorothy getting on? The New Forest must have been lovely – till to-day.

My love
ERM

1 4 April 1920.
2 The wedding of Dorothy Smith and Sid Gillum in Clent on 12 February. Jean was a bridesmaid.
3 The Rev. Walter Smith, Vicar of Andover, who conducted the marriage service with assistance from two other clergymen, was an elder brother of Dorothy's and Jean's father. He had intended to enter the diplomatic service on leaving Oxford, but changed his mind after falling in love with Emily Babington, a cousin ten years his senior, who told him that she would only contemplate marriage with a clergyman. He determined to fulfil her condition, but she died and, when dying, revealed that she loved another man. After this reverse, Walter married another cousin, Margaret Vaughan, who favoured a life of strict austerity and saw to it that the family home was as uncomfortable as possible.
4 The wife of Edward Conybeare, Grace's brother. His diary records that Frances's visit to Beaconsfield was on 16 February.
5 According to the report in a local newspaper, *The County Express*, 21 February 1920, 'the bride wore a draped dress of white satin, trimmed with pearls, and a lovely Honiton lace veil, which had been worn by her mother and grandmother at their weddings'.
6 Eleanor (*L*12 n. 4) was teaching in Ranchi on the Chota Nagpur plateau in Bihar state in a mission school of the Society for the Propagation of the Gospel. She continued to work in Ranchi and nearby Murhu until her death in 1952. As well as teaching, she produced translations of Bible notes and other Christian literature into Hindi (*Oversea News* 129 (September 1952) 4). The identity of 'the Fletchers' cannot be established.
7 Novel by Mary Agnes Hamilton (London, 1919).
8 The first novel of John Cournos (London, 1919).
9 In this case the author of the book Rose reviewed was not just a friend, but also the man she loved. Her review, in *The Daily News*, 18 February 1920, 5, mixes praise with

some criticism. She calls it 'the harshest indictment of Government methods which has yet appeared in fictional form' and says that it makes 'interesting reading', despite 'certain faults of form, style and construction'. The novel owes much to Gerald's experience of the Ministry of Munitions, in which he served in 1915–1916.

10 On Regi's successful business career, see L6 n. 2. During the First World War he was an adviser to the Lands Department of the Ministry of Munitions.

11 On the Department of Propaganda in Enemy Countries, based at Crewe House and directed by Lord Northcliffe, and on Gerald O'Donovan's and Rose's membership of it, see Introd. I.5 and L3 n. 19. Sir Campbell Stuart was Deputy Director of the Department and Deputy Chairman of its advisory committee of eminent public figures and publicists. Soon after the war he wrote *Secrets of Crewe House: The Story of a Famous Campaign* (London, 1920). H. Wickham Steed, Foreign Editor, and from February 1919 Editor, of *The Times*, was also a member of the advisory committee, and he and the historian R.W. Seton-Watson were the co-directors of the Department's Austro-Hungarian section. Steed describes his involvement in *Through Thirty Years, 1892–1922: A Personal Narrative* (London, 1924) II 185–258. C.J. Phillips, who before and after the war worked for the Board of Education as an inspector of schools, had been transferred to the Foreign Office and was responsible for liaison between it and Crewe House. Gerald was Secretary of the Italian Committee at Crewe House, while Steed was its Chairman. Gerald's tenure of his office was not without controversy. In July 1918 he visited Italy as an emissary from the Committee. He was accompanied by his wife, Beryl, who had been brought up in Italy and acted as his interpreter. The selection of a man who had left the Catholic priesthood and married did not go down well in Italy, and Gerald caused consternation among British diplomats in Rome by interesting himself not only in matters of propaganda but also in internal Italian politics. (See J. Rennell Rodd, *Social and Diplomatic Memories (Third Series) 1902–1919* (London, 1925) 356–357; J.F. Ryan, 'Gerald O'Donovan: Priest, Novelist, and Irish Revivalist', *Journal of the Galway Archaeological and Historical Society* 48 (1996) 1–47, at 39–41.) Moreover, a letter of 5 June 1919 from G. Gale Thomas, for the liquidator of the Ministry of Information, to the Treasury, complains that Gerald, during his mission, exceeded his authority in approving increases in the salaries and allowances of several British government employees in Italy and in sanctioning excessive expenditure on furniture for the British Institute in Naples (National Archives file T1/12469).

12 See *The Daily News*, 9 March 1920, 5, for Rose's reviews of Helen Rootham (trans.), *Kossovo: Heroic Songs of the Serbs* (Oxford, 1920), Matilda Botham-Edwards (trans.), *French Fireside Poetry* (London, 1919), and Christian Malloch (trans.), *Lyrics from the French* (London, 1919). In the same place she reviews four other volumes of poetry.

13 *Limbo* (London, 1920) contains seven stories. Although it is not attributed to her, Rose's review is undoubtedly the one printed in *The Daily News*, 9 February 1920, 5. The style and vocabulary are unmistakably hers: compare, for example, 'his stories have a touch of the elfish humour and the elfish fantasticalness of Mr. E.M. Forster's' with phrases in another review of hers in *The Daily News*, 9 March 1920, 5: 'something at once elfin and homely' and 'this domesticity touched with fantasticalness'.

14 Elizabeth, the County-Dublin-born wife of the mathematician Horace Lamb.

15 Rose was 38 when she wrote this letter. The interest she mentions here was explored in her portrayal of 43-year-old Neville Bendish in her next novel, *Dangerous Ages* (1921).
16 The etiquette was that an eldest unmarried daughter was addressed as plain Miss Jones, while a younger unmarried daughter was also given her Christian name or initial.
17 Margaret evidently had the company of the Walter Smiths!

17

[No address]
5 March 1920

Dearest Jean

Thank you very much for your letter and for *Potterism*.[1] I *am* glad you like it. As you don't mention the thing I feel most qualms about – whether the melo-drama, such as it is, is too much out of keeping with the rest – I am hoping it didn't strike you too forcibly. I did my best to piece it on and point out that it came in to my idea of Potterism – but I fear not very successfully. Why I really put it in was, of course, to give them all an opportunity of talking, and something to talk about. Yes, it is true that my sub-authors are rather subdued in tone. I subdued them, slaying the incongruous jests and quiddities upon their lips. You see I didn't want people to say it was really R.M. all through.[2] But I don't think even R.M.'s part is really very gay. I felt it such a solemn and such a sad subject and deplored it so deeply – as Gideon did.

The chief difference in the corrected proofs is that I have cast some doubt on whether Clare had really pushed Hobart downstairs or only imagined it. I haven't said that she didn't, or that she did – I've just left people doubtful. You see I'm not really, myself, sure which it was, as I wasn't there when it happened – she might have done it, or she might only have seen him fall for himself and romanced about the rest. What I feel is really wrong is that Juke had no manner of right to write all that down about her and leave it about where I could get it and publish it – but that can't be helped.[3]

I'm sorry about the date of the League of Nations meeting – stupid of me, because I was there, and might easily have looked it up.[4] As to the other meeting, I didn't really know there'd been only one like that. But I think the danger of Madeleine Symons or anyone who knows her thinking I meant Jane for her is remote, don't you? As a matter of fact it is, of course, the sort of detail one would carefully avoid mentioning if it had been a portrait – which is what a good many readers fail to realise always. I hope she won't mind, in this case![5]

I am glad of your comments, which are always to the point – I suppose because you always know what I am trying to do in a book, and so judge it by how far that comes off, not by other standards – which is the only helpful criticism, of course. Incidentally, I am v. glad you don't think Leila Yorke farcically over-drawn, as I am half afraid she may be – that sort of person so easily becomes a conventional type, not 1st hand – the fact being that I don't know her from the inside, of course – and people aren't *really* mere fools, whatever they may appear.

How dull *The Mercury* is this month! And what bad poetry! Who *are* Martin Armstrong and the other man,[6] and why does J.C. S[quire] admit them, I wonder? I begin to fear he is losing his critical faculty. I hoped Robert Graves was going to have one – [7] didn't he say so? But perhaps he proposes and Mr Squire disposes – in fact, certainly. I like your 'Feb: Morning'[8] much better than any of these.

The family is going to Mr Shackleton this afternoon, to see Epstein and so forth – a nice mixture.[9]

My love. Come again soon.

R.

1 The book had not yet been published, and, as the first words of the next paragraph shows, Jean has been reading a copy of the uncorrected proofs.

2 *Potterism* is in six parts. Parts I and VI are 'told by R.M.'; Parts II, III, IV, and V are told by, respectively, Gideon, Leila Yorke, Katherine Varick, and Juke.

3 Clare Potter confessed to Laurence Juke, a young clergyman, that she had pushed Oliver Hobart down the stairs to his death (*Potterism* 186–187), and he recorded the confession 'in his private journal' (167). But, like Rose, Juke is uncertain whether she had actually done this: 'I was puzzled. That she had truly repeated what had passed between her and Hobart I believed. But whether she had pushed him, or whether he had lost his own balance, seemed to me still an open question' (187).

4 On the League of Nations meeting in the Albert Hall, see *L4*. It was on 13 June 1919. In *Potterism* 59 it is put in May.

5 'The other meeting' is that 'of a section of the Society for Equal Citizenship' at which Jane Potter took the chair. It is described in *Potterism* 84. The speakers were all female, all under thirty, and mostly university-educated. Evidently, Madeleine Symons, who at Cambridge had been president of Newnham College's branch of the National Union of Women's Suffrage Societies and had gone on to work for the Women's Trade Union League, had chaired just such a meeting. One can certainly accept that Jane Potter is not a portrait of Madeleine: for one thing, Jane is a rather selfish person, which Madeleine certainly was not, but the detail to which Jean drew attention is not the only one that might have made Madeleine wonder if she had not been in Rose's mind from time to time. It may be a coincidence that Jane was Madeleine's second name. It is much less likely to be a coincidence that Jane's parents had 'a lordly mansion' at Potters Bar, and Madeleine's, until her father's death in October 1917, an impressive mansion (Hadley Lodge) only a couple of miles south of Potters Bar.

6 Armstrong wrote novels and short stories as well as poetry. There are two poems of his in *The London Mercury* 1, 5 (March 1920) 521–523: 'The Senses' and 'The Coming of Green'. Several other male contributors have poems in the same issue, and it is not clear which of them is 'the other man'. In 'Coming to London – XIII' (Bibliog. I.7)

34, Rose writes that she forgets whether she heard Armstrong reading poetry before the First World War or later. Her remark to Jean strongly suggests it was later.

7 By 'one' Rose means not a critical faculty (!) but a poem in *The London Mercury*. The poem may be the 'The Stake', published in 1, 8 (June 1920) 138. Graves had recently enjoyed J.C. Squire's encouragement and collaboration in connection with the two numbers of *The Owl* that appeared in 1919. Graves and his father-in-law, William Nicholson, were the literary editor and art editor respectively of this short-lived miscellany of poetry and prose, with illustrations. (Only one more number, *The Winter Owl* (1923) was to appear.) Squire contributed to both issues in 1919 and gave some editorial assistance.

8 'Charing Cross Bridge, February Morning' is in Jean's *Shepherd of Souls* 11.

9 The home and studio of the symbolist artist William Shackleton were in New King's Road, Fulham, but the two exhibitions Rose and her family were going to see in his company were at the Leicester Galleries, Leicester Square. One was of Epstein's sculptures, including a controversial bronze of Christ (*L*18 n. 12). The other was the tenth exhibition of the Senefelder Club, which existed to celebrate and promote the art of lithography. Artists represented in that exhibition included Gauguin, Manet, Renoir, and Goya.

18

Hedgerley End
Beaconsfield
17th March [1920]

Dearest Jean

Thank you for sending me 'Statistics', which I return. I think it very good. You've got so much heat and Mexico-ishness into it – especially into the 2nd stanza. I think I do like the end – no, I don't think it is Matthew Arnoldish. What are you going to do with it?[1]

Thank you also for your last letter and for sending *Limbo*. Mother and I laughed over you and *Limbo* and the Murrays. It's quite true about reading aloud, of course, and a thing to be remembered. It's rather stupid of him to put in the jarring things he does sometimes – I hope he'll drop them.[2] Did you see Naomi's review of him in the *S.W.G.* last week?[3] I met him last week at a party – but I hardly spoke to him, I was too taken up with trying to soften away my review of Douglas Goldring's *Fight for Freedom* to him (to D.G., I mean – such a nice man, he is, and writes such bad books!)[4] and he with talking to Arnold Bennett about both of their new plays, that seem to be coming out almost simultaneously.[5] A queer-looking person, isn't he?[6] He's going to be one of a party the Sitwells are getting up to go to *Boy of my Heart* at the Lyceum next week. It ought to be rather funny.[7]

I am also next week going to the Brooke wedding, which is to be at

St Margaret's, Westminster.[8] Dorothy has apparently only just made close acquaintance with the marriage service, and thinks it very common indeed, which I suppose it is. I've told her that she'll probably have a homily composed by the clergyman instead of the prayer-book one – not that she'll like it any better, I fancy – and if he makes the comparison that is sometimes made of the bride and bridegroom to the Church etc. – I think she'll hardly survive it.[9] She won't be able to see either J.R. or herself in their respective roles.

Did Uncle Kenneth (who is with us now) tell you of Uncle Willie's verdict on the homily addressed to Dorothy and her groom? Mr Todd asked him, walking away from the church 'What did you think of the address?'[10] Uncle Willie thought for a moment, then replied concisely. 'Rot. Rot. Stuff and nonsense'. Mr. Todd, who apparently had regarded him as more academic in language than that, was rather amused.

I am glad you think the *Potterism* melodrama doesn't fit in too badly. As for Gideon and Jane, I know it's wrong – of course they won't have been so deceived about each other – but I had to make it so. I think you are right that if either *had* done it, the other would have been sure – one would, I know – but it is just *possible* one mightn't be sure they hadn't. Just possible – but I fear it is very near the edge of the psychologically impossible, if not over it.

Jane married Oliver from worldly ambition, and because she liked his looks. Perhaps that isn't really likely, either.

I've just been shown a lovely poem by Graham Royde Smith (Naomi's brother) on the lines of Edgell Rickword's *Mercury* poem about how, since seeing his lady dressing, he 'hadn't troubled much about his food'.[11] G.R.S.'s ends

'But though the whole affair's most nauseating
My appetite for food shows no abating'.

It's really rather nice. Naomi asked Edward Shanks why they put in such things, and he replied that the author is a young man they want to encourage – which seems a bad reason on the whole!

I went to the *Challenge* and retrieved my article on 'Blasphemy' which I thought it was time I had back again. I met a woman who had met you, and told me you had told her I was very angry with her, which was embarrassing! I told them I was going to send it to *The Church Times* instead. However, I didn't, but to *The Nation* as on reading it over, I thought it had the suitably solemn touch for that, [and] wasn't sure the *C.T.* would altogether fancy it. It's very dull and solemn and pious – but *The Nation* says it is suggestive and have taken it – for this week, I gather, or next. I stuck in a story about Mrs Pankhurst, and made it à propos of an article by Clutton Brock – otherwise it remains as it was, and very dull too.[12]

I've just been to such a nice lecture on the Technique of Poetry by Mr de la Mare – a lovely combination of abstruse philosophy and idiotcy – he read the most fatuous poems, composed by himself, to illustrate his points.[13]

Train getting in[14] – sorry to write so abominably – you know how it is, don't you, my love.

Always yours,

R.

I was sorry I missed Dorothy[15] yesterday.

1 Jean's poem, described by Gilbert Murray as 'a real beauty' (letter to Jean, 14 July 1920), first appeared in the *The New Statesman*, 10 July 1920, 391. She included a significantly revised version of it in *Shepherd of Souls* 33–34. In both places the title is followed by the bracketed words 'Royal Commission on the Sugar Supply'. Jean worked for the Commission as a statistical officer in 1918–1919.

2 The passage that apparently caused embarrassment when read aloud in the Murrays' house is most likely to have been one early in the first story, 'Farcical History of Richard Greenow', pp. 4–5: 'If this were a Public School story, I should record the fact that, while at Aesop ['one of our Greatest Public Schools'], Dick swore, lied, blasphemed, repeated dirty stories, read the articles in *John Bull* about brothels disguised as nursing-homes and satyrs disguised as curates.' It sounds as though Jean was doing the reading, although this is not absolutely clear. In any case, the passage would have gone down particularly badly with Lady Mary, who lacked any sense of humour. Mary Midgley, who was Murray's secretary for a while in the 1940s, describes the difficulty of reading aloud to Lady Mary (and indeed the difficulty of Lady Mary!) in *The Owl of Minerva: A Memoir* 144–146. See Introd. II.4.

3 The unsigned review, in the issue of 13 March 1920, is very favourable. It begins: 'There is no English writer under the age of thirty more interesting than Mr. Aldous Huxley.'

4 Rose's review of *The Fight for Freedom, a Play* (London, 1919) is in *The Daily News*, 21 January 1920, 5. She finds it 'not, to say the truth, a good play', being 'full of propaganda' and having 'characters [that] are too manifestly mouthpieces for good or evil sentiments'. Goldring had been a publisher as well as a poet and novelist. His novels included *The Fortune* (Dublin, 1917), critically acclaimed but little read at the time, in which the hero becomes a wartime pacifist, as Goldring himself did.

5 Arnold Bennett, a very prolific and versatile writer, had been Director of Propaganda in the Ministry of Information in 1918, at the time when Gerald O'Donovan and Rose were working in the Department of Propaganda in Enemy Countries. Storm Jameson, *Journey from the North* I (London, 1969) 161, gives a vivid picture of Rose and him together at one of the soirées at 44 Princes Gardens: 'One Thursday evening, I watched her with Arnold Bennett. He hung over her, mouth slightly open, like a great fish mesmerized by the flickering tongue of a water-snake.' The identity of the new plays he and Huxley are said to have been talking about is uncertain: Bennett's next ones were *Body and Soul: A Play in Four Acts* and *The Love Match: A Play in Five Scenes*, both published by Chatto and Windus in 1922 and first performed early that year. The first play by Huxley to be published (also by Chatto and Windus), an adaptation of Frances Sheridan's *The Discovery: A Comedy in Five Acts*, did not appear until 1924.

6 Huxley was 6 feet 4 inches tall, thin, with a large head. What has been called his 'otherworldly look' was at least partly attributable to his very bad eyesight.

7 *The Boy of My Heart*, a melodrama by Walter Howard, combined excitement and amusement.

8 The 'parish church' of the city of Westminster and the Houses of Parliament. Dorothy Lamb and Reeve Brooke were married on 23 March 1920. A notice in *The Times*, 16 March 1920, 19, announces: 'The marriage . . . will take place quietly . . . There will be no reception.' For Dorothy's wish for a quiet wedding, see *L*16.

9 More than thirty years later Rose attended another marriage service in the same church and commented: 'A beautiful service and singing. But what an *odd* service the marriage service in some ways is! I can't help feeling that the Christ and Church analogy, kept on all these centuries, is pretty blasphemous and silly' (*LLF* 105; 30 July 1953).

10 The address was given by the Rev. J.A.H. Law, Rector of Fleet in Lincolnshire and the bridegroom's brother-in-law. R. Stuart Todd, a prominent resident of Clent, where the marriage took place, was to be High Sheriff of Worcestershire in 1926.

11 'Intimacy', the sixteen-line poem parodied by Graham Royde Smith, was printed in *The London Mercury* 1, 5 (March 1920) 527. It includes the lines: 'Since I have seen you do those intimate things | That other men but dream of; . . . | I have not troubled overmuch with food | And wine has seemed like water from a well' (1–2, 10–11). Graham Royde Smith (unlike his sister, he did not hyphenate himself) left school at 15 and spent most of his career with railway companies. He was the last secretary of the London, Midland and Scottish Railway and wrote about the railways. He had a great love of poetry and composed some himself. One of his poems, 'Here, There, and Everywhere', was printed in *The Westminster Gazette*, 29 January 1900, 12, when he was only seventeen. He is the dedicatee of Naomi's anthology *Poets of Our Day* (London, 1908), and a poem of his is included in her *A Private Anthology* (London, 1924) 57.

12 See *The Nation*, 27 March 1920, 888, where the author of an unsigned article entitled 'The Blasphemy of Religious People' can now be identified as Rose. In an article entitled 'Father Vaughan and Mr. Epstein', published in *The Nation*, 6 March 1920, 769–770, Arthur Clutton-Brock, a distinguished essayist, critic, and journalist with a profound interest in aesthetics and religion, had discussed the condemnation of Epstein's portrayal of Christ by Fr Bernard Vaughan SJ, and Rose makes his comment that 'Father Vaughan will not be able to understand why his Carlo Dolci Christ seems blasphemy to others' the starting-point of her article. Incidentally, Clutton-Brock too disapproved of the statue, but not for the same reasons that Vaughan did.

13 'Poetic Technique' was the last of a series of four public lectures delivered by Walter de la Mare at fortnightly intervals in Bedford College for Women, University of London, Regent's Park. Rose first met de la Mare through Naomi Royde-Smith not later than 12 May 1912 (lunch-meeting mentioned in Naomi's diary). For several years from 1911, when he started reviewing for *SWG*, he was infatuated with Naomi. She called him Binns. The relationship, for all its passion, was never physically consummated, but inspired his writing. In 'Coming to London – XIII' (Bibliog. I.7) Rose writes admiringly of his poetry (32), but says that he 'read his poetry deplorably' (34). He can be heard reading two of his poems on a compact disc, *Historic Recordings of Poets Born in the 19th Century*, issued by the British Library in 2003. On the same disc Rose can be heard reading her poem 'The Alien'.

14 Since Rose 'has just been to' de la Mare's lecture, it may be assumed that she is travelling home to Beaconsfield.
15 Jean's sister, not Dorothy Lamb.

19

University Club for Ladies,
4, George Street,
Hanover Square,
W.1.
Friday [30 April 1920]

This is only to leave my love and Mother's, and these tulips from Naomi –
someone gave them her yesterday for her birthday.[1] I didn't expect they'd let me
see you to-day – I'm going to ring up to-morrow and find out if I can see you for
a minute before I go down to Romford for the afternoon. Monday I'm going to
Cambridge till Wednesday or Thursday,[2] but I want to call in the morning first if
I may. Naomi sent messages – would have liked to come and see you, but is going
out of town next week for her holiday, which lasts through May. She has five
separate diseases, poor dear, including dilated heart, gout in the toe, and anaemia.

They tell me you are going on as well as is expected – but I know it is bad at
first – I'm so sorry my dear. Shall I bring or leave you some books on Sat: or
Monday? I've several rather good review books, and more bad ones. I must show
you two comic letters I have from 2 of the Reviewed. Poor fools, what *is* one to
do with them? I really do try and not hurt their feelings more than need be.

My love – get better quickly.

Rose.

1 Naomi's birthday was 30 April. Rose has delivered the flowers and this note to the
London hospital in which Jean has just had a hysterectomy – a drastic operation for
a woman still in her twenties. Later there was speculation in the family as to whether
it was necessary.
2 We learn from Edward Conybeare's diary that on Monday 3 May Rose made the journey
from Beaconsfield to his house in Cambridge by bicycle, arriving at 8 pm, and that on
5 May she left early for Thetford (Norfolk) and Southwold (Suffolk), again by bicycle.

20

Beac[on]s[field]
6 June [1920]

Dearest Jean

Thank you for your letter. I'm sorry about the dentist; also the clergyman's
throat. You don't say anything about the convalescence process, but I hope it

goes on as well as may be. About Kirnan, I shan't, anyhow, be there in July – I shall be away a good part of it and rather busy the rest – and probably, I think, not at all: September would be the only chance, but it is rather an off one, I fear. I seem to have so many other different things I have engaged to do, and you can't just go there for the inside of a week and come back. I have a great scheme for staying with Jeanie at Deal and lingering along the south coast sometime, but that must wait till it's really steaming hot, because of bathing. But it's a lovely plan.

I'll show you the *Potterism* reviews when next you come here. They are quite entertaining reading. It is edifying to see how it strikes such different minds as Rebecca West's and *The Times Lit[erary] Sup[plement]* man, who, Naomi says she is sure, is either a clergyman or Clutton-Brock:[1] either way she is certain he wrote it on a Sunday afternoon, with the church bells going. It rather pleased me; I felt it lifted the book to the plane of a book with a high (even if unachieved) Christian purpose. And so it has! As to R.W., I thought her review quite amiable, for her, though I don't know how W.L. George will like her saying that I wrote *The Making of an Englishman*.[2] She is an inaccurate person, though clever. I didn't agree with her that Mr and Mrs Potter were academic, did you? She does not know our universities well. I don't think it was she who complained of the end – someone else, I think – perhaps *The M[orning] Post* or [*The Daily*] *Telegraph*.[3]

That poem about truth is J.C. Squire.[4]

Did you see Naomi's review of *Potterism*?[5] She liked the detective story in it, I'm glad to say – they mostly complain that it shouldn't really be there – (as of course I know it shouldn't, at least I knew they'd all think so, bless them, but it was to please myself and Will.)

I had tea with Edith Sitwell the other day, and she talked all the time about Robert Nichols, who, it seems, has now got engaged to a nice girl he's only met twice, and his friends are all hoping that is the end of Aurelia and quite time too. E.S. says he never really loved her at all, but posed about it, as he liked the idea of a grande (and rather disreputable) passion. She, and all his friends, can't bear the Sonnets, both on literary and moral grounds.[6]

I fell in love with two people at once the other night, when I dined with the English Association.[7] Sir Henry Newbolt took me in and on the other side was Dr Alington – such charmers, they both were. Middle-aged men *are* nice, when they are. Dr A. talked about your family. He likes Uncle Charlie tremendously.[8] He told me he had been taking with his Division the part of *What Not* about the different reasons why people didn't read the Bible – I suppose it must have been a scripture class, but it seems an odd one. As for Newbolt, I fell over both ears, but it's no use, as he's married, with a son of 27. He has such beautiful manners! I had an awful moment when I found I was put down on the menu to reply to the Guests' Toast that he was proposing, though I had written beforehand to refuse this – but I was firm, and Dr Alington was made by Newbolt to do it instead – 'butchered to make a holiday for Miss Macaulay', as he said in his speech.[9] Could you make an after dinner speech in a large room? I know I couldn't. And if I did, no-one would hear it. All the other speakers were wonderful – brimming with anecdotes and polite references to those present – I should be incapable of either.

I must stop and work. I've taken over the reviewing page of *Time and Tide* – not a bad job, because I can choose any book I like to do each week. And Mr Forster has sent me *The Vanity Girl* for the [*Daily*] *Herald*,[10] when I've said all I can think of about it for *The* [*Daily*] *News* long ago.[11]

We are settling down after a rush of disturbed rooms and cleaning, but the spare room is still unpapered as yet, and all the damp is coming through the walls. Mother's been away at Holmbury,[12] but is now back. And it's bitterly cold. I do want summer so badly, don't you. To-morrow I'm meeting a dramatist who wants to turn *Potterism* into a play. I wonder if he'll really do it.[13] I don't think it would be a good play at all. By the way, Naomi points out truly that I've given myself hopelessly away socially by making the Honourable Clare Potter take the bus from Covent Garden to King's X, just as one of us might. Of course really she'd never be seen in a bus of any sort. It was very inept of me; N. refrained from referring to it in her review out of regard for me, as it might indicate too plainly how far I am from knowing the ways of the Best People.

What are you doing, reading etc.? Can you go walks at all, I wonder? I wish we could be at Kirnan together: as it is I think you'd better make your plan independently of me, as Sept: is such a vague chance.

My love please to Aunt Nannie, and much to yourself.

ERM.

---

1 Naomi was mistaken. The unnamed author of the review, in *TLS*, 3 June 1920, 348, was Orlando ('Orlo') Williams, a versatile writer, translator, and critic.

2 See *The New Statesman*, 29 May 1920, 226. Rebecca West acknowledges that *Potterism* is funny, but finds it 'a disappointing book', arguing that Rose's 'story does not hang together'. Although she slipped up in assigning the title of W.L. George's novel *The Making of an Englishman* (London, 1914) to Rose, the book on which she is commenting is not George's, but Rose's *The Making of a Bigot*, also published in 1914.

3 It was *The Morning Post*, 28 May 1920, 4: 'It is only in the last few pages that her [Miss Macaulay's] complete coolness and aplomb desert her for a moment. "R.M.", we feel, might have contrived a braver and wittier farewell comment.'

4 The poem, composed in 1913, is entitled 'Faith'. It begins: 'When I see truth, do I seek truth | Only that I may things denote, | And, rich by striving, deck my youth | As with a vain unusual coat?'

5 *SWG*, 5 June 1920, 18. The review is unsigned. Naomi was also to review *Potterism* in *Time and Tide*, 16 July 1920, 209–210.

6 For two years, from October 1917 to November 1919, Edith Sitwell was a friend and correspondent of Robert Nichols, one of the soldier-poets of the First World War, who had just seen the publication of his *Aurelia and Other Poems* (London, 1920). The collection includes a sequence of 27 'Sonnets to Aurelia', inspired by the writer's brief affair with the poet Nancy Cunard, who was to establish the Hours Press (1928) and become a militant civil rights activist. She had collaborated with Edith in organising the first *Wheels* anthology in 1916 and was the author of the poem that gave the series its title. The 'nice girl' whom Nichols was to marry, although not until July 1922, is Norah Denny. She too was a poet, but not associated with the Sitwells and very different from Nancy in personality, being gentle and unassertive. It is most unlikely that she and Robert had 'only met twice'. He knew her well enough by the beginning of 1918 to make her the dedicatee of a slim volume of his poems, *The Budded Branch*, published in the spring of that year. On Robert's relationship with Nancy, his biographers make a comment that fairly well accords with Edith's opinion as reported by Rose: '[They] were perhaps both more or less unconsciously playing the part of people having a love affair for the benefit of themselves as audience' (Anne and William Charlton, *Putting Poetry First: A Life of Robert Nichols 1893–1944* (Norwich, 2003) 102). By the time Rose wrote this letter, Nichols had moved to Boars Hill. He stayed until January 1921. His near neighbour Robert Graves describes him as 'one more neurasthenic ex-soldier, with his flame-opal ring, his wide-brimmed hat, his flapping arms and a "mournful grandeur in repose"' (*Goodbye to All That* rev. ed. (1957) 261).

7 The 1920 Annual Dinner of the English Association was held on Friday 28 May at the Royal Adelaide Rooms in the Strand. Rose was one of five guests.

8 From 1908 to 1916 the Rev. Dr C.A. Alington had been headmaster of Shrewsbury School, which Jean's brothers Bill and Henry had attended. In 1917 he had become headmaster of Eton.

9 Newbolt, best known for his poems 'Drake's Drum' and 'Vitaï Lampada', was chairman at the dinner in the absence, through illness, of the English Association's president, Charles H. Herford. The Association's *Bulletin* for September 1920 includes the following report: 'He [Newbolt] welcomed Miss Rose Macaulay, whose works were known to everybody in the only way that works of literature should be known, namely, by the intensity of the pleasure they produced. He shrank from discussing Miss Macaulay's poems, and he hoped Miss Macaulay would not mention his own. But of Miss Macaulay's novel, *What Not*, he could speak, because the subject of that book was a Ministry in which they had both been employed for a time. What Miss Macaulay did not know about that Ministry was not knowledge, and what Miss Macaulay had not said about that Ministry was not wit or humour. She was a guest they were particularly delighted to meet.' The report confirms Alington's joke about being 'butchered to make a holiday for Miss Macaulay'. The comment recalls Byron, *Childe Harold's Pilgrimage* 4.141.7: 'Butcher'd to make a Roman holiday'. The Ministry in which both Rose and Newbolt worked was that of Information in 1918 (Introd. I.5). After its liquidation in December 1918, they were both employees of the Foreign Office, from which Newbolt resigned on 1 April 1919, Rose about a month later (*L3* n. 19). Newbolt was indeed married, but his marriage involved an unorthodox, although harmonious and happy, arrangement. His wife, Margaret Edina, a

daughter of the Rev. (William) Arthur Duckworth, had consented to marry him only on condition that he accepted her cousin Ella Coltman as well. About two years into the marriage Ella became his lover and thenceforth the two women shared him on a fair and amicable basis. He even kept accounts, recording how often he had slept with each woman each month. See Susan Chitty, *Playing the Game: A Biography of Sir Henry Newbolt* (London, 1997) 91. Although Rose says that she could never make an after-dinner speech in a large room, she was to do this on future occasions. One such occasion was the 143rd anniversary dinner of the Royal Literary Fund, presided over by the Prime Minister, on 22 May 1933. Writing to Horace Vachell, who was also to speak at the dinner, she confesses: 'the prospect of trying to pronounce my R's in the presence of Mr Ramsay MacDonald rather daunts me' (letter, dated 25 April 1933, in the possession of the present editor).

10 Forster was the paper's literary editor. Rose accepted his invitation: her review of *The Vanity Girl*, a novel by Compton Mackenzie (London, 1920), is in the issue of 16 June 1920, 7.

11 *The Daily News*, 8 May 1920, 2.

12 In rural Surrey (not Sussex, as CBS 83 and Emery 161 say). Naomi had a cottage there. She was a not infrequent visitor to Hedgerley End (Letters 25, 36) and got on well with Grace.

13 It seems that he did not do it. A radio play based on *Orphan Island* was broadcast by the BBC Home Service on 13 June 1957, but the only novel by Rose to have been adapted for the stage, to the present editor's knowledge, is *The Towers of Trebizond*. Hugh Whitemore's dramatisation of the book was performed, as a one-woman show, by Rohan McCullough at the Edinburgh International Festival in August 1991 under the direction of Wyn Jones.

21

Hedgerley End
Beaconsfield
2 August 1920

Dearest Jean

Thank you very much for your letter.[1] The Icelandic depressions would seem to be worse than ever to-day, and I expect you ate your sandwiches in the dining room. Yes, it's a funny atmosphere up there, though agreeable.[2] There are so many things it would be worse than useless to say, aren't there. Uncle Willie is the most comprehending, in some ways; certainly about books. I love to hear him on the books he is reading; he throws himself into them with such zest – as he did into the M.S. of Mrs. Lynd's[3] that I had to read when he was here.

It was nice at Oxford, and rather funny.[4] I dashed down to it late, after the Hawthornden award, which I felt I must stay for. Mr Murray did the presentation, you know – I don't know why Miss Warrender thought him suitable.[5] He did it very nicely, and told Mr Freeman how nice it would be for him in later years, when he felt depressed about himself, to be able to think 'Well anyhow in 1920 a committee of four intelligent people thought my book of verse the best thing of the year'.[6] So now we're all going to give each other medals, to cheer us up in our darker hours. We all knew pretty well that Freeman was going to have it, though fear still lingered that it might be Robert Nichols,[7] which no-one could have borne. However, I gather from J.C. Squire that there was no danger of this. Freeman is rather bad and very dull, but a harmless creature. I think the whole idea of a cash prize is silly, and doesn't produce a good effect.[8] People oughtn't to be thinking of that when they write. I hope it won't go on always; I don't suppose it will, though they say now it will continue after Miss Warrender's demise. She is rather an engaging lady, I thought.[9]

Now I'm at home, en famille, not going to town at all, and writing *Ages*,[10] which interests me vastly, and I'm starting for Devon and the Duchy[11] in the middle of the month. It's rained so much that it can't rain always, I'm thinking. I've fixed the J.R. Brookes (I hope) at Porlock,[12] Carpenters at Port Isaac,[13] Rebecca West at Ruan Minor,[14] Lady Rhondda at Rottingdean[15] – but want several more inns still. Lady Rhondda suddenly wrote and asked me to her bungalow for a week-end. I said no, but might I stop a night when bicycling through Rottingdean at the end of August. I shall be absolutely disreputable by then, and have no clothes but a jersey and a bathing-dress; and I don't feel I know her well enough to invade her probably comme-il-faut bungalow – but never mind, it's her fault, and she's quite jolly and sporting and nice. Think of me rushing up and down the Cornish hill roads, and diving into rock pools – I wish you could come too! It really will be fun. Rather hard work though: I must get into good training first. I'm so glad being old – 'in the vale of years', as Aunt Ellen[16] puts it so happily – doesn't mean one gets any less active and robust, so far. But 39! *Eheu fugaces*,[17] as Will remarks in his birthday letter. Time flies by – cannot think why it <goes>[18] so quickly. Oxford reminded me of my lost youth – Somerville, and Summertown, and 3 Clarendon Villas, into which I peered.[19] So small; and so large a family of noisy children it held; what a nuisance we must have been to our neighbours.

We had rather a nice and funny evening at 44 [Princes Gardens] the last Thursday we were there. We had G.K. Chesterton and J.C. Squire and a young rationalist off *The Westminster* and other rationalists (e.g. the J.R. Brookes) and 2 parsons (one of whom was Arthur Duncan-Jones) and got them all discussing whether social progress and humanity was derived from Xianity or not. G.K.C. talked and talked and talked – you may imagine on which side – and was backed by charmingly Xian utterances from J.C. Squire – but Mr Usher,[20] the young rationalist, pluckily held his end up, and Naomi sat on the floor and smoothed everyone down and drew them out and said 'Of course he is' when G.K.C. said that man was the image of God and everyone else looked bewildered and as if they hoped not. It does sound an awful idea, certainly![21] G.K. enjoyed himself hugely, and broke the springs of the settee on which we had arranged he was not to sit; we kept him on a big arm-chair all the time except for 5 minutes, but in that 5 minutes the damage was done. He is really rather a darling. And it's so nice when people are so sure of what they believe.[22] The Anglican Fellowship hadn't a notion what it believed, from Canon Streeter (the chairman) downwards.[23] The only people who had were the two R.C. visitors, Father McNabb (an Irish Dominican priest of great charm and firm convictions, who said he was glad to note that we had anyhow a sense of humour, because that was the younger daughter of humility) and Miss Ward, who of course is R.C. too, and was rather shocked at us.[24] Percy Dearmer[25] failed to turn up. I was interested and entertained on the whole, though bored in parts.

This is a fearful scrawl – it's because it's a wet afternoon and I can't go out and can't write any more of *Ages* till tea-time and won't write any reviews. You'd better wait to read it till it's a wet day with you too, which I expect happens sometimes. Margaret said it was horribly cold. How goes life? Not very grand, I'm afraid. I'm sorry you can't fish; or, I suppose, walk a great deal. Kirnan exists for that; its indoor life is nil. Much love; and from Mother and Margaret too.

Rose.

1 Jean will have written for Rose's 39th birthday on 1 August.
2 Jean is staying at Kirnan (*L6* and n. 2).
3 Sylvia Lynd's manuscript was almost certainly of *The Swallow Dive* (London, 1921). For Rose's good opinion of this novel, see *L23*.
4 The reason for Rose's visit is not known. There is no record of any Somerville College or University function on 27 or 28 July 1920.
5 The presentation, by Gilbert Murray, was at the Wigmore Hall, London, on 27 July 1920. Alice Warrender, a friend of J.C. Squire and Edward Shanks, had founded the Hawthornden Prize, the oldest of the famous literary prizes, in 1919, when the winner was Shanks. A wealthy spinster, whose aristocratic family was from Edinburgh, she named the award in honour of the Scottish poet William Drummond (1585–1649), whose home was Hawthornden Castle, south-east of the city. The place is now the Hawthornden International Retreat for Writers. In the early years the Prize was £100, plus, from 1920, a silver medal. It was awarded to a writer, who must not be over forty years of age (which ruled out Rose after 1921), who had produced some distinguished work of imaginative literature, either in prose or in verse. For a memorandum on the prize, written by Edward Marsh and dated 19 June 1919, together with a letter from Marsh about the first competition, see Susan Lowndes (ed.), *Diaries and Letters of Marie Belloc Lowndes 1911–1947* (London, 1971) 90–91. See also Peter Lewis, 'The Hawthornden Prize', *The Henry Williamson Society Journal* 26 (September 1992) 32–49 – a useful account, although the writer is mistaken in thinking that the first award was made in 1920.
6 John Freeman, largely self-educated (he left school before he was thirteen) and a

remarkable combination of poet and businessman, was a friend of J.C. Squire and belonged to the 'Georgian' circle of poets. He won the prize with *Poems Old and New* (London, 1920). The awarding committee consisted of the prizegiver, Squire, Laurence Binyon, and Edward Marsh.

7 Misspelt Nicholls by Rose.

8 In 1912 Rose had won, with her novel *The Lee Shore*, the first prize of £600 in a fiction competition organised by Hodder and Stoughton. In a letter of 6 May 1913 to Katharine Tynan (KTH 1/656/13), she expresses her delight, as well as her surprise, at the award, but refers only to the usefulness of the money. In 1931 she accepted Methuen's invitation to be one of the three adjudicators in its Competition for Novels of Modern English Life, which offered a first prize of £1,000.

9 A letter dated '28 August' from Rose to Miss Warrender was offered for sale by John Wilson Manuscripts Ltd of Cheltenham in 2004. Rose, writing from Beaconsfield, expresses disappointment that she will 'be away from home again this Thursday, over the week-end', but hopes that 'you will be able to come sometime later, when you get back. It would give me and my mother so much pleasure'. Since Grace died in May 1925, the year cannot be later than 1924, and it is very likely to be 1920, soon after Rose's first meeting with Warrender, who had recently moved to Bayman Manor, Chesham, in Buckinghamshire and just north of Beaconsfield.

10 This may be an abbreviation of *Dangerous Ages*, but it may be that Rose had not yet decided on that title.

11 Cornwall.

12 In Somerset, between Exmoor and the sea.

13 On the north coast of Cornwall. The Rev. Spencer Carpenter, an Anglo-Catholic, was married to Silvia, sister of Arthur Duncan-Jones, his contemporary at Caius College, Cambridge (*L4* n. 4). After her death in 1941, he married again. A historian and theologian who wrote, lectured, and preached interestingly, he was at this time tutor and lecturer at Selwyn College, Cambridge. From 1935 to 1950 he was Dean of Exeter. In a letter to Jeanie dated 26 January 1957, Rose recalls: 'It was to him that I made my last confession, in 1921 or 2, before giving it up for 30 years. He has always had a very nice sense of humour, and tells amusing stories about people' (*LS* 211). That last confession may well have been on Good Friday, 14 April 1922, for in an unpublished letter to Jeanie, of 15 April 1922, Rose writes: 'I went to Mr Carpenter's 3 hours – he was very good, as he always is. I also went to confession to him, and he is always good at that too. He expects so little, and takes the line that one has to make something of a bad business and that God will be thankful for anything he can get, though he has to give up the hope of getting anything but a 2nd best. He is very practical too' (ERM 9.3).

14 On the east coast of the Lizard peninsula in south Cornwall. Rebecca West had been having an unhappy time. In the spring she fell into a water-cistern in the garden of the Cornish home of G.B. Stern and her husband. A wound sustained in the accident turned septic, and she spent several weeks in a nursing home in Redruth, where she experienced insomnia and, when she did manage to sleep, disturbing dreams. H.G. Wells added to her troubles by being unsympathetic and unfaithful.

15 On the Sussex coast. Margaret Haig Thomas, Viscountess Rhondda, had recently

founded *Time and Tide*, an independent political and literary weekly for both men and women, but run by women. The first issue appeared on 14 May 1920. Although *Time and Tide* had seven directors at its birth, it was Lady Rhondda's child, and she subsidised it with her own money. She was very much in charge from the beginning, although she did not become the editor until 1926. She continued to be in charge until her sudden death on 20 July 1958. Very shortly after her marriage in 1908 to Humphrey Mackworth, a Conservative, she had joined the Women's Social and Political Union and enthusiastically participated in its militant campaign for women's suffrage. In its early period *Time and Tide* reflected her left-wing and feminist views, but over the years her views changed and the paper's line changed with them. Her marriage was dissolved in 1923.

16 Ellen Rose (*L*6 n. 6). She was to die on 28 February 1921, aged 89.

17 The first words of Horace, *Odes* 2.14, on the shortness of life and the inevitability of death.

18 Unless the preceding words have been misread, some such supplement is necessary.

19 On the Macaulays' years in Oxford and Rose's time at Somerville, see Introd. I.2.

20 Herbert Usher was Assistant Editor of the *Westminster Gazette*. Although not yet an occupant of 44 Princes Gardens, he was to move into a flat there on 1 November 1920 (Naomi Royde-Smith's diary). A member of the Labour Party, he twice stood unsuccessfully for Parliament before serving, in 1929–1935, as Personal Private Secretary to the Prime Minister Ramsay MacDonald. Later he held senior posts in the Treasury, and after the Second World War on the War Damage Commission. On his marriage to Grace Barker, who also had a flat in no. 44, see *L*23 n. 5. Naomi's diary reveals that the date of the gathering described by Rose was Thursday 15 July.

21 In her article 'The Blasphemy of Religious People' (*L*18 and n. 12 there), Rose discusses 'that very common kind of blasphemy which believes that humanity was created in God's image, that God is a kind of glorified human being', and concludes: 'There is only one remedy for blasphemy. The human race should not talk about God at all, except in his aspect to us of the Voice of Conscience – the only aspect we can know anything about.'

22 Chesterton certainly was sure of what he believed. At this time he was moving ever closer to the Roman Catholic Church, into which he was received on 30 July 1922. As for the settee incident, a sedentary lifestyle and overeating (much of it, apparently, due to his famous absent-mindedness) had turned him from a slim youth into an obese man.

23 A New Testament scholar, Burnett Streeter was at this time Fellow of Queen's College, Oxford, and Canon of Hereford. He became Provost of Queen's in 1933.

24 Vincent McNabb, like Chesterton and Hilaire Belloc, was a proponent of 'Distributism', a socio-political philosophy based on religious and ethical principles and intended to be a third way between capitalism and socialism. His devotion to the simple life manifested itself in 'wearing homespun robes and refusing to use a typewriter because it is a machine' (Alzina Stone Dale, *The Outline of Sanity: A Biography of G.K. Chesterton* (Grand Rapids, Michigan, 1983) 155). Maisie Ward's books were to include *Gilbert Keith Chesterton* (London, 1944).

25 Dearmer, Arthur Duncan-Jones's predecessor as Vicar of St Mary's Church, Primrose

Hill, was the author of *The Parson's Handbook* (London, 1899) and an expert on English ecclesiastical art, music, and liturgy. He saw art and music as intrinsically important components of religious worship, and not surprisingly attracted artists and musicians to his church and congregation. He was the General Editor of *The English Hymnal* (1906) and engaged Ralph Vaughan Williams as the Musical Editor. In 1919 he was appointed Professor of Ecclesiastical Art at King's College, London. Rose mentions him in *Potterism* 15.

22

Beaconsfield
15 September 1920

Dearest Jean

Many happy returns, and a fine day for the time of year, and my love and best wishes, and all other good things, and *Lady Adela*,[1] which made me laugh and may you. It's so hopelessly silly; also has more bad jokes to a page than any other book I've come across. I wish I'd written it!

I'm just back from the South West. I enjoyed myself. Too lovely, the Cornish fishing-towns are. Do you know them? Like nothing else: all pale whitewash and old grey slate roofs, huddled close together up steep crooked streets, with green doors and outside stone staircases, like in Italy, and climbing down to little harbours full of fishing-boats. St Ives was like that, and Polperro, and Port Isaac, and lots more. And Fowey is a dream of romance. I spent a Sunday with the Carpenters at Port Isaac, and we bathed twice in the day and went to church 3 times – both so unusual for me that I was quite upset by Monday morning. Lovely bathing: you plunge into a blue tossing sea off rocks. Do you know Veronica?[2] She really *is* attractive. We discussed the future of the Church when not bathing or praying. Mr C. says he becomes more anti-clerical each year he lives. How wise that is. The only antidote. I arranged other hosts and hostesses at intervals along the Cornish and Devon coasts, and at times when there weren't any always managed to get a room somewhere. If I'd been two instead of one I wouldn't have, hardly ever; they always had just one bed left, or knew of some cottage which could take in one woman. It wasn't as warm as I could have wished, but fine on the whole. Now I'm back, and found piles and piles of work waiting, not having had any books sent after me naturally. One was Edmund Blunden's *Waggoner*.[3] I like it very much in many ways, though he has too many queer Kentish words and doesn't always make you care about what he describes in such detail. But then it will suddenly be poetry, you never know when. Now I've got Edward Thomas' *Collected Poems*[4] – I do think he is fine. You should get them sometime. And *The House by the River*[5] (very bad) and *The Tragic Bride*[6] (rather bad) and Margaret Storm Jameson's new novel (exactly like *The Pot Boils*).[7] And piles and stacks of rubbish. I'm bored with it all. But in Cornwall I had a lovely time in the evenings, getting on with my own book[8] and no interruptions.

Are you at Clent still? I suppose so. I wonder how you are, my dear. Tell me, when next you write. Are you going back to Oxford at the beginning of term? And shall you be at Yatscombe at first?[9]

Eleanor is sailing[10] early in October.

Mother sends her love and greetings, and here are all mine. My love, please, to Aunt Nannie. Your loving E.R.M.

1   The book, for Jean's birthday, is by Gerald Gould, with drawings by Will Dyson (London, 1920).
2   The Carpenters' adopted daughter. When she married Dorrien Alastair Douglas Young, a 29-year-old army officer, in Exeter Cathedral on 27 July 1938, she was aged nineteen, and so was only one or two years old in the late summer of 1920. Rose was one of the witnesses of her marriage.
3   *The Waggoner and Other Poems* (London, 1920). Blunden spent most of his childhood in Kent. The experience had a lasting influence upon him, instilling a deep interest in rural life and the natural world. Another powerful and enduring influence was the war, in which he had served with distinction, winning the Military Cross. Like Robert Graves and Robert Nichols, he lived briefly at Boars Hill after the war, but during the summer of 1920 abandoned his English course at Oxford and moved on to a part-time editorial post with *The Athenaeum*.
4   Thomas was killed at Arras on 9 April 1917. Before the war he wrote prose. His switch to poetry probably owed much to the advice and encouragement of Robert Frost. Most of his poems were published posthumously. *Collected Poems* (London, 1920) had a foreword by Walter de la Mare.
5   Novel by A.P. Herbert (London, 1920). See *L*23 and n. 10 there.
6   Novel by Francis Brett Young (London, 1920). It is about Gabrielle Hewish, a baronet's only child, who, after her lover slips and accidentally shoots himself dead when they are out walking, marries the Rev. Marmaduke Considine, whom she does not love. He has the bright idea of offering to board and educate, for high fees, a small number of boys, including ones that are backward or difficult. One of his first pupils is the good-looking but wild Arthur Payne. Gabrielle tames him, and they fall in love. The relationship is discovered by his mother and has to end. Arthur travels abroad and goes to university. After he announces his engagement to a suitable young lady, Gabrielle accompanies her husband one evening when he is rabbit-shooting. He slips, his gun goes off, and he is shot dead. The coroner's jury in Devonshire, 'a county where juries are more than usually slow of apprehension', concludes that it was a tragic accident.
7   See *L*4. Storm Jameson's 'new novel', her second, is *The Happy Highways* (London, 1920).
8   *Dangerous Ages*, part of which (Chapters VIII–IX) is set in Cornwall.
9   Jean did indeed resume working for Gilbert Murray in the autumn of 1920, and lived at Yatscombe, the Murrays' house.
10 For India.

23

Hedgerley End
Beaconsfield
9 March 1921

Dearest Jean

Yes, I know it's longer since I wrote, and I've been meaning to for weeks, because I wanted to know how you were, and all sorts of things. But, what with work and what with social life,[1] even the letters one really wants to write slip out. Anyhow it will be splendid to see you on Monday. I can lunch, and I'll get Naomi if possible, but I have an idea she always lunches with Aldous Huxley on Mondays, to arrange the dramatic criticism.[2] However, I'll see her again to-morrow, and will try and make her come. I know she'd like to see you – and she always likes to meet intelligent young men. Perhaps Mr M<a>cdonell can come to 44[3] some Thursday later on, can he? It's no use at present, as this next one is the last till May. Naomi is going to Switzerland for 6 weeks. And Margaret and I are going to Italy for 3 weeks in April – isn't it a lovely plan – on my *Potterism* money. *Potterism* has sold fabulously in America, it seems, for some reason, and I ought to roll when the money comes in. It's my lovely publisher there, Horace B. Liveright, and his Live Methods.[4] Anyhow, somehow it's caught on in the Middle West.

Dangerous Ages (a silly name, but it can't be helped) is coming at the end of April, I believe. I've just got the proofs. A baddish book, it looks in galley slips.

It was very nice having Madeleine that Thursday. It seems that she works with Grace Barker (of our establishment).[5] She came on a rather crazy evening when we did charades and weren't being at all grown-up or intelligent – at least only Aldous Huxley, in a corner, was trying to be. I hope she'll come again sometime. It will be nice to know Agnes Murray, too.[6] One gets into a stupid way of meeting no-one but writers, journalists, reviewers and publishers. I was at a party at the Beresfords[7] last night, and I believe every person in the room (except some wives, of course) did one of these things, or two, or three. The J.R. Brookes are the only ones of my friends (in London) who open the windows onto a different view, and one rather needs more, not that the writers aren't the best really – that is, one feels more at home with them – but I sometimes fear one gets provincial, which would be awful, as the Roberts' at Shelford used to say.

I append a list of possibly readable novels. I'll send you some, too (you might return them sometime, will you?) but I'm afraid I've been sending the best all away to Rome, to feed Gerald O'Donovan,[8] who has an insatiable appetite. *Helena Cass*[9] is thrilling, rather, but not well-written of course. I'll send you *The House by the River* when I get it back from the Carpenters, who borrowed it. It's by A.P. Herbert, and about J.C. Squire murdering his housemaid. A.P.H. says he didn't mean it for Squire, but we all know he did, as it's the same house, and a poet and all.[10] He's rather a nice creature. I'll send you *Revolution*[11] and *The Swallow Dive*[12] – *Revolution* is v. dull, though. *The Swallow Dive* is very gay and clever. But not a thriller, so I dare say the Murrays wouldn't care for it. Mrs Lynd is a lovely person, and she has put in Robert[13] as the hero, and described him beautifully – as she said, you can't have anything so decorative in the house without using it! They are an adorable family – nearly the nicest people I know.

About lunch – can you and they manage the 1917 [Club]? It would suit me far best, as I have to be there anyhow, to see someone else. It's 4 Gerrard St, as you know. It's rather a low hole – will they mind? If they would, I'll manage somewhere else, only in that case may it be 1.30 instead of 1.15?

I've just been attending a Psychoanalysis lecture, by Dr Hadfield. He's not a Freudian, and not absurd, but really interesting.[14] According to him, *anything* can be cured: it's the key to the kingdom of heaven on earth, obviously, and certainly treatment should be provided free by the State. You are hypnotised, and cured of all your mental diseases (or what clergymen call, wrongly, sins). It sounds to me too good to be true, and as if there must be a hitch somewhere. I think Aunt M[ary] should be done. Not that we haven't all our diseases, but she would be a good subject for experiment, being rather an obvious invalid. We might all subscribe and send her. Probably her disease is the result of some circumstance of her 1st 2 or 3 years of life, and if, under hypnosis, she could be brought to remember this, she could be cured by suggestion.

We are so glad about Dorothy's son-to-be (we hear that is its sex).[15] And very much interested in Regie's change of career.[16] I'm glad one member of our two families is to go into the Church (as mother has never let us call it).

You didn't say how you are, but tell me on Monday. My love always

ERM

Mother sends her love.

1 Rose's socialising in the preceding weeks included being a dinner-guest, for the first time, of Virginia and Leonard Woolf. Virginia records her not entirely favourable impressions of her guest in her diary for 18 February 1921: 'Something like a lean sheep dog in appearance – harum scarum – humble – too much of a professional, yet just on the intellectual side of the border. Might be religious though: mystical perhaps. Not at all dominating or impressive: I daresay she observes more than one thinks for. Clear pale mystical eyes. A kind of faded moon of beauty: oh and badly dressed. I don't suppose we shall ever meet for she lives with Royd Smith, and somehow won't come to grips with us.' See A.O. Bell and A. McNeillie (eds), *The Diary of Virginia Woolf* II (London, 1978) 93. On Virginia's unfavourable report of one of Naomi Royde-Smith's soirées at which Rose was present, see *L*25 n. 3, and on the Woolfs as guests of Rose, *L*45 n. 3.

2 In 1920–1921 Huxley was drama critic of the *Westminster Gazette*. Naomi did not meet either Rose and Jean or Huxley for lunch; instead (as her diary reveals), she met Walter de la Mare at Charing Cross and left London on a 1.20 pm train.

3 44 Princes Gardens. Rose writes 'McDonnell' – a double misspelling. A. G. Macdonell's wartime service was followed by participation in Quaker relief work in Poland and Russia (1921–1922). He then worked at the headquarters of the League of Nations Union (1922–1927) before embarking on a successful career as a writer and critic. He is best known for his detective stories and satirical writings, especially for *England, Their England* (London, 1933), in which he caricatures the English social and sporting scene. He was a friend of Agnes Murray, mentioned later in this letter.

4 Rose wrote in a similar way to Sydney Castle Roberts on 2 February. After mentioning 'my American publishers' big advertising campaign', she says: 'They seem by these live methods to have succeeded in disposing of 20,000 copies of the book up to date – little did I think I should ever come to be a big success in the Middle West!' (ERM 15.126). Horace Liveright and Albert Boni decided to go into publishing together late in 1916, and the first titles in their 'Modern Library' appeared in 1917. For several years their company was remarkably successful: Liveright was good both at choosing authors and at promoting books. But a combination of his financial recklessness and alcoholism brought about the decline and fall both of himself and the business. His colourful life and career inspired *The Scoundrel* (1935), a Hollywood film in which the publisher is played by Noel Coward. Writing to her mother on 26 January [1922], Rose describes how, over lunch with her and Dorothy Brooke in London, Liveright tried to persuade her 'to write a fine strong love-story for the American Public' (ERM 9.1).

5 At this time Madeleine Symons was working for the National Federation of Women Workers (NFWW), with which the Women's Trade Union League (WTUL) had been amalgamated on 1 January 1921. According to M.A. Hamilton, *Remembering My Good Friends* 138, Grace Barker worked during the war with Mary Macarthur (Secretary of WTUL) and Madeleine on industrial arbitration tribunals. She also says (207) that Grace was a nurse in Vosges in 1917–1918. Grace was to marry Herbert Usher, the 'young rationalist' of *L*21, in 1923. The couple had three daughters, and Grace, with whom Rose remained friendly until her death in 1958, went on to live to 102. By 'our establishment' Rose means 44 Princes Gardens. Naomi's diary reveals that the evening of charades was that of 3 February, and that those present included Storm Jameson, Dorothy and Reeve Brooke, Michael Sadleir (*L*56, 60), and his wife, Edith.

6 The Murrays' younger daughter had taken a Third Class in Classical Moderations at Somerville College, Oxford, in 1915, but, instead of going on to complete the Greats course, had worked first as a nurse, then as a lorry-driver. In 1916 she became engaged to a young officer, but he was killed in France. After the war she failed to find a permanent job, and although, being attractive and vivacious, she had many male friends and suitors, she did not marry. In the summer of 1922 tragedy struck: while she was on holiday in the Auvergne with a young Greek man, she contracted peritonitis. Her mother, accompanied by Archie Macdonell (n. 3), went out from England to be with her, and her father travelled from Geneva, but she died on 21 August.

7 Beresford (*L*15 n. 4) and his second wife, Beatrice ('Trissie'), had moved from East Claydon, Buckinghamshire, to a house in Notting Hill.

8 Gerald and Beryl and their three young children went to Rome in March 1920 and stayed in Italy until autumn 1921, although Gerald returned to England from time

to time to see his publisher – and Rose. One such visit was in the autumn of 1920: Naomi Royde-Smith's diary reveals that she met him, either with or without Rose, at least six times between 17 October and 2 December.

9 Lawrence Rising, *She Who Was Helena Cass* (New York, 1920).
10 Squire's house on the river was Swan House, Chiswick Mall, London W8, on the north bank of the Thames. In the novel the poet (Stephen Byrne), after strangling the maid, puts her body in a sack and dumps it in the river. Herbert, who had a lifelong love affair with the Thames, lived at 12 Hammersmith Terrace, also on the north bank of the river and extremely close to Swan House.
11 *Revolution: A Story of the Near Future in England* (London, 1921), a futuristic socio-political novel by J.D. Beresford.
12 Rose reviewed *The Swallow Dive* (London, 1921) in *Time and Tide*, 28 January 1921, 89, summing it up as 'altogether, within its compass, a brilliant, gay, whimsical, alive book'.
13 Sylvia Lynd's husband.
14 J.A. Hadfield was a distinguished psychiatrist, who did not belong to any of the 'schools', but based his theories above all on his first-hand experience of the patients who consulted him. He had a reputation for being a lucid and persuasive lecturer. Rose's interest in psychoanalysis at this time is reflected in *Dangerous Ages*, which was about to be published.
15 The 'son-to-be' of Jean's sister was in fact a daughter, Anne, born in Bombay on 25 April 1921.
16 Since the autumn of 1919 Jean's brother Regie had been a trainee farmworker in Worcestershire. He had now decided to study for holy orders and, after a term at Bristol University, enrolled at Salisbury Theological College.

24

1917 Club,
4, Gerrard Street,
W.1
10 May [1921]

Dearest Jean

I've sent a card to Miss Murray not to come this Thursday but some other – I shall be away for this. We shall be delighted to see her, and of course also anyone she brings, as I have told her. Naomi and I are both back, she from Switzerland, I from Italy. Varazze[1] was divine. It hasn't, I think, heard of Lenin, and is all for Gesù Cristo, Mary and the Saints – particularly Santa Caterina, our patroness,[2] who looked after all the Varazze soldiers during the war so that hardly any were killed. The war didn't make what is called a deep impress on the natives, I fancy. Our landlady asked us which side the English had been on, and was quite prepared to be affable either way. A terrible pity, all the poor young men suffering so on both sides, and all for nothing of any importance, seems the point of view.

It was lovely to be there. We climbed the hill paths and walked about the town, and everyone clasped us by the hand and recalled the *bambini inglesi* and their *cavallo*, and their *babbo*[3] with whom they all used to go walks every afternoon. Our own house is painted new and wonderful colours, and a great sea has washed away the beach in front of it, so that the garden is raised high above sea level now. I bathed all the last part of the time – it was far warmer than the Cornish seas last August, but the residents watched with me with interest, as no-one but *inglesi* (of whom we are still the only specimens, fortunately) ever begin bathing till June. It is wonderful how free it has kept from English visitors. I don't know why it is – fashion, I suppose. They all go to Rapallo and the other places, but not there. But the place has grown – there are a lot more villas now all round it. It was chilly at first, but later it warmed up, and the hills were hot and sweet with lemon-trees or thyme and myrtle and juniper. Margaret got quite well there of her back, and walked a lot. Now we're both back at work and feeling rather bored. My dear Thomas died while I was away, in a nursing-home, of gastritis. It is empty not to have him – and dreadful to come back each day when I go to town and not have his absurd transports of joy and love. I hate walks without him. However, he was 10 years old, and that is old – about seventy for a human, they say.[4]

How are you? When shall we see you? I'm going to Cambridge for Whitsun, if trains anyhow permit, which perhaps they won't. *D[angerous] A[ges]* should have been out in April, but was held up by the strike, and probably won't be now till the end of May.[5] I can't feel any interest in it, somehow. I must try and work some up. All books bore me, I think – a nice state of mind for a critic. I've read nothing good for months except *Queen Victoria*. You've seen that I expect? It really is excellent. A brilliant character study. But, my word, what a manful woman! Strachey curbs his dislike well, and is beautifully commentless; it is really on the whole a sympathetic study.[6] And one of the most entertaining books I have often[7] read. There are no good novels just now, and little verse. Romer Wilson's new novel[8] is liked by some, but others (including me) find it silly, though prettily told. She is rather a little donkey, I believe – full of unrequited affections of which she makes no secret – or was, anyhow. Her new novel is emotional fantasy, and the heroine talks in Norwegian and the hero in English and neither understand a word the other says, only they understand all that matters. Have you seen Virginia Woolf's little book *Monday or Tuesday*?[9] It is attractive. I do think she is good.

I've received an invitation to attend Wednesday lunches at Gatti's and discuss the League of Nations.[10] I expect you have heard all about this scheme already. I doubt it's doing any good. Anyhow, what's the use of *interesting* people in the League? The thing is to make it function if possible. I think I shall go to lunch one Wed: and hear what they suggest. I don't know why I'm asked – perhaps that I may write novels about it. It might be a theme. A very hypothetical fantasy, it would be, in which wars were averted by the League in action.[11]

Aunt Mary and Uncle R[egi] came down here [to Beaconsfield] the other day, but (if that is the right conjunction) I was out. Aunt M. is very keen and hot over the Wakeford case, i.e. his innocence.[12] This makes me doubt it more deeply than before. It is queer, though. Everyone who knows him (including the Duncan-Jones', who worked with him for years in Lincolnshire)[13] says he is such a really splendid and spiritual person, and that it is inconceivable. My friend at Lincoln[14] who knows him very well (I think he has been her director) is beginning now to be shaken (unlike most of his Lincoln friends) and finds it difficult to know what line to take when they meet. She is inclined to the mental aberration theory, on the whole. Meanwhile Mr Bottomley is offering £1000 for the missing lady – a chance, as Dorothy Brooke says, for all of us. I should think there'd be thousands of them. No-one can disprove their claim, anyhow, nor prove it either, so I expect the £1000 is safe enough.[15] *John Bull* offered the Archdeacon £100 each for three articles on the case – but, as his wife said, though they are very poor they aren't as poor as all that yet. She appears to believe in him absolutely – but this may be merely the front she presents to the world.[16] What did you think of the daughter who was at Newnham?[17] She didn't attract me much when I met her. Poor things, it is a horrible position for them all, whatever is at the bottom of it.

I began this letter in the train, on club paper, and am finishing it at home, and it seems to have stretched to an unwieldy bulk. It's turned into a golden evening, full of cuckoos and sunshine. The green of the trees is incredible this May – but it always is, every May. When are you coming for a week-end? Next time you're in town, go to *Bull-Dog Drummond*.[18] It's 1st class melodrama.

My love always R.

1 See Introd. I.1. For accounts of later visits to Varazze, see *L*76, 93.

2 St Catherine (Caterina Benincasa) of Siena.

3 'the English children and their pony, and their daddy'. The pony was a gift from Regi Macaulay in January 1890, when Rose was eight.

4 Few who encountered Thomas (Fig. 2) would have shared Rose's sorrow at his passing. A mongrel, but predominantly chow, he fought other dogs and attacked people. Edward Conybeare was among his human victims: 'Bitten by Rose's beastly chow' (*Diary*, 14 March 1912). Thomas's behaviour did not improve when his mistress moved from Great Shelford to Beaconsfield, for in April 1919 he had to be muzzled (letter of 22 April 1919, in the editor's possession, from Rose to Mary Roberts). His chief claim to distinction is that he inspired the closing poem of Rose's *Three Days* (1919): 'To Thomas: An Easter Address'.

5 Coal miners were on strike, or rather locked out, after rejecting new employment terms, during April, May, and June 1921. The dispute had a knock-on effect on other areas of the economy, although a threatened sympathy strike by railwaymen and other transport workers did not materialise. *Dangerous Ages* was published on 20 May.

6 Lytton Strachey's *Queen Victoria* (London, 1921) was significantly gentler in tone than his *Eminent Victorians* (London, 1918).

7 'Often' is a little unexpected.

8 *The Death of Society* (London, 1921). It was to be awarded the Hawthornden Prize on 29 June 1921. For Rose's opinion of it, see also *L*25 and n. 10 there.

9 A collection of eight short stories, including the one that gives the book its title, it was published by Hogarth Press (London, 1921).

10 A. & S. Gatti Ltd had three restaurants on or just off the Strand. The premises at 436 Strand were for many years a favoured venue for luncheons and dinners arranged by societies and other organisations.

11 Four months later Rose was to attend the Second Assembly of the League of Nations (*L*26), but the resulting book, *Mystery at Geneva* (1922), was not at all like the one she is thinking of here. For her earlier interest in writing a peace conference book, see *L*3 and n. 13 there.

12 This was the *cause célèbre* of 1921. John Wakeford, Precentor of Lincoln Cathedral and Archdeacon of Stow, was accused, under the Clergy Discipline Act of 1892, of immoral conduct. It was alleged that, on two occasions in March–April 1920, when staying at the Bull Hotel, Peterborough, he shared a bedroom with a woman who was not his wife – a woman with whom he was also seen in Peterborough Cathedral. What made the allegation extra-sensational was that the clergyman who brought it to the attention of the Bishop of Lincoln was none other than Wakeford's brother-in-law, the Rev. Herbert E. Worthington. At a Consistory Court hearing in Lincoln he was found guilty. An appeal was heard by the Judicial Committee of the Privy Council at 9 Downing Street, but the Committee's judgement, delivered by the Lord Chancellor, Lord Birkenhead (F.E. Smith), on 26 April 1921, upheld the verdict of the Consistory Court.

13 Arthur and Caroline Duncan-Jones. In 1915–1916 he was the incumbent of Louth, Lincolnshire.

14 Unidentified. Perhaps the wife of Peter (also unidentified) from Lincoln, who was Rose's guest on 7 February 1925 (*L*45).

15 Horatio Bottomley's campaign on behalf of Wakeford was launched in *John Bull*, his weekly newspaper, on 7 May 1921. The reward mentioned by Rose was offered either for production of 'the girl in the cathedral' or to any woman who could prove that she stayed with Wakeford at the Bull Hotel. In its issue of 14 May *John Bull* increased the reward to £2,000. A fortnight later it announced that 'the girl in the cathedral' had been traced. She turned out to be a young married woman, Freda Hansen. She confirmed Wakeford's testimony that their meeting in the cathedral had been by chance and wholly innocent, and that she never accompanied him to the Bull Hotel. The campaign for justice for Wakeford continued until April 1922, culminating in the delivery of a huge petition to the Home Office, but the petition failed, whereupon *John Bull* lost interest in the case. It never paid Mrs Hansen the promised reward. That Wakeford was innocent of the charge, and the victim of a conspiracy to ruin him, is convincingly, as well as entertainingly, argued by John Treherne, *Dangerous Precincts: The Mystery of the Wakeford Case* (London, 1987).

16 Wakeford's wife, Evelyn Mary, continued to stand by him, and any suggestion that she was not wholly convinced of his innocence seems to be unjustified.

17 Evelyn Katharine Wakeford was at Newnham in 1914–1917.

18 A play based on the novel by 'Sapper' (H.C. McNeile), adapted by the author with assistance from Gerald du Maurier, who acted the part of the hero, Capt. Hugh Drummond. It was running at Wyndham's Theatre, Charing Cross Road.

25

Beaconsfield.
30 May [1921]

Dearest Jean

Thank you for your letter, and for letting me see the 'Spring Storm',[1] which is very good. It came this morning, just before Naomi left, and I gave it her to take with her and look at, in case they want it for the [*Saturday*] *W.G.* She hasn't seen anything of yours for a long time, and was probably abroad when you sent the last. That notice about being full up is their more respectful form of rejection: the other is merely the editor regrets he can't use this. N. liked the 'Spring Storm' herself, in the brief read she had of it at breakfast.

Secondly – yes, do come for June 12th – that will be good. Thirdly, do let me know more about the Summer School – or, no, don't bother, I'll get Miss Murray to send me a notice of it.[2] She is coming again this Thursday (I hope), when we are getting up a private and informal discussion as to means of bringing pressure to bear on the Government about Ireland,[3] by private and concerted action – such as refusing to pay our income-tax and rates, or to have our dust-bins cleared or something. We're asking people of all shades of political opinion – Irish nationalists and one Ulsterman, archdeacons priests and bishops, as well as the usual literary riff-raff[4] – the idea is to have it[5] an effort of right-minded people, not a party thing – the only view we shall all share is that the scandal must be stopped. So we may all spend the summer in prison! Will you join, and get the Murrays to join too?

Yes, Robert Lynd, the darling, can't review novels, except to say how nice they are. His forte is Elizabethan verse and 18th century prose. I thought his remarks on mine charming and kind, but certainly not a review or criticism.[6] Do you agree with Naomi that I have returned to the human novel proper,[7] or with H.C. Harwood in *The Outlook* that I am still writing satiric commentaries, – what he calls my Annual Register of our follies and ideals? I think he's wrong, and that D[*angerous*] A[*ges*] isn't a contemporary satire at all – and certainly growing old, which he says it's mainly about, is a primeval problem.[8] But people get ideas into their heads about authors and can't get rid of them. *The Morning Post* says I sit in the seat of the scorner, clever and gay.[9] Surely not, in this book. It's neither scornful, clever nor gay. A serious and rather sentimental book, I call it. I've done it myself for *Time and Tide*, with *The Death of Society* – have you seen that? It's rather attractive, though grotesque: I didn't say much about my own, of course, only what it is about, and that it was rather thin in parts, but painstaking. I didn't like to find many faults, it might encourage others to do the same.[10]

I'm so sorry about you, my dear. I wish you could be better more quickly. It is horribly hard luck. I think of you often and wish you well. Mother too. She sends her love, and wants to see you. The 12th is really better than 26th, if it's the same for you.

Shall you be there for the L[eague] of N[ations] Summer School? I suppose not – in fact, of course you won't.

Very much love – Rose.

1 The poem is in *Shepherd of Souls* 20. An earlier publication of it has not been traced.
2 The summer school, it emerges, is of the League of Nations Union, of which Gilbert Murray was Vice-Chairman. It was held in Oxford from 21 to 28 July 1921, with over two hundred participants.
3 Among those present at 44 Princes Gardens on Thursday 2 June were Virginia and Leonard Woolf. The former gives an unfavourable account of it in her diary (5 June 1921): 'We went to Miss Royde Smith's party on Thursday. Never did I see a less attractive woman than Naomi. Her face might have been cut out of cardboard by blunt scissors. . . . It was a queer mixture of the intelligent and the respectable. . . . I detest the mixture of ideas and South Kensington. Then Rose chipped in with her witticism all in character at which the clergyman, Duncan Jones, said "Oh Rose!" and everyone laughed loud, as if Rose had done the thing they expected. Yes, I disliked it all a good deal – and the furniture and the pictures – the marriage of conventionality and the Saturday Westminster.' See A.O. Bell and A. McNeillie (eds), *The Diary of Virginia Woolf* II (London, 1978) 122–123. The 'Troubles' in Ireland had been in progress for over two years. The pattern of events was that guerrilla attacks by the IRA led to British reprisals, which in turn triggered more violence, especially after the deployment of the infamous Black and Tans in the summer of 1920, and the situation provoked widespread outrage in Britain and overseas. A truce, offered by Lloyd George to the Sinn Féin leader, Éamon de Valera, was agreed on 8 July 1921 and came into effect on 11 July.
4 Virginia Woolf, writing to Vanessa Bell on 25 May 1928, uses the same expression when lamenting that Rose is like a house that has 'gone too far to be repaired' because she 'has lived with the riff raff of South Kensington Culture for 15 years'. See N. Nicolson and J. Trautmann (eds), *A Change of Perspective: The Letters of Virginia Woolf* III (London, 1977) 501.
5 Above 'it' Rose has written 'what action we take', but this seems to be a gloss rather than a substitution.
6 Lynd's review of *Dangerous Ages* in *The Daily News*, 28 May 1921, 8, is indeed kind, but the greater part of it consists of quotations from the novel.
7 Unsigned review in *SWG*, 28 May 1921, 18.
8 Harwood's review, in *The Outlook*, 28 May 1921, 459, is favourable, but he thinks that 'the style itself seems a little inferior to the romantic and delicate sensibility of the author's earlier work' and says: 'It is high time that Miss Macaulay wrote another novel'.

9 *The Morning Post*, 27 May 1921, 4. The words of which Rose complains come at the end of the anonymous review: 'But although the all-liveliness and present-dayness of Miss Macaulay's illustration and comment pack the book with amusement, as well as wisdom, the tragic implications of its thesis are not hid. And in developing them she displays a growing pessimism. We should like to suggest to her that this is the danger in sitting too long and perhaps too comfortably in the seat of the scorner, however clever and gay.'

10 Rose's reviews of Romer Wilson's *The Death of Society* and of *Dangerous Ages* are in *Time and Tide*, 3 June 1921, 533–534. After summing up Wilson's novel as 'an earnest, emotional, original and uncommon book', she makes the following remarks on her own: '"Dangerous Ages" is, on the other hand, an ordinary novel about ordinary people behaving in ordinary ways. The theme is the reaction of a group of people to their ages, which range from eighty-four to twenty. There is so much to say on this theme that volumes would not exhaust it. "Dangerous Ages" is a slight study enough. One feels that it would be better for more body, that it is a little thin in parts. There is even, here and there, a rather glib facility of thought and method. But it aims at being a careful record of different characters and the psychology of their different ages. Of course the worst of it is that age has really very little to do with psychology. One has to exaggerate these things for fictitional purposes. It may be added that there is no moral to this tale, and that it gives a painstaking account of psychoanalysis, bathing, love and family life. Some people may like it, others had better not try.' Authors often write the blurbs for their own books. They do not often publish signed reviews critical of them. Two readers who disliked *Dangerous Ages* were Rose's mother (*L2* n. 1) and her uncle Edward Conybeare. The latter calls it 'nasty story with *hideous* jacket' (*Diary*, 20 May 1921). His low opinion of the book was not shared by the Femina-Vie Heureuse Committee, which in February 1922 awarded it the prize of 1,000 francs for the best English work of imagination published between 30 June 1920 and 29 June 1921.

26

Hotel Touring Balance,
Place Longemalle,
Geneva.
15 September 1921

Dearest Jean

This is to bring my love and very best wishes for your birthday. I made a mistake in thinking the lion was the Geneva beast, I was thinking of Lucerne.[1] So I am sending you a bear, who I hope will arrive all right.

It is great fun here – a nice, absurd show the Assembly is.[2] All the work is done behind the scenes – on Commissions and at lunches and dinners in hotels, and, mainly, by the Permanent Secretariat, an industrious, capable body who regard the Delegates rather cynically, like a schoolroom of children who have to be managed. They are very kind to me, and give me all journalistic facilities (as a matter of fact I am doing some journalism) which includes being asked to *enormous* lunches by Delegations – these are rather fun. We lunched yesterday with the Canadian Delegation; I sat next to Mr Walter, the *Times* correspondent,[3] who was, I think, a little chagrined at being put on the left of the chief Delegate, while Wilson Harris[4] of *The D[aily] N[ews]* was on his right.

Wilson Harris is the kindest and friendliest person in the world. He knows everyone and has private information on everything, so he is very enlightening. He is being extraordinarily nice to me, and brings all kinds of exciting people to dine on the balcony of my hotel with me. Last night Gen. Sir F. Maurice,[5] who was out here seeing after artificial legs, had us both to dinner (such a nice, chivalric General!) before he caught the train to Paris, and afterwards W.H. and I rowed out on the lake, which is the loveliest thing imaginable both by day and night.[6] By night it is smooth and still and lit by boats with Chinese lanterns. By day all kinds of shades of blue, with the mountains behind the town standing round it. One rows far out into it, and bathes from the boat – when there's time, but this seldom happens. Life is a scramble.

Thank you for telling Wilfrid Roberts to look me up – he found me out in the Press gallery, and next week I am dining with them.[7] They sit in the Press gallery opposite mine, *en famille* – Mr Roberts, Lady Cecilia (who is writing for *The White Ribbon*[8] or something), Master Roberts, who says he is writing for the *Women's International Journal*[9] or some such paper, I forget exactly what, and Miss Roberts, a nice chubby thing in pink, who sits on meetings of oppressed nationalities, in connection with the Women's International League at home.[10] They all look such a nice family party, so pleased with it all.

Mr Murray[11] kindly called on me the other day at my hotel, but I was out unfortunately. We are going to try a lunch one day, if ever he isn't lunching on Reports, Commissions and Covenant articles. It will be nice if it comes off. It was kind of him to call, and he a delegate and up to his eyes in work day and night.

The Assembly speeches are, for the most part, windy and lacking in practical point – Delegates getting up to praise or blame the League, the Council, the Secretariat or what not. But there have been some good speeches – Balfour,[12] Lord R. Cecil,[13] Nansen,[14] Wellington Koo,[15] and Sastri of India,[16] and to-day Bp. Noli of Albania.[17] And an exciting quarrel between Chile and Bolivia about their treaty of 1904. The South Americans are rather fun – no more idea of internationalism than (say) Maxse[18] or *The M[orning] Post*, though they can talk eloquently about it. They have to be smoothed down by the others – though, to say the truth, internationalism is an empty enough cry with most of the Assembly, however loud a one.

Did you hear about the *W[estminster] G[azette]* turning itself into a morning liberal 2d paper on Oct: 11th, to run Grey and the so-called new Liberal Party? Spender is to edit it, of course.[19] Wilson Harris is rather fuming at being out here so that he can't go and look them up and make them take him on – he is sick of

The D[aily] N[ews], which sticks his political correspondence on a back page to leave room for Charlie Chaplin, Widow's Sad Illusion, and Cat's Strange Fate. I should think they would be thankful to get him – he's much the best political correspondent going. The *S.W.G.* is going on as before – it's for a long time been the only *W.G.* that really paid its way, and I daresay it will continue to be that. Spender is a good leader-writer but a rotten editor, he can't get the news. However, H.B. Usher, his assistant, is a bright youth.

I am at the moment at the Assembly, where a Delegate has been holding forth for an hour in very slow French and not saying one word that could or should be reported or remembered – why can't these people be stopped? We get the speeches circulated next morning anyhow, so why utter them and waste the Assembly's time? Last night a stormy session on the Judgeship elections was closed by orations on Dante, started by Sir Rennell Rodd – very flowery and moving.[20]

I really can't stand this man any longer, I must go out and get yesterday's English papers.

My love to you always. I hope you'll have a nice birthday – and a very nice year – a nicer one than last, which was really hampered by circumstances.

I wish you were out here too – you'd love it.

Y[ou]r loving ERM.

1 The famous Lion Monument in Lucerne commemorates the loyalty and courage of the Swiss Guards who died defending les Tuileries in Paris in 1792.

2 The Second Assembly of the League of Nations. Rose tells Jean below that she is 'doing some journalism'. On a postcard she wrote to her brother, Will, a few days earlier she is more informative: 'I am reporting for *The Daily Chronicle*, for the time being, besides being League official novelist' (ERM 15.113. The card is dated 11 September 1921, but postmarked 10 September). It is not clear how seriously 'League official novelist' is to be taken, but certainly the most important product of Rose's attendance at the Assembly was her next novel, *Mystery at Geneva* (1922); moreover, in a postcard she wrote to Gilbert Murray from Geneva on 28 August 1950 she recalls that she was actually writing her 'mystery novel about the League' during the 1921 Assembly. In a prefatory note in the book she writes: 'It has for its setting an imaginary session of the League of Nations Assembly, but it is in no sense a study of, still less a skit on, actual conditions at Geneva, of which I know little.' Nevertheless it owes much to her stay in Geneva and to her observation of the delegates. Several characters in the novel are based on real people who attended the Assembly (n. 11 below). The book was published on 30 October 1922. About four months into the writing of it, Rose was fortunate not to lose her manuscript, for, writing from London to her mother in Beaconsfield on 26 January [1922], she says: 'They *had* found and retrieved my little red novel at the station, so the hand of fate has not intervened to stop my writing it after all' (ERM 9.1).

3 Hubert Walter had joined *The Times* in 1894. From 1907 until his retirement in 1930 he represented it at special events in Europe on many occasions.

4 Harris had joined *The Daily News* in 1908 and went on to serve it as news editor, then as leader writer, then as diplomatic correspondent. He was editor of *The Spectator* from 1932 to 1953. He wrote two books on the League of Nations.

5 Major-General Sir Frederick Maurice's army career came to an abrupt end when he wrote a letter, printed in *The Times* and other newspapers on 7 May 1918, in which he accused the government, led by Lloyd George, of deceiving Parliament and the people about various matters to do with the war, including the strength of the British army on the western front. He went on to have a distinguished academic career, but also worked tirelessly, through the Royal British Legion, on behalf of former members of the fighting services.

6 At the end of *Mystery at Geneva*, Miss Montana, known until the final pages as 'Henry Beechtree', comes down to the lake's edge, to 'take a boat and have a last moonlit row' (259).

7 The Roberts family: Lady Cecilia was a daughter of George James Howard, ninth Earl of Carlisle, and a younger sister of Gilbert Murray's wife, Lady Mary. Her husband, Charles Roberts, had been Liberal MP for Lincoln in 1906–1918 and Under-Secretary of State for India in 1914–1915. Wilfrid ('Master Roberts') was born on 28 August 1900 and so was just 21. He was about to commence his third year at Balliol College, Oxford. He was Liberal MP for North Cumberland in 1935–1950, but joined the Labour Party in 1956. Christina Roberts was aged 25 at this time.

8 The official organ of the National British Women's Temperance Association. Lady Cecilia was at this time Acting Vice-President of the Association. In 1922 she became its President.

9 Rose may mean *The International Woman Suffrage News*, the monthly organ of the International Woman Suffrage Alliance. There is an unsigned piece on the Assembly in 16, 2 (November 1921) 18–19, but nothing attributed to Wilfrid Roberts.

10 The Women's International League for Peace and Freedom was founded in The Hague in 1915. Along with (among others) 'The Non-Alcoholic Drink Society', the WILPF is represented at the fictional session of the League of Nations Assembly in *Mystery at Geneva* (13). Rose had already mentioned it in 'Woman; What Is She? Some Popular Fallacies', *The Daily Telegraph*, 5 July 1919, 14: 'The theory that women are likely to think alike is the basis of such anomalies as women's parties, and women's societies of all sorts. Even in such a well-educated society as, for instance, the Women's International League, one of the main premises is that women of all nations should somehow be associated politically through their sex, that frailest of bonds. Temperament, according to such thinkers, counts for little; so do education, heredity, environment, and economic position.'

11 Gilbert Murray, represented in *Mystery at Geneva* by Professor Arnold Inglis, 'that most gentle, high-minded and engaging of scholars' (127), who loved the ancient Greeks (129). Other leading delegates to the Assembly who appear in the novel include Lord Balfour (Lord Burnley), Lord Robert Cecil (Lord John Lester), Nansen (Svensen, 'an eminent Norwegian explorer' (36)), Dr Koo (Dr Chang), and Fan Noli of Albania ('a placid Albanian bishop' (117; see also 24, 36)). It may be noted that Murray was not averse to making fun of the League of Nations, as is shown in his anonymously published 'Old Moore's League Almanack', *The New Statesman*

and Nation, 31 December 1932, 851–852, and in an undated and unpublished farce entitled *Saved Again, or, the Assembly as it Might Be: A Serious Drama*. On the farce, see Christopher Stray (ed.), *Gilbert Murray Reassessed: Hellenism, Theatre, and International Politics* (Oxford, 2007) 11.

12 Lord Balfour, Conservative politician and philosopher, was Prime Minister in 1902–1905. As Foreign Secretary under Lloyd George (1916–1919), he was the author of the Balfour Declaration (2 November 1917), supporting the establishment of a national Jewish home in Palestine. He was a cousin of Lord Robert Cecil.

13 See *L4* n. 12. He is mentioned also in Rose's postcard to Will (n. 2 above), but Babington Smith, in her typed transcript of the message, kept with the original in Trinity College, Cambridge, misreads 'R. Cecil' as 'H. Caine', and is followed by Crawford 180. Lord Robert Cecil attended the first three Assemblies of the League of Nations as a representative of South Africa, which explains why in *Mystery at Geneva* Lord John Lester is 'one of the delegates from Central Africa' (118–119).

14 Fridtjof Nansen, Norwegian explorer, zoologist, and statesman, directed the League's High Commission for Refugees, established on 27 June 1921. He was awarded the Nobel Peace Prize in 1922. In *Told by an Idiot*, the novel Rose wrote after *Mystery at Geneva*, Victoria Carrington takes her children to hear Nansen speak in the Albert Hall about his exploration of the Arctic (146–149). Through their work for the League of Nations Nansen and Gilbert Murray became friends. In his bold play *Fram*, staged at the National Theatre, London, in 2008, Tony Harrison makes Murray's ghost emerge from his tomb in Westminster Abbey, rouse the shade of the actress Sybil Thorndike, and engage her assistance in presenting his (Murray's) play (a play within a play) that tells Nansen's story.

15 Chinese statesman and diplomat, partly educated in the USA. He was to be his country's Foreign Minister and its Ambassador in Paris, London, and Washington.

16 V.S. Srinivasa Sastri, a schoolteacher before he went into politics, was a highly cultured man and brilliant orator. Although he sought Home Rule for his country, he disagreed with Gandhi and his followers that a campaign of civil disobedience was the right way to achieve it. So, along with other 'moderates', he left the Indian National Congress in 1919 and exercised his influence in the newly established Indian Liberal Federation. He was the first Indian to be made a member of the Privy Council (1921). He was also made a Companion of Honour (1930).

17 Fan Noli, Albanian patriot and democratic politician, was another highly cultured man, who had spent most of his life in the USA, where he studied at Harvard University. Of the Orthodox faith, he objected to the refusal by the Greek Patriarch at Constantinople to allow the use of the Albanian language in services. So he was ordained priest by the Russian Metropolitan in New York and later proclaimed a bishop by members of the Albanian community. Despite his eloquence in Geneva, he was largely ineffective in domestic politics. He was Prime Minister for six months in 1924 before his government was overthrown by force.

18 Leo Maxse, editor of the influential monthly *The National Review* since 1893, was anti-German, pro-French, and a passionate believer in the value of the British Empire. He was opposed to the League of Nations and advocated increased spending on armaments to deter Germany from starting a second world war. His elder brother, General

Sir Ivor Maxse, took a similar line, declaring in November 1919: 'I prefer a League of Tanks to a League of Nations' (see J. Baynes, *Far from a Donkey: The Life of General Sir Ivor Maxse, KCB, CVO, DSO* (London, 1995) 222).

19 *Westminster Gazette*, a Liberal evening paper, started life on 31 January 1893. John Alfred Spender was on its staff from the beginning and became its editor in 1896. The paper, whose circulation never exceeded 27,000 copies and often not even 20,000, was not a commercial success, but had a reputation and influence that was out of all proportion to its small readership. That readership included many people who 'mattered' in British politics, the chief attraction being Spender's well-informed, well-argued, constructive editorials. The fortunes of the paper, like those of the Liberal Party itself, declined after the split between Asquith and Lloyd George in 1916. Its conversion into a morning paper was not a success. Spender's long editorship came to an end in February 1922. The *WG* limped on until 1928, when it was taken over by *The Daily News*, which in turn was amalgamated with *The Daily Chronicle* in 1930. Edward Grey, Viscount Grey of Fallodon from 1916, was Foreign Secretary in 1905–1916. He had been President of The League of Nations Union since November 1918. Although he was not quite 60 in the autumn of 1921, his poor health combined with increasing blindness meant that he would not have been a suitable candidate for leadership of the Liberal Party, even if he had wanted to be one.

20 The election was of judges for the Permanent Court of International Justice, which was to hold its first session at The Hague on 15 February 1922. The reason for the tribute to Dante on 14 September 1921 is that it was the six-hundredth anniversary of his death. Rodd had been British Ambassador in Rome in 1908–1919. At the League of Nations Assembly, he was representing the British government, having just retired from the diplomatic service. According to the report in *The Times* (15 September 1921, 7), he said of Dante: 'This universal poet had earned the universal worship of all mankind.' He was followed by three other speakers. 'Finally, at the suggestion of the President, the Assembly rose in honour of the great poet.'

27

[No address]
Wednesday.[1]

Dearest Jean

I am not easy about mother, and think I must get home to-night, as she has no-one but servants, and I don't quite know how bad she is feeling. She told me not to worry, but I can't well help it. I think I shall stay till after the 4.30 address and then catch a train. It is a pity, because I am loving the retreat rather. But it's no use staying with a divided mind, feeling I ought to be elsewhere. Also, I have a friend far more seriously ill in London, whom I can visit on my way home. I have a lonely and depressed note from him this morning – so altogether, you see, I am but a poor retreatant at the moment.

Perhaps some day you would show me any notes you have of the later addresses.

We haven't communicated much, but it has been nice seeing you about. I hope you are liking it, and not feeling tired.

I wanted rather to speak to Fr. Cary[2] – but as it is his off afternoon and I leave after the address, I see no chance. He *is* good this time.

Bless you always, and my love. I'll write soon and tell you how mother is. There's no need for anxiety, only she wants taking care of.

R.

1 This letter, occupying two sides of a small, lined page torn out of a notebook, was written during a retreat, held in or near London, that Jean was also attending. Since Rose's mother is alive, it cannot be later than the early months of 1925: Grace died that year on 5 May, and during the three weeks preceding her death Rose was abroad. The reason for tentatively placing the letter here is that it seemingly predates Rose's long period of estrangement from the Church. This estrangement, associated with her affair with Gerald, began, according to her own testimony, more than two years before her mother died, and the last time she went to confession may well have been Good Friday, 1922 (*L*21 n. 13). Admittedly, one cannot be sure that she gave up attending retreats at the same time as she gave up going to confession, and the present letter could be earlier or later than April 1922. One possibility is that the retreat she and Jean attended is the one she mentions in an unpublished letter to Jeanie of 6 January [1922] (ERM 9.2). (Hitherto that letter has been dated to 1921 or 1922, but 1922 is certain, because Rose's mention of newspaper reports of unusual influenza symptoms tallies exactly with an article in *The Times*, 5 January 1922, 10.)

2 Lucius Cary was a member of the Society of St John the Evangelist, an Anglican order established in 1866 by the Rev. Richard Meux Benson. Benson was Vicar of Cowley, Oxford, and the Society's members are often called the Cowley Fathers. Before and during the First World War Rose was a not infrequent visitor to St Edward's House, Great College Street, Westminster, the Society's base in London, where she made her confession to Fr Cary or sometimes, if he was not available, to Fr Hamilton Johnson, the priest who was to bring her back to the Anglican Church towards the end of her life.

28

Beaconsfield.
9 March [1923]

Dearest Jean

Thanks so much for your letter. I was wondering whether you had moved on to Rome yet or not.[1] And now you are in the train, due to get there to-morrow morning – how exciting. I hope the Italian exchange still is as good as ever. A friend of mine was there for a month in Jan. and Feb., and found it pretty cheap.

Prices are high: a letter to England costs a franc, but it only came to about 3d then. He said Mussolini has terrorised – or subsidized – nearly the whole Roman press, and every morning they all have leaders beginning 'The wise Mussolini has a plan. The great conciliator[2] will take action. . .' And the Fascisti officers swagger about as offensively as Black and Tans.

Did you find Paris desperately anglophobe? I believe Italy is: the press, that is; of course the people are always all that is charming and amicable. I wish I could be in Rome with you. Mind you go out to Albano, and Tusculum, and Tivoli, and Frascati, and Veii,[3] and if possible to some of the hills beyond these. I think all the time one spends going out from Rome one is glad of, though expeditions take a whole day from seeing Rome itself of course, and it is difficult to spare any. Do you know people there, and are you staying with them?[4] I shall love to hear all about everything when you come back. I suppose you'll be fluent in Italian by then. I hope the French cold is quite gone. It's *bitterly* cold here – to-day anyhow. Rome can be cold in March, you know, very. But you get glorious hot sunny days often. When do you return? Will you go souther yet?

Will is still with us.[5] He and I are doing all the theatres, and it's great fun.

I must write my play soon: I have an idea for one scene – in a jury-room – but I must get onto a jury before I can write it, and I don't know <how> this is done.[6] A lawyer I know offered to help me, but I don't know if he can. I ought to be eligible in London, but may have to wait years unless I take steps.

I've just been reading and reviewing Amber Blanco-White's novel, *Give and Take*, which is entirely about the Labour and Wages section of the M[inistry] of M[unitions] during the war, and the hero is Gordon Campbell. When you come home I will send it you, as you probably know all the people.[7] It is very informative and rather ponderous, but I found it interesting, and it's certainly clever. Dorothy Brooke can't bear it, but then she does so hate being bored. She brings out her characters well, and people who know him say G.C. is very true to life – I wonder what you'd think. It is a surprising novel, from her, because it's quite devoid of sex interest – I suppose she lives all that, and gets rid of it that way. I gather she's still going strong, in that direction.[8]

Did you say you know one Marjorie Gabain, and is she an actress? There is one of that name acting in Milne's new play (a very poor play) and acting very well, too, in a small part. I thought her one of the best people in the cast.[9] It's the Reandean Company.[10]

Next week we want to see *The Bad Man*[11] and *Rats*.[12] So, you see, we are not idle. Besides the local movie, which we frequently attend now in the evenings. I'm not getting much work done – one can't, with a brother in the house, I find, except when he's away for week-ends. And I'm awfully behind, too.

America doesn't like [*Mystery at*] *Geneva* quite so much as England did, I fear. One reviewer thought me 'a very shallow thinker', as I did not seem to know how to define or understand 'News', which any newspaper man could have explained to me! They take one's feeble jokes and solemnly turn them inside out like this, seeking sense and finding none.

Well, my dear. I hope very much you'll find Rome agreeable. Your Paris pension must have been great fun.[13] I wish I'd been there too! Have a very nice time; and always my love. Will was sorry to miss you at Clent.

R.

1 Jean had resigned as Gilbert Murray's secretary early in 1922–'on account of health', in her mother's words. In February and early March 1923 she spent five weeks in Paris, where two people dear to her were studying. One was her brother Jim, who was there to improve his French. The other was a friend from her Newnham days, Dorothy Garrod, who, having studied anthropology in Oxford after the war, was now a pupil of Abbé Henri Breuil at l'Institut de Paléontologie Humaine. She became an archaeologist and palaeolithic historian of great distinction. From Paris Jean went on to Rome on her own and remained there until May.

2 Mussolini had become Prime Minister of Italy on 31 October 1922, heading a government composed not only of Fascists, but also of Liberals and Nationalists. A week earlier, at the Fascist Conference in Naples, he stressed the need 'conciliare la Nazione', and this remained his stated policy after he achieved power.

3 Albano Laziale, Tusculum, and Frascati are to the south-east of Rome, Tivoli to the east, and Veii to the north.

4 Jean stayed in the British School at Rome.

5 Will Macaulay had returned to his farm in Canada in the spring of 1920, but was on holiday in Britain from December 1922 until March 1923.

6 The play was *Bunkum*, a farce. It was never produced or published. Rose's typescript (ERM 5.1) is dated April 1924. There is no jury scene.

7 Rose's favourable review is in *The Daily News*, 23 February 1923, 8. (She was also to praise the book in 'The Quarter's Fiction', *The Guardian*, 13 April 1923, 314.) Amber Blanco White wrote *Give and Take: A Novel of Intrigue* (London, 1923) under her maiden name, Amber Reeves, with 'Mrs Blanco White' following in brackets. It was her fourth and last novel. The first sentence reads: 'Of all the Ministries in Britain the Board of Reconciliation summoned the most conferences and possessed the prettiest stairs.' In the last years of the First World War Amber was a Sub-Section Director in the Labour Regulation Department of the Ministry of Munitions, the same Department in which Jean had been employed. Earlier she had a post in the Admiralty. Captain (later Vice-Admiral) Gordon Campbell received the Victoria Cross and other awards for the dangerous operations he undertook in command of Q-ships–ships that appeared to be merchantmen or fishing vessels, but actually were armed. On three occasions he destroyed German U-boats after allowing his ship to be torpedoed and then waiting for the enemy submarine to come within range of his hidden guns. Amber was still a student at Newnham College, Cambridge, when she became involved intellectually, emotionally, and physically with H.G. Wells, advocate of free love and collector of 'new' women. His affair with Amber was particularly passionate. The fruits of it included a daughter, Anna Jane, born on 31 December 1909, when Amber was aged 22, and his novel *Ann Veronica: A Modern Love Story*

(London, 1909), about a girl who, in defiance of parental disapproval and traditional morality, goes off with the man she loves. Amber was a few weeks pregnant by Wells when she married Rivers Blanco White on 9 May 1909. She and her husband had two children and brought up Anna Jane as if she too were theirs. After the Great War Amber developed her interests in social, economic, psychological, and philosophical problems. From 1928 she taught at Morley College, an adult-education establishment near Waterloo. She assisted Wells with his encyclopaedic *The Work, Wealth and Happiness of Mankind* (New York, 1931; London, 1932). Her own writings included *The New Propaganda* (London, 1939) and *Ethics for Unbelievers* (London, 1949).

8 The most significant affair Amber had in the 1920s was with Sir Matthew Nathan, the dedicatee of *Give and Take* and the model for its chief character, Sir Adrian Heath, Secretary to the Ministry of Reconciliation. Her senior by 25 years, he was a bachelor, who, in the words of his *ODNB* biographer, was 'not averse to the companionship and affection of women'. Amber and he had few opportunities to meet at this time, when he was serving as Governor of Queensland (1920–1925), so it is not at all clear that Rose is alluding to their relationship, an account of which is given by Ruth Fry, *Maud and Amber* (Christchurch, NZ, 1992) 83–88.

9 Rose misspells 'caste'. The play, a comedy, was A.A. Milne's *The Great Broxopp: Four Chapters in His Life*, at St Martin's Theatre. Gabain, who acted the part of Honoria Johns, had been a contemporary of Jean both at the Godolphin School, Salisbury, and at Newnham College, Cambridge. Born in Le Havre to a French father and Scottish mother, she was a younger sister of the artist Ethel Léontine Gabain. She made regular appearances on the London stage between 1915 and 1939, usually playing minor roles in productions that had short runs. She also appeared with Peggy Ann Wood's Rapier Players at the Little Theatre, Bristol, in the 1930s and with la Comédie Française in Paris.

10 The company derived its name from the surnames of its founders, Alec Rea and Basil Dean. They went into partnership in 1919 and broke up, after disagreements, in 1929.

11 A comic melodrama, 'a Texas brigand play' (*The Times*), by Porter Emerson Browne. It had begun its run at the New Theatre, St Martin's Lane, on 3 March.

12 A revue, with words by Ronald Jeans and music by Philip Braham, at the Vaudeville Theatre, Strand. *The Times* critic calls it as 'a very uneven production'.

13 Jean joined Jim in staying with a couple called Beuzart in Meudon on the south-west side of Paris. Jim describes the husband as 'a Protestant pastor, very friendly and rather solemn', his wife as 'much more vivacious and a good sort' (J.S. Smith, *The Last Time* 57).

29

[No address]
18 July [1923]

Dearest Jean

I am so glad about the Press job. It sounds very much what you want. And Oxford will be nice to work in, and you may be able to do some writing and reading at the Bodleian besides. It will be good to have the Murrays at hand, too. And the Clarendon Press is such a splendid press to be connected with.[1] I wish the Newnham job could have dropped your way, but I suppose it's not settled yet, so there is still a hope?[2] This seems to me a good second, though nothing could be like a job that takes you to Italy, I suppose. Anyhow, I'm very glad. Will it be only in term-time, or all the year?

Of course that's what literary agents exist for, to place stuff of all kinds. Try Curtis Brown, 6 Henrietta Street, Covent Garden.[3] I'll speak of you to him. Of course I'm not sure what they'd do with serious and scholarly articles such as yours – but I'll talk to their magazine dept. about it.[4] At present that dept. is engaged in vainly striving to serialise my new novel[5] for me, before it comes out – but the daily press declines to think it what their public desire, and say (a) it isn't serial stuff (b) the religious aspect alarms them! I didn't know it had one – except that one character (Papa)[6] takes on a new creed about once a year – perhaps they think that too often or something. *I* think it makes it a very religious book.[7] But perhaps the public don't like so much religion in a serial.

Mother's *much* better, now the heat is over. Not well yet, but quite different from a month ago.[8] She sent you much love, and is so glad about the job. She keeps enquiring after D's baby, but I told her I *thought* it wasn't due till August. Poor Dorothy, it is a pity the little creatures can't do their job quicker; she must be getting very tired of Isaac Israel on the way.[9]

How did Regie like the A[nglo-]C[atholic] Congress?[10] I lunched with Kenneth Mozley one day; he is now quite an A.C.[11]

We're so sorry about Uncle Charlie's fall, and sprained wrist. I hope it is progressing well. It will be easier now to keep cold winter bandages on it than a few days ago. I wish I could have seen you in London.

Next week Margaret's holidays begin, and the week after Jeanie's.

My love always, and I do so hope the Press will be a nice job. R.

I've just finished my book. It's bad, but I'm glad it's through.

1 With the support of testimonials from Gilbert Murray and J.C. Smith (*L*78 n. 11), Jean had been offered the post of secretary to Robert W. Chapman, Secretary to the Delegates of the Clarendon Press. His main scholarly interests were Jane Austen and Samuel Johnson. Being his secretary was not entirely straightforward, to judge from *DNB*: 'He never used a typewriter or wrote with a fountain pen. He wrote rapidly: what he wrote was not always legible, even to his secretaries, his close friends, or the printer'. Jean remained in the post until July 1926. At this time the Clarendon Press had a separate existence within Oxford University Press and was not, as it became in 1978, just an imprint of it.

2 'The Newnham job' for which Jean had applied was a three-year Research Fellowship. In 1923 no candidate was judged to be deserving of the award.

3 Rose's literary agents. Albert Curtis Brown was an American, who came to London in 1899 as a journalist, but soon established the firm that still bears his name.

4 The scholarly article Jean hoped to have published was probably 'Notes on the Fletchers (with Special Reference to Giles Fletcher the Younger)', a revised and abbreviated version of a thesis she presented for her English Tripos at Cambridge in 1915. It is mentioned by J.C. Smith in the testimonial he wrote for her on 14 April 1923. It survives in a typescript copy, but seems never to have been published.

5 *Told by an Idiot*, published in late October 1923.

6 Mr Garden.

7 On the face of it, this statement seems inconsistent with Rose's comment, in the previous sentence, that she did not know the book had a religious aspect.

8 According to Edward Conybeare, Grace was having 'fits of giddiness' (*Diary*, 20 June).

9 Dorothy Gillum's second child, Kenneth, was born in Winchester on 31 July 1923. On D Day, 6 June 1944, he was one of those dropped by parachute with the task of guiding in the following gliders. He was killed in action three days later, aged twenty.

10 The congress, marking the ninetieth anniversary of the initiation of the Oxford Movement, was held in London. A week of events began on Saturday 7 July, and the opening session of the congress itself took place in the Albert Hall on 10 July.

11 The Rev. J.K. Mozley, a prolific writer on Christian thought and belief, was at this time Principal of Leeds Clergy School. In 1907–1919 he had held a fellowship at Pembroke College, Cambridge, and Rose probably got to know him when she and her family were living at Great Shelford. The two were cousins: his maternal grandmother, Lydia Rose, and her maternal grandmother, Eliza Rose, were sisters. He addressed the Anglo-Catholic Congress on 'The Meaning of Calvary'.

30

Hedgerley End,
Beaconsfield.
8 October [1923]

Dearest Jean

I am *very* sorry about your débâcle – it is bad luck.[1] But I'm glad you think the work was more of a coincidence than a cause; if so, it was bad luck that it happened to coincide, but gives hope. You won't go back till you really feel fit, will you. I do feel sorry, though. It is maddening being cut off like that at the outset of a thing.

I wonder if it really is all right that you should do the work yet? What does your doctor say, if anything?

I suppose now you are resting all you can. I hope so.

I'm glad you saw mother at Eton.[2] She liked being there, and seeing people. She liked seeing you (I mean literally seeing, for she said how very nice you and Dorothy both looked) and the short scrap of talk she had with you. It's rather wonderful, considering her state of health all the summer, that she was able for such events and not the least over-tired. She is now being treated by inoculation,[3] and has had the 1st of 12 goes – and as each go makes her feel ill, and she will have one every 4 days for 7 weeks, it is a depressing prospect. However, her life is cheered by the thought of changing the Ford for a brighter and a better car. All day and each day they arrive in droves to the door to be seen. Second-hand ones, they are, and it is all most exciting. When in doubt, we send for the Brookes, who are our experts, and settle the applicants summarily.

Jim (what a dear he is, by the way) dined with the Brookes and me and we went to a melodrama at Drury Lane.[4] I had a hopeless cold and no voice, and do hope I've not given it to him. I'm still afflicted, though better. We burn incense in the diningroom to disinfect it, and feel very holy. Dorothy Brooke (who was here yesterday) didn't like the incense, and felt as Satan feels when he sees the weakest saint upon his knees;[5] she would, of course. But mother and I are well suited by it.

I am living a life of mingled toil and dissipation, as usual, and have no time to retire into my cold. The articles I write under its pall are of the silliest; however, I keep on writing them. Two this morning, and now for another . . . What a disease!

I like your guitar lady and gentleman.[6] I wish people would play it more now. I learnt it when I was small. A lady at Varazze came and taught it me. Why me (no-one else learnt it) I can't say. I was especially strong on 'The Blue Bells of Scotland', I remember. But that, of course, was in the guitar period, somewhere round 1835.[7]

Very much love: and mother sends much too. Let us know when you go to Oxford again. And I do hope things will be better. I do think it is rotten luck. Do take things absolutely easy this month, won't you.

Goodbye, my dear.

R.

1 It is not known what Jean's illness was on this occasion. Anyhow, she was soon able to return to her new job in Oxford.

2 The occasion was the funeral, on 2 October 1923, of Jean's uncle Sir Henry Babington Smith, a Fellow of Eton College, who had a distinguished career as a civil servant and in international finance. In 1898 he married Lady Elisabeth Bruce, eldest daughter of Victor Alexander Bruce, ninth Earl of Elgin, whose private secretary he was while Lord Elgin was Viceroy of India (1894–1899). The couple had ten children. One of their six daughters was Constance Babington Smith.

3 Misspelt 'innoculation'. Edward Conybeare reports: 'Grace tells of her bad bacillus tracked down, and of triumphant ride at HBS funeral' (*Diary*, 9 October).

4 *Good Luck* by Seymour Hicks and Ian Hay (pseudonym of John Hay Beith) at the Drury Lane Theatre. *The Times* describes it as 'thrilling sporting drama' and 'a prodigious entertainment'. Jim, aged 23, had been offered an appointment in the Nigerian Administrative Service, and was taking a three-month preparatory course in London.

5 William Cowper, *Olney Hymns* 29.11–12: 'And Satan trembles, when he sees | The weakest saint upon his knees'.

6 The picture is very likely to have been *The Duet* (1836) by the Dutch painter Cornelis Bernardus Buys (1808–1872), showing a woman playing a guitar and a man playing a violin. See F.V. Grunfeld, *The Art and Times of the Guitar: An Illustrated History of Guitars and Guitarists* (New York and London, 1969) 232 pl. 167. Its date is in line with Rose's playful reference to 'the guitar period, somewhere around 1835'.

7 Grace Macaulay's diary for January–May 1890 reveals that Rose's guitar teacher was Signorina Erminia. She gave Rose, then aged eight, lessons on Thursday mornings. Grace does not mention 'The Blue Bells of Scotland', but records (23 January) that the teacher 'sang "Sono Orfanella" to R[osie]'s accompaniment and children were amused'. The same entry explains why Rose's elder sister, Margaret, did not play the instrument on the same occasion: 'M.'s hands not steady enough', but a later entry (22 May: 'Guitar mistress to M & R as usual in morn') suggests that Margaret too did receive some instruction.

31

Hedgerley End,
Beaconsfield.
24 October 1923

Dearest Jean

I have been asked for advice about what school to send a child of twelve to. Among others, the parents are considering the Godolphin School.[1] Could you tell me (a) the fees (but I suppose these would be quite changed in these days) (b) size – i.e. are the houses and forms very large? (c) are the houses close to the School, so that the girls don't have far to walk in the mornings? (The child gets coughs in the winter).

I'm so sorry to bother you – and perhaps your information isn't up to date enough to be of use now, but I know no quite recent Godolphians. It is a good school, isn't it? Is it specially Church or anything?

You'll get my *Idiot* to-morrow or so – it comes out to-morrow, I believe.[2] Do you like the wrapper? The Idiot's face is almost too unpleasant, I think. That idiot could never have told the tale of life, which, after all, has gleams of intelligence and virtue – in fact, a great many. But I suppose it was difficult to indicate everything in one face. I don't know if you'll like the book – it looks to me dreadfully heavy, and like an unmade pudding.

My love always. Jim is coming to Tedworth Square (Naomi's new house) this Thursday.[3] He can't come here for a Sunday yet. It will be nice when he can. E.R.M.

1 On the Godolphin School, Salisbury, and Jean as a pupil there, see Introd. II.1. The child whose education is under discussion is Brigid O'Donovan, the elder daughter of Gerald and Beryl. She was born on 14 December 1911 and so was nearly twelve. She

was to be educated not at the Godolphin, but at Cheltenham Ladies' College, which she entered in May 1924. Since both Jean's mother and Rose's and her aunt Mary Macaulay had been pupils at the College, it is possible that Brigid was sent there in response to Jean's advice. It is also possible that she influenced the O'Donovans' decision to send their son, Dermod, to Shrewsbury School in 1927, two of her brothers having been educated there.

2 Jean's presentation copy from Rose is dated 30 October 1923.

3 Naomi had moved from 44 Princes Gardens to 2 Tedworth Square, Chelsea, at the beginning of October.

32

Beaconsfield.
9 November [1923]

Dearest Jean

Your good letter to hand, waiting for me last night when I came back to Needle and Home[1] from Deal, where I had been to see how Jeanie and her finger were – she has got it badly poisoned – the first of the right hand, which is awkward. They are afraid she may have to lose the tip of it, but think not the whole finger. However, she is now well in herself, and goes about.

You are a dear about the *Idiot*. I note that you recognised bits of Imogen,[2] even through the various circumstantial disguises in which I enveloped her: which was clever of you, as I didn't think anyone beyond my immediate family (who knew, of course, about the navy and other things) would. It's not that she's a portrait of me – I couldn't do that – but merely that I've given her a lot of my own inward experiences, childish imaginings (and mature ones too, I suppose) and points of view – and the games we used to play on the underground and in the streets, and so forth. But, as you weren't there, I think it was penetrating of you. Dorothea Conybeare[3] recognised it too. Of course all that about the ships (which I knew by heart) and the Story of a boy or young man which my life always was, and the slim green volume, is pure autobiography.[4] I'm glad you like it, my dear.

Reviewers and others have been mostly very kind, though I note that I have made Raymond Mortimer, of *The New Statesman*, very angry indeed. But of course I knew he would be, as I parodied and subverted some of his own most loudly expressed views on sex differences. Even allowing for the natural chagrin caused by that, I think his review lacks good taste – he is so obviously trying to be personally offensive, not criticizing the book or describing it. I've never met him (except in print) but I am told he is a bumptious and offensive youth. So I think on the whole it is well to have got his goat.[5] Other criticisms have been kindly and well-meant – except that one or two alluded to my 'chilly cynicism and superiority'. I like *The Outlook*'s statement that 'from some cold star Miss Macaulay observes our passions' – it sounds so grand, though chilly, this weather.[6] Most people (who don't know me) write and tell me I am Rome![7]

Yes, the attitude towards children is interesting in its development. One can't think how the little dears of 1520 ever grew beyond six at all, they must have been so kept under and maltreated and disdained and birch-rodded. How are the modern generation treated – the new babies, I mean, like Dorothy's? But then Dorothy is no test of her time – she would always have her own good sense. I do think some parents are immoral idiots, don't you.

Well, I'm glad the job is figuring out fairly well, and that you haven't been knocked over again. It will develope more, of course, as time goes on – personally I hate all jobs for the first few weeks. But the people being the right sort is almost more important than anything else. And it is jolly to be part of a thing like the Clarendon Press. Don't you love their new Jane Austen? The pictures are so gorgeous.[8] Who are the people you see most of? In the Press, I mean. One advantage of Oxford is, there are so many people in it who are worth seeing – the incoming undergraduates and others. I hope the Murrays are well.

I'd love to come and stay sometime. At the moment I'm having bother with glands, and may have to have something done to them. I get so many sore throats, and am told the glands and the ear are inflamed or something. But it's nothing much, and will probably pass off of itself.

Mother is as pleased as a queen, with her new car.[9] I'm on my way home to Beacs, where Jim and the Brookes come too this afternoon for the week-end. The Brookes wanted to come too for this one, and I thought Jim wouldn't mind, and they'd like to see him.

All my love and best wishes. I do hope you are looking after yourself. I think too many early moves a *mistake*, by the way!

ERM

1   Rose uses the same expression, in reference to her London base at 63 Edgware Road, in *L*43. Presumably it derives from the magazine *Needle and Home*, which appeared between January 1913 and February 1930.

2   Imogen Carrington, daughter of the eldest of Mr and Mrs Garden's six children, Victoria.

3   Rose's first cousin, the youngest of the five children of Edward and Frances Conybeare.

4   For 'all that about the ships', see *Told by an Idiot* 195, where Imogen, having told Billy that she doesn't share his interest in 'how babies come', declares: '*I'd* rather know the displacement and horsepower and knots of all the battleships and first-class cruisers', and, when Billy tests her knowledge, rattles off the answers. Imogen, like Rose in her childhood, longed to be a sailor (*Told by an Idiot* 154), and 'the slim green volume' contained the poems she imagined she wrote as a brilliant young naval officer called Denis Carton: '"Few people knew", said Imogen, within herself, "that this slender book of verse, *Questionings*, bound in green, with gold edges, which made such a stir in lit'ry London, was by a wiry, brown-faced, blue-eyed young lieutenant-commander,

composed while he navigated his first-class gunboat . . . among the Pacific Islands, taking soundings.'"

5 In his review (*The New Statesman*, 10 November 1923, 146, 148) Mortimer, aged 28 at this time, certainly says some harsh things, claiming, for example, that 'Never was there such remorseless flogging of dead horses, such fearless tilting at obsolete windmills', and concluding: 'But one rises from *Told by an Idiot* as from a boudoir, reassured. The minds of women, after all, are not becoming like the minds of men. For no man could conceivably combine so much cleverness with so little logic, so much intelligence with so little intellect.' A notable critic of literature and the visual arts, he was literary editor of *The New Statesman* from 1935 to 1947. In 1948 he moved to *The Sunday Times*, and from 1952 was that paper's chief reviewer. He and Rose were to become good friends (*L*108 n. 6).

6 *The Outlook*, 3 November 1923, 337. The reviewer is H.C. Harwood.

7 Rome, Mr Garden's second daughter, was named after the Church of which he was a member when she was born. Like Rose, she falls in love with a married man, although her dilemma as to whether to accept his proposal, made to her on a bench in the garden in Bloomsbury Square, to run off to Italy with him is solved when a man armed with a knife deals him a mortal wound in the back just as she is about to reply.

8 *The Novels of Jane Austen: The Text Based on Collation of the Early Editions* (Oxford, 1923), edited by R.W. Chapman, whose secretary Jean had just become. Printed on large paper and limited to 1,000 copies, the work is in five volumes, each of which has a colour frontispiece.

9 The car, acquired on 29 October, was a Benz. When Grace visited her brother, Edward Conybeare, in Cambridge the following summer, he described her as arriving 'in triumphal car (super taxi) with man, maid and dog' (*Diary*, 23 June 1924). It was the second car she owned. The Ford it replaced had been bought in spring 1920 and soon suffered the indignity of being 'run over by fire engine' (Edward's *Diary*, 7 August 1920). Grace usually, if not always, had herself driven by a chauffeur.

33

Beaconsfield
28 November [1923]

Dearest Jean

Jim says you and he can come for the 15th and 16th week-end. That will be splendid. We do want to have you both.

I was sorry about last Sunday, and hope you had to be in town in any case. Jeanie went away on Monday, not cured, but better. The top of her finger bone had to be taken off, which was bad luck, though she says she won't miss it.

How is everything? I'm in bed to-day with a temperature, due, I think, to throat and glands, which keep afflicting me in these days. It is a bore, as I wanted to get to town. But I shall be all right to-morrow, no doubt. I hope life and work are as they should be with you. Are you going to vote? I shall vote for Mr Murray for Oxford, of course.[1] For Bucks I don't know – both our candidates are duds, and I do hate all the parties so, and don't know enough about tariff duties to vote on those,[2] though I *think* they're all wrong. And I hate Baldwin and Asquith and Lloyd George. I like Ramsay,[3] but I'm not going to help put Labour in just now, it's such an ass. So there I am.

My love always. R.

1 Gilbert Murray stood unsuccessfully as a parliamentary candidate for the University of Oxford in the general elections of 1919, 1922, 1923, 1924, and 1929 – as an Independent in 1924, on the other occasions as a Liberal. It was in the election of 6 December 1923 that he came closest to success. Although Jean was now 32, she had been eligible to vote only for two years. Until July 1928 women were not eligible until they were 30, whereas men were at 21. Oxford and Cambridge had each had two seats in Parliament since 1603, and in the nineteenth and twentieth centuries other universities were enfranchised. Graduates formed the electorates, and they were entitled to vote in their geographical constituency as well as in their university one. University constituencies were abolished in 1950.

2 In the 1923 general election campaign the Conservatives, led by Stanley Baldwin, proposed to relieve unemployment by the introduction of protective tariffs. However, they fared badly: although they remained the largest party in the House of Commons, they lost the comfortable majority they had gained over other parties in 1922, and on 23 January 1924 Ramsay MacDonald, with support from the Liberals, formed the first Labour government.

3 Rose would have met Ramsay MacDonald at the 1917 Club. He was its President, and his friend and biographer Molly Hamilton was a friend of Rose as well.

34

Beaconsfield.
Monday. [18 February 1924][1]

Dearest Jean

I got home for lunch, in rain and thaw, and read *The Holy War*[2] (which I borrowed after all) in the train. I'll send it back very soon, with the Walpole.[3] I thought of a lot more ideas for the *Island* – it will be the most unsaleable novel ever, but it is fun writing it.[4] You were a great help to me. I hope Fr. Cary will like it!

Mother says she sent me a p.c. but it hadn't come at 10.30, when I started: however, it is of no importance, I gather. Well, thank you, my dear, for having me, and being so most nice to me–I loved it. You are the best of hostesses; I only hope you weren't tired yesterday, trapesing around after my friends in the frost. Come here soon. And I do hope you may feel fitter before long, and not have temperature-fits; I hate your being disabled, even for a few minutes at a time. My love and thanks. R

1 This letter was written exactly one week before the next one. The references to the reading and return of *The Holy War* indicate a short interval, and the matter is clinched by Rose's description of the weather during her Sunday in Oxford and her return to Beaconsfield on the Monday morning: data kindly provided by the Radcliffe Meteorological Station, Oxford, show that her account perfectly suits 17–18 February, but not 10–11 February.

2 By John Bunyan, first published in 1682. It is mentioned in Rose's next novel, *Orphan Island* (59–60, 109, 169–170), being one of the very few books that the governess, Charlotte Smith, managed to rescue from the shipwreck.

3 One can only guess what book is meant, but if, as is probable, Rose had borrowed it, like *The Holy War*, in connection with the writing of *Orphan Island*, a work by, or about, Horace Walpole seems much less likely than one of the novels in which Hugh Walpole explores the psychology of boys – *Mr. Perrin and Mr. Traill* (1911), *Jeremy* (1919), and *Jeremy and Hamlet* (1923).

4 In a letter of 18 January 1951 to Hamilton Johnson, Rose says of *Orphan Island*: 'It was the one of my novels I enjoyed writing most (except *They Were Defeated*) because I indulged in it my morbid passion for coral islands, lagoons, bread-fruit and coconut trees, and island fauna and flora' (*LLF* 59). An article of hers entitled 'Island Fiction', in praise of the genre, was published in *The Guardian*, 19 October 1923, 950. Significantly, this appeared a few days before the publication of *Told by an Idiot*, just at the time when her thoughts are likely to have been turning towards the subject of her next novel.

35

Hedgerley End
Beaconsfield
Monday. [25 February 1924][1]

Dearest Jean

These[2] with my thanks. And thank you for the *Large Room*,[3] which came to-day. *The Holy War* amused my journey home very much.

I am now wrestling with What the Public Wants, having just returned from an idle and festive (and very cold) week-end at Holmbury,[4] and having this fearful discourse upon me to-morrow afternoon. 'God help us both', as A.P. Herbert remarked over the telephone on Friday. Yes indeed.

Mother has the other photograph of Jim from the one you have.[5] I think it is pleasing, don't you. Don't forget to ask him about the detective stories. My love, and thank you again. R.

1 This letter can be precisely dated, thanks to Rose's mention of her performance alongside A.P. Herbert 'to-morrow afternoon'. It was on 26 February 1924, at 5.30 pm, that the two discussed 'What the Public Wants–and Why', with Rose as the lec-turer and A.P.H. as the counter-lecturer. The meeting, held at the London School of

Economics and presided over by J.C. Squire, was one of a series of six organised in aid of King Edward's Hospital Fund. In her lecture Rose contended that most people did not know what they wanted, but could be made to believe that they wanted anything. The lecture (with A.P.H.'s response) is summarised in *The Times*, 27 February 1924, 16, and she included a revised version of it in *A Casual Commentary* 209–218.

2 *The Holy War* and the Walpole book.

3 S.C. Carpenter, *A Large Room: A Plea for a More Inclusive Christianity* (London, 1923).

4 Where Naomi had a cottage.

5 Jim had sailed from Liverpool on his way to his new post in Nigeria on 23 January 1924.

36

Beacs.
Sunday. [6 April 1924][1]

Dearest Jean

Thanks so much for *Tales for Me to Read to Myself* – they are v.g. I will return them directly. Uncle Willie didn't know them, as they came rather after his day.[2]

I'm so sorry you were laid low by Saturday's exploit, but I don't wonder. I'm thankful you didn't get bronchitis or pneumonia. I do hope you are really all right now and so having a nice week-end this heavenly weather. Such a lovely spring day here. Naomi only got down for the inside of to-day – she and Uncle Willie made quite a good thing of it, and she loved him. Mr Milner White[3] and Mr Trevelyan[4] only came for a very brief call – and then arrived Uncle Regie and Harry Babington Smith.[5] So tea was rather a crowd. But very nice. The clergymen weren't there for it, of course. And Naomi and the uncles talked about conjuring tricks and acrobats and the Way of the World. N. has now gone – so have uncle R. and H.B.S.

I wonder what about the Henley house. Uncle Willie said it was *not* going to be bought – but I don't suppose he knew. He is in a lovely mood – but is now talking so consecutively and audibly to himself in the next room that he is rather disturbing me.

I dined with the E.V. Knoxes[6] on Friday, and we prepared a lovely 'Conversation' for him to do about me in *The Queen* – (did I tell you about that before? It's a series Naomi has – Conversations with authors, by one another) I am going to appear in it as a very genteel and pompous Leader of Women, with the responsibilities of Empire heavy on me, and I even propose to visit Wembley, *not* for the wiggle-waggle, but to support our Colonies.[7] Also, he is going to make me blush when he says 'serviette'.[8] ('At this Miss Macaulay blushed a little'). I will send you a copy of whatever issue it appears in, if he really does it like that.[9] The nice thing is that most of *The Queen* readers will probably take it quite seriously.

Post going – probably even gone. My much love – I do like seeing you a lot. So does mother. Yes, I will come to Oxford in the summer and stay in Iffley Rd.
ERM

1   The content of the letter shows that Rose is writing in the spring of 1924, and the exact date of the gathering in Beaconsfield is given in Naomi's diary.

2   This collection of four stories, written for young children to read to themselves, was first published by Joseph Masters, London, in 1863, when W.H. Macaulay was about ten. None of the words used contains more than six letters.

3   The Very Rev. Eric Milner-White, Fellow and Dean of King's College, Cambridge, later (from 1941 until his death in 1963) Dean of York. He was an ardent Anglo-Catholic. It was he who inaugurated in 1918 the King's tradition of holding a Festival of Nine Lessons and Carols on Christmas Eve, and who supervised the restoration of the medieval glass windows in York Minster after the Second World War. The reason for the gathering at Hedgerley End in the afternoon of 6 April 1924 is not revealed, but one may reasonably assume that it was organised to coincide with the visit of W.H. Macaulay, who seems to have been a staying guest.

4   The Rev. William Bouverie Trevelyan, another Anglo-Catholic clergyman, had been Warden of the House of Retreat, Beaconsfield, since 1914. Before that (1907–1913) he had been the first Warden of Liddon House in London (see *L*95, 99). He was related to Rose and Jean, being a nephew of Sir Charles Edward Trevelyan (1807–1886), who married Hannah More (not 'Moore' as given by *DNB* and *ODNB*) Macaulay (1810–1873), a daughter of Zachary Macaulay and a sister of Thomas Babington Macaulay.

5   A son of Henry and Elisabeth Babington Smith, aged 21. Educated at Eton College and King's College, Cambridge, he was to return to Eton as a teacher.

6   The writer and journalist Edmund Knox and his first wife, Christina, parents of the novelist Penelope Fitzgerald (1916–2000), who was to write a book about her father and three uncles, *The Knox Brothers* (London, 1977). The youngest brother was Ronald Arbuthnott Knox (1888–1957), who became a Roman Catholic and translated the Bible. Using the pseudonym Evoe, Edmund was a frequent contributor to *Punch*, of which he was to be editor (1932–1949).

7   The Empire Stadium at Wembley, later called Wembley Stadium, in London, was erected in 1922–1923 in connection with the British Empire Exhibition of 1924–1925. The exhibition, opened by King George V on 23 April 1924, was designed to show the strength, wealth, prosperity, and unity of the British Empire. Rose wrote an article on 'Causes at Wembley', first published in *The Guardian*, 4 July 1924, 614, and reprinted in *A Casual Commentary* 163–166. *The Guardian* was a weekly Anglican newspaper, to which Rose contributed at least 23 articles between October 1922 and 1925. In 1922–1923 she concentrated on reviewing books and discussing various sorts and aspects of fiction, but in 1924–1925 she wrote on a variety of topics, and no fewer than eight of her articles from those years were reprinted in *A Casual Commentary*, although the book gives no indication of their source.

8   According to H.W. Fowler, *A Dictionary of Modern English Usage* (Oxford, 1926), 'napkin should be preferred to serviette' (370), the latter being a genteelism (213).

9 'Conversations V: E.V. Knox and Rose Macaulay', appeared in *The Queen*, 14 May 1924, 10–11. It is a light-hearted and amusing piece, but there is no mention either of Wembley or of serviettes and napkins.

37

Beaconsfield
2 May [1924]

Dearest Jean

Thank you so much for yours. Mother is better, but still gets relapses into bed and weakness.[1] It is a bother. Margaret was home for Easter week, and I was away, walking about the Mendips. It was so nice. Glastonbury is an exquisite dream. So is Avebury (not on a Mendip, but I went there). I loved it all.

I'm glad you had a good Easter.[2] I did too, because of the lovely weather. I put on a panama hat and a cotton shirt and walked and lay about the fields and woods. Now it's damp again, and chilly. I'm so glad about the new rooms.[3] They do sound pleasant. I will surely come a week-end, when I can disentangle my life a little from jobs and engagements. I shall love it. I want to go to Cambridge some time this month, if possible. Probably Oxford in June.

Life has just begun again – that is, Naomi is back from a holiday, and so am I, and people ask one to dinner and parties and things, and one has to work. Of course, life is like that – but I did like Somerset and leisure and possessing my soul a little.

Do you mean May morning is *nominally* 6? For a moment I thought you had got it the wrong way up, and meant to say that it happened at 4 – but I expect they've changed the hour, to avoid such excruciating earliness. I used to love it. I went in punts afterwards, and had breakfast on the river.[4]

Oh, how I wish I had more *time*. I am distraught for lack of it.

How are you, darling? Well, I do hope. Always yours, with my love R.

The Brookes are back from Spain. They only ½ liked it. Rather sinister and queer the lovely D[orothy] says.

1 Grace had suffered a heart attack on 2 April 1924.
2 Easter Day in 1924 was 20 April.
3 At 204 Iffley Road, Oxford.
4 Around 6 am on May Day the choir of Magdalen College, Oxford, sings a Latin hymn at the top of Magdalen Tower. Many assemble to hear it, some in punts on the river Cherwell at Magdalen Bridge.

38

Monday [23 June 1924][1]

'The Schis<m>atic' is not, apparently, in our Cleveland (published by your Press and at Yale, in 1911) and is perhaps among the spurious poems this editor has ejected, that are to be found in the early editions.[2] I daresay it is among the 'other exquisite Remains of most eminent Wits of both the universities that were his Contemporaries' which used to be published with his poems.[3] So you might send me a copy if you have time ever – or part of it.

Joseph Warton died in 1800, so *Minor Morals* is before that anyhow.[4]

The day is still exquisite, and I wish you here and myself free to spend the day in woods again. It was a nice Sunday. I love you much. ERM. 'The peculiar smells that float in the air in copses'. (*Minor Morals*, even, notices these.)[5]

1 This message is written on a postcard addressed to Jean at 204 Iffley Road, Oxford. The postmark is: 'Paddington, W.2 2.45 p.m. 23 June 1924'.

2 'The Schismatic' (Rose has written 'Schistratic') is not admitted by B. Morris and Eleanor Withington (eds), *The Poems of John Cleveland* (Oxford, 1967) either. A seventeenth-century edition that does contain 'The Schismatick' is J. Lake and S. Drake (eds), *The Works of Mr. John Cleveland* (London, 1687) 378–379. Rose quotes nine lines of the poem in *Orphan Island* (161). When Miss Smith cannot remember who wrote them, Charles Thinkwell, who 'always knew things like that', murmured 'a pseudo John Cleveland' (162). Rose was to make Cleveland, best known for his political satires and staunch supporter of the royalist cause, a leading character in *They Were Defeated*.

3 Rose's quotation is of part of the title of E. Williamson (ed.), *J. Cleaveland* [*sic*] *Revived* (London, 1659).

4 *Minor Morals, Interspersed with Sketches of Natural History, Historical Anecdotes, and Original Stories*, by Charlotte Smith, was first published in 1798 (London), with further editions in 1799 (London) and 1800 (Dublin). The connection between her book and Warton is that, towards the end of Dialogue VIII (1798 ed., II 46–47; 1800 ed., 127), she quotes two stanzas of his 'Ode to Evening', mentioning that they are 'by a poet still living'. Warton, as Rose says, died in 1800. It is clear that Rose is using a later edition of *Minor Morals* – either that of 1816 or that of 1825 (both London). It may be noted that the governess in *Orphan Island* is called Charlotte Smith.

5 The quotation is from Dialogue XII of *Minor Morals* (1798 ed., II 130; 1800 ed., 179): 'The peculiar smells that float in the air in copses, and which arise from the exhalation of innumerable leaves; the variety of colours those leaves presented, either from the change of season or their native hues . . .'

39

Hedgerley End,
Beaconsfield.
1 July 1924

My dearest Jean

This <is> one of the 1st moments I have had free from labours or dissipations since you went. Thank you for your nice card, as well as letter and Schismatik, which I love. I am disappointed about the 13th – mother returned from Cambridge having bidden Dorothea[1] here for it, and at the same time Dorothy Brooke wrote to say it was their only July week-end and might they come – so now we have them and D. both – I hope they'll suit. And this next week-end is no good for me, and all July after 13th I am tied here with a friend – so Oxford will have to wait, which saddens me. Of course there's next week – but that's not to Iffley Road and you.

I shall like seeing Regie on Friday. I must send him a card of directions, as I gather he's not very good at topography. I said the 1917, but didn't say how to get there.

Goodbye darling – it was a joy to have you. I found more wild strawberries on Sunday, and larger and redder ones. You haven't a Dr Watts, have you? I've lost mine, and want The Voice of the Sluggard![2]

We have Uncle Willie here to-day and to-morrow – in great form, but too full of cricket.[3] He thinks *A Passage to India* far E.M.F.'s best book.[4]

All my love – and mother's love and thanks for your letter to her.

R.

---

1   Conybeare.
2   Isaac Watts's poem, first printed in *Divine Songs Attempted in Easy Verse for the Use of Children* (London, 1715) 46–47, is called 'The Sluggard', but starts with the words ''Tis the voice of the sluggard. I heard him complain | You have wak'd me too soon, I must slumber again.' Rose quotes the first two stanzas of the poem in *The Minor Pleasures of Life* (1934) under the heading 'Lying Late'. But she wanted Watts now for *Orphan Island*. Carved on the island's trees 'were . . . maxims and comments on life, of which some were biblical, and several by Dr. Isaac Watts, a poet with whom Miss Smith would seem to have had a close acquaintance' (130). Passages of *Divine Songs* are quoted on pp. 131, 247, 298–299. See also 255. 'The Sluggard' is not quoted. Instead Rose prefers 'Go to the Ant, Thou Sluggard' (131) from Proverbs 6.6. Sluggard quotations from both Watts and Proverbs are made in her *Personal Pleasures* (1935) 65, in the course of an essay that is entitled 'Bed' and divided into two parts, 'Getting into it' and 'Not getting out of it'. The essay was reprinted in *The Queen*, 21 January 1958, 24–25.
3   Given that W.H. Macaulay was keen on cricket, his excitement was understandable. On 1 July, in the second Test Match between England and South Africa at Lord's, the

home side had made 531 for 2 declared and was on its way to victory by an innings and 18 runs. In an article 'On Thinking Well of Ourselves', first published in *The Guardian*, 8 August 1924, and reprinted in *A Casual Commentary* 205–208, Rose was to discuss the way devotees of cricket 'have, in their limitless conceit, coined the phrase "Not cricket", and applied it to mean any unfair conduct', and 'succeeded in imposing on their countrymen the notion that to play this game implies some peculiar virtue'.

4 E.M. Forster's book was published on 4 June 1924. At the end of her entirely favourable review (*The Daily News*, 4 June 1924, 8), Rose wrote: 'it is, I think, the best and most interesting book he has written'.

40

Beaconsfield
29 July [1924]

My dearest Jean

Your letter was nice, as always. I am *much* better: in fact, getting about again now – about the garden and even village. I feel daily stronger, and shall soon feel quite strong. Though I suppose this always takes time. I feel I've missed the summer in bed, and get up to find it is autumn. But that may mend.

I'm glad you are getting away so soon. I hope you will successfully stalk Miss Jane Austen, and avoid the police station. I know all about how to steal letters and everything else, from the books I read. No crime I am now not familiar with.[1]

I am now busy writing *Orphan Island* again. By the way, the 1st part is, J.C. Squire told me the other day, coming out in the August *Mercury*.[2] He said he didn't send me a proof, because he heard I was ill, but did them himself, so they must be full of mistakes I was going to alter, with, I dare say, a lot of new ones added. However, it doesn't matter in *The Mercury*; I shall re-write it for the book.

The family come home this week – M[argaret] and J[eanie], that is. M. is at Kirnan, getting daily better, and being walked by Uncle W[illie] daily a little further up the hills. I hope he won't kill her. She says Mr Impey is too noisy, though quite nice.[3]

Well, I hope you'll have a nice time – but I expect you will.[4] Write more poetry, if any offers – and get very fit and be very happy.

I am chiefly troubled by arrears of the letters I failed to write while sick – on top of thousands of books I should review, an article for *The Guardian* I should write,[5] and the novel that I should be getting on with. But I'm not letting any of it bother me, as I want to get fat again. I find one shrinks while in bed – crossways, but mother says I have increased vertically, to make up.

Goodbye, darling – and here is a poem Naomi sends me, which I suppose was sent for *The Queen*.[6]

ERM

1   Since Jean's letter does not survive, it is not clear what is going on here. But Rose's mention of stealing *letters* suggests that Jean may have made a playful reference to her involvement, prior to the book's publication, with *Five Letters from Jane Austen to Her Niece, Fanny Knight*, printed in facsimile (Oxford: Clarendon Press, 1924). It is to be remembered that Jean was at this time employed by the Clarendon Press as secretary to R.W. Chapman, the expert on Jane Austen, whose 'baby' the book was.

2   *The London Mercury* 10, 58 (August 1924) 350–359.

3   On Edward Impey, see *L*53 (and n. 1 there), 54.

4   Jean was going to France.

5   The article mentioned in *L*39 n. 3.

6   Naomi had resigned as literary editor of *SWG* in 1922. That she was doing some work for *The Queen* has been mentioned in *L*36.

41

Beaconsfield
17 September [1924]

My dearest Jean

Wherever you are for your birthday, this brings you all I can wish you of good, and, besides, my love. Also the *Week-End Book*, which you may or mayn't like – I think it a nice collection of poems, and, though the games are foolish, the cooking and medical recipes are useful, or might be. I had it away with me on Exmoor, and it pleased me. I read with joy the Song of Solomon – it's better, really, when free of the humorous turn given it by the Fathers in the headings.[1] And I love the Donnes, many of them, and other poems.[2]

I wonder where you are – I shall send this to Oxford. For my part, I am just this moment home from Exmoor and Porlock, where I spent a fortnight after August's feverish literary activities; directly I got off the *Orphans*, off I dashed for the Minehead train – or rather the Taunton train, for I was in the Quantocks first for a few days. Exmoor was glorious. I walked all day. Do you know that part – the Horner valley, and Porlock, and Dunkery Beacon, and Cloutsham, and Malmsmead and the Doone valley, and the Oare valley, and all.[3] I learnt afterwards that the uncles were at Exford – but I didn't know that, and did not join them at their cruel sport, of which I can scarcely approve.[4] It rained some, but also shone some, and the heather on the hills, and the woods and streams in the combes, and the purple sky leaning on it all, and the sun gleaming through were exquisitely lovely, and I was exquisitely happy. Now, I'm back, and must settle in and be busy again – in fact, I am already too busy. But this week-end, if mother's health allows, she and I visit Clent. I wonder if, by any chance, you'll be there?[5] I don't know if you're back from your holidays yet – or even back from France – or perhaps you are in Scotland somewhere – I don't think Uncle Kenneth said when he wrote to mother. It is a sudden plan of mother's, this week-end, and I hope it comes off. On the Monday, she goes on to Lichfield[6] to see the Moncriefs,[7] and I go home by train. But none of this may occur: she's not very well this week, as a matter of fact, and it may have to be deferred.

August was nice, but for over-work on my part, with those infernal *Orphans*, who had to be both finished *and* typed. I made Margaret do my reviewing for *The D[aily] N[ews]*, under my signature – a gross fraud! I typed it out, and altered anything that didn't seem quite likely for me, but on the whole the results were most life-like. I hadn't the face to keep so many books hung up unreviewed, nor yet the time to review them.[8] For the rest, we had a nice time *en famille*, and a lovely picnic on August 6th – and, by the way, how clever and kind of you to send us a pot of cream just in time for it! It was very luscious and festive.

I do hope you've had splendid holidays, darling, and will have a really attractive term, and, indeed, year. Mother sends a great deal of love for your birthday. And so do I, and wish you very happy.

Rose.

P.S. Uncle K. says that Aunt Nannie and Uncle Charlie will be away for Regie's ordination this week-end, and I suppose you too, for which I am sorry.[9]

1 'The Song of Songs, Which Is Solomon's' is printed in *The Week-end Book* (London, 1924) 17–25. 'The humorous turn given it by the fathers in the headings' refers to the interpretation, first propounded by Origen in the third century AD, that *The Song of Solomon* is not a celebration of sexual love but an allegory of the relationship between Christ and his Church.

2 The poems in *The Week-end Book* include seven by John Donne.

3 All the places mentioned are in Somerset, except Malmsmead, which is just in Devon. Rose had Gerald's company on her holiday. In 'Miss Anstruther's Letters' (Bibliog. I.7) 307, Miss A. remembers 'climbing Dunkery Beacon to Porlock' with her lover.

4 The uncles are Willie and Kenneth. 'Their cruel sport' is hunting. For Rose's opposition to it, see also *L75*. Both uncles rode to hounds up to the outbreak of the First World War. After the war Kenneth no longer rode, but Willie continued to hunt with the Devon and Somerset Staghounds until at least 1924, when he was 70. John Maynard Keynes, his colleague and friend at King's College, Cambridge, describes a stag-hunting holiday he had with him in September 1923, staying in Exford at the Crown Hotel. Kenneth joined them, but did not hunt. On this occasion Willie found 'the game rather severe for his old bones', but in a letter of 10 October 1924 Keynes reports that 'Vice Provost Macaulay is very well and has been hunting the stags furiously'. See P. Hill and R. Keynes (eds), *Lydia and Maynard* (London, 1989) 100, 103, 107, 233. In his obituary of Willie in *The Cambridge Review* 58, 1419 (15 January 1937) 169–170, at 170, Keynes mentions that 'he was the last Fellow of [King's] College to follow the old practice of keeping a horse'.

5 The plan would have been to stay with Kenneth Macaulay at Walton House. Jean's family home, Cross Bank, is also in Clent.

6 Misspelt 'Litchfield'.

7 The Rev. Canon Archibald Moncrief and his wife Louisa. Louisa, whose maiden name was Rose, was Grace's first cousin and a sister of Emilie Rose, after whom Grace and George called their second daughter. She was one of Rose's three godparents. Archibald had been Canon Residentiary, Lichfield Cathedral, since 1916 and Precentor since 1919.

8 Two reviews under Rose's name are printed in *The Daily News* on 14 August 1924, 6, and seven on 22 August 1924, 7.

9 Jean's brother was ordained Anglican priest on Sunday 21 September 1924. One would certainly expect his devout-Anglican parents and Jean to have wanted to be present.

42

Train to Beacs.
Friday [7 November 1924]

My dear, I got your note and poem last night in London, too late to answer till now, when I am on my way down to Denham, there to get out and walk.[1] Thank you for both. I want dreadfully to meet; we've been hoping you might propose a week-end and come down. I've been wanting, too, to come to you, but so far I've been either smothered in work at week-ends or they've been taken up elsehow–often both. This one is bad, because Saturday night I have to spend in town.[2] If you could come for it, we should all the same love it, and I'd be home Sunday morning, but of course I'd rather have you for a better one. Next week-end is no use, as I shall be in the north for five days. The one after that (22nd) the Brookes are booked for, but if you could come too it would be splendid–what of it? They'd love it – if you didn't mind. We wouldn't see so much of you quite as if no B's were there – but it would be fun, and would do to go on with. Or, there's the one after that quite free – 29th. But do come.[3]

I like St Hubert – though I feel as if it still wanted things doing to it (a) to elucidate here and there an obscurity (b) to remove what look like rather careless rhymes, such as in stanza 4. I think it's rather beautiful, but hasn't (to me) got the force and fire of some of your things.[4] But I'll meditate further on it. Where do you send your things, if anywhere? When we meet, we will talk of lots of things. Myself, I saw E.V. Lucas yesterday, and he wants my essay-book by the end of the year, and I have now to work and weep till then.[5] *Orphan Island* comes on the 14th, I think. You'll get your copy before that, possibly. I'm not sure.

I saw *The Duenna*[6] on Wednesday – so enchanting.

Soon it will be Denham – and a fine breezy morning for a walk. My dear love all the time; I like you a lot. Rose.

1 The attractive Buckinghamshire village of Denham is about seven miles before Beaconsfield, if one is travelling from London. Was Rose going to walk by herself or with Gerald? One cannot be sure, but, given that she had so much work to do, it is easier to imagine her taking the morning off to be with him than to be alone. Among the memories Miss Anstruther had was of 'sauntering in Buckinghamshire beech-woods' with her lover ('Miss Anstruther's Letters' 307), probably in reference to Burnham Beeches. In Rose's next novel, *Crewe Train*, Mr Dobie's daughter, Denham, was 'named after her mother's favourite Buckinghamshire village' (3), but she had already used Denham as a surname in her first novel, *Abbots Verney* (1906), ten years before she went to live in Buckinghamshire.

2 The engagement is described by Dorothy Brookes in her diary for Saturday 8 November: 'Rose and Naomi came to dinner and we went to dreadfully bad play at Fortune Theatre *Sinners*'. The Fortune was the first London theatre to be built after the war, and this was the first performance of the first play performed in it.

3 Jean did not come. Instead, Rose visited her in Oxford (*L*43).

4 The poem is not among Jean's surviving papers.

5 Lucas became chairman, in 1924, of Methuen, the publisher of Rose's *A Casual Commentary* (1925). She did not send him the book until July 1925 (*L*53).

6 Comic opera, with words by R.B. Sheridan and music by his father-in-law Thomas Linley, first produced in 1775. In the production attended by Rose, at the Lyric Theatre, Hammersmith, Linley's music was adapted by Alfred Reynolds.

43

Beaconsfield.
2 December 1924

Dearest Jean

Thank you so much: I did love my week-end. You are the nicest person to stay with anywhere, and Oxford always Oxford.

I hope Dorchester[1] was good. For me, I encountered Humbert Wolfe[2] on Oxford platform, and we travelled up together. Our (mainly, as you may guess, his) incessant bright babble drove one lady from the compartment early, which seemed to please him. He is a good travelling companion, however – really entertaining. Arrived in town, I was led by St Andrew (whose transferred feast it was[3]) to a block of exquisite flats called St Andrew's Mansions, off Baker Street,[4] close to Mme Tussaud's, the Wallace Collection, Great Central Station,[5] Oxford Street, the Times Book Club,[6] and not bad for Paddington. I enquired of the porter – and actually one was empty that minute – or not empty, but obtainable from January. Same rent as Needle and home, and with two real bedrooms instead of a cubby-hole behind a curtain, self-contained, water h. and c., electric light, gas cooker, kitchen, . . .[7]

The rest of the letter is missing.

1 Almost certainly the village a few miles south of Oxford rather than the county town of Dorset.

2 Civil servant and poet. From 1915 until the end of the First World War he worked in the Ministry of Munitions as a controller of labour regulations. Jean will surely have seen him in action there, and, according to Naomi Royde-Smith, writing to Viola Garvin on 20 September 1943 (ERM 15.173), Jean's and Rose's friend Madeleine Symons 'knew him intimately just after the war'. He and Rose were, and remained, good friends. Selections of her poetry were reprinted in 1927 in *The Augustan Books of English Poetry* series edited by Wolfe. Correspondence between the two, comprising 11 letters or postcards from her to him and five letters from him to her, is preserved in the Berg Collection in The New York Public Library.

3 St Andrew's Day, 30 November, was a Sunday in 1924. Rose travelled to London on Monday 1 December. In connection with Rose chancing upon St Andrews Mansions on St Andrews Day, neither she nor Jean is likely to have forgotten that the poems in Rose's *The Two Blind Countries* include 'Two Hymns for St. Andrew's Day'.

4 Dorset Street, in which St Andrews Mansions stands, crosses Baker Street at approximately the halfway point. The block of flats, still well preserved, is on the north side of the street at the east end of it. Rose first occupied no. 2, the entrance to which is down a few steps on the left side of the courtyard (Fig. 6), but some time between May and December 1926 she moved to no. 10, the entrance to which is on the right side of a narrow passage beyond the courtyard. Rose's study overlooked the courtyard. An article by Louise Morgan, 'Rose Macaulay', *Everyman*, 31 July 1930, 3–5, part of a series on 'How Writers Work', is illustrated with photographs of Rose in her study, standing outside its window, and planting flowers in the nearby flower bed that contains a small statue mounted on a pedestal. Rose's change of flat also involved a change of telephone number, from Mayfair 1938 to Langham 4107.

5 A station on the Bakerloo line of the London Underground. The name Rose gives it is out of date: opened as Great Central Station on 27 March 1907, it was renamed Marylebone on 15 April 1917.

6 42 Wigmore Street.

7 From *L*45 we learn that there were two 'parlours', one of which was larger than the other, and a hall. There was also a bathroom (*L*54).

44

Beaconsfield
29 December [1924]

Dearest Jean

Thank you a great deal for the perfectly lovely cuirass – what finish, what chic, what *haut ton*! It is divinely warm, beautifully made, and the strings exactly the right hue. I feel *so* cosy about chest and lungs as I walk about. Being colder than you, I even wear it over jerseys when out, under a coat. Not that I've walked very much lately, partly from weather, partly from a tedious cold which I yet have.

Chiefly I walk Benjamin down the lane and over very soggy fields – he adores it, absurd little bear.[1]

I *am* sorry about your knee. For goodness sake look after it well, as knees are very dangerous to neglect. I knew someone who . . . however, it is no moment for cautionary tales. But really be careful, won't you, and don't use it too soon or too hard.

Poor Regie: imagine having to preach to all the uncles and aunts in a room! Could you? I should die, I am sure I should. But I expect he is less self-conscious and much braver – I suppose they get used to it, poor dears. Anyhow, I'm so glad he is home for Christmas.[2] Here we have been 3 – but mother mostly in bed, rather sadly. We've been reading Boswell's letters.[3] I love all his courtships. But what a creature!

All my love for 1925 – and give some of it to Aunt Nannie and Uncle Charlie please. R.

1 From Dorothy Brooke's diary we learn that Benjamin was acquired on 24 September 1924 immediately after the death of a dog called Dickon. She describes the new puppy as 'a funny little rough black one'. After Grace's death in 1925, Benjamin lived with Margaret in Petersfield.
2 Regie was at this time a curate in Dewsbury, Yorkshire.
3 C.B. Tinker (ed.), *Letters of James Boswell* (Oxford, 1924).

45

Beacs.
8 February [1925]

Dearest Jean

Andrew has arrived: he is *so* nice. Very beautiful and decorative and fine. Thank you a lot for him. I found him here to-day when I got home, and shall take him up to-morrow.[1] It is a very stirring question where to put him. If the hall, he must have a little bracket. I incline to over one of the doors–perhaps the larger parlour. But I shall try him about. Of course he really ought to be outside, over the door, but I don't know if he would be safe. Though I could nail him, perhaps. Anyhow, he is lovely, and I shall feel thoroughly protected under his wing. I love his green fishes.

I had a visitor there last night – Peter, from Lincoln.[2] I sleep in the front bedroom, and the spare one is the little back one. I love it all, but especially the Orangery, the small parlour with the orange and lemon paper. It has now an oranges and lemons lamp shade which I found; and my San Remo plate with a lemon on it; and a pile of real o. and l. in a bowl; and your Spanish burin on a shelf. And a huge divan. It is most lovely. Peter and I calculate that the divan could seat 8, if they crossed up their legs and sat two in a row.[3] I am having a house warming party sometime, you see, and it will be something of a squeeze, if many come! Peter says I must settle them down to a paper game, or they will 'get wild', and damage the flat. I do hope they won't! Perhaps, after all, I'd better not have a party at all.

Uncle Regi is coming to tea with me on Wednesday: I hope he'll like it. I think it's nicer than Eton Avenue,[4] but I expect he won't.

I feel I ought to have Aunt Mary sometime, as she had me, but will wait a bit.

When are you coming to London again? Do come and have a night at Andrew's soon. Or (and) a week-end at Beacs. Mother improves, but rather slowly. I wish she were better. She is greatly taken with St. A.

I haven't got a char yet, so spend all my time when in the flat cleaning it. I must get hold of one, or my income will fail.[5] I have forgotten that ever I wrote books and articles. But I must remember again, and fall to. How terribly little *time* we all have, don't we. I do so want lots more. Death will take us before we are nearly ready and while I am still struggling with my white woodwork and floors. All my love in the mean-time, and my thanks.

R.

1 Rose had obtained the tenancy of 2 St Andrews Mansions in early January 1925. CBS 100 and Emery 192 misdate the move to 1922.

2 Unidentified, but perhaps the husband of the unnamed female friend mentioned in *L*24.

3 There is a photograph of Rose reclining and reading on the divan in *Everyman*, 31 July 1930, 3. This item of furniture is mentioned by Virginia Woolf in her diary under 27 March 1926: 'Lodged on a low sofa in Rose's underground cheerful, sane, breezy room I talked to . . .'. She, Leonard, and several other guests had been entertained to dinner by Rose at a nearby restaurant (almost certainly the Rowan Tree, 44 Dorset Street, practically opposite St Andrews Mansions) and had gone to her flat after the meal. The date was 27 February 1926. Virginia did not enjoy the evening, which she describes not only in her diary, but also in a letter of 29 March 1926 to Vita Sackville-West. In the letter she calls it 'a ghastly party' and says that 'in the whirl of meaningless words I thought Mr O'Donovan said Holy Ghost, whereas he said "The Whole Coast" and I asking "Where is the Holy Ghost" got the reply "Where ever the sea is" "Am I mad", I thought, or is this wit? "The Holy Ghost?" I repeated. "The Whole Coast" he shouted, and so we went on, in an atmosphere so repellent that it became, like the smell of bad cheese, repulsively fascinating.' Leonard Woolf, *Beginning Again: An Autobiography of the Years 1911–1918* (London, 1964) 127–128, describes the same party, even though, as he acknowledges, it did not take place during the period covered in his book. He even describes the same incident, but confuses Gerald O'Donovan with another Irish writer, Conal O'Riordan. He did not enjoy the party either, partly on account of an incident in which he himself was involved. He thought the lady sitting next to him had dropped her napkin on the floor, but, when he gallantly leant down to pick it up for her, found he was mistaken. According

to him, the lady was Sylvia Lynd and the 'napkin' was part of her petticoat. Virginia's version is more sensational: the lady was Barbara Ayrton Gould and the item was her sanitary towel.

4 R.H. Macaulay lived at 11 Eton Avenue, London NW3.

5 The char Rose engaged was Mrs Trowles (*L*69; *LS* 30, 32).

46

2, St. Andrews Mansions,
Dorset Street, W.1.
2 April 1925

My dearest Jean

Thank you for your lovely and useful letter – also for the lovely and useful guide,[1] which I will cherish carefully and restore faithfully. I have been reading it yesterday in the train up to town; it seems full of information and charm, tho' dating from days when Turismo was less developed there than now – would it was so still. But I believe one can get right away from coasts into the remoter parts of the hills.

Your letter I shall keep by me for further reference on the spots mentioned. It is like you to have written it, and exactly what one wants to have. What exquisiteness! You are as generous as one would expect with it – I only wish you were coming too. We will go to Soller, and perhaps stay with the pulley well and the flat roof,[2] and anyhow walk up the mountains. It sounds like paradise – and we shall be arrived on the island a fortnight to-day! I shall bathe everywhere – Pollensa[3] and Alcudia beach, and all round the coast. And, I hope, stay at Nuestra Señora de Lluch.[4] Did you see Valldemosa,[5] I wonder? Or visit Ibiza? That sounds so difficult and lengthy a voyage that I expect we shan't. Especially as it is obviously going to be quite impossible to see all Mallorca in the time. I do hope it will be blue and hot and shining all the time. I shall take what Jeanie describes as 'both furs and muslins' – I suppose both will be necessary.

I went to the Coliseum last night. They had a Spanish show – dancing, singing, Toreadors, etc. – very nice.[6] Next me was a group of 5 young Spanish sailors from their ship – rather solemn and grave until the Spanish turn, and then seized with ec<st>a<s>y,[7] almost falling over the rail with shouts of 'Evviva'[8] and thoughts of home. They obviously thought the rest of the evening poor – and so it was, except for Lopokova and the Postman[9] (lovely) and the Cambridge Madrigal singers[10] – also lovely. (By the way, for the first time I saw, on these, the Oxford trouser[11] – I suppose you know it well. It is very ungraceful!)

Now I must go out. I shall write to you from the Island, and send picture cards. I am glad you know it – you will know what it's like when I say what we're doing. Thank you again, and bless you. I do hope you'll get to Olive's cottage.[12] It must be exquisite.

All my love. R.

1 A guide to Mallorca.
2 That is, in the pension in which Jean and Regie stayed in 1919 (*L*3 and n. 18 there).
3 Pollença.
4 Lluc. A monastery and pilgrimage centre in the Serra de Tramuntana.
5 Valldemossa: a small town in the mountains, south-west of Sóller, famous for its connection with Chopin and George Sand, who spent an unhappy winter there in 1838–1839.
6 'Women and Flowers of Spain'. Described as 'a choreographic and lyrical fantasy', it was in 11 parts and was the last item in the programme.
7 Misspelt 'ectsasy'.
8 'Evviva' is Italian, not Spanish. The sailors will have shouted '¡Viva!'.
9 'The Postman', described as 'a ballet comedy', was performed by Stanislas Idzikowski in the title role and by Lydia Lopokova as the maid who wants the postman to return to her a letter she regrets having written to her lover terminating their relationship. It was danced to the music of Beethoven's Piano Sonata No. 18 in E flat major, Opus 31 No. 3 ('The Hunt'). Lopokova was leading ballerina (when she chose) in Diaghilev's Ballets Russes. At the time of her Coliseum performance, she was awaiting the completion of proceedings to annul her marriage to Randolfo Barocchi. The decree nisi had been granted on 15 January 1925. The decree was made absolute on 27 July, leaving the way clear for her marriage to John Maynard Keynes on 4 August. There is a photograph of Lopokova and Idzikowski performing 'The Postman' in P. Hill and R. Keynes (eds), *Lydia and Maynard* illustration 14. Lopokova's life and career are described and assessed by Judith Mackrell, *Bloomsbury Ballerina: Lydia Lopokova, Imperial Dancer and Mrs John Maynard Keynes* (London, 2008).
10 The Trinity Madrigal Club, Cambridge.
11 Oxford trousers or bags were a new style very wide at the ankles.
12 Olive Willis owned Holcombe Cottage, Aisholt, Somerset, on the eastern side of the Quantock Hills. Ancient and with a thatched roof, it is vividly described by Anne Ridler, *Olive Willis and Downe House: An Adventure in Education* (London, 1967) 65–66, and there is a photograph opposite 136.

47

Fonda Ca's Pentinadó
Calle de Castañer, n.º 7
Al lado de la estación del ferrocarril
Sóller-(Mallorca)
18 April 1925

My dearest Jean
  I am sure you will like to see this note-paper! We have been here for 2 days, and adore it. All (except for the *cabinete?*)[1] is perfect. There is a charming youth

who appears to manage the inn – I don't know if he is Antonio Magraner or some subordinate[2] – and lovely food, and exquisite plants in the courtyard, and everything of the best – and, as a fellow guest from Madrid remarks, far fewer pesetas than the other inns here. Thank you so much for mentioning it.

Soller is divine.[3] Words fail us to say how much we love it. You know it, so I won't describe it to you. But oh! I don't know which part is best, the streets of the town, or the sweet-smelling paths of the hills behind, or the little port, or the mountains, or the charming, kind, gentle, people (who have the extra grace of understanding my Spanish and talking a Spanish I can understand). Today we hired a horse and shay, and drove and walked to Valdemosa, past Deyà[4] and Miramar. Such exquisite views all the way. Valdemosa and Deyà are wonderful. To-morrow (Sunday) we hope to do your walk.[5] At odd moments we stroll through the streets and shop, go to the church, talk to the population, and climb the hill paths behind. It is all too heavenly for real life. On Monday we go to Pollensa, via Palma. Pollensa too is reported perfect.

How enchanting the people here are, aren't they – so courteous and gentle and helpful. In Barcelona they were noisy, rather, and grasping – but here they are angelic. If only they would learn better sanitary arrangements, they would lead the world in civilisation, we have decided. One doesn't ask for a chain to pull, but they might keep a can of water to pour. However, I will blame them for nothing.

We are infinitely happy. I wish you were here too. It is the perfect life. It is sad to think how soon it must end. There seem no other English in Soller – at least I think I saw two in the distance once, but they don't seem to be staying here. And there weren't many apparent in Palma. We get to Pollensa by train from Palma to Inca, and diligence[6] from Inca, which runs through Lluch. It will be a lovely journey.

Now I must get to bed. Isn't it lovely the way the torrent murmurs all night. And there are frogs in the hills. It's very like Varazze in some ways, you know. My dear love. R.

Margaret sends much love.[7]

1 The query is Rose's. Her word seems to be a conflation of the French *cabinets* and the Spanish *gabinete*, but the Spanish word, unlike the French, does not mean 'loo'.

2 Printed alongside the inn's address, at the head of the letter, is 'Vda. de Antonio Magraner'. Rose has not realised that Vda. is an abbreviation for Viuda, 'Widow'. The proprietress was already widowed when Jean stayed in the inn in 1919.

3 Sóller is where Mr Dobie in Rose's next novel, *Crewe Train*, goes to live after his wife's death (3–5), and where his daughter, Denham, and Arnold Chapel spend part of their honeymoon (126).

4 Deià; where Robert Graves went to live in 1929.

5 The walk, which Jean made with Regie on 11 April 1919, is described poetically and in detail in a journal she kept during their visit to Mallorca. It took them inland, first

up to Biniaraix and then up again, in the direction of Orient, until they reached the summit of a steep and lofty ridge and obtained a magnificent view.

6 Stagecoach.

7 Although only Margaret's love is sent, Jeanie was there too: see *LS* 28–29.

48

Beaconsfield.
7 May [1925][1]

My dearest Jean, Thank you for your two notes – the one I found when I came home, and the one to-day.

It is all too dazing still to write much – but you, who knew her, will understand. She loved you very much, you know, and always wanted to see you. She was like nothing on earth – all that love and life. Mothers are, I suppose; but she was intensified, somehow. To all of us home and love, and to me my intimate daily companion, and to everyone a kind of lamp of radiance. She loved living, but didn't mind dying either – you know her intense and vivid faith.

Well, we shall all get used to doing without her in time, but so far it seems a dizzy business looking ahead. It's Will's home winter, too – the poor darling.[2]

Anyhow, it wasn't the long drawn-out illness and helplessness she sometimes feared, and that it might have been. But just now small things seem to hurt rather a lot – as that we weren't with her for her last few weeks. If only we had known – but no-one could, of course. She made us go, and it was like her – but still it hurts rather.

But these are the small things, and don't really matter. My dear love. I rather dread to-morrow.[3]

R.

Father Cary wrote me such a kind note.

1 After the time in Mallorca with Margaret and Jeanie, Rose was with Gerald in Andorra and France and was contacted with difficulty when her mother suffered a heart attack on 2 May. She rushed home, but her mother was unconscious and died on 5 May.

2 Rose refers to the coming winter, when Will was to be home from Canada.

3 Grace's funeral took place in Great Shelford on 8 May. In his diary Edward Conybeare writes: 'Grace's last triumphal ride from Beaconsfield to Shelford there to lie by George. All went well, though cold and showery day.' Jean was among the mourners.

49

Dearest Jean

In clearing things up I came on this,[1] and will send it back now for fear of getting it mislaid, buried, or burnt in the bonfire in the field. Thank you so much for it: it afforded me much good reading in the island. I hope its condition has not much depreciated; it did a lot of travelling in a rucksa<c>k.

Margaret and Jeanie have gone back to work. M. comes down sometimes, and will till we let the house. The maids and Hooper[2] and I are desperately busy clearing out the house, burning rubbish (accumulations of over 40 years), disposing of jumble, rags and bones, getting chimneys swept, boilers mended, ceilings whitewashed, etc. etc. I am to and fro between here and the flat, but mostly here. I am too busy to think much, which is for the best: also it's best really to have the others gone, as it leaves more rooms free to be dealt with. It is a serious business, this clearing out for furnished letting, and involves much thought. More thought will occur in the winter when we resume the house again for 3 months or so and then finally sell it and find a cottage somewhere for some of the furniture and for a family resort where we can meet. But Will and Eleanor will have to be here for that, too.

A little later, when the stress lessens, I wish you would come for a night to the flat. Perhaps June is better than May, as now I can't easily make arrangements for nights away, not knowing when I may have to be here for something. I should so love to see you. My mind by then will, I hope, be a little restored and less chaotic. I am probably going down to Margaret, to All Saints House,[3] on Saturday or Sunday. Life is a tangle of complicated business, further increased by people's kindness in writing letters which must be answered. One is glad of the letters, though; so many people, even quite slight acquaintances, did so love her, and one likes that. And if there was nothing to do, the ache of it would be, I suppose, more than one could bear.

My dear love to you. I'm glad you loved her, and she you. She did, you know, a lot. So do I, always.

R.

1 The guide book to Mallorca lent by Jean.
2 The gardener/chauffeur.
3 The home of the East London Community of Deaconesses to which Margaret belonged. According to CBS 104 n. 2 and LeFanu 171, she retired in 1924, when the community was dissolved, but not only is she still living in its house, but Rose has spoken of her going back to work. However, four months later she is reported to have found a house in Petersfield (*L*55). In retirement she continued to wear her

religious habit–a practice that caused a difficulty when she was holidaying with Rose and Will in America in December 1929–February 1930: they had hoped to cross into Mexico, where anticlerical measures were in force, and frontier officials, believing that Margaret was a nun, refused her entry.

50

Hedgerley End,
Beaconsfield.
21 May [1925]

My dearest Jean

Did you mean it about Whitsun? If so, would you come and walk with me in the Cotswolds? More details when I know them – but we might meet at some station on Saturday, spend Sat: and Sunday nights somewhere, with rucksacks, home-hunting (with a view to our futures) and I'd have to get back here Monday evening.[1] This only if fine, of course. I think, though Whit, we could get taken in at inns all right, don't you? I will write again when I have time to look at maps – I have where I want to go in my head but not planned out yet. This is in haste for post. It would be lovely if you could come. We needn't do more walking than we want.

Much love. R.

P.S. We wondered if you would care to have a little copy of *The Imitation of Christ*[2] that mother used. She had several: this was given to her by Father in 1890. I am sure you have it already, but I think she would like you to have this one, and we would too. I am sending it by separate post.

1 In 1925 Whitsunday was 31 May.
2 A translation of Thomas à Kempis, *De imitatione Christi*. Rose had her own copy of the work, a present from a godmother when she was 13. In *LF* 97 she describes the strong impression it made on her at the time.

51

Hedgerley End,
Beaconsfield.
3 June [1925]

My Dearest Jean

How lovely to have *Essex*,[1] and how *nice* of you to think of it! I have had a read in it, and it is ever such nice country. I waver between Chipping Ongar and the Dunmow region. There seem plenty of Rodings to choose from.[2] Forthwith I shall trip there. Meanwhile, I shall take *Essex* to bed nightly.

Thank you for Whitting with me, my dear – I loved it. Let's do it again some-times. Meanwhile, we will meet on Monday the 15th or so, but that won't be moving, and not so good. You are good to move with – pace, desires, company, everything right and as it should be. Except that we ought really to have opposite biases, whereas we seem both to have one to the left, hence circles. I have been informed before that mine is to the left. I expect you caught yours from me. My friend Gerald rolls straight on and corrects mine, being very firm about direc-tions. But on the whole we did beautifully, and I did love it. Dorothy B[rooke] wants you to go to Mrs Strong's dinner. Do, and spend the night with me. It seems a duty.[3]

All my love. R.

1 Almost certainly J. Charles Cox, *Essex*, in Methuen's 'Little Guides' series, probably the third edition (London, 1919).

2 Abbess Roding, Aythorpe Roding, Beauchamp Roding, High Roding, Leaden Roding, Margaret Roding.

3 Eugénie Strong, archaeologist and Roman art historian, was assistant director of the British School at Rome from 1909 to 1925. Both her contract and that of Thomas Ashby, the School's Director since 1906, were terminated, in controversial circum-stances, with effect from 1 July 1925. The dinner, at the Cecil Hotel, Strand, on 14 July 1925, was to honour her on her departure from the post. Presided over by Herbert Asquith, former prime minister, it was attended by people prominent in politics and public affairs as well as in academic and cultural circles, and not only by Strong's friends and supporters but also, as she did not fail to notice, by some of those respon-sible for her dismissal, including Jean's uncle Arthur Hamilton Smith, Keeper of the Department of Greek and Roman Antiquities in the British Museum. The list of those present is preserved in Girton College Archives (GCPP Strong 6/3). Although Jean's name is on the list, Rose's is not. On Strong's life and career, see Stephen L. Dyson, *Eugénie Sellers Strong: Portrait of an Archaeologist* (London, 2004). Dorothy Brooke had classical and archaeological interests. After reading Classics at Newnham College, Cambridge, she had been a student of the British School at Athens (1910–1911) and lecturer in Classical Archaeology at Bryn Mawr College, Pennsylvania (1912–1913). In 1913–1914, when she had a travelling scholarship from Newnham, she returned to Greece and also visited Paris, Rome, and Turkey, studying in museums and visit-ing archaeological sites. Although she did not participate in any excavations after the Great War, she maintained her interest in the ancient world and produced two books. See, further, David W.J. Gill, '"The Passion of Hazard": Women at the British School at Athens Before the First World War', *Annual of the British School at Athens* 97 (2002) 491–510; 'Dorothy Lamb (1887–1967): A Pioneering Mediterranean Field-Archaeologist', in *Breaking Ground: Women in Old World Archaeology*, at: www.brown.edu/Research/Breaking_Ground/.

52

Hedgerley End,
Beaconsfield.
25 June 1925

Dearest Jean

Thanks so much for this[1] –most useful. It is a lovely county, isn't it.

This is our last week in the Old Home. I leave it finally next Wednesday,[2] and the problem of how to convey from it all I shall require for 6 months varied climes and occasions is serious. I expect I shall have to raid it secretly by night after Isaacs[3] are in residence.

I now go and count linen and put it in presses, etc. etc. Any news of the poems yet, I wonder? I expect not yet. Publishers have great deliberations as a rule. Much love. R.

1 The guide to Essex.
2 1 July.
3 Not the tenants' real name any more than Isaac Israel was the real name of Dorothy Gillum's expected baby (*L*29).

53

Kirnan,
Kilmichael Glassary,
Argyll.
28 July 1925

Dearest Jean

It is nice up here, and I wish you were here. The weather has been lovely, mostly, from my point of view, and n.g. for sport. No uncles but Uncle Regie, who is being a dear. The Impeys are here – he is a noisy, rude man, as you know, though very friendly. She is a nice quiet person whom I like.[1] Bill[2] came on Saturday: what a dear. And so engaging to look at. He is such a refreshing element in the party, and so nice to talk to. It is satisfactory getting to know one's cousins one by one.

We play rummy in the evenings for shilling stakes, as Uncle R. won't play for less (we'd prefer pennies) and we get slightly impoverished thereby, but what matter? Mr Impey is full of vulgar laugh and ill-bred chaff and if I were his wife I'd control him. I think he thinks that having been at school with Uncle R. excuses anything. However, he is a lively soul. To-day is chilly and wet, and only fit for arm-chairs and pen and paper. I am trying to get on with my novel,[3] having got the essays[4] safely off my hands before I left London. I leave here Friday, spend Sat: and Sunday nights in the flat, and start for Switzerland Monday. What are your plans?

I love walking about these hills, with the sun and shadows sweeping over them and the curlews crying – the quiet and peace makes London seem like a lunatic asylum. The only thing is, one can't, for long, do without one's fellow lunatics, who happen to be the people one really needs to see often. I wish some of them were here on the moors.

I hope you are happy, my dear, and well, as it leaves me at present. My love always.

ERM.

1 Edward Impey, a contemporary of R.H. Macaulay both at Eton and at King's College, Cambridge, was a master at Eton from 1884 to 1913. His obituary in *The Times* (7 January 1946, 7) describes him as 'an admirable schoolmaster' and emphasises the affection with which he was regarded by pupils and colleagues, but mentions that 'in his dealings with grown-ups his tongue could sometimes be a little trenchant and unguarded'. See also *L*40 and 54. He married Kathleen Austen-Leigh in 1891.

2 The third of Jean's five brothers, Bill Smith was educated at Shrewsbury School and the Royal Military College, Sandhurst. From 1916 he served on the Western Front as an officer in the Gloucestershire Regiment and was wounded three times. In 1919 he was a member of the British Military Mission to south Russia in support of the White Army forces commanded by General Anton Ivanovich Denikin. He also saw service on the north-west frontier of India. In 1921 he left the army and joined the Bombay Burmah Trading Corporation. He resigned from the BBTC at the beginning of 1929, whereupon he and his American wife (*L*54 n. 4) went to live in Massachusetts, first in Boston, then in Ipswich. He returned to Britain on his own in 1939 to undertake wartime duties (*L*79 n. 13). After the Second World War he became an American citizen. Among his writings were five novels published in the 1930s and *A Gardener's Dictionary of Plant Names* (New York, 1963).

3 *Crewe Train* (1926).

4 *A Casual Commentary.*

54

2, St. Andrews Mansions,
Dorset Street, W.1.
1 August 1925

My Dearest Jean

The mats are lovely, and quite the correct ideas for Andrew – thank you a lot. I got here this morning at 8, after not a bad train night,[1] and plunged into a hot bath, and immediately everyone came ringing at the door – the postman, the porter, and I don't know who else – so I had to leap in and out of the water like a porpoise: – the one drawback, this, of being servantless and alone. Opening the front door an inch I stretched a naked and dripping arm to receive their offerings, and plunged below water again leaving no trace but a bubble. I feel restored now, but very sleepy. I go to Switz: on Monday.

What made F.S. turn down the poems?[2] Weren't they enough in bulk, I wonder, or does he not wish for religion, or what does he feel? I'm rather sorry about it – he is a nice publisher, but stupid. What next? What of Constable? Or Methuen? Tell me sometime what you think. Or should you write a few more first, do you think?

I'll send you p.c.'s from Switzerland and tell you what it's like – rather fussy, I expect it may be. But very beautiful. I go 1st to Mürren, then to Maloja.[3] Back here about the 23rd, when Margaret joins me in Andrew's for a little while.

I am hoping to be introduced to Bill's young lady then, if they go to town en route for her return to America. I am very much interested in that – I gather she is charming. So is he, so that's all right.[4]

He hadn't yet told Uncle Regie when I came away, but was going to, with some trepidation as to the comments that might greet the news. I do hope the uncle will be nice about it – after all, it really isn't his affair. And he's extraordinarily kind, beneath all that nagging that sometimes is tiresome.

He was very sweet this time, mostly. Kirnan was a lovely comedy – the absurd Mr Impey, and his effect on everyone separately. He drives Bill rather wild sometimes. And me too sometimes, and Margaret when he says to her 'You may be very holy and all that, but . . .' He is a silly old ass. But it was nice there – the heavenly hills and walks, and Uncle R. being funny and absurd, and Bill with his infectious laugh and nice face, and lots of time to talk for Margaret and me, which we used well. I hope your time in Inverness will be as good. Where shall you be in early Sept: and late August? You might let me know sometime – either here, to await return, or to the Palace Hotel, Maloja, between the 8th and 14th. After 14th I shall be wandering about rather.[5]

My love always, and grateful thanks. R

1 Overnight train from Glasgow.
2 Frank Sidgwick, co-director of Sidgwick & Jackson Ltd, had published poetry of Rupert Brooke as well as Rose's first volume of poetry, *The Two Blind Countries* (1914). The letter (24 July 1925) rejecting Jean's poetry survives among her papers. Reading the poems had given them 'a great pleasure, very unusual in the ordinary course of reading MSS. of poetry. But it appears commercially hopeless to attempt to launch a new poet.'
3 Together with Gustav Holst, the composer, Rose was accompanying a Lunn tour as a lecturer, but, after fulfilling this commitment, met up with Gerald.
4 Bill had recently become engaged to Isadore Leighton Luce of Portsmouth, New Hampshire. They were to be married in Bombay on 16 December 1926. She became an expert on early American gardens, about which she published three books and

many articles. She wrote under the name of Ann Leighton. On her wartime book, *While We Are Absent*, see *L*79 and n. 10 there.

5 Rose might have added 'and with Gerald'!

55

My Dearest Jean

This with my love and greetings and a tile stand for kettle or tea-pot, which may go off to you either to-day or to-morrow, as I'm not sure if they've finished it yet. I'm sending it to the Press,[1] which seems inappropriate, because Bill says you've left 204 Iffley Road, and I'm not sure of the other address he suggested, nor, I think, was he.[2] He says you have Jim with you – how is he?[3] I'd love to see him again – also you.

I expect you got a letter I wrote to you from Switzerland, in reply to yours, and caused to be posted at Coire by a porter – if you didn't, by any chance, you might tell me, as with it I posted another, which I rather wanted to arrive, and I'm not sure has – the porter offered to take them for me as there wasn't time to get out, and I'm not sure what the cupidity of French[4] porters may not lead to. But I expect they were both all right.[5]

Switzerland was glorious, and great fun, and after it I explored Normandy for a time, which I loved. I didn't know before how charming the little old villages and towns were, with their mediaeval timbered houses and narrow streets, and 14th century farm-houses standing among orchards. I went to Bec, Bernay, Lisieux, etc. I was at Lisieux on a bad day – the festival of a horrid little new saint they've made – Thérèse – an idiotic little nun, smirking to heaven and clasping roses.[6] She seems to have quite superseded the B[lessed] V[irgin] M[ary] in Norman favour just now.

After I got back, I was first at Deal with Jeanie, then Margaret was with me here, house-hunting. I think she's found a home at Petersfield – a rather lovely place, and a nice conveniently sized house for herself and friend and spare room for family and room for Hedgerley End furniture, which is what she wanted.[7]

Since she left me I've been very busy with proofs of the essays and a smother of tiresome articles for various destinies – including one I am now struggling with for the Glasgow Rectorial magazine to help G K Chesterton to be elected Rector![8] I am tired of all this, and want to write my novel, but can't get onto it.

It was great fun last night, Bill and his young lady and I dined together and went to *Hay Fever*.[9] She is very charming, isn't she. I saw her before this, of course. I like to see her and Bill together – such a pretty pair! Bill is a dear – I'm glad she is going to Oxford.[10]

I must stop and work. You know how I love you, and wish you all the best things this year and all the years. Love to Jim too, please. Bless you always.

R.

1 Clarendon Press, Oxford. The gift is for Jean's 34th birthday.
2 Jean had moved to 188 Iffley Road.
3 Jim had just come back from his first tour of duty in Nigeria. Physically, he was rather run down, and he remained in England until March 1926.
4 A slip: Coire (Chur) is in Switzerland.
5 The letter to Jean is not preserved.
6 St Thérèse of Lisieux, a Carmelite nun, had been canonised by Pope Pius XI on 17 May 1925. The celebration witnessed by Rose cannot have been to mark her Feast Day, which is 1 October. She was clasping roses, because, in reference to favours promised to those who sought her intercession, she said: 'I will let fall a shower of roses.' She is the patron saint of florists. Sheila Kaye-Smith, who with her husband built a small Catholic church, dedicated to her, in the grounds of their home near Northiam in East Sussex, writes about her in *Quartet in Heaven* (London, 1952). Rose's and Gerald's visit to Lisieux is recalled in 'Miss Anstruther's Letters' (Bibliog. 7.I) 307: 'Lisieux, with ancient crazy-floored inn, huge four-poster, and preposterous little saint (before the grandiose white temple in her honour had arisen on the hill outside the town)'.
7 The house was called Heathlands.
8 Chesterton was not elected. There were three candidates. Austen Chamberlain topped the poll with 1,242 votes. Chesterton was second with 968, Sidney Webb a poor third with 285.
9 Comedy by Noel Coward. It opened at the Ambassadors Theatre on 8 June and was transferred to the Criterion Theatre, Piccadilly, on 7 September.
10 'Going to Oxford', in the sense of visiting it.

56

This letter is incomplete: the beginning, occupying at least two sides, is missing, and so is the end.

[Late September (?) 1925][1]

. . . What about the poems? I think I suggested Constable in my last letter[2] – what about it? Have you done any more, or completed more. I do want them out – I love them so much. Sidgwick & Jackson are feeling cautious, I suppose, and they are always rather hard-up, not being commercial publishers. Constable might be better, and Michael Sadleir[3] is a nice person. I wonder what stage you are in about them.

Shall I see you soon? Aren't you and Jim coming up to see the metropolis? I've been treated by a dentist for teeth and by an osteopath for spine – (I mean, I am being treated for spine now) so am doing very well. I went to the ost: for a pain in the hip, and he said my spine curved to the right and shouldn't, so he thinks he is putting it straight, I don't know if he really is.

He says it was probably infantile bronchitis <that> began it – it doesn't seem to have hampered me much in a long and active career. However, he says it will, if neglected. I should be sorry for that, so must see it doesn't.

The Brookes and I are starting a tennis club, to play in the Parks – do you know of anyone who'd join? (Not too good, but good enough). . .[4]

1 This fragment is later, but probably only a little later, than *L*55.
2 Rose mentioned Constable, as well as Methuen, in Letter 54. That was not her last letter; indeed, given that a letter Rose wrote to Jean from Switzerland (see *L*54) is missing, it was not even her last letter but one. There are two possibilities: either Rose's memory was at fault, or she suggested Constable again in another missing letter.
3 Sadleir, mentioned also in Letter 60, joined Constable in 1912. He became a director in 1920 and chairman in 1954. He was a notable book-collector and bibliographer, and he wrote novels, the most popular of which was *Fanny by Gaslight* (London, 1940).
4 Dorothy Brooke's diary reveals that Rose stayed with her from 11 to 14 September, and that there was much playing of tennis – all day on the 12th and in the morning of the 13th. This well suits the proposed dating of this letter.

57

2 St. Andrews [Mansions]
3 November 1925

Dearest Jean

Thank you so much for yours. I'm glad you like the *Commentary*.[1] I hope people will find it helpful.

I'm glad to say Uncle Regie seemed quite pleased at having it his book[2] – I should never dare to dedicate a novel to him! Unless a detective story or something similar. But these light musings on life are different. I dined there last night and met a nice gardening girl called Colvin.[3]

I got a bad shock last week on reading in *The Daily News* that Madeleine Symons had married Will Thorne![4] The most incredible feature in the amazing case was that they were going to live at Hammersmith – I concluded Madeleine had gone insane, to be not only marrying poor old Will Thorne but to be leaving the Adelphi for Hammersmith.[5] I was greatly relieved to see the withdrawal next day. Did you hear of the affair? It was all so very circumstantial and detailed.[6]

'Beds and 'Omes'[7] I wrote somewhere about 1919, when the muzzling order was on[8] – it came out in some weekly, I forget which. He was a touching old man, and I was sorry for him – it was all just as I said, and the authorities were all so pained and stern at the idea of 'sleeping rough'. It is an odd world.

It is nice to have Jim about the place. We are going to a play together next week, and this Thursday (I hope) to see *The Gold Rush*,[9] dine here after it, together with the Brookes, and proceed, if we still have energy, to Naomi's in the Temple.[10] I haven't yet had his assent to this, but I hope he'll be able.

I was sorry about the 27th, but felt that you were wise. Are you very much rushed with books? I wonder if the packers' strike is interfering much with Christmas books.[11] Don't work too hard, will you. Is there any chance of your coming up at all this month, I wonder? And how is the Rome plan progressing?[12]

I sat at table with Prof. Murray last Tuesday (to-day in the room with him, but different tables). He complained that he seldom saw you. I said you were very busy, and that I didn't either much. He spoke to-day, on the Pact – very nice, as usual.[13]

Isn't it pleasant warm November weather, full of chrysanthemums. I'm so glad. My love always. R.

1 *A Casual Commentary*, published by Methuen on 29 October 1925, contains 40 short essays.

2 The dedication in *A Casual Commentary* is: 'To R.H.M.'.

3 Brenda Colvin, aged 28 when Rose met her at Regi's house in Eton Avenue, was born in India. In or about 1922, after studies at a horticultural college, she set up her own garden-design business. Over the years she established a national and indeed international reputation as an architect not only of gardens but also of landscapes. She undertook numerous projects for private customers and public bodies and wrote *Trees for Town and Country* (London, 1947) and *Land and Landscape* (London, 1948). It is likely that Regi was consulting her mainly about his fine garden at Kirnan in Argyllshire. His speciality was rock plants and alpines. He was a pioneer in the creation of hybrid gentians, one of which bears his name: *gentiana macaulayi*. Details are given by Jim Jermyn, *The Himalayan Garden: Growing Plants from the Roof of the World* (Portland, 2001) 195–196.

4 Will Thorne, trade union leader and Labour politician, was aged 68, Madeleine 30.

5 The Adelphi, the famous development (begun in 1769) of the four Adam brothers, between the Strand and Victoria Embankment, includes Buckingham Street, where Madeleine was living at no. 14.

6 The reports in *The Daily News* are in the issues of 28 and 29 October 1925, in each case on p. 7. The first report is headed: 'WILL THORNE'S WEDDING. SURPRISE FOR HIS COLLEAGUES. MARRIED TO MISS M. SYMONS, J.P.' Occupying almost a complete column, it describes how the previous day Thorne had sent messages to meetings of the General Council of the Trade Union Congress and West Ham Town Council, informing them that he could not be present because he was getting married that morning. In neither message did he name his bride, but *The Daily News* had been informed by 'a friend of Mr. Thorne' that she was 'Miss Madeleine Symons, a Justice of the Peace for London, and a well-known woman trade union leader.' Information about Madeleine's age, education, career, and character follows. In the second report, under the headline 'WILL THORNE'S WEDDING. THE

IDENTITY OF THE BRIDE', *The Daily News* prints a letter of complaint from Madeleine's solicitors and, in response to it, states that it 'deeply regrets having published the statement complained of, which is recognised to be without foundation, and offers to Miss Symons the most sincere apologies for any inconvenience she has been caused'. It goes on to reveal that the bride was actually Rebecca Cecilia Sinclair, aged 46, and, quickly recovering from its embarrassing gaffe, gives its readers a spirited account of her big day, the most sensational snippet of information being that she was a Conservative. When she died the following year, Thorne was widowed for the third time, but he was survived by his fourth wife, Beatrice Nellie Collins, whom he married in 1930.

7 *A Casual Commentary* 158–162.

8 The reference is to the trouble that delayed the publication of *What Not* (*L3* n. 17).

9 Charlie Chaplin film (1924). It was showing at Tivoli in the Strand.

10 At this time Naomi was living at 2 Mitre Court, just off the south side of Fleet Street. In her diary Dorothy Brooke confirms that the party made it there on 5 November, but is unenthusiastic about the evening: 'Dined with Rose and Jim at Maple Tree, went to Naomi. Very dull.' The restaurant, actually the Rowan Tree, was close to Rose's flat (*L45* n. 3). Except that the title of a book by Naomi is given in *L73*, this is the last mention of her in Rose's surviving letters to Jean. The friendship between the two women was soon to come under some strain. Rose's biographers mention a row provoked by Naomi's alleged indiscretion about Rose and Gerald. According to CBS 102, 'at some point during the first half of the 1920s . . . Rose and Naomi had a violent quarrel'. LeFanu (154) describes 'a painful break-up', placing it 'some time in the mid-1920s', probably around the time that Rose's *Crewe Train* appeared. That novel was published in October 1926. On the 26th of that month Rose wrote to Sylvia Lynd complaining that Naomi had written to say that one of the characters in the book, Evelyn Gresham, a romantic novelist whose aptitude for fiction is manifested not only in her writings but also in everyday life, was 'a portrait of Mrs Garvin'. Rose denies that Mrs Gresham, described in the novel as 'an incurable gossip, a sympathetic and intelligent scandal-monger' (196), is a portrait of Mrs Garvin, adding: 'As to scandal-mongering, Naomi does much more of that herself.' The implication seems to be that Mrs Gresham is more similar to Naomi than to Mrs Garvin. Mrs Garvin is Viola, the second wife of J.L. Garvin, editor of *The Observer* from 1908 to 1942, and the stepmother of Rose's friend Viola Gerard Garvin, literary editor of *The Observer* from 1926 to 1942. (LeFanu, as her index entry confirms, is under the misapprehension that 'Mrs Garvin' is the younger Viola, who never married.) Although Rose and Naomi continued to keep in touch, their friendship was never again as close as it had been in earlier times, and, in a letter of 20 September 1943 (ERM 15.173) to the younger Viola Garvin, Naomi reveals a surprising degree of resentment towards Rose and several of those with whom Rose associated, including Viola herself. Viola, who was about to give a talk to the English Association on 'Two *Observer* reviewers: Gerald Gould and Humbert Wolfe', had asked Naomi to communicate some recollections of them. Naomi refused: 'Alas! Your letter has called up the Bruno Walter dinner-party and the awful pencil game you and Rose and Humbert and the Lynds organized against my novel *The Bridge* on the eve of publication and the *Observer* review

by Elizabeth Bibesco of *Jake* – all things against which I have tried to raise a wall of oblivion, letting my acquaintanceship with all of you begin *after* these horrors. So I can't delve into the days when I was useful enough to Humbert and to Rose for them to play at being friends.' Interestingly, Naomi's bitter (and, in Viola's opinion (ERM 15.174), highly inaccurate) recollection is of events not in the 1920s but in the 1930s. Contrary to the impression given by some of Rose's biographers, there was, it seems, never a complete rift between the two women. Naomi's diaries and Rose's letters to her show that they continued to meet. Shortly after the publication of *Crewe Train* and the writing of Rose's letter to Sylvia Lynd, the two (Rose and Naomi) had lunch together (16 November 1926), and three days later Naomi and her fiancé, Ernest Milton, were guests at a dinner party given by Rose.

11 A strike of packers and porters employed by publishers began on 31 October 1925 and dragged on into 1926.

12 Jean and Jim visited Italy for three weeks in December 1925. As well as going to Rome, they met up with Fr Lucius Cary, who was convalescing in Sorrento, and afterwards spent Christmas in Florence (ERM 13.167).

13 The security pact agreed at the Locarno Conference (5–16 October 1925). Murray, as Chairman of the Executive of the League of Nations Union, welcomed it. His talk on 3 November was to the Grotius Society in Gray's Inn.

58

Beacs.
30 January 1926

Dearest Jean

Thank you so much for yours, which finds me immersed in the chaos of last days – vans about to run off in all directions laden with objects for all our different homes.

We have had an arduous job breaking up the home and choosing its contents – books were the worst, as we knew we must part with a lot, so went through them sheeping and goating them, meaning to goat herds and herds – but, as it took 5 votes[1] to make a goat and only one to make a sheep, it didn't fall out quite as we had hoped. 'Ninety and nine lay safe in the fold',[2] – but *what* fold we cannot yet imagine! However, Petersfield[3] will really take a good lot and Andrew's more than you'd think. The move occurs actually on Monday.[4] Margaret, Will and Eleanor then are off to Petersfield in the car (which Will has retrieved and drives), and I stay like Casabianca on the wreck while fragments strew the sea,[5] and go up to Andrew's late in the day to recoup. Will and Eleanor will be to and fro till March 20th or so, between Petersfield and me, and the various visits they're proposing – I don't yet know quite which week-ends I'll have, both because of this and because I've promised all I can manage to Petersfield while he is there.[6] But there are sure to be some free ones, which I will know about as time goes on, and I would simply love you to come – or any other times you could. This next one I am booked for – I wanted to go to Petersfield for it, but unfortunately have someone staying for Saturday night.

Do make the Press send you up to the B[ritish] M[useum].

Where is Jim? Is he at Exmouth, taking care of his nephew and nieces,[7] or with you? We've had 2 uncles and 1 aunt[8] over here, selecting a few books – priceless people.

Have you read *The Cantab*, by Shane Leslie? Uncle Willie comes in, and all the King's people – otherwise, however, it isn't v.g. Uncle W. is well done, though only very briefly – he emerges as very attractive and like himself.[9]

I feel you were very right to leave 188 Iffley Rd – I always thought it a mistake, living in the house with someone not a great friend, with whom you may, nevertheless, have to be companionable. I know I could never do it – but then, I am more of a Diogenes than you, I fancy. Living Alone – it is a great and important thing – unless one can be living with precisely the right person or persons. Anyhow, I gather you are only temporarily settled so far: I hope you will find something nearer in time.

I am lamentably behind in my profession, alas, having idled (literarily speaking) since before Xmas, and now must work like niggers and try and get the novel[10] finished and a thousand articles written.

All my love to you – and do come up soon. I'll write again when I know more about week-ends.

R.

1 The votes of Rose, Margaret, Jeanie, Eleanor, and Will. Rose wrote from Hedgerley End to Katharine Tynan Hinkson on 7 January: 'All this month I am down here, with my brother and sisters, very busy sorting, dividing and disposing of our household goods, as we have sold the house from the end of January. It is a melancholy job' (KTH 1/656/9).

2 Cf. Luke 15.4, but Rose is recalling Elizabeth Clephane, *The Lost Sheep*: 'There were ninety-and-nine that safely lay | In the shelter of the fold; | But one was out in the hills away, | . . .'

3 Margaret's house.

4 1 February 1926.

5 During the Battle of the Nile on 1 August 1798 Giacomo Jocante de Casabianca perished with his father, Louis, who, to avoid surrender to Nelson, blew up his ship after the crew had been saved. The act of heroism is the theme of Felicia Hemans's poem 'Casabianca', first published in the second edition of *The Forest Sanctuary and Other Poems* (1829). Rose is echoing the first stanza and the last line of the penultimate stanza: 'The boy stood on the burning deck | Whence all but he had fled; | The flame that lit the battle's wreck | Shone round him o'er the dead' (1–4); 'There came a burst of thunder-sound – | The boy – oh! where was he? | Ask of the winds that far around | With fragments strewed the sea!' (33–36).

6 'He' is of course Will. Originally Rose started the sentence 'Will will be to and fro' and inserted 'and Eleanor' afterwards. It's clear too that she originally wrote '. . . the various visits he's proposing'. To complete the correction of the sentence, she should have ended: 'to Petersfield while they are there'. The focus on Will and the mention of Eleanor as an afterthought reflect the priority her brother had over Eleanor in her mind and heart. As a child, Eleanor was largely excluded from the family circle (Introd. I.1), and, although Rose was undoubtedly unhappy about her sister's treatment in childhood, the two never became close.

7 Anne, Kenneth, and Helen Gillum, who were being looked after in Exmouth by Jean's parents while their mother, Dorothy, was out in India with their father. The enquiry about Jim taking care of them may be slightly mischievous, given that, despite being a kind uncle, he never exhibited any inclination or capacity to take care of small children.

8 Mary Macaulay and two of the three Macaulay uncles (Willie, Kenneth, Regi).

9 *The Cantab* (London, 1926) is a novel describing the experiences of a Cambridge undergraduate. The author (real name John Randolph Leslie) read Classics at King's College, Cambridge, in 1904–1907. W.H. Macaulay appears as 'Mr. MacKennon', the Tutor of King's (57–58, 174–175, 202).

10 *Crewe Train.* On 26 March 1997 Judge William Crawford QC was formally rebuked by the Lord Chancellor, Lord Mackay of Clashfern, for saying 'work like niggers', on the ground that 'use of such expressions is likely to give offence and did, in fact, give offence to members of the ethnic minorities'. However, to criticise Rose for an expression that was widely used in her day without any intention to make a racial slur would be anachronistic.

59

St A[ndrew]'s [Mansions]
1 July [1926]

Dearest Jean

Many thanks for the cheque. Yes, let us go and eat again at Tina's.[1] Perhaps next spring?

I like to plan exploits with you for next spring, somehow: it reduces the sense of impending doom.[2] I like to think, also, that if one does at each moment what seems the thing to do, it's bound to come out all right. And I feel you've got your thing to do now, without prejudice to the future. In that way, these steps are wiser and less rash than matrimony, say, which, though not necessarily permanent, is so much so as to leave bad scars behind when renounced. This may be for life, for years, or for a month, equally rightly and fitly. Anyway, I expect you know what's the thing to do, bless you always.[3]

I dined last night with Roger Hinks – nice child – and went to the [Royal] Academy [of Arts] Soirée with him.[4] He is rather sweet. I said I had lived in Italy as a child. How exciting, he said, those Garibaldi times must have been! I protested that the Garibaldi times were in the 60's, but when one is that age I don't think it makes much difference – past times are all one.

My love always, my dear. It was good to see you.

R.

1 Tina is Christian Anne Curror, one of the proprietresses of the Rowan Tree (*L*45 n. 3; 57 n. 10). It is likely that Jean timed her visit to Rose to coincide with attendance at the bicentenary celebration, in the cloisters of Westminster Abbey on 24 June, of the foundation of the Godolphin School, Salisbury.

2 The reference here and below is to Jean's intention to enter an Anglican convent – an intention she fulfilled in June 1927. She left the Clarendon Press in July 1926.

3 Gilbert Murray's reaction to Jean's decision had some similarities to Rose's. In a letter to her of 24 September 1926 he wrote: 'It is hard to hold out against your letter. Indeed it – I will not say, converts me, but – makes me wonder whether, after all, you may be more right than I and the rest of the world. All I should say is: If the door does not seem, after trial, to lead into the Garden, do not feel that you are eating your words or failing in your purpose if you turn back and try other doors. There is so little clear light anywhere, but remember that you have the love of M[ary] and me always with you.'

4 The Royal Academy of Arts soirée was at Burlington House, Piccadilly. Roger Hinks was the elder son of Arthur Robert Hinks, astronomer and geographer, and his wife, Lily Mary. In 1926 he was appointed Assistant Keeper in the Department of Greek and Roman Antiquities in the British Museum – a post in which he remained until 1939. He then went to the Warburg Institute, and in 1942 to the British Embassy in Stockholm as second secretary. He wrote on Caravaggio as well as on ancient art. His first book was a joint enterprise with Naomi Royde-Smith: *Pictures and People: A Transatlantic Criss-cross Between Roger Hinks in London and Naomi Royde-Smith in New York, Boston, Philadelphia During the Months of January, February, March 1930* (London, 1930).

60

10, St. Andrews Mansions,[1]
Dorset Street, W.1
11 January 1927

Dearest Jean

Thank you for sending the poems.[2] I only remember (I think) seeing one of them before – 'Whitehall Gardens [Floodtide]', which I like much. 'Paschal New Moon [in March]' is a lovely thing – the best of all, I think – really exquisite.

Am I wrong, I wonder, in thinking that 'Flight from Cologne' would be better <for>[3] a word of explanation at its head?[4] Unless you can get it into the lines somewhere, but I think you can't. Few people will remember, at the moment of reading it, that he was escaping with his translation – and it makes it better to know it. In itself, it is admirable, particularly the river and the rowing – though I'm not sure (are you?) that 'bringing strong, Blown from Arcturus on the upstream wind, The bells' etc. goes well – but this may be all right after a moment's reflection.[5] But what an effect of dark and wind and river and bells and haste in the night – very good indeed.

'Cambridge [from the Oxford Road]' is delightful. So is 'Turris Davidica', though less un-ordinary. 'Bugles' I am inclined to share your view of![6] Pleasant, but much what appears quite often in the *Mercury* and other magazines, merely written because someone has heard a sound or seen a sight that moved them less to thought than to a record of their impressions. All right, but not good enough for you. On the other hand, another sight ('[Whitehall Gardens,] Flood Tide') emerges as something very attractive and alive. I love the boats 'lowing all together' down the ebb. As I say, I've seen this before and liked it.

'Challenge' and 'The Life-time' moved me very much, and I can't think of them objectively as verse – only as further evidence that you have to do what you mean to do.[7]

Well, I shall be very proud that they will be dedicated to me: I do hope Constable will take them. If they should boggle at the tone of some of them ('– as much religion as my William likes'[8] is what they *may* want, and no more; and I imagine that Michael Sadleir, anyhow, is an agnostic) – if they should, I suppose you may have to try some publisher who is *not* an agnostic, such as Faber & Gwyer (?)[9] or Longmans. Both these are quite good; but after all, there is no reason why Constable's should feel this. The mass of the poems are lay. When do you send them?

Have a good time in the blessed island.[10] I'm sorry it was put off, and for the reason. Poor Tom, what bad luck.[11] Did I say we lunched together before Xmas? I loved it; and him. I hope to see him again soon after he is about and back at work. My love to him, please, and I hope he's recovering, and that no-one else will get it. Hadn't you and Uncle Charlie better flee at once – quick, quick, like Tyndale?[12]

The Brookes and E.V. Knoxes are going to Banyul<s>[13] (close to Collioure and Port-Vendres), a sea place near the Spanish frontier. They wanted me to go too, but I can't just now. I am of the school of thought which goes abroad when abroad is best, not when England is worst. I was at Collioure in August – an exquisite coloured fishing-port piled above a bay.[14] Send me p.c.'s of Mallorca. And, if it comes in handy, give my love (best brand) to Fr. Cary.

I supped with the Hinkses on Sunday, and went on to a party to meet Sara Allgood and Maire O'Neill – enchanting women.[15] I liked the Hinks family, especially Mr H. and the schoolboy.[16] Mrs H. I'm sure is nice, but with a touch of the blight which sometimes descends on matrons – that nameless blight, what is it? A quenching of some spark of life – or was it never lit? When I'm with girls – all alive and keen and jolly – I feel sometimes quite moved for them, to think that perhaps they will take the blight sometime. But perhaps they won't; the best don't, of course; only those whose spark is mainly youngness and high spirits. That seems to go out, but not real intelligence and humour, which lasts.

Your family in Bombay seems to be being very good to Eleanor.[17] She has had a wretched time, poor dear, but I hope is mending now.

I had a nice yokel Xmas, walking all over Hants, Surrey, and Sussex. I lunched with the Squires and dandled Julia, who is exquisite (aged 10 months).[18] Other free meals I secured, – tramping over three counties, and I was given a globe of the world, and some 6 in: scale maps of Hants – *so* nice. Every ditch revealed. The wayfaring woman tho' a fool shall not err.[19]

My love and thanks, I do love your poetry.

R.

1 For Rose's move from 2 St Andrews Mansions to no. 10, see *L*43 n. 4.

2 A preliminary version of *Shepherd of Souls*.

3 Rose has written 'of'.

4 The published version has the note '(*Tyndale, December 1525*)' below the title. William Tyndale had gone to Cologne to have his translation of the New Testament printed, but the printer had not yet reached the end of St Matthew's gospel when, after the hostile intervention of the anti-Lutheran Cochlaeus (Johann Dobneck), work was stopped. Late in 1525 Tyndale fled south up the Rhine to Worms and got the work printed there in 1526.

5 The published version has 'still' for 'strong'.

6 The poem is among Jean's papers, but not in *Shepherd of Souls*.

7 Neither of the poems mentioned here is in *Shepherd of Souls*, but 'Challenge' is pre-served among Jean's papers, with a note indicating that it was composed in 1917 and revised in 1926.

8 The quotation is from a letter, dated 29 June 1784, from Hannah Godwin to her brother William. She is reciting the 'internal accomplishments' of a Miss Gay, who, she thinks, would be a suitable wife for him. The original reads: 'with about as much religion . . .'. The letter was published by Charles Kegan Paul, *William Godwin: His Friends and Contemporaries* (London, 1876) I 30–31, and Hannah's advice became more widely known through Robert Louis Stevenson's quotation of it in *Virginibus Puerisque, and Other Papers* (London, 1881) ch. 1, pt. 1.

9 The query is Rose's.

10 Mallorca. Jean revisited it and Spain with her father in February–March 1927.

11 Tom Smith, the eldest of Jean's brothers, spent his career in the Royal Navy. He had been promoted to lieutenant-commander in 1924 and was now taking a course at the Royal Naval College, Greenwich. Rose comments 'Poor Tom' because he had been suffering from influenza, but he was soon to be happy Tom, for on 16 January he became engaged to Prue Martin, the younger daughter of a doctor in Exmouth.

12 'Quick, quick' is a recurring phrase in Jean's 'Flight from Cologne'.

13 Rose writes 'Bannyul (?)'.

14 Rose revisited Collioure, probably, as on her first visit, with Gerald, in September

1938 (*L*77). The visits are recalled in 'Miss Anstruther's Letters' (Bibliog. I.7) 306: 'the little harbour at Collioure, with its painted boats'; and the place is the setting of the first chapters of *The World My Wilderness* (1950).

15 Sara (Rose writes 'Sarah') Allgood and Maire O'Neill were brilliant Irish actresses. Maire was Sara's younger sister and adopted her pseudonym to distinguish herself from Sara. Her first name was Mary, but she was usually called Molly, while Sara was called Sally. They were in London for a revival of the triumphant 1925 production of Sean O'Casey's *Juno and the Paycock*. It was to open at the Criterion Theatre on 24 January, with Sara playing Juno Boyle, Maire Maisie Madigan, and Maire's second husband, Arthur Sinclair, Jack Boyle (the Paycock). When *The Times* reviewed the original production at the Royalty Theatre, it called them 'an incomparable trio' (18 November 1925, 12).

16 On the Hinks family, see *L*59 n. 4. 'The schoolboy' is David, who was a month short of his fourteenth birthday. He became Junior Bursar of Trinity College, Cambridge.

17 Jean's family in Bombay comprised Dorothy and Sid Gillum, and Bill and Isadore Smith. Henry Smith (*L*61) was also in India, but probably in Calcutta. In later years he was to be very supportive of Eleanor and her work.

18 Jack and Eileen Squire lived at Frith Cottage, Bowlers Green, in the Surrey village of Thurley. Julia, born on 25 February 1926, was their only daughter. After studying at the Central School of Arts and Crafts in London, she worked on many films as a costume designer. She was working on her first major film, *The Magic Box*, in 1950, when she married the actor George Baker, with whom she had four daughters. The marriage was dissolved in 1974. Eileen Squire's third name was Anstruther, and it is possible that it inspired the title of Rose's 'Miss Anstruther's Letters'. The author's corrected typescript of the story (ERM 5.4) reveals that she had first intended to call the woman 'Miss Ashley', perhaps taking the name from Ashley Court, the building in which Jean had her London flat at the time.

19 An adaptation of Isaiah 35.8: 'The wayfaring men, though fools, shall not err therein.'

61

10 St Andrews [Mansions].
18 June 1927

My dearest Jean

Thank you more than I can tell you for your letter. I don't feel that it is, so to speak, answerable, in any sense of the word – but to be kept. All this terrific tangle and wilderness – does the way lead out of it into something alive, or only, as it now feels, into a dark void, I wonder. Anyhow I suppose that should make no difference to the way itself.[1]

Well, Fr. Cary wrote to me (before I wrote) and proposed calling on Tuesday afternoon, which was extraordinarily nice of him. I shall like to see him very much.[2]

As to Henry,[3] I loved him. He was *so* charming and gentle and (as you say) precise. A lovely sort of rationality and fastidious *niceness* – and, I do think, with a touch of Uncle Willie – (don't tell him I said so, he mightn't like it). But I did like him, and hope to meet him again in the autumn. What a nice family you are, aren't you.

I feel pleased about the Poems. C.W.[4] might be wrong about their saleability, even. They are more attractive than his – much – so might attract more, tho' this doesn't always follow. I do hope they'll take trouble with them. I hope you suggested to them the vase-drawing: why not?[5]

About my dedication – is it initials only, or name? Unless you think initials more chaste (I admit I have always used them) it would make me proud to have Rose Macaulay in full[6] – but this is your affair, and I should like either. I shall love that book. Tell the Press to be as quick as they can with the proofs, if I am to do them, which I should like very much (unless Fairacres[7] will let you yourself). I shall be abroad from mid-July for three weeks, then here for a while, then Petersfield – but at Petersfield I could do proofs as well as here, of course, only not in Switzerland. You will tell them what you want by way of type etc. And I *hope* they'll let you do the proofs because not to do the proofs of one's own poems would be heart-breaking, and the theme of them wouldn't at all be incongruous with your way of life – in fact, would well fit in. But if not, I shall cleave meticulously to your script, so it will be all right.

Perhaps as well not trouble Dorothy with advances. Especially as Henry tells me that they will be at Reigate and I expect the children will seldom come up to London. Perhaps some day when I'm walking in Surrey or something I'll call and see them all.[8]

By dint of being in Switzerland this year, I shall miss Kirnan. Mr Ford has just gone there. Uncle Regie does manage to collect a set of tiresome old men about him, somehow. Why, I wonder?[9]

Darling, I do love you a great deal. I'm not sure where you are this week, but send this to Clent. My blessings and thanks.

R.

1   Jean, who was to enter the Anglican convent at Fairacres, Oxford, in a few days' time, evidently commented in her letter on the matter about which Rose had recently confided in her during a weekend of walking on the Chilterns – her relationship with Gerald – and assured her that she would be in her prayers. Rose's confession to Jean and her request for her prayers are mentioned by Jean in a letter of 8 February 1972 (ERM 4.208) to Constance Babington Smith, who had brought Rose's affair with Gerald to public attention ten years earlier. Jean never revealed to anyone the secret with which she had been entrusted.

2   It looks as though Jean had mentioned to Lucius Cary, the Father Director of Fairacres, that Rose would like to see him. It is not clear, from Rose's report in *L63*, how much she told him about her situation.

3   Jean's youngest brother, aged 25 at this time. Educated at Shrewsbury School, he had

joined the Bombay Company in India in January 1924 after serving an apprentice-ship with Glazebrooke, Steel & Company, a Manchester firm closely linked to the Bombay Company in the cotton and textile trade. He continued to serve the company until 1948 and was managing director of its Calcutta branch from 1941. Rose makes a less flattering assessment of him in an unpublished letter to Jeanie of 14 September 1939: 'I saw Bill and Henry Smith the other day – Bill very charming, Henry nice but dullish, as usual' (ERM 9.72). Bill, with his literary interests and abilities, was always likely to be more on Rose's wavelength than Henry the businessman.

4   Charles Williams. A prolific writer and lecturer and a staunch member of the Church of England, he was from 1908 to 1945 a reader for Oxford University Press, which had accepted *Shepherd of Souls* for publication. Among Jean's papers are several letters from him, including one of 13 June 1927, in which, after tentatively suggesting some minor alterations in Jean's poems, he praises them generously and, like Rose, expresses the opinion that they are superior to his own: '[Your poems] are very beautiful and so far beyond my own scope that I can do nothing but admire. The very technique of them is a technique I cannot attain to – those delicate prolongations and inflections and stillnesses.' Unfortunately his doubts about the saleability of Jean's book turned out to be all too well-founded.

5   If this suggestion was made to Oxford University Press, it was not accepted.

6   Jean granted Rose's wish.

7   The nuns at Fairacres, the Anglican Convent of the Incarnation, were – and are – the Community of the Sisters of the Love of God, a contemplative order established in 1906 by Fr George Seymour Hollings of the Society of St John the Evangelist or 'Cowley Fathers'.

8   Sid Gillum, who had been with the Bombay Company since 1899, left India in 1927 and became a partner in Wyer & Hawke, the Bombay Company's London Agents. He and Dorothy bought Quarry Hill, Reigate.

9   No doubt Rose considered Edward Impey the most prominent member of her uncle's 'set of tiresome old men'. One might have expected her to be less disapproving of Henry Justice Ford, best known as the illustrator of Andrew Lang's fairy books. A contemporary of R.H. Macaulay at Cambridge, he was one of seven brothers, six of whom were educated at Repton and Cambridge, and all of whom, including Henry, were very good cricketers.

62

10 St. Andrews [Mansions].
26 June 1927

Darling, thank you for typescript[1] and your letter. Also for file-box, and for the photograph. I like to have it – but it's nothing like nice enough, of course, and somehow not altogether you. However, photographs seldom are just right. I'd rather have a painting of you, of course, – colour being so important with you. But this is better than nothing.

Of course you must have a contract properly drawn up, with a royalty clause, so that you get profits if any. Curtis Brown had better see to your end of it, don't you think – my agents, I mean. They always do mine and, tho' they get 10% commission on any profits, they more than repay that in the extra money they get for one. If you don't say no, may I put the contract up to them to do, when the Press write about it. I should never dare to make a contract myself with a publisher – lamb standing up to wolf, it could be. I did it with Sidgwick with my book,[2] and have been sorry ever since. Even the nicest publishers have to be matched by agents, as a rule.

I'll keep the duplicate safely, and your list of addresses.[3] I wonder what date they suggest for publication? I'm glad about my dedication in full – I do like to think of it, I shall feel *so* proud and pleased.

I didn't see Fr Cary after all, as I expect you know. He was overdone, and couldn't leave Oxford. I hope he will come when he can; I'd like to see him.

My dear, I've been thinking so much of you these last few days – I do pray all is and will be well with you. When you can easily spare a letter, let me have news, won't you. Bless you: you mean extraordinarily much to me, now and always.

Thank you for being what you are – to me and in yourself.

R.

1 Of *Shepherd of Souls*.
2 Rose's first volume of poetry, *The Two Blind Countries*, published by Sidgwick & Jackson in 1914.
3 In *L*68 Rose has to confess that she has lost the list.

63

10, St. Andrews Mansions,
Dorset Street, W.1.
10 July [1927]

My dearest Jean,

I had meant to write before, but have been so beset about with occupations that I didn't; but I have been thinking about you a great deal. Father Cary came, and was so nice; what he said about the life made me understand better, I think – tho' I did understand before. He was unspeakably kind, and made me feel so much that he was there if one should need him in any way, later on.[1]

I wonder how you are, and how life is. Both well, I hope. I gather from the Press that there is no chance of proofs till after August – but I told them I should be ready for them any time after the middle of the month, when I get back from Switzerland. I am going there at the end of this week, to join Margaret, and shall be glad. Life is arduous, difficult, and (to-day) rather hot. (Not that there is much hope of *that* lasting long.) I have to spend the week finishing up jobs, and running round after foreign money etc etc – and arranging for the bath to be enamelled while I am away. Yes, I am to have a white and shining bath when I return. I also during the week have two dinner-parties, a thousand lunches, and a party here,[2] so many people that I must put them in the courtyard I think – or on the roof, as Sir Wm Beveridge put us when I dined there last week, a lovely roof with a view of London.[3] Can you in any way bear Mrs Mair?[4] I really can't! She complains so of the clothes of female dons, and of how it must influence badly the students. Of course it doesn't – and even if it did, well, good heavens, mayn't the children be allowed 3 short years in which to think other things more exciting than what they have on their backs? I gently implied this, and that all their lives they'd doubtless give fully its due importance to wearing apparel, but she would have her way – women should realise the importance of clothes. How funny the angels and other beings not on this planet must find the human animal, mustn't they.

I heard from Madeleine Symons, from Sheringham, asking me if I could go down there sometime before Sept: 15th to the house she has with the Ushers. I'd like to visit them if I can fit it in, but don't yet know. She says her daughter laughs all the time she doesn't sleep, which sounds good.[5] Aren't the Babington Smiths at Sheringham?[6] I must get their address if I do go, and see them. But I may never get there; I do find it, you know, difficult to get to places! Easier to get abroad than anywhere else, which is queer. When you are seeing people more, I shall get to Oxford, however.

S<i>lvia Carpenter[7] asked for your address, and I will send it; I told her you couldn't write, but could get letters. I fancy she partly wanted to greet you, and partly perhaps to use you as a kind of clearing-house for objects of prayer. I suppose people are always ready to do that, and perhaps it is quite in order.

Goodbye darling. I love you. Heaven knows there's plenty of trouble wants healing, both by prayer and otherwise. I shan't expect any answer to this, I needn't say – in fact, I'm going away at the end of the week, and shan't get letters at present. My love always. Rose.

1 Originally, Rose went on to say: 'At present I feel that I . . .'. But she changed her mind and deleted the words. One can only guess at how the sentence would have continued. Perhaps something like: '. . . must reflect on my situation and try to deal with it myself'.

2 Rose's party, mentioned in Dorothy Brooke's diary, was on 13 July.

3 Beveridge, social reformer and economist, was Director of the London School of Economics from 1919 to 1937. Rose first met him through Naomi Royde-Smith during the First World War. He lived at 53 Campden House Road, Kensington.

4 Janet ('Jessy') Mair was a Scot and the wife of David Beveridge Mair, a cousin of William Beveridge. With DBM she had three sons and a daughter, Lucy, who at one stage was, like Jean, secretary to Gilbert Murray, and later became Professor

of Applied Anthropology at the London School of Economics. Mrs Mair, who had been Beveridge's secretary and aide when he was a senior civil servant during the war, moved on to the LSE with him, her appointment being that of Academic Secretary. In *DNB* (and *ODNB*) she is described as 'overbearing and temperamental' and, like Beveridge himself, 'highly unpopular with many of the School's professors', who complained about what they called the 'Beveridge–Mair dictatorship'. In December 1942, after the death of her husband, she became Beveridge's wife. Rose's poor opinion of her was shared by Naomi, who writes in her diary for 29 July 1920: 'Lunched with Molly [Hamilton] and Mrs. Mair who was *dis-gust*ingly hypocritical', underlining 'dis-' once and '-gust-' twice.

5 On the birth and paternity of Madeleine's daughter, see *L*65 n. 5. It is not known when Madeleine moved from London to Sheringham on the Norfolk coast. She was back in London by November 1927 (*L*68).

6 After the death of Jean's uncle Sir Henry Babington Smith (*L*30 n. 2), his widow and children lived at Loudwater, Sheringham.

7 See *L*21 n. 13. Rose writes 'Sylvia'.

64

10 St Andrews [Mansions].
Tuesday [12 July 1927]

My dearest Jean

I wrote to 276 Iffley Rd on Sunday – stupid of me, I thought that was the convent address. But I expect you will have got it. And now I have yours of the 10th, which I loved to get. I *am* glad you are happy and well, and that the people are the right kind. Good. Can you, or do, write any poetry, I wonder? It must, in a way, be the right condition for that, just as it is for things producing their right shapes and smells. Everything sharpened and more vivid, I mean, and set free of our confused entanglement and muddle, and striking to the heart of beauty. Darling, I'm glad you have it.

For my part, I go to join M[argaret] in Switzerland on Saturday. I shall write from there. Now no more. It is all right for me to write as often as I like, isn't it, even though you can't usually answer. I shall do so unless advised not. I don't feel that getting an answer actually matters: I mean, I feel I do get an answer, though not on paper. My love and thanks.

Rose.

65

Geneva.
31 July 1927

My dearest Jean

I am week-ending here – a brief space between mountain walking in the Oberland and mountain walking in the Savoy passes, which I start to-morrow, hoping to get to the Italian frontier and across it, if the weather is good. Here and now it is very hot and fine, but it may not last.

Kandersteg was glorious – a village where five mountain valleys meet, so that there are many quite different directions for walks. And such walks! Mountain paths climbing up to blue lakes, or to green and white glaciers, or merely up piney mountain slopes, above white and rushing rivers, and waterfalls like heavenly ladders all the way, and the air like strawberry ices (wild strawberries abounded) and alpenrosen and gentians and little starry Alp flowers everywhere. And such nice, lusty brown people wishing one grüss gott on the way. It *was* nice, all of it. I walked and climbed all day, Margaret a little; she got much stronger there.

The Savoy passes will be good; probably less beautiful, but very exciting. Beyond the Italian frontier (I hope to walk over the Mont Cenis pass) there is interesting country, and hill towns such as Susa and S. Michele.[1] Margaret has gone home now, and I am alone.[2] I rather like being here again, on this blue lake, though it is a town.[3]

I wonder how you are, and how is life. Both well, I hope. I had thoughts of you this morning, in the horrid English church I attended. Why are English churches abroad as they are? To-morrow, you know, is my birthday, which always gives me to think. I don't like them much. All the same, I think they are good for one.

Did I tell you both Madeleine and the Ushers had asked me to go down to them in August if I could? I don't know if I can, as I go to Petersfield almost at once on getting back to London. But I'd like to see Madeleine and her daughter. Grace is a little peevish about it all – I gather she feels that it has all rather come on her, and that she and H.B. are being a little compromised in the eyes of the world – Grace, of course, tho' the kindest hearted and best of friends, in action, *would* take this line about it, and would rather feel the affront to respectability (that's middle-class midlands, I fancy)[4] than any other aspect of it. But I expect she doesn't let on to Madeleine that she feels this – if she does, it must be uncomfortable for poor M. The worst of it is that she says people are saying H.B. is the father! I can hardly believe this – but still, people will and do say anything. Grace is far too loyal to tell people who it really is, of course, but she wishes Madeleine would. However, as I told her, these things soon die down, and usually the less said the better. Poor Ushers – they *are* so respectable. And so kind with it. It would be so odd to feel *respectable*, wouldn't it, of all things. But so many people do.[5]

Well, Tom got married all right, I hear.[6] I'm so glad. Also that they will be in London, so that I can see them sometimes. I hope I'll see Jim too, when he comes – but that's not till the autumn, I think.

Now I must wash such hair as I have – it's incredibly short just now, for travel – in order to start next year clean in person. An elderly but well-washed woman, I shall be described, if I am killed to-morrow in the train to Chambéry.

Good-night, darling – how much I love you, and how much think of you, you know. Please pray for me sometimes.

Yours always,

Rose.

1 The abbey of San Michele is spectacularly situated on a high hill near the small towns of Avigliana and Sant' Ambrogio, west of Turin.

2 Not alone for long, for the next stage of her holiday was to be spent with Gerald. The days they spent together are recalled in 'Miss Anstruther's Letters' 307: ' villages in the Haute-Savoie, jumbled among mountain rocks over brawling streams, the motor bus over the Alps down into Susa and Italy'. It is noticeable that Rose avoids mentioning Gerald in this letter, even though she has told Jean of their relationship.

3 For Rose's visit to Geneva in September 1921, see *L*26. There too she remarks on the blueness of the lake.

4 Given that both Grace and her husband came from Yorkshire, 'midlands' seems not entirely appropriate.

5 The father of Madeleine's daughter, Teresa, was not H.B. Usher, but James ('Jimmy') Mallon. Madeleine's senior by twenty years, he is shown on Teresa's birth certificate as 'journalist'. That description is misleading (deliberately so, no doubt), for, although he did some writing for newspapers, his real work was social reform, in which cause he was an energetic, able, and prominent campaigner throughout his adult life. From 1906 until 1954 he worked at Toynbee Hall, the universities' settlement established in East London with the aim of improving the lives of the poor, and he was its Warden from 1919 on. A charming and eloquent man, he was as popular as he was persuasive. Madeleine probably first came into professional contact with him very soon after she became an official of the Women's Trade Union League in 1916, in which capacity she was much involved with the wages of women in the munitions factories and served on several Trade Boards. For several years before she came on the scene, Jimmy had been campaigning alongside the WTUL for improved conditions for women workers, and he sat on many of the Trade Boards. After the war the two continued their professional contacts: for example, in 1920–1921 Madeleine gave a course at Toynbee Hall on 'Problems of Women's Employment', and in 1921 they were two of the three Trade Union representatives elected to serve on a committee of six formed to draw up a scheme for co-ordinating the work of the various Trade Boards (*The Woman Worker* 60 (March 1921) 7). At the time of his affair with Madeleine, Jimmy was no longer a bachelor, having married on 10 August 1921 Stella Katherine Gardiner. She was a daughter of Alfred George Gardiner, editor of *The Daily News* from 1902 to 1919. There had been, and were to be, no children of the marriage, which ended only with Jimmy's death in 1961. His fathering of an

illegitimate child seems never to have been made public before, which shows how well the secret was kept. Teresa was born in a nursing-home, run by Miss Ellen Simpson, at 27 Welbeck Street, London W1, on 14 November 1926. The birth was registered by both parents on 24 December 1926, Jimmy's 52nd birthday. Perhaps at this stage the couple were thinking of bringing up their daughter together. But this was not to happen. Madeleine adopted Teresa on 29 July 1927 and brought her up alone until her marriage in October 1940, when Teresa was aged fourteen. On 21 January 1929 she also adopted a boy, Terence Richard ('Dickie') Symons, who was born 7 February 1925. She was not his biological mother. Dickie, serving as a lieutenant in the Coldstream Guards, was killed in action near Gennep on the Dutch–German border on 20 February 1945, aged twenty.

6   Tom Smith and Prue Martin were married at Holy Trinity Church, Exmouth, on 16 July 1927.

66

10, St. Andrews Mansions,
Dorset Street, W.1
17 September 1927

My Dearest Jean

I wish I had written yesterday – I forgot that the 18th was a Sunday, and now you won't get this till the day after your birthday. Just the same, it can wish you the joy of the day, and does, and brings moreover all my love, for now and the year it begins.

I have a book for you, but won't send it until I hear (either from you or from one of your family) that you may be sent things – I expect so, but am not quite sure, and don't want you to have the bother of sending it back again. But if I *don't* hear, I will send it during next week.

I heard of you from Henry, who wrote me such a nice letter after he'd seen you. I am so glad of his report: it sounded all right, very much all right. What a wise boy that must be! I hope to see him before long, when he leaves his stags and comes to London.[1]

Well, I had a very exciting holiday, first Switzerland (which was really beautiful and great fun – I walked and climbed all day – I forget if I wrote to you from there?) then scrambling about the French and Italian Alps, climbing over the Mont Cenis pass and coming down on the Italian side, and staying at little mountain towns – Susa and Sant' Ambrogio. It was from 80 to 90 in the shade all that time, and I loved it, though climbing up to the monastery of San Michele, above St Ambrogio, up a very steep track in the sun for several hours on end *was* a little warm. Then I went to Petersfield, and walked about rural England in the rain for a change, which was lovely too. I'm only just back, and not liking London much yet, except for my friends. What oh what a place. One gets so tired if one walks 3 miles, instead of feeling fresh after 10, as in the country. I suppose it's the drab ugliness that fatigues physically. Still, temptations to waste of time are lessened by that, and I really ought to be sitting at my delayed book,[2] not roaming country fields.

Well, Henry says you are well and happy, so I won't ask as to that. If ever you can write, tell me a lot of things – as, can you and do you read much – general reading, I mean, not devotional? Are you gardening, and do you like it, and do you walk in the grounds much, and – oh well, anything you do and feel, because I do want to know about you. Myself, I am very well and robust after my simple and wholesome holiday in God's great out o' doors – very different from Roger Hinks, who writes from various continental metropolises, Vienna, Prague, Dresden etc. – of visiting the opera each night and going over Palaces and galleries each day. Not what I call rest.

Did I tell you I've learnt some Greek since last year? I used only to know the letters, and I suddenly thought I'd better know more of the language than that, so I attacked it, and do so in my spare time and get on fairly easily. Also some German! Humbert Wolfe has just brought out a verse rendering of a selection from *The Greek Anthology* – good, I think, though not literal.[3] He is a very versatile creature.

Bless you always – I do love you.

An elderly cousin, Mrs Fred Conybeare,[4] has written to say, 'Will I take her to the dentist's, and what does Life mean?' I will take her, but I can't tell her that, I fear.

Yours always
Rose.

1 Henry was on Exmoor, riding with or, like his and Rose's uncles Kenneth and Willie (*L*41), following the Devon and Somerset Staghounds.
2 *Keeping up Appearances*. American title: *Daisy and Daphne*.
3 *Others Abide* (London, 1927).
4 Jane Conybeare, second wife of Frederick Cornwallis Conybeare, a distinguished Armenian and biblical scholar, had been widowed in 1924 and was now in her late sixties. Rose's portrait of a seventeenth-century Dr Conybeare in *They were Defeated* (1932) is, she says, partly modelled on Fred Conybeare (*LF* 35, 300).

67

10, St. Andrews Mansions,
Dorset Street, W.1.
19 October 1927

My dearest Jean

Since I last wrote I've seen Jim, Henry, Tom, and Prue, so it seems time I saw you too! Jim was just going to Oxford, but I hear fell sick and never got there – or perhaps he has now.

Prue and Tom I had tea with yesterday. She is rather a darling child, isn't she – *so* pretty, and such a well-bred, competent hostess – rather like a child playing (very well) at being a wife. I loved them both. She is awfully fond of you, as you know. But then who isn't?

We are trying to get up a theatre party – they, I and Uncle Regie, for a crook drama. But so far we haven't found the night. However, we shall all meet (if he asks us) at Uncle R.'s on Nov 2nd for Henry's last evening.[1] At present we've only been invited by Henry, and I doubt if the uncle knows about it yet!

I'm terribly busy with this book, which I really *am* working at feverishly now, to get it finished by Christmas if possible. I like writing it, and especially when I do enough of it at once (like this) to get saturated; it's only then that ideas flow; why I halt so mostly is that I only do so little, and so many other things, that I never get into it. Perhaps one needs a rush at the end to make one concentrate – or I do.

Darling, when is your – and my – book coming? They sent me a proof: I love it more than ever, and want to see it out. I shall write and ask them when it's coming, I think. I do hope in time for Xmas. I want to give it to people so much.

I wonder very much how you are, how is everything, if it's still all right, if you're happy, and everything else. I hope Jim will tell me something of you when we next meet – I forget if he's coming up with Henry or not?

Margaret is quite alone at the moment, (Miss Haines[2] being away on a rest-cure) and liking it. I was down there[3] on Sunday week – it was so lovely, golden woods and misty downs. I walked all day. Walking time seems rather over now, alas; well, all the more time for working, I suppose – but what a poor substitute!

Darling, you have all my love. Don't bother to try and write, of course, but send me a thought over the aether.

Rose.

I wish Fr. Cary would come to tea with me again sometime! Do you think I could ask him? Is he ever in town now?

---

1 Henry was returning to India.
2 Fanny Haines, a friend of Margaret, had been a governess. In an unpublished letter to her sister Jeanie (ERM 9.20), written five days before the present letter to Jean,

Rose makes some unflattering remarks about Fanny and wishes that she would make
a home for herself, or be someone's housekeeper, rather than live with Margaret. In
L87, written five years after Margaret's death, Rose mentions that she has visited her.
3 At Heathlands, Petersfield.

68

10, St. Andrews Mansions,
Dorset Street, W.1.
4 November 1927

My darling Jean

Your letter was good to get. I sent your messages to the people concerned.
Also I wrote to Charles Williams and asked could I see to preliminaries, and he
will send me a revise of them in a few days, when he gets them. I want to see the
dedication. But I fear there is no chance of its coming out by Xmas, which is sad.
I hope it will be not too long after.

Now I have an outrageous and shocking confession to make – I've gone and
been and lost your list of addresses for the book. I put it away carefully, but it
has apparently somehow got lost or thrown away – anyhow I've looked in all
possible places, and it isn't anywhere. I *am* so sorry. So, before the date of publication, could you send me another list – you could send it via Jim or someone
to whom you were writing. I do hope it won't be a bother, and that you have
the addresses at hand – if not, give me the names, and I'll find out the addresses
easily. And please forgive me, I'm so ashamed of myself! I've noted the alteration
you've made.

Well, I'm glad about the life: good. And it's interesting about the maps being
right. Oh dear, well it all looks very much like your being on the right track. I *am*
glad really; only sometimes the other side has a look in in one's feelings about it.

Vera Fraser[1] writes an answer to my message, and says 'Will you give her my
love when you write, and tell her that I shall never lose the vision of the Church
which she gave me'. She is very pleased about you – she wants to have a Te Deum
in Westminster Cathedral – which looks a little like her having got hold of a
vision of some other church since she saw you.[2] But perhaps she meant Abbey.
Or perhaps she quite rightly takes the Christian church to be all one, as it is. She
asks me what day your profession was; I told her I thought, if you ever decided
on that, it would be in some years – isn't that so? Also, might you receive greetings at Christmas. I said yes, any greetings any time, only that you couldn't write.

Yes, I *am* busy with that accursed book – trying to finish it by end of the year,
working night and day (or so I see it just now, though I do seem to have done a
few other things both by day and night this week). I am liking writing it. What
a good invention writing books is – it keeps one's thoughts so employed. I wish

Madeleine would write something – but she says she doesn't and never has. I had tea with her yesterday, and gave her your love. Teresa is as fat as butter and very engaging, and rolls on the carpet like a puppy. Madeleine I thought sad, and was sorry. I think she feels it a mistake to have settled again in London, and I gathered (though she didn't say anything of that) that perhaps this was because of associations, and what is over, and missing it horribly. But of this I know nothing – only that she was rather on the edge of tears, I think, before Teresa entered. I think for one thing T. isn't a whole time job, with that efficient nurse, and that she misses her work. I wish she'd get a job. She says she is stupid now in her brain and can't concentrate. I suppose it's having been through all that. I am very sorry about her. She said that with most people she liked to seem very cheerful, and I think she does, so I shan't speak of her like this to anyone, only of course you. Life is a queer, wry business, and she's got to a bad place in it, but she'll get through it of course. She's so much pluck.[3] No religion, of course, which is unlucky.

Well, it's just on midnight, and I must stop. I had a nice evening at Uncle R.'s, with Henry, Tom and Prue. H. and T. were most charming. So was Prue. But I suppose a little conventional? Or will be, when she's quite grown up. After all, why not? *How* pretty and nice she is, though. Uncle R. was a jewel.

Good night, darling. I love you a great deal. Be happy, and every good thing happen to you. I like to feel your prayers.

R.

1 Probably Vera Sylvia Mathieson Fraser, who had been an undergraduate and post-graduate student in English at University College, London, during and after the First World War. She was to produce a translation of André Maurois, *Chateaubriand* (London, 1938). Reviews by her in *TLS*, 5 February 1938, 89, suggest that she had expertise in medieval Latin as well as in English and the Romance languages. She seems to have been Roman Catholic when she died in 1978.

2 Westminster Cathedral is Roman Catholic.

3 Pregnancy and single motherhood had interrupted an impressive career: as well as having been a prominent trade unionist, Madeleine had been a member of the Executive Committee of the Labour Party (1922–1923), a Justice of the Peace for the County of London (1924), and a member of the Royal Commission on Lunacy and Mental Disorder (1924–1926). However, Rose was right to forecast that she would get through a difficult period. Although she never returned to a trade union post, from 1932 until shortly before her death in March 1957 she gave outstanding service as a Magistrate in the Juvenile Courts and as a member of numerous committees concerned with social welfare. The remarkable tributes to her published in *The Times* after her death make moving reading, presenting a vivid picture of a woman who was not only much respected for her wisdom, energy, and clarity of thought and speech but also much loved for her kindness, modesty, sense of humour, and charm (issues of 22 March 1957, 10; 26 March, 13; 29 March, 13; 3 April, 13). As for her private life, on 25 October 1940 she married the recently widowed Harold Robinson, Professor

of Physics at Queen Mary College, University of London. He died in November 1955.

69

10, St. Andrews Mansions,
Dorset Street, W.1.
8 January [1928]

My dearest Jean

It will be good to see you whenever it occurs: soon, I hope. I wonder how you are – and what, if any, are your immediate, and later, plans.[1] The book comes in February, doesn't it? That will be joyful.

I hope you've had a nice restful Christmas. I suppose Jim is now gadding on the continent with the gay Father Cary[2] – I think Cowley Fathers manage their lives so well![3] Though I'm not *quite* sure that Fr. Waggett hasn't made a mistake in temporarily alighting at Great St Mary's – Cambridge seems a little to think so.[4] He does get himself into such queer positions. I rather hoped you'd be able to go abroad too with Jim – it would have been fun. I'm afraid he is really going back this month, isn't he?[5]

For my part, I've just despatched *Keeping Up Appearances* to its English and American publishers – (I forget if you knew I had a novel called that coming out?) – and am awaiting proofs. I liked Christmas – we were snow-bound and rather romantic. Since I returned I've been living in a turmoil – household chores (Mrs Trowles[6] having been laid up, and everything in the world needing seeing to at once, such as gas pipes, curtains, etc. etc.), visitors, work, and what not. Life is very odtaa,[7] and I can scarcely squeeze into it time for the things I have to write. I want *space* – one gets 'That Breathless Feeling' so badly, all c<l>uttered up and choked with jobs and people and things. I wonder if you feel that specially now, after a more ordered life – I imagine one might. And so many of my friends seem entangled in troubles, of one sort or another. The devil tempts one at times to incredibly selfish withdrawals from these, telling one that the mix up in them is incompatible with any life of one's own at all – but this cannot be true in a well-ordered career (which is so far from any career of mine!). Well well, I suppose everyone is in the same boat – no, not quite, because some people are so much more competent and quick and clever, and can do everything at once – and then again some people don't seem to have so strongly developed that selfish craving for getting on with one's own affairs. But women are unfortunate, for they have to see that their net curtains go to the cleaner's at the right time, and that their white paint doesn't get too dirty. Men don't seem to care about these things.

My dear love to you anyhow. You remember I have a file of yours? Shall I send it, or keep it for you for the moment?

R.

I hope you're happy, and feeling everything all right and worth while.

1 Jean gave up convent life in December 1927. Sometime in 1928 she joined the staff of Downe House School.
2 In 1928 this did not mean what it might be taken to mean today!
3 Compare remarks Rose makes in *LF* 184. But after that volume of letters was published, Jean informed Constance Babington Smith that Rose's recollection of Fr Cary 'going off for a holiday in Italy at Christmas time' with her and Jim was inaccurate. In fact, he was already there, convalescing after an illness, and their visit to him in Sorrento was before Christmas (1925), not at it (ERM 13.167).
4 Philip Waggett, who had joined the Society of St John the Evangelist, Cowley, in 1892, was a charismatic preacher and conductor of missions and retreats. Rose, who had heard him preach in Cambridge before the First World War, much admired him. See especially *LF* 39–40. It is indicative of his influence on her at that time that she uses quotations of him as epigraphs in both *The Valley Captives* (1911) and *The Lee Shore* (1912). Great St Mary's, Cambridge, which he served from 1927 to 1930, is Cambridge's University church as well as a parish one. Rose's doubts seem to have been justified, for, according to *DNB*: 'by now he was physically a broken man, and he failed to exercise the influence in the university which had been expected'.
5 Jim was returning to Africa. If one asks why Jean did not accompany him on the continental trip, part of the answer may be that, given that Lucius Cary was the 'Father Director' of the convent she had just left, she might have felt uncomfortable in his company, particularly if, as is not unlikely, she was already thinking that her true home might be the Catholic Church. According to Rose, 'he was very grieved when she went over, knowing what Anglicanism had been to her' (unpublished passage of the letter of 4 August 1954 to Fr Johnson, preserved because Constance Babington Smith quoted it in a letter to Jean (ERM 14.132)).
6 Rose's charlady was in her late 60s.
7 One damn thing after another. *Odtaa* is the title of a novel by John Masefield (London, 1926).

70

This letter is incomplete.

10, St. Andrews Mansions,
Dorset Street, W.1.
5 February 1928

My dearest Jean

My *Shepherd of Souls* has now arrived: staying in to-day with a cold, I have been reading it through again, and love it very much. The title-poem I believe I almost like the best – but I don't know. I love 'Paschal New Moon [in March]', and 'Moths', – and what a beautiful and satisfying thing 'The Requiem Mass' is – and how lovely is 'Scythes'; and 'Flight from Cologne', even though curtailed.[1] But they are all good. So many have that quality of poignant life-hidden-in-darkness that Novembers have sometimes – and others have April sun and colour. (Perhaps this is according as they were written in England or in foreign parts!) Anyhow, they are good stuff, and I was that proud you can't think, to see my name on the dedication page. Someday you will put it also on the page where it should be written in ink, won't you.

I suppose it came out on Friday, did it?[2] I do wonder what other people will think of it.[3] When I get out again (to-morrow, I imagine) I shall buy some of it to give to people. I think it presents a good appearance – not so thin, and daintily mottled, and nicely printed and margined. Altogether a book to be proud of. I'm so glad you've done it.

What are you now doing, I wonder? I am trying to prepare an address on Literary Standards – a perplexing subject. I have spent to-day reading (besides *Shepherd of Souls*) Longinus,[4] Burke,[5] and Saintsbury,[6] but am not much forwarder in forming my own theory of aesthetics. Stupid things one speaks about. But it gives a reason for reading all kinds of . . .[7]

1 'Flight from Cologne' ends with four dots, as if it were a fragment.
2 Rose is writing on Sunday. The book was published on Thursday 2 February.
3 Reviews of *Shepherd of Souls* were favourable (Introd. II.5). One of those who praised it was Naomi Royde-Smith. She reviewed it for *Time and Tide*, 22 June 1928, 608–609, and in the Special Christmas Number of *The Bookman*, December 1928, 4, in response to the editor's request for a note on an 'overlooked book', made it her choice, calling it 'one of the most remarkable volumes of poetry that has come into my hands for some years'.
4 The name, but not the true one, of the author of *On the Sublime*, a literary treatise written in Greek, probably in the first century AD.
5 Edmund Burke. Presumably Rose was reading *A Philosophical Enquiry into the Origin of Our Ideas of the Sublime and Beautiful*, first published in 1757.
6 George Saintsbury wrote many works on literary theory and history, including *A History of Criticism and Literary Taste in Europe from the Earliest Texts to the Present Day* (Edinburgh, 1900–1904) in three volumes.
7 The rest of the letter is missing. The next words may have been something like '. . . works one wouldn't otherwise read'.

71

10 St Andrews Mansions
Dorset St, W.1.
20 April 1929

Dearest Jean

Thank you so much for yours from the Caffè Alpino of the 11th. How lovely a place Brunate sounds.[1] All those hills are the most exquisite walking-country in April and May.

Yes, I'm afraid all the Riviera places are getting spoilt and noisy and be-villa'd, since the war. Did you go to Lévanto – a tiny fishing place huddled beneath cliffs? Even our darling Varazze has got spoilt and built about – tho' no English go there. Aren't the little hill-villages behind nice, though.

I've had rather a poor spring. I got better of flue [*sic*], though never *quite* well, but then was struck down by some different bacilli, of a very annoying kind – something to do with the kidney and colon – anyhow, they cause high temperatures for some days, and then leave you feeling rather weak. I get up now, in the afternoons, and hope to be quite well next week, but shall still have to be careful for a time. I don't know what woke the bacilli to this morbid life: probably I did too much in Hampshire when I was there.

I am glad to say that before this occurred I saw Bill and Isadore – most charming, they were.[2] I read the 1st bit of Bill's novel,[3] and thought it interesting and well-told. I didn't know he wrote so well.

I now am installed (since Nurse went yesterday) with a stately elderly dame called Mrs Brown, who sleeps in and gets my meals and all – very grand. It's only for a week, till I'm well and fit. Then I shall go down for a little country air to Petersfield, then try and take up my normal life for a change.[4]

I am reading Professor Murray's tilts against Obscene Literature in *The Nation* week by week. More power to him. He has, unfortunately, practically the whole of the literary intelligentsia under 50 against him and his cause. Bloomsbury solidly takes up arms for Obscenity. For my part I wish there was no such thing. But still, we have made these taboos, and till they are broken down I am for their observance, merely on personal and aesthetic grounds. If I had more energy and health I think I should write in on his side. Especially this week, because such a rude vulgarian imbecile wrote such a rude letter and made me angry. However, I don't suppose he'll mind.[5]

I hope, my love, you are still having a lovely time. I'd better send this to Clent, I think – they'll have some address, I dare say. It will be fun hearing about everything. Love and love and love.

R.

1 The village of Brunate, 500 m above Como, affords a magnificent view of the lake. In March Jean had had the company in Italy of Gilbert Murray and his daughter Rosalind Toynbee. On a postcard, postmarked 3 April 1929, to Margaret, Rose reports: 'Lady Mary Murray writes that she (Jean) has gone back to Rome after having Mr Murray and his daughter at Lerici, and she (Lady M.) will not be surprised if she were to go to Rome in *more senses than one*. As for me, I am never surprised by anyone in these days' (ERM 15.119). Jean was indeed to become a Roman Catholic in 1933. So was Rosalind.

2 Bill Smith had resigned from the Bombay Burmah Trading Corporation after Isadore had been taken ill in Burma. In the early months of 1929 the couple holidayed in Britain and Europe before going to the USA together.

3 *Bandar-Log*, Bill's first novel, was to be published in 1930.

4 On 3 May, the day Rose went to Petersfield, she was seen in London by a heart specialist and had an electrocardiogram. The specialist's verdict on her heart was unfavourable. See *LS* 49, where she declares her determination to carry on as usual.

5 A letter from Gilbert Murray, published in *The Nation and Athenaeum*, 23 March 1929, 876, under the title 'Obscenity in Literature', provoked a lively correspondence that continued for ten weeks, until it was terminated by editorial decree. The broader context of the correspondence was the campaign, led by the Home Secretary William Joynson-Hicks ('Jix'), against 'pornography' and 'obscenity'. Among those who wrote were Lytton Strachey (30 March) and Leonard Woolf (30 March; 18 May). A second letter from Murray, written while he was in Italy, was printed on 13 April. The 'rude letter' that angered Rose is in the issue of 20 April, 72. Written from Paris by Darsie Yapp, it concludes: 'To be indecent is to be unseemly; it is unseemly that the Home Secretary should have inserted a hyphen between Joynson and Hicks, it is unseemly that Professor Gilbert Murray should have translated Greek tragedy into his priggish verse, but it is criminal flapdoodle that James Joyce's "Ulysses", which is a present glory of our English tongue, should not be allowed free access to every library in England.' (Joynson-Hicks was plain Hicks until 1896, the year after his marriage to Grace Lynn Joynson.)

72

7, Luxboro' House,
N[orthumberla]nd St,
W.1
5 October [1930]

Oh darling, what a darling lark! I do love it, above the blowing golden wheat and in the windy blue sky – and, as you say, just like Luxboro'. You *are* nice, to send it me. I am so happy here, I feel like a lark myself, in all this sunshine and trees – here I am, 5.30 (winter time) sitting by my window and writing by the full light of day (such as the day is – I can't say much for it, but all the more credit to Luxboro' for transmitting it so well).[1]

I am really pretty straight now, tho' I've not yet done any work here – I must now begin, I've wasted weeks and weeks. It's *lovely* here – you *must* come and see it soon. I am at the moment engaged in piecing together, cleaning and restoring a lot of ancient door-plates found in Caledonian Market[2] – nice warm-cream china, with gold squiggles – lovely. But many are broken. I got the lot cheap; they are very costly as a rule, as you know. They're going to look charming when they are all cleaned up and mended, and just suit the room. I still hold morning receptions of geyser men, carpenters, plumbers, electricians, and what not, and shall feel quite lonely when the tumult and the shouting dies.[3]

That book has got to sell, or ruin stares me in the face. I sincerely hope it is doing so. I notice a tendency among the low-brow critics to complain of too much jungle[4] – I hope that won't sink the ship; curse the people who want people, people all the time and are bored by peccaries and alligator pears. Still, there are plenty of people as well for them.

I must stop and brew my tea, long overdue, but I am snowed under by letters and door-plates.

My love and great thanks for the little *alouette*, bless him.

I hope all goes well with you. By the way, what of Bill's novel? I am lunching with Collins to-morrow, and will enquire.[5]

R.

1 Rose's 'new' flat, very close to her previous one, differed from it in being on an upper floor. She praises its sunniness and leafy views in writing to other correspondents, as well as to Jean. The present letter shows that her biographers have misdated her move to Luxborough House. LeFanu 197 gives the date as 1932 and, although CBS 122 and Emery 229 are not precise, they seem to think that it was 1931 or 1932. Although, in dating her letter to Jean, Rose does not give the year, the mention of her hopes for the success of *Staying with Relations* proves that she is writing in October 1930. The book was published on 22 September 1930. In the late 1930s Northumberland Street was renamed, and Rose's address became Flat 7, 8 Luxborough Street, W1.

2 In Islington.

3 'the tumult . . . dies' – Rose is quoting Rudyard Kipling, 'Recessional', line 7.

4 *Staying with Relations* is set in Guatemala, a country which Rose hoped, but was unable, to visit during a transatlantic holiday with Margaret and Will between December 1929 and February 1930. As CBS 111 says, the novel 'is . . . notable as the first of her books to display her gifts as a travel writer'.

5 The enquiry is about Bill's second novel, *West Is West*. It was to be published not by Collins but by John Lane, The Bodley Head (London, 1931).

73

7 Luxborough House,
Northumberland St. W.1
7 January 1933

My dearest Jean

It *was* good to see your hand again and to have your letter – tho' I don't suppose you should write, actually. But I have been wanting much to know how you were going on. It sounds fairly promising – but a long time to be in bed; I wish you were better. And if you can't read a great deal, time must creep rather.[1] If you'd like me to send you any books, send a card. I have Elizabeth Bowen's novel *To the North*,[2] which I think clever, charming, and good, and could send it if you'd like to read it and haven't. I *like* it. I like Margaret Kennedy's too, but less; it is quite amusing, and quite to be read, but that's all. Yes, get it from Boots.[3] I haven't got that.

What I could send you I don't quite know. But say the word; I could send you Thomas Gage his missionary travels in Guatemala,[4] or Bernal Díaz his soldierings in Mexico,[5] or Mary Kingsley her adventures in Africa[6] (she is a charmer) or *Faraway*[7] (bad) or *The Delicate Situation*[8] (Naomi Royde-Smith) or what not. But I expect you get plenty from the library. If you read *Poc<a>hontas*,[9] David Garnett's new book, *skip all the 2nd chapter*. I did, seeing in time that I should hate it. There are some other things one doesn't like, scattered about – but that chapter I should spurn like the devil, at any time, but more particularly when laid up. If you would fancy any book you think I could send you, send a p.c., whenever you have a mind to.

I've met Helen Waddell, but only slightly. I feel I know her much better by correspondence. She wrote me a beautiful letter when she was just after reading *They Were Defeated*.[10] She was unhappy because Julian[11] hadn't loved and married Mr Milton – she thought it would have been such a good plan for both of them. Milton is a special love of hers,[12] and she can't bear him to have wed with a loutish girl who was no use to him and ran away. I rather wish he had married Julian myself; she would have loved it. [*The*] *Wandering Scholars*[13] is enchanting stuff. She gives the impression of having been so thrilled with her subject that she doesn't always finish her sentences – like St Paul. She is just finishing a novel about Abelard[14] – or was, when she wrote to me. It sounded fine, and very moving. She is a Somervillian, an Ulsterwoman, and about 40, I suppose.[15] Aren't her translations of mediaeval Latin lyrics pretty?[16] 'An exciting mind'[17] is what she has exactly. I am hoping to meet her soon again.

I'm glad you like things in *The Bedside Book*.[18] I do, too. Some of the Chinese lyrics are rather lovely, and else.

Are you going to be well when Jim arrives?[19] I do hope so. We heard he was sailing about now. When you arise strong and well, how splendid it will be. But

<one>[20] can't hurry hearts. I'm glad your doctor is good and knows his job, and will cure you. I don't like you to be laid low like this. Madeleine and Teresa are recovering from their whoops, and off to Bournemouth for a week, I think. Flu is everywhere – but not in Luxbro' so far.

All my love and have a hale 1933. I do hope things aren't too dreadfully tedious. Bless you.

    R.

1 Before the end of 1931 Jean had left her teaching post at Downe House. In 1932, probably in the late summer or early autumn, she was admitted to a nursing home in Birmingham. She was to stay there for several months under the care of Dr Theodore Stacey Wilson, whose main interest was in the study and treatment of mild chronic illnesses, including those connected with the heart, stomach, and colon. In her case, as the last paragraph of this letter reveals, he had diagnosed a heart problem. He was an original and enthusiastic physician, but some of his ideas and methods were controversial at the time, and it is hard to believe that any doctor today would have ordered Jean to bed for so long. Family belief is that her illness was partly, perhaps largely, psychosomatic. At this time the struggle with her conscience, about whether or not to become a Catholic, was intense and still unresolved (Introd. II.5). In a letter of 25 September 1932 to Jeanie, Rose says: 'I wrote to Jean for her birthday and sent a book, but no answer. She has become very strange' (ERM 9.54). Jean was almost certainly in the nursing home by then. The birthday letter does not survive.

2 London, 1932. Rose and Elizabeth Bowen were friends. They met through Olive Willis, Rose's friend from her Somerville days and headmistress of Downe House, at which Bowen was educated. (When Bowen attended the school, it was in Kent. It moved to its present location in Berkshire in 1922.) The encouragement Rose gave Bowen, who had written some short stories, but not yet published anything, was much valued by its recipient, as she acknowledges in William Plomer et al., *Coming to London* (Bibliog. I.7) 79. Moreover, she introduced her to Naomi Royde-Smith, who printed her first story in *SWG*, and she recommended Sidgwick and Jackson to publish her first book, *Encounters* (1923), a collection of short stories.

3 Although Boots sold books, Rose almost certainly means Boots Booklover's Library, a very popular and successful subscription library. The novel was probably *A Long Time Ago*, published by Heinemann in October 1932.

4 Thomas Gage was author of *The English-American his Travail by Sea and Land; or, A New Survey of the West-India's* (London, 1648). Rose's book is likely to have been a modern edition, perhaps A.P. Newton (ed.), *Thomas Gage, the English-American: A New Survey of the West Indies* (London, 1928).

5 Bernal Díaz del Castillo, Spanish soldier and author of *Historia verdadera de la conquista de la Nueva España*. The book Rose is offering Jean is most likely to be *The Discovery and Conquest of Mexico*, ed. Genaro García, trans. A.P. Maudsley (London, 1928). It may be assumed that her reading of both Gage and Díaz was connected with her recent American travels and the writing of *Staying with Relations*.

6 Mary Kingsley wrote *Travels in West Africa, Congo français, Corisco and Cameroons*

(London, 1897), but the book offered was almost certainly Stephen Gwynn, *The Life of Mary Kingsley* (London, 1932). Writing to Jeanie on 25 September 1932, Rose reports: 'I have just been reviewing a Life of Mary Kingsley' (*LS* 59).

7 By J.B. Priestley (London, 1932).

8 London, 1931.

9 Misspelt '*Pocohontas*'. The full title is *Pocahontas; or, The Nonpareil of Virginia* (London, 1933). Chapter 2 contains a gruesome description of how a male prisoner, a warrior from another tribe, is tortured to death by Red Indian women.

10 Published in October 1932, *They Were Defeated* (American title: *The Shadow Flies*) was Rose's favourite among her own novels. It is set in the seventeenth century, which she loved, and much of the action takes place in Cambridge, which she loved too. One of her characters is the poet Robert Herrick, with whom she had an ancestral link on the Macaulay side, and she dedicated the book to her uncle William *Herrick* Macaulay, who had spent most of his adult life in the service of King's College, Cambridge. Another character is Dr Conybeare, an imaginary ancestor on her mother's side of the family, whom she partly modelled on a deceased cousin (*L*66 n. 4). The letter Helen Waddell wrote to Rose does not survive, but Rose's reply, dated 1 November 1932, is preserved (ERM 15.188). In writing to Jean about Waddell, Rose playfully uses the Irish-English idiom 'she was . . . after reading', Waddell being Irish.

11 Julian ('July') Conybeare, daughter of Dr Conybeare, is the fictional tragic heroine of *They Were Defeated*. Taken by her father to Cambridge, where her brother Christopher ('Kit') is an undergraduate, the attractive and serious-minded girl is seduced by Kit's tutor, the poet John Cleveland (Letter 38). To her bitter disappointment, Cleveland is not interested in her mind at all, only in her body, and pours scorn on her passion for poetry and learning. Moreover, she loses not only her virginity but also her life: she is accidentally killed during a fight between Cleveland and her brother Francis.

12 Waddell chose to write her MA dissertation on 'John Milton the Epicurist'. A year after the present letter was written, Rose's *Milton* was published in Duckworth's 'Great Lives' series (London, 1934).

13 London, 1927.

14 *Peter Abelard* (London, 1933).

15 Waddell was indeed an Ulsterwoman, the family being from Co. Down. But her father was a missionary, and she was born in Tokyo. That was on 31 May 1889, which means that she was 43 when Rose wrote this letter. She obtained her BA and MA degrees at Queen's University, Belfast. It was not until late in 1920 that she registered as a postgraduate student at Somerville.

16 *Mediaeval Latin Lyrics* (London, 1929).

17 Evidently Rose is echoing Jean's description.

18 Arthur Stanley, *The Bedside Book, a Miscellany for the Quiet Hours* (London, 1932). The publisher was Rose's friend Victor Gollancz.

19 Jim was home on leave from Nigeria in January–June 1933.

20 The bottom-right corner of the page is torn off. The missing word may have been 'you' rather than 'one'.

74

Wood End[1]
Liss
Hants
10 August [1935]

Darling, what *nice* sachets! They lie sweetly in my drawer, scenting everything; thank you so much for them. And for your two letters – birthday one and to-day's. By the way, if Miss Kelleher[2] should send *They Were Defeated* to London, could she please write *Not to be forwarded* on it, or it will come on here – no, I see you leave to-day, so don't bother; it's too small to matter, anyhow.

Your comments on Elizabeth's book[3] are, as always, very acute and good. I think I feel much as you do about it – and I did feel that Leopold was too articulate, in thought and emotion, for 9, even for his race and parentage.[4] Because he hadn't been *reared* to be articulate – probably to be simple and childish. It strikes a false note, I felt when I came to it; and one notices it because most of it is so right. Naomi Fisher[5] is strange, but I think I believe in her, or nearly. Some people felt the book should have been extended, to cover the return of Leopold and his step-father to Karen, and let us see how it was going to work out, but I don't feel that. She says she might do that in a sequel; but I expect not. I'm glad you feel she has more control and grip than before; I do, too, and I think she does. She is a little, I think, too much under E.M.F[orster]'s influence – almost, here and there, echoes him; I think she'll shed that, and develope [*sic*] entirely on her own presently. I think this book will do her reputation good. The reviewers, or most of the chief ones, are all going to praise it, I gather.

Have you left Hillingdon, teeth and all?[6] I hope they're nice and comfortable! And did you meet Sir Charles Strachey at lunch, and isn't he rather attractive?[7]

I had a hectic last few days finishing off my *Pleasures*,[8] and am now in golden Hampshire weather and peace, but, alas, not idle, for I now have to compose an article on *Euphues* for a book someone is editing on Novelists by Novelists.[9] I am supposed to be doing Lyly, and Sidney if I like too, but the *Arcadia*[10] is a bore, and I don't know if I'll say much of it. *Euphues*,[11] on the other hand, is fun, in spite of its idiotic plot. I like the comical similes, and the absurd style. I lie in the garden and read it in the mornings, and the rest of the day wander about this glorious paradise by car and leg. To-day I spent on Selborne common.[12] *Such* views of ripe corn-fields and steep deep-green beech hangers and blue rolling hills far off, and such smells.

I do hope Clent is being nice, my dear, and you well. Do keep so. It was extraordinarily agreeable to see you. Margaret enjoyed Kirnan among the uncle-and-auntery. I wonder if Uncle Willie is back yet.

M[argaret] and J[eanie] and I v. well and bright, and send you love: I a great deal of it, and my thanks again.

R.

1 Margaret moved the few miles from Petersfield to this house on St Mary's Road, Liss, in August 1929.

2 Miss Kelleher cannot be identified, unless she is the 23-year-old dressmaker daughter of a dressmaker in Rose's surviving address book (ERM 3.259), begun at Christmas 1944. The address-book entry reads: 'Mrs Kelliher (and daughter, Mrs Coppin) 16 Pandora Road, W. Hampstead'. It may be reasonably assumed that the daughter is the Kathleen Keleher (*sic*) who married William Coppin, a chauffeur, in Marylebone on 16 April 1938.

3 Elizabeth Bowen, *The House in Paris* (London, 1935).

4 Leopold is the product of the affair his upper-class English mother, Karen Michaelis, had with Max Ebhart, who is Anglo-French and half-Jewish. Karen married Ray Forrestier, and Leopold was adopted by a childless expatriate couple living in Italy.

5 Karen's friend and Max's fiancée, who shares the house in Paris with her dying mother.

6 Hillingdon Hospital, Uxbridge, Middlesex. Jean, her mother records, 'was unwell during the summer of 1935 and spent some months' there in the summer of 1935. The nature of her illness is not revealed. Despite the reference to teeth, it can be assumed that dental problems were not the reason for such a long spell of hospitalisation.

7 Charles Strachey served first in the Foreign Office, then in the Colonial Office. In 1924–1927 he was Assistant Under-Secretary of State for Colonies. The lunch may have been at Walton House, Clent, which, since the death of K.A. Macaulay in 1933, had been the home of W.H. Macaulay. Strachey had been educated at King's, Cambridge, the college to which WHM had devoted his career.

8 *Personal Pleasures* (London, 1935). The book contains short essays by Rose on sixty subjects, arranged alphabetically, from 'Abroad' to 'Writing'.

9 Derek Verschoyle (ed.), *The English Novelists: A Survey of the Novel by Twenty Contemporary Novelists* (London and New York, 1936). Rose's contribution, 'Lyly and Sidney', occupies pp. 29–47 of the London edition, pp. 33–50 of the New York one. Derek Verschoyle joined *The Spectator* as drama critic in 1932 and was its literary editor from 1933 to 1940. Gerald's wife, Beryl, was a Verschoyle, but it does not appear that she was related to Derek.

10 Prose romance, interspersed with poems, by Sir Philip Sidney.

11 John Lyly's prose romance. It was published in two parts: *Euphues: The Anatomy of Wyt* (London, 1578) and *Euphues and His England* (London, 1580). So strikingly peculiar is its style that 'euphuism' came to denote an affected and bombastic manner of writing.

12 Selborne, a few miles from Margaret's house at Liss, is celebrated as the home of Gilbert White (1720–1793), author of *The Natural History and Antiquities of Selborne*. Selborne Common, above the village, is an attractive area of heath and woodland.

75

7 Luxboro'
Whit Monday [17 May 1937]

My dearest Jean

I'm glad you are in that nice nunnery – I know where it is, but don't remember the house itself. To be by the Cherwell in May – what pleasure![1] But I wish it could be *warm*, as it used to be long ago in the Mays when I was young. Perhaps it will suddenly turn so, and the buttercups will shine in the sun.

Yes: isn't *Abinger Harvest*[2] nice. I love some of the quite early ones – the historical ones. And all the Eastern ones – yes, 'The Suppliant'. To me, to be able to charm me about India is a supreme test of charm, because how I do dislike it! As a pacifist, I shouldn't feel this, but – I don't like Indians. I write it, as you see, very small, and hope to conquer the – I was going to say prejudice, but really I've met a lot of them and it is a *post*judice,[3] which is much more unpacifist, I fear. But then I've not seen them at home, only the trippers, or the expatriates, or the earnest young students. I should probably like the northern races better than the southerns, and the Mohammedans better than the Hindus – or shouldn't I? Eleanor says her aboriginals (of Chota Nagpur)[4] are delightful – but then any people one lives among are delightful, which is nice for the human race. (I am so glad to have lived among Italians, because they are being made to appear so hateful now, and so ill-mannered, by their horrid controlled press, and a lot of English who don't know them at home think they must be – in so far as they are, just now, it's worked up by propaganda – their broadcasts and newspapers about us are really dreadfully rude and spiteful and untruthful. I hate it all. Alas, the days when the English were in love with the Italian race, the days when E.M. Forster wrote his first books, are long past.[5] But the poor there have the same charm, surely – or not? How far can a nation's temper be distorted and perverted by its government and press? It is a dreadful subject for speculation.)

But Indians. Why don't I like them as much as Africans? Perhaps it's all nonsense. Still less one is apt to like those whom we may no longer call Anglo-Indians (with glorious exceptions). E.M.F. hated these too much; I wish, when he went to India in 1912 (after which he began the *Passage*)[6] he hadn't been with Lowes Dickinson.[7] He has himself the minority mind, as you say; but G.L.D. had a minimus mind – really distorted a little – and an immense influence over E.M.F. I *think* he got – must have got – some of it skew-eyed. Of course Anglo-Indians nearly all say it's utterly wrong. That garden party, e.g. Eleanor is reading it again, at my request, to tell me her views. What she said before is that (published 1923)[8] it was out of date, and reflected much more of 1912.[9] Now it is probably still more out of date, as she says English manners and feelings about Indians are steadily improving. She is the fairest-minded person I know, nearly; and, being a missionary and yet English, stands between the two camps. She says she *has* often been shocked by English manners to, and talk about, Indians, but less now than once. I mean, she has heard them say to each other, looking into a train-compartment containing English-speaking Indians, 'Oh don't let's get in there, there are Indians'. Rudeness can no further go, it would seem. I'm glad it is decreasing. Do we grow more civilised? (I mean we English: it is apparent that many nations don't, alas.) I am debating for the B.B.C. next Wednesday on 'Should blood-sports be forbidden?' I am saying they should. Particularly hunting animals with dogs. I do think that feeling is growing stronger against this. A boy of 23 – Tristram Beresford – at the B.B.C. says that, with him and his friends it's not even arguable, they all agree.[10] But there are plenty of sporting young left, of course, and particularly in the country. I think it *must* be only a question of time before fox and deer and hare hunting join bear and bull baiting as forbidden incivilities.

I meant to go to Liss for Whitsun, but got wet on Coronation Day[11] and lost my voice completely and went to bed instead. I can speak again now, a little, and my chest feels less straitened. I'm not speaking much, as fortunately there's no occasion, and hope by Wednesday to be as sonorous as Great Tom[12] or Big Ben. I am up and about now. I had a nice, busy, quiet 3 days in bed, writing this and that. Kingsley Martin asked me to write an answer to Joad in *The New Statesman* about Pacificism, and I struggled with this, but not very intelligently, I fear.[13] And letters, and E.M.F. and all – how time is always too short! *Eheu!*[14]

Those first novels (of EMF's) are so interesting. They couldn't have been written after the war: so intensely period. Imagine Lucy, Caroline Abbott, any of them, in a modern novel.[15] I wish he'd write one now. How far would his people come up to 1937 – or rather, to the fictional 1937 idea of people, which isn't, of course, the same? Of course they would be much too *nice* – fastidious, I mean, and virginal; perhaps too intellectual; people in most novels now are so *physical*, and so often and so easily in bed with each other, a situation in which E.M.F. would be both bored and embarrassed to find them, though, with his conscientious integrity, he might feel he must deal with it. 'Oh dear', I can hear him saying, 'Well, I suppose they must do it. Here goes'. But then he would think, how would this affect and re-orientate their lives and views, and that it surely must.[16] As it did in *Howards End*.[17] This alone would make him oddly unmodern (cf. Evelyn Waugh and his school). To my mind, much truer; but then I'm not modern either. To grasp the new point of view, one must (I think) be under 40 (or under 45, is it? Aldous Huxley has grasped it quite thoroughly).[18]

Forgive all this half-baked raw material for comments which I am still thinking about EMF as I write. I want to place him, and to have a piece about how he fits in with to-day – but don't quite yet know what I do think. I wonder what he would say himself.

Bless you and my love.

R.

1 The 'nice nunnery' is St Frideswide's, Cherwell Edge, situated on the corner of
   Oxford's South Parks Road and Saint Cross Road and separated from the River
   Cherwell by part of New College Playing Fields. Cherwell Edge had been tenanted
   by the Society of the Holy Child Jesus since 1905. From 1907 until 1969 it offered
   accommodation to Roman Catholic women students attending the University as well
   as to visiting students and scholars. In 1970 the Society moved to its present home at
   14 and 16 Norham Gardens, where it remains, and in 1977 Linacre College moved
   to Cherwell Edge. In the Society's archives are a *Scribbling Diary* and *House Diary* for
   1937. They record that Jean was in residence from 6 May until 6 July, but on several
   occasions went away for one night or for several nights. At this time Cross Bank
   was undergoing substantial alterations. Jean's widowed mother went away for three
   months while these were carried out. Jean too needed to escape somewhere, but was
   obliged to make several visits to Clent to check on the progress of the work.

2 A collection of essays by E.M. Forster. The book, published in 1936, takes its name
   from the village of Abinger Hammer in Surrey, where the author lived with his mother
   from 1925 until her death in 1945, in a house (West Hackhurst) that had been
   designed by his father.

3 'Postjudice' had already been used by John Ruskin and G.K Chesterton. One wonders
   whether Rose's unfavourable opinion of Indians was in any way connected, even if she
   was not conscious of the link, with the murder of her brother Aulay in India in 1909
   (Introd. I.4).

4 A highland region of the north Indian state of Bihar.

5 *Where Angels Fear to Tread* (1905) and *A Room with a View* (1908), Forster's first
   and third novels, have Italian, as well as English, settings and characters. What Rose
   writes here is to be compared with remarks of hers in the *The Writings of E.M. Forster*
   35–36. The book was published the following year. After referring to the habit the
   English have of falling in love with Italy, and to current problems such as 'Fascism,
   Signor Mussolini, . . . [and] Italian broadcast views on Britain', she writes: 'Mr.
   Forster, residing for a time in Italy in more felicitous days than these, fell deeply in love
   with it and with its denizens, with this enchanting, unaffected, cynical, callous, gay
   and somewhat barbaric Latin people, whose very humbug is emitted with a glorious
   gesture of eloquent absurdity, so different from the stiff, stilted, half-muted humbug
   of the fog-bound and inhibited British.'

6 *A Passage to India*, the last of the five novels published in Forster's lifetime. *Maurice*,
   completed in 1914, appeared posthumously in 1971.

7 Goldsworthy Lowes Dickinson, historian, philosopher, and essayist, was a Fellow of
   King's College, Cambridge, when Forster was an undergraduate there.

8 1923 is a mistake for 1924.

9 Like Forster, Eleanor first went to India in 1912.

10 'Should Blood Sports Be Prohibited?' was broadcast by the BBC National Service on
    19 May, 9.20–10 pm. There were three other participants in the discussion. Tristram
    Beresford was the eldest son of J.D. Beresford (*L*15). After working as a producer for
    the BBC in Birmingham, he registered as a conscientious objector at the beginning of
    the Second World War and embarked on a career in agriculture. As well as becoming
    a successful farmer, he distinguished himself as an agricultural economist, serving

as agriculture correspondent of *The Financial Times* for 14 years, writing regularly for *The Countryman*, lecturing, and broadcasting. His book *We Plough the Fields: Agriculture in Britain Today*, published by Penguin Books (Harmondsworth, 1975), had a wide readership.

11 The coronation of King George VI took place in Westminster Abbey on 12 May 1937. Heavy rain began to fall shortly before the royal procession reached Buckingham Palace after the ceremony. Whitsunday was 16 May.

12 The great bell, weighing over six tons, brought from Osney Abbey to Christ Church, Oxford, at the dissolution of the monasteries.

13 Rose's contribution, a letter printed under the heading 'Mr. Joad and the P[eace] P[ledge] U[nion]', is in *The New Statesman and Nation*, 22 May 1937, 844–845. The article to which it was a reply is in the issue of 15 May, 802–804. It is entitled 'What Is Happening in the Peace Movement?'. C.E.M. Joad, head of the Department of Philosophy at Birkbeck College, University of London, where he was a stimulating teacher, was a prolific writer and (in the 1940s) broadcaster, who did more than any of his contemporaries to popularise philosophy. Kingsley Martin was editor of *The New Statesman and Nation* from 1931 (the year in which the two magazines were amalgamated) to 1960. The PPU was founded by Dick Sheppard (*L*83 n. 3) and others in 1934, but membership was at first open only to men. When women were admitted in 1936, Rose became one of its sponsors. But she found it hard to be consistent and thoroughgoing in her advocacy of pacifism, as her six-page PPU pamphlet *An Open Letter to a Non-Pacifist* (London, 1937) shows, and she resigned her sponsorship in March 1938, when German troops marched into Austria. (Her PPU pamphlet is reprinted, with minor alterations, from her article in *Time and Tide*, 5 December 1936, 1695–1697, where she was replying to a piece by Malcolm Muggeridge in the issue of 28 November 1936, 1660–1662. Both articles appear under the heading 'Notes on the Way'.)

14 See *L*21 and n. 17 there.

15 Lucy Honeychurch is a character in *A Room with a View*, Caroline Abbott in *Where Angels Fear to Tread*. What Rose says here is echoed in *The Writings of E.M. Forster* 42: 'There could, of course, be no Miss Abbott in a novel of to-day. . . . A new kind of young woman has got into our novels, uninhibited, philandrous, high-geared, for ever in and out of bed.'

16 Compare *The Writings of E.M. Forster* 274–275: 'What we call (with a rather crude and impudent exclusiveness) Love, or (with a rather callow and ungrammatical ellipsis) Sex, does not loom with the conventional and tedious predominance given it by most imaginative writers. He handles it now casually, now with a gingerly aloofness, now with a welcome in which its particular incidence appears submerged or sublimated by reverence for it as a token coin of further and more important immensities.'

17 Published in 1910.

18 Huxley was 42 at this time. Rose was 55, Jean 45.

76

Varazze.

15 September [1938][1]

My dearest Jean

This is to bring my love for your birthday – lots and lots of it. I am, as you see, at Varazze, and very nice it is to be here. The people are as engaging and kind as ever – the town has grown enormously, and is now quite half new villas etc, but the sea and the hills are the same. I divide my time between them; the one is silky and blue and smooth and warm, and incredibly buoyant compared with all other water; I swim to and fro in front of our house[2] (my *albergo* is on the shore, quite close) – the other (the hills, I mean) are hot and piney and olivey and smell immensely sweet and the *cicali*[3] sing. I try and find the old walks, and the old paths – I sometimes can't remember how each walk began, it's rather like chasing dreams, or ghosts. Ghosts, of course, everywhere. Our little house is changed a lot, and has a high wall all round the garden, and the beach has sunk, but it is the same building, tho' a new colour; the interlopers long since painted it yellow with brown stripes, and the *orto*[4] is full of sand. Well well.

I don't get much news here, as I only see the Italian press. From that one would gather that such massacres of Sudetens[5] occurred daily that few Sudetens can be left to be oppressed or freed. I don't think we care in Varazze. Who are these *Sudetici*,[6] who are being so ill-treated by the *Cechi*,[7] and what are they to us, and what is all the fuss about, is what we feel. We don't listen much to wireless news. We feel, possibly, like the landlord of an inn I stayed in in France, who told me he did not want to hear of the doings of 'tous ces hommes terribles, Stalin, Hitler, Mussolini, Runciman' – he preferred Beethoven and Mozart. Poor mild little Runciman has got into fearful company![8]

I fear the situation is grave, in fact, I know it is; and perhaps it is selfish and escapist to be lapped in this peace and pleasure, far from the fray. I heard Hitler's speech,[9] relaid with admiring comments from Milan; it didn't seem to me that it amounted to much, but my German is very frail.

We finished our Peace and War anthology[10] before I came away, and I do think it is rather good. I'll send it you for a birthday present when it comes out, shall I?

I'm here for a few days more, then back to France, where I have still some things to do and people to see. I do hope I shall manage to see Isadore and Tom[11] before they go? – in fact I mean to. I hope they, Aunt Nannie, and you, all flourish. I read of 'intense military preparations' in England – but then I read many a curious thing here. I gorge myself with peaches and figs, which are absurdly cheap, and try to forget everything else – or most other things.

It's rather lovely to be here with the car, which has never occurred before; it brings lots of places within easy reach, though of course most of the walks are *not* helped by a car.

My love always. I hope this year will be a good one. Oh, how I do hope so. The world is incredible, I can't believe in it.

    R.

1 Rose wrote to Daniel George (Bunting) as well on the same date (ERM 16.43). Unsurprisingly, there are some close similarities between the two letters. Her visit to Varazze was (see also *L77*) part of a motoring holiday in France and Italy. Gerald was with her for at least part of the time. It was the last occasion they were abroad together. Emery 255 and LeFanu 205 say that Rose was in Varazze when Hitler and Chamberlain met in Munich. This is incorrect. Her Varazze letters to Daniel George and Jean were written on the day the two leaders met at Berchtesgaden. The Munich conference was a fortnight later, on 29–30 September, and Rose was back home by then.

2 The house in which Rose and her family lived from May 1891 until July 1894. Rose describes her family's idyllic time there in 'Villa Macolai', in Ethel Smyth et al., *Little Innocents: Childhood Reminiscences* (London, 1932) 46–49. Her parents sold the house in September 1911.

3 A mistake: the Italian for 'cicadas' is *cicale*.

4 'Kitchen garden' or 'orchard'.

5 Sudeten Germans.

6 Rose would have more correctly written *Sudeti*, the noun.

7 Czechs.

8 Lord Runciman was invited by the British Foreign Secretary, Lord Halifax, to mediate between the Czech government and the Sudetenland Germans. He commenced his futile mission in Prague on 3 August 1938.

9 The speech, made at Nuremberg on 12 September 1938, in which Hitler demanded self-determination for the Sudetens. It brought Runciman's mediation effort to an end.

10 *All in a Maze: A Collection of Prose and Verse Chronologically Arranged by Daniel George, with Some Assistance from Rose Macaulay* (London, 1938). The book's publication in November 1938 was not well timed, with the threat of war hanging over the country, and it was not a success.

11 Tom, aged eight, was the eldest of Isadore's and Bill's three children. His mother and he had arrived in England from the USA in August and were now staying with Jean's mother at Cross Bank.

77

Flat 7
8 Northumberland St.
W.1
2 October 1938

My dearest Jean

Your letter was so good to get, on my arrival here last Wednesday,[1] in a black hour, to a London full of trenches and gas-masks, all hope nearly gone. Yes, it's true about recovery. I saw Reims the other day – so beautifully built up again. And all those quiet little yellow-ochre villages and towns north of Paris, which were trampled mud and blood. Still, how one hates destruction; there are lovely things which can't be mended again so as to be the same. France and Italy was a dream of pleasure – Laon, Cluny, Sisteron, Aix, Arles, Marseille (which is noisy to a degree incredible, and *not* a dream of pleasure) – then over the mountains to beyond Toulon, and so along the Côte d'Azur, hunting up little places for Margaret to winter in (and this now seems on the map again) and into Italy, where I was for a week, and it *was* lovely, though Varazze is terribly grown and smartened – but I wrote to you from there. I came back by the Pyrenees – Narbonne, Collioure and those lovely Côte Vermeil places, and Foix,[2] and drove home up the western coast, partly to visit La Rochelle (so glorious!) and partly because I could have the news better there. And I met on the way huge cathedrals, and Romanesque gateways in tiny villages, and fat old peasant-women to whom I gave lifts, and who kept crying 'Ah, comme les Anglais sont gentils!' (it seems the French, perhaps wisely, don't give lifts much). At Beauvais I met the rain and *la guerre*, and so home and to more of these.

I was so sorry I missed Isadore. I wish I *had* met her in London, because she seems to have gone to pieces rather, and I might have cheered her up – but you did that when she returned, no doubt.[3] What made her crack up so? Her account of London has no relation to anything I found; I think she must have seen it through eyes of fear, and attributed her own feelings to people at large. I found cheerful, stolid crowds, watching the trenches in the parks and making jokes about them and about their gas-masks and about the war – I saw no panicky people, though no doubt there were some, there always are. Perhaps Isadore is demoralised by motherhood. Mother always said it was disintegrating, mentally and physically – partly the actual process, partly having such precious hostages to fortune. But I was sorry she felt it so badly.

Were you threatened with Birmingham refugees? Margaret was;[4] they were going to evacuate Portsmouth so far as they could, and each unoccupied room of each house was to contain a refugee. M. was considering coming to me for the duration, but scarcely liked to leave Wood End to the refugees altogether. For my part, being above the age-limit for most of the female war activities[5] (even if

I fancied them) I purposed to join (directly Luxborough House fell) one of the marauding[6] gangs that they said would roam about and loot among the ruins.[7] What a war! With all those amateur pilots of both sexes dashing about the sky, and all the homes-from-home in trenches and gas-proof shelters, and all the rest of it – it seems to have been organised in a thoroughly romantic spirit. Well, I'm glad it's deferred. Only deferred, all the best people say, with this boost we've given to Hitler, and the wealth and dominion that will now accrue to him in Eastern Europe. It's an infamous peace, of course – so, perhaps, are most peaces. It did make one rather sick, all that ovation in the streets from excited crowds when Chamberlain came home, and not a thought or a word for the poor Czechs he'd sold.[8] It wasn't – and isn't – decent. All the good are sick and ashamed, I think. Because he could have got decent terms out of H[itler] – we really had him more or less in a corner. The Czech protest to-day is pathetic. I'm glad ministers have begun to resign over it.[9] Harold Nicolson gives the peace six months only.[10] But I have a feeling that Hitler will fall before that. The Germans dread war as much as we do, obviously. The Italians, far more!

All my love. What a person you are, aren't you.[11]

R.

1 28 September.
2 Collioure was first visited by Rose and Gerald in August 1926 (*L*60 and n. 14 there). Both it and Foix ('The balcony where they dined at the Foix inn, leaning over the green river, eating trout just caught in it') are among the places Miss Anstruther remembered visiting with her lover ('Miss Anstruther's Letters' 306).
3 Rose means when Isadore returned to Clent from London.
4 That is, Margaret was threatened with refugees, not with Birmingham ones: Rose inserted 'Birmingham' as an afterthought. Clent is close to that city. Liss, where Margaret lived, is not far from Portsmouth.
5 The contribution Rose made to the war effort was as a volunteer ambulance driver, using her own car.
6 Misspelt 'maurauding'.
7 This light-hearted remark calls for two serious comments. The first is that it was no light matter for Rose when in May 1941 a bomb caused Luxborough House to fall, destroying her home, her books, her letters, and most of her other possessions. The second is that she had a fascination with ruins. This fascination is prominently manifested not only in *The Pleasure of Ruins* (1953) but also in *The World My Wilderness* (1950), in which Barbary and Raoul find themselves most at home among petty criminals and drop-outs inhabiting the ruins around St Paul's Cathedral just after the 1939–1945 war. See also *L*92 n. 1.
8 The British Prime Minister, Neville Chamberlain, returned to London, from the two-day Munich conference with Hitler, Mussolini, and the French Prime Minister, Édouard Daladier, in the evening of 30 September 1938. The Munich Agreement accepted Germany's occupation of the Sudetenland, but guaranteed the borders of the rest of Czechoslovakia.

9 (Alfred) Duff Cooper resigned as First Lord of the Admiralty on 1 October 1938 in protest against Chamberlain's policy of appeasement. He served as Minister of Information under Churchill (1940–1941) and as Ambassador to France (1944–1947).

10 Harold Nicolson, writer and critic, spent twenty years in the diplomatic service (1909–1929) before turning to journalism. From 1935 to 1945 he was National Labour MP for Leicester West. He was the husband of Vita Sackville-West.

11 This comment, together with Rose's opening words ('Your letter was so good to get'), suggests that Jean, realising that events during Rose's absence abroad might make her return home something of a shock, had struck exactly the right notes in writing to her.

78

[20] Hinde [House]
[Hinde Street]
[Manchester Square]
[London W.1][1]
25 February [1942][2]

Darling Jean

Your card just come. And your letter before, which I liked so much to get. It arrived rather in the midst of anxieties and stress: since I wrote last, Gerald O'Donovan came into King's Coll: Hospital to be examined for what his g.p. thought was kidney trouble. It proved not, but an inoperable malignant growth.[3] They thought they had better operate, but only as a palliative, and to prevent great pain in near future. The surgeon told me he didn't think he would get through the op., which was Monday evening.[4] He did get through it, and is now doing as well as he can; but they found the growth to be more wide-spread than had been thought, and have shortened the expectation of life from perhaps 18 months or so, to a good deal less.[5] The only thing is, they hope he won't suffer much. I haven't seen him since the op:, but hope to be let to by end of week – perhaps Friday or Saturday. He is still critically weak, of course.

Though he knew, I think, when I last saw him, that he might likely not come through the op:, he doesn't know that it's not a cure. So it's not too easy talking on that basis. I suppose, when strong enough, he will go home.[6]

All this rather gets in Dryden's way, though, as a divergent course, I have been trying to concentrate on him. It gives one a queer dazed feeling – a sudden precipice yawning across a road that has run for nearly 25 years. First Margaret, then he. No doubt life must be thus, when one reaches my age. Perhaps, for him (as for her) it may be better to slip out before worse befall us all. I find it is minor things that stab deepest – the destruction of all his letters at Luxborough, for instance. Why didn't I move them in time?[7]

Well, let us try not to be maudlin.

I was interested in your Dryden comments. I feel myself he was a natural and fundamental sceptic – but think you are right that he easily fell into the socially agreed (as at the Restoration). And your remarks on the translator's mind are illuminating. I'm glad Grierson is doing D. in that book.[8] I forget now what he said of him in *17th Century Cross Currents*.[9] T.S. Eliot is rather exaggerated: he says 'it is hardly too much to say that D. found the English speechless and gave them speech'.[10] Speechless? I think it *is* too much to say! T.S.E., whom I do like and admire, at times has a curious myopia, and baffles one. Tho' he can usually explain himself when one talks to him.

Poetry: yes. The time is nearly due for a history of the poetry of the last century – I mean since about 1850 to now, with all its movements and currents. I hope J.C. Smith[11] includes this.

I am reading an interesting American (Louis Bredvold) on Dryden's intellectual milieu and 17th c. background.[12] It is good. The biog: you read was perhaps Christopher Hollis – and a goose he is indeed! 'A comedy of errors', as some American professor calls it – and of superficialities and nonsense.[13] Why do people attempt what they haven't the means for? I don't know when Elizabeth's 'New Judgment' is to be.[14] The father-literature says Jane[15] transferred her paternal passion to Knightley, Mr Bennet, even Darcy, I think.[16] Your idea of reconstruction would be much brighter.

I hope much to see you. Will you ring when you are up (Wel[beck] 4107, as usual). Then we can arrange times. Come to Hinde for tea – or evening. I shall know more very soon about when I can go to K[ing's] C[ollege] H[ospital]. Meanwhile, dear love.

R.

---

1 Luxborough House, where Rose had lived since 1930, was destroyed by an enemy bomb during the night of 10–11 May 1941. The Germans took advantage of a full moon to launch their heaviest raid on London, using high explosive and incendiary bombs. The damage and loss of life were severe. Among the historic buildings damaged were Westminster Abbey, the Houses of Parliament, and the British Museum. Fortunately, Rose was staying in Margaret's house at Liss, helping Jeanie to sort belongings and prepare for the sale of the property and some of its contents. She discovered the destruction of her flat only when she returned to London in the evening of 13 May. After renting a bedsitting room in nearby Manchester Street for a few weeks, she took up residence in June 1941 in Hinde House. Her third flat in the section of London W1 bounded by Marylebone Road to the north and by Oxford Street to the south was to be her last home. Several other significant happenings in Rose's life since October 1938 may be briefly mentioned. On 26 June 1939, while holidaying with Gerald in northern England, her bad driving caused a car crash at Hartside near Alston in Cumberland. She swerved and collided with an oncoming car driven by the District Auditor for the Ministry of Health. Gerald

suffered head injuries and soon afterwards a minor stroke. Although he recovered, the incident deeply affected her. She appeared in Penrith Police Court on 18 July 1939, giving her name as Emily Macaulay, on a charge of driving a car without due care and attention. She was fined £2 with £1 6s 3d costs, and, despite a plea that her membership of the Women's Voluntary Ambulance Service meant that there were 'special circumstances', had her driving licence endorsed. (The case is reported under the heading 'HARTSIDE COLLISION. Woman Motorist Whose Attention was Diverted' in *Cumberland and Westmorland Herald*, 22 July 1939, 13.) On a brighter note, *And No Man's Wit*, about the Spanish civil war, was published in June 1940 – her first novel for three years, and her last for ten. But 1941 delivered a severe blow in each of three successive months: the death, from cancer, of Margaret at the age of 60 on 1 March; the death of Beryl's and Gerald's younger daughter, Mary, from septicaemia, at the age of 23 on 18 April; and the bombing of her flat in May. Also, Virginia Woolf drowned herself on 28 March. Another death, on 14 July, was that of her cousin Donald Macaulay, the husband of her Great Shelford friend Gladys Fanshawe.

2 The gap between this letter and the last one is long one, but it is not to be supposed that Rose and Jean stopped corresponding or keeping in touch in other ways. In fact, Rose's words 'since I last wrote', at the beginning of the letter, indicate that there was correspondence between them that has not been preserved. Moreover, Jean was one of those who gave Rose practical as well as moral support when she lost her flat and possessions in May 1941. In a letter of 28 May 1941 to Gilbert Murray, Rose mentions her kindness, and how she 'lends me black clothes when I have to attend funerals, and helps me to get curtains for my next flat' (GM 151.6).

·3 Colorectal cancer.

4 Rose is writing to Jean on Wednesday.

5 Gerald was to live for another five months. He died on 26 July 1942.

6 He did indeed go to his and his wife's home at Albury, Surrey, and it was there that he died.

7 See also *L79*, written almost a year after Gerald's death, in which Rose envies Isadore Smith for having her man still alive, despite being separated from him by the events of war, *and* for having his letters. For her pain over the loss of her lover's letters in the bombing of Luxborough House, and her remorse over her failure to save them, see also 'Miss Anstruther's Letters' (Bibliog. I.7). The autobiographical character of that short story is very marked and obvious, and attention has already been drawn to passages that recall experiences described in the letters to Jean. Rose's corrected typescript (ERM 5.4) reveals that the bombed building in which Miss Anstruther had her flat was originally to be called not Mortimer House, as in the published version, but Mexborough House.

8 'That book' is H.J.C. Grierson and J.C. Smith, *A Critical History of English Poetry*. It was to be published by Chatto and Windus (London, 1944). Grierson was an expert on John Donne and seventeenth-century poetry as well as on Sir Walter Scott. On J.C. Smith, see n. 11.

9 Full and correct title: *Cross Currents in English Literature of the XVIIth Century: or, the World, the Flesh and the Spirit, their Actions and Reactions: Being the Messenger*

Lectures on the Evolution of Civilization, Cornell University 1926–1927. The book was published by Chatto and Windus (London, 1929).

10 T.S. Eliot, *John Dryden: The Poet, the Dramatist, the Critic* (New York, 1932) 24.

11 James Cruickshank Smith had collaborated with Ernest de Selincourt in editing Edmund Spenser for Oxford University Press and had produced, among other things, several selections of poetry, some of them for schools. He was Jean's immediate boss in the Ministry of Munitions during the First World War. After the war, when he returned to his work in the Scottish Education Department in Edinburgh, the two continued to keep in touch. His surviving letters to Jean, written in 1919 and 1920, are mostly about their chief common interest, poetry, but show that he and his wife, Edith, had a great affection for her. They and a testimonial he wrote for her on 14 April 1923 also reveal that he admired her poems. In the testimonial he writes: 'I have read all or most of the verse that she has written since 1915, and can say with confidence that her vein of poetry is so pure and fine as to make one complain only that it is not more abundant. Her poems are not mere emotional rhapsodies, like so much contemporary verse: they contain a firm core of thought, high, austere and delicate.'

12 L.I. Bredvold, *The Intellectual Milieu of John Dryden: Studies in Some Aspects of Seventeenth-Century Thought* (Ann Arbor, 1934).

13 C. Hollis, *Dryden* (London, 1933).

14 'New Judgment' is the title of a half-hour talk, by Elizabeth Bowen on Jane Austen, broadcast by the BBC Home Service on Sunday 8 March 1942.

15 Jane Austen.

16 The first of these three characters is in *Emma*, the other two in *Pride and Prejudice*.

79

20 Hinde
10 [and 12] June [1943]

Darling Jean,

Thank you so much, for the book, your letter, and the kind copying of the Lisbon priests.[1] I feel deeply with Wm Lloyd – I wonder what he ate and drank. He was braver than I; I should never win applause for divinity while thus suffering in the stomach.[2] I wish we knew more details of these Lisbon seminarists. They now walk about Lisbon two by two in black gowns and birettas and scarlet oars sewn on their gowns (I was told why this, but have forgotten).[3] A large proportion of red-heads, there seemed to be the Sunday I went to a service in the College church, so no doubt many are Irish. But I don't know exactly *why* they come to train in Lisbon, with so many British and Irish colleges now available. I would like it myself, because I like Lisbon and the Inglesinhos[4] itself is so pretty, and they have a pleasant quinta across the Tagus to go to too.[5]

Actually, there would seem to have been more English Protestants martyred *in* Lisbon than English Catholics *from* Lisbon: the worst time for these was during the Spanish Captivity.[6] The Portuguese never really liked the Inquisition, and accepted it without enthusiasm.

I would like to find out more about Father Nicholas Aston, S.J. (early 17th c) and Father Floyd, or Fludd (same period).[7] Both their jobs seem to have been to keep an eye on their countrymen in Lisbon, make converts among them, and report Protestant religious assemblings to the Inquisition, or any cases of proselytizing or indiscreet remarks. Fr. Aston was generally liked, Father Floyd hated. Fr. Aston projected the English College, but died before he could found it. Father Floyd lived, apparently, in the monastery of San Roque, in Lisbon. Both would board the English ships in the Tagus, interview the sailors, and warn them not to bring their Bibles or Prayer Books on land. There is a good deal about them in the correspondence of the then English Consul, Hugh Lee,[8] which makes interesting reading. His job was to try and extract the English from the clutches of the Inquisition when they fell into them and, as you may imagine, he had a worrying time. Fortunately, that didn't have to be one of Uncle Charlie's jobs in Spain![9]

I have now finished Isadore. I think it is very charming – so beautifully written.[10] Aunt Nannie is right about the odd things people say to her! I suppose that is American – all that fuss, I mean, about adultery, the facts of life, sex, etc. Or is it just modern? I'm glad no one bothered *us* about them. I can't help feeling that children can't really be anything like so concerned about such things as grown-ups now make out. I remember, when I was about 15, Jeanie and me asking mother 'What makes people have babies?' She told us, we thought it a little odd, but I never remember either discussing it or brooding over it, though I did think it (with Sir T. Browne) rather a mistake of nature's, and would there had been some nicer way.[11] But it never really bothered me. And before that, one supposed it happened when a man and woman (unrelated) lived together – which seems to indicate weak reasoning power; perhaps the younger now are smarter.

What fun it will be to get to know those children. I love the picture of Emily, in her neat grey shorts.[12] It must have been comforting for Isadore to write all that. How much she is in love, isn't she. And how fortunate to have Bill's letters intact.[13] I suppose those children are the most attractive of all your nephews and nieces: perhaps one would expect it, with their parents. Yes indeed; heaven send no bad disappointment overtakes them.

Gilbert Murray (you may see the thought-sequence)[14] came in on Wednesday, and we went on to a conversazione of the Authors' Society where he made a charming speech.[15] We talked of all kinds of things – including Arnold Toynbee and Chatham House a little – but he made no reference to the Toynbee domestic affairs, nor have I heard any elsewhere, so I suppose it isn't much about yet.[16]

I am getting rather better, I think. I had an X-ray this morning, but no news yet of results, of course. I get about as usual now, but don't do anything wildly energetic. B[ritish] M[useum] research is exasperating: so many slips come back marked 'not available' – which means either destroyed, or secreted in Welsh mountains, both equally final, for the moment. Mine will be a weak and crippled book for lack of proper reading. The books are mostly in Portuguese, so difficult to find elsewhere. However, I hope the Public Records[17] are where they should be. And my Portuguese friend here has a good library.[18]

12th. I meant to post this, but obviously I didn't.

I had a partial report from K.C.H., fuller later. Same old ulcer in same old spot (which surprised me) but quite small, as it was last time it broke out. I don't know why the pain-timing is different this time. But they say it sometimes is. Anyhow, I suppose I shall be told to go along quietly, imbibing milk and resting – not away or in bed, I expect. I have this good char now, and life is quite easy, and I like to get on with my work if I can. I expect I will be recovered before long. Heart already better, they said. Blood pressure 128–30, which is of course too low for my age,[19] and they think me anaemic, but that is harmless if so; most women are, unless they have the opposite trouble, of high pressure, which is *much* more tiresome.

Will is out of hospital in Vancouver, and is staying with friends there, pottering about the house and garden and feeling quite cheerful. No farming for him this year, naturally. He looks forward to it again next year, but I doubt it, I fear the hour has struck for the end of that, though we don't say this to him, he loves his farm so much. Of course we are anxious still, as coronary thrombosis is dangerous even when it seems better.[20]

A fine Whitsun. I hope you are enjoying it, and feeling fairly good, and Aunt Nannie too. My love to her, please: that is a thing I would like to do, to see her again before very long, when travelling days return. You too. Are you ever jealous? I believe not. I found myself envying Isadore, who has her man *and* his letters. What matter being absent for 3 or 4 years? It is nothing, and will make it all the better when they are together again – like getting married all over again, bless them. My love always.

R.

---

1 The period after Gerald's death was, naturally, one of deep unhappiness for Rose. Her way of coping with her grief was not to write a novel – something she says she could not have done (*LF* 116) – but to busy herself with research on British people (not just English people, as most of her biographers say) who over the centuries went to Portugal for various reasons. The research resulted in *They Went to Portugal* (1946). The book contained only about half of what Rose had written, and the other half was published, more than thirty years after her death, under the title *They Went to Portugal Too* (1990). Portugal was neutral during the war, and between 6 March and 7 May 1943 Rose had a happy and productive stay there, getting the feel of the country and of course collecting material for the proposed book. Her expenses were paid by Collins, her publishers, although, when she delivered the book to them, they refused to accept it, and it was taken on by Jonathan Cape instead. During and just

after her visit to Lisbon, she wrote three articles: 'Lisbon Day, London Day', *The Anglo-Portuguese News*, 6 May 1943, 5; 'Looking in on Lisbon', *The Spectator*, 2 July 1943, 8; 'A Happy Neutral', *The Spectator*, 9 July 1943, 33. The last two of these are reprinted in *They Went to Portugal Too* 305–311.

2 William Lloyd or Floyd, born in Carmarthenshire, arrived in Lisbon on 1 October 1635, when he was aged 21, was ordained priest on 26 April 1639, and remained in the English College until 29 June 1642. The College's Annals describe him as able, but as suffering from a severe weakness of the stomach. He returned to Wales, and in 1679 became a victim of the reaction to the 'Popish Plot' invented by Titus Oates and Israel Tonge. He died in prison in Brecon six days before the day appointed for his execution. See [William] Croft, *Historical Account of Lisbon College* (Barnet, 1902) 19–21, 198.

3 See *They Went to Portugal Too* 81: 'the students [of the English College] donned the uniform in which they today walk the Lisbon streets – cassock, biretta, sleeveless habit, bearing the design of an oar in scarlet, for under SS Peter and Paul, they were to go fishing for men'.

4 Colégio dos Inglesinhos, the English College in Lisbon, was first occupied in 1628. For Rose's published account of it, see *They Went to Portugal Too* 77–94. Its last students were dispersed in 1971, although its 24th and last President, Mgr James Sullivan, remained in his post until 1975.

5 On the country house and estate at Pera, south of the Tagus, see *They Went to Portugal Too* 87–88.

6 1580–1640.

7 See *They Went to Portugal* 190–203; *They Went to Portugal Too* 98–109. Henry Floyd, from the diocese of Norwich, studied at the English Colleges in Reims, Valladolid, and Seville before becoming Superior of the English Residence in Lisbon. He was ordained in Valladolid in 1590 (probably) and became a Jesuit in 1599. Aston (or Ashton), from the diocese of Lichfield, also studied in Reims (1589–1590), using the name of Anthony Walwin, and was ordained in Valladolid, to which he was transferred in September 1590, but, contrary to Rose's indication in this letter (not repeated in her books), does not seem to have become a Jesuit. He succeeded Floyd as Superior of the English Residence in Lisbon in 1597. He died about 1605, with his wish to see an English College in Lisbon unfulfilled. Most of the above information about him is derived from Godfrey Anstruther, *The Seminary Priests: A Dictionary of the Secular Clergy of England and Wales 1558–1603. I Elizabethan 1558–1603* (Ware/ Durham, [1969]) 11–12.

8 See *They Went to Portugal* 191–202; *They Went to Portugal Too* 95–116.

9 Jean's father had been British Consul in Bilbao and, later, Consul-General in Barcelona.

10 The reference is to Ann Leighton (Isadore's pen-name), *While We Are Absent* (Boston, 1943), an account of being a wife and mother in Massachusetts during the war, with her husband away.

11 See Thomas Browne, *Religio Medici* 2.9: 'I could be content that we might procreate like trees, without conjunction, or that there were any way to perpetuate the World without this trivial and vulgar way of coition: it is the foolishest act a wise

man commits in all his life; nor is there any thing that will more deject his cooled imagination, when he shall consider what an odd and unworthy piece of folly he hath committed.' Rose recalls the same passage in a letter to Jeanie in 1957 (*LS* 236).

12 Emily Jean Macaulay Smith, the youngest of Isadore's and Bill's three children and Rose's god-daughter, was aged seven at this time. In *While We Are Absent* she is 'Lucy', described as being 'in smart grey shorts' (157).

13 Despite having lived in the USA since 1929, Bill spent most of the war, from 1939 until the autumn of 1944, in the British army, attached to MI5. He was based in England, but his duties took him to other parts of the world as well, including Africa and Australia.

14 Murray was predeceased by three of his five children – Agnes in 1922, Denis in 1930, and Basil in 1937.

15 The event was held in Grosvenor House on 9 June. Murray was one of three hosts, the others being G.M. Trevelyan and H.G. Wells. Rose's friendship with Murray, whom she had known since at least 1919 (*L*10 n. 6) developed considerably during the Second World War and continued until his death in 1957. He and his wife were among those who assisted Rose with gifts of books after the bombing of her flat.

16 The historian Arnold Toynbee was the husband of Murray's elder (and only surviving) daughter, Rosalind. The couple married in 1913 and had three sons, the eldest of whom committed suicide in 1939. They had now separated, and were to be divorced in 1946. Also in 1946 Arnold married Veronica Marjorie Boulter, his assistant throughout his years as Director of Studies at the Royal Institute of International Affairs, Chatham House (1926–1955).

17 Public Record Office, Chancery Lane.

18 See *L*82 and n. 12 there.

19 Rose's report of her blood pressure is puzzling: if her systolic blood pressure was in the range 128–130, it was not low; and if her diastolic reading was 30, she was not alive!

20 Will, whom Rose had last seen when he visited England in 1938, died of a heart attack on 16 November 1945 a few days short of his 61st birthday.

80

20 Hinde [House]
4 July [1943]

Darling Jean

I meant to write before, to thank you for yours: and now I have your p.c. My Floyd was Henry: he is in the *D.N.B.*,[1] and I read something else about his Lisbon activities. Perhaps Canon Collingwood[2] might know something both of him and Fr Aston (who projected, but didn't live to found, the Lisbon College). Both he and Fr <F>loyd[3] were posted, I gather, in Lisbon to keep an eye on the English there (Jacobean). I would very much like to approach Canon Collingwood, if you think I might. If he lectured at Lisbon, he would be sure to be helpful about the College, anyhow. If your kind Abbess[4] would really give me an introduction to him, I should be most grateful to her, him, and (above all) you. Thank you so much.

Yes, Portugal traded hugely with Bristol and Wales and the west: also of course with Ireland. With London too, of course; but particularly with the West. The Lisbon English Factory of Merchants had all kinds – English, Scotch, Welsh, Irish.[5]

Well, I have been up now for three or four days – since last Friday – and feel quite restored, pain quite gone. I now get out again, and have been to the B.M. etc. My doctor wanted me to go and lie in bed at Romford, as before, for a fort-night (so did Jeanie), but I felt I couldn't be so far from my books – Clent would have been still further, of course, and the journey not a good plan I suppose – so I stayed here, and a nice stout daily woman came in and did all my errands, and I was able to get on with Portugal quite a bit. Now I feel almost well, tho' still cautious. Such lovely weather to creep about in.

Una Pope-Hennessy[6] told me the other day that Fr. Burdett had been very ill (heart attack).[7] But he was better, and I hope is now better still.

This horrible smashing and bombing – it is ghastly. I am glad to see all the protesters – among them Dr Inge,[8] who complained of the destruction of so much beauty – Palermo, Genoa, Naples, Cologne, the old German towns. One of the Sunday papers had a leader on him, called 'Silly Dean', and saying what do beautiful buildings matter? We do, I gather, try to avoid them: but in the night how can we? What kind of a shambles will Europe be after this war? And, alas, what hate everywhere. Do you see *The Christian News Letter* ever? I send some-thing out of it which really was rather consoling to me – a spot of brotherly love in the darkness. There is a good number this week too. I wish our propagandists wouldn't so often talk as if Germany and the Nazis had thrown off Christianity (I mean church Xianity, not Xian conduct). I am told it is not so in the least: church worship and attendance, in all the communions, go on quite freely and copiously, as much as here. Their fault (like every one else's) is in not seeing the discrepancy. One gets so tired of our silly propaganda.

I was in Regent's Park yesterday: several leaves fell!

How are you, love? And Aunt N[annie], to whom my love. A great deal to yourself.

R.

---

1 Jean may have mentioned the Jesuit theologian John Floyd, Henry's younger brother.
2 Cuthbert Collingwood was at this time Chaplain of Westminster Cathedral and editor of *Westminster Cathedral Chronicle*.
3 Rose has mistakenly written 'Lloyd'.
4 Laurentia McLachlan, Abbess of Stanbrook Abbey. See *L*103 n. 6.
5 See the first chapter of *They Went to Portugal Too* (3–13), entitled 'Medieval Traders: Merchants in Lisbon (Twelfth to Mid-sixteenth Centuries)'.

6 The widow of Major-General Richard Pope-Hennessy, who had died in 1942, Una had been created DBE in 1920 in recognition of her work for the Central Prisoners of War Committee of the British Red Cross Society. She was a versatile writer, best known for her works of literary and historical biography. Her husband was a Roman Catholic, and she became one. They had two sons, John and James, with whom Rose remained very friendly after Una's death (17 August 1949). John became a distinguished art historian and museum director. James, the younger son, was also highly talented. Following in his mother's footsteps, he became a writer specialising in biography. He became best known to the public for his *Queen Mary, 1867–1953* (1959). But of particular interest, in the context of Rose's friendship with the Pope-Hennessy family, is his *West Indian Summer: A Retrospect* (1943), a book inspired by his prewar employment as private secretary to the Governor of Trinidad and Tobago. In it he describes the experiences of nine visitors to the West Indies. The parallel with Rose's *They Went to Portugal* is obvious. It is possible, as Emery 277 tentatively suggests, that the two writers discussed with one another the basic structure of their books. (Emery is under the misapprehension that *West Indian Summer* was written by John.) James was a homosexual who increasingly associated with low company, and in the evening of 25 January 1974 he was killed in his home by three young men, who were convicted of his manslaughter.

7 Francis Burdett had been a Jesuit priest, but had resigned on account of poor health and become a secular priest. He spent his last years in London as a semi-invalid. Among Jean's papers is a letter, dated 6 September 1943 and written to her when she was staying in a convent, in which he thanks her 'for the beautiful note-paper and much else' and gives her spiritual advice. He died on 21 December 1943. On his obituary in *The Catholic Herald* and a response to it, see *L*86 n. 9–10.

8 W.R. Inge, Dean of St Paul's Cathedral from 1911 to 1934, 'the gloomy dean' as he was often called, was well known for his outspoken and often controversial opinions. He expressed these not only in his sermons and books but also in *The Evening Standard*, for which he wrote for 25 years (1921–1946). His journalistic activity and influence prompted the quip that he was 'a pillar of the Church of England and two columns of *The Evening Standard*'.

81

All that survives is this postscript.

[Summer 1943[1]]

P.S. À propos my remark about not trusting the Pope's judgment, I was thinking why – partly it is his[2] early support of Hitler and the Nazi party – Thyssen[3] says he influenced the Catholic Centre Party to vote Hitler into power, at a time when his anti-Jew and anti-Democrat policy had long made him revolting to many of us. But I think this was part of the anti-Socialist and anti-Left business, which perhaps it is v. difficult for the Catholic Church to escape. The same applies to his past and present goodwill towards Franco and his revolution, which perhaps it is scarcely fair to hold against him (and here even you and I I think differ). I don't know at what point he became anti-Nazi; I am sure he is now. As to Italian nationalist feeling, I don't see how he can hope to be unaffected by this – I mean, wouldn't any of us be? I am a little myself – I don't mean by English nationalism, for this goes without saying, I fear, and one has to be continually on one's guard against it – but by Italian, because I love them so much. I can't bear the thought of those two little islands being smashed up like that.[4] Did you see that a group of returned Italian prisoners on being disembarked in Italy shouted '*Pace! Pace!*' and the crowd joined in, and the police had to interfere and cancel the planned celebrations?[5] If only they will go on shouting it, bless them.

Forgive my doubts about the Pope: you can have them about Canterbury[6] if you like!

1 This fragment follows on naturally after Letter 80, with its remarks on bombing and on Christianity in Germany. The reference to the bombardment of two small Italian islands (see n. 4) indicates the summer of 1943, probably not much later than mid-July.

2 Eugenio Pacelli, who became Pope Pius XII on 2 March 1939, was Papal Nuncio in Germany from 1917 to 1929 – first in Munich, then (from 1920) in Berlin. In December 1929 he was made a Cardinal and in February 1930 became the Holy See's Secretary of State. On 20 July 1933 he signed a concordat between the Vatican and the Nazi government defining the position of the Roman Catholic Church in Germany. A few days before that, the Catholic Centre Party (Zentrumspartei) went into voluntary liquidation.

3 Fritz Thyssen, a Catholic and wealthy industrialist, who, having earlier given Hitler financial support, became strongly critical of him in the late 1930s. He fled to Switzerland in September 1939, then sought refuge in France, but was extradited to Germany in 1941. He spent the rest of the war in concentration camps and the last year of his life in Argentina. He wrote *I Paid Hitler* (London, 1941), but the book does not contain the claim Rose attributes to him.

4 The Italian islands of Pantelleria and Lampedusa, situated between Sicily and North Africa. The bombardment of Pantelleria began on 8 May 1943 and continued until its surrender to the allies on 11 June. Lampedusa surrendered on 12 June. By the time Pentelleria was taken, allied bombers had flown over 5,000 sorties against it and dropped more than 6,000 tons of bombs. Much the heaviest bombardment was in the last days of the operation, and it is unlikely that Rose was writing before, or much before, it was completed.

5 Italian prisoners taken on Pantelleria and Lampedusa were transported either to Medjez el Bab in Tunisia or to Casablanca in Morocco, and the identity of the group mentioned by Rose has not been established. Probably they were a mixture of the sick and wounded and of those classed as 'protected personnel' under the terms of the Geneva Convention. Examples of exchanges of British and Italian prisoners in these categories are those that took place in Turkish ports on 21 March 1943 (at Mersin) and 8–9 May (at Izmir).

6 The Archbishop of Canterbury was William Temple.

82

20 Hinde House
Hinde St.
W.1
4 August 1943

Darling Jean

Thank you so much for your letter and beautiful string bag – did you net it – or knot it – I don't know what the word is, do you know the song about how Phyllis answered nought but went on knotting? Perhaps she made a string bag.[1]

I am leading the quiet industrious life suited to my years – writing daily at the Record Office, where I still peruse MS letters of Consuls and ambassadors in Lisbon, cursing this vile bunch. But it is nice stuff, much of it. I am getting a lot about Fr. Henry Fludd out of it.

When in Hinde, I write the book (now to be called *Going to Portugal*).[2] I am now on Philippa of Lancaster, who married John I of Portugal – she is in the section called 'Royalty',[3] along with a brief stop at Estoril by Edward VIII,[4] a yachting call from his grandfather,[5] and a visit from the Duke of Kent in 1940.[6] Philippa was rather nice. The Portuguese historians say that her 'glacial English influx' was passed down to her sons, who were all amazingly cold and chaste in matters of love – so unlike the Portuguese. Rather interesting.

I shall be in Romford for a week or so from 14th, lying in the garden. At present I feel indescribably exhausted, as if at the bottom of a deep pit, and every movement like a climb up a steep bank. Tired heart, my doctor says; and you know about that yourself. It is collapsing, and makes one very lethargic and inclined to despair. My only activities are gentle bicycle rides to the Record Office, B.M. and London Library,[7] and up the High St to get my food. I am seeing a few friends over from Portugal now and then. The state of things there has been bad – rioting for food and against Salazar, particularly since Mussolini fell.[8] But they parade the troops about Lisbon, and that quietens the Portuguese, who are easily intimidated. I suppose in the end there will be an upset of some kind, as in the other countries; I hope not a bloody one.

I had a long letter from Aunt Mary, who says London is so quiet and empty after the rush to the sea. It has seldom seemed to me more full. But what torments people will endure to get elsewhere than where they are! It shows a great, even if a rather wrong, spirit, which one must admire, though not emulate. I have so little spirit myself these days but I gape in wonder at these endeavours and endurances. As to those who are contending in the heat round Etna,[9] imagination boggles. Oh dear, why doesn't Badoglio yield?[10] And why must Churchill say such ill-bred, bullying things about stewing and hotting up?[11]

I had a reply from Canon Collingwood, but unfortunately he professes little knowledge of his alma mater; he only knows what he has read in Canon Croft's dull book. And of 17th cent. English Catholic Lisbon, nothing. I know much more, it seems. But he has told me someone who might give me more information, and writes pleasantly. A mine of Portuguese information is Professor Prestage, who inhabits a charming little Queen Anne house in Holland Street,[12] and lets me go there to refer to the Portuguese Chronicles he has that the B.M. has sent away. He thinks I am approaching this book (to be called *Going to Portugal*) in the right spirit, and that it may well take 20 years! I agree. I hope it won't outlast me.

I hope you are feeling reasonably well and cheerful. Myself, I rather like being alone in the house – so much liberty and space all to oneself but for the housemaid, who more than repays the space she fills, and whom one couldn't be without. My love, blessings and thanks. R.

1 'Phyllis Knotting', by Charles Sedley (c. 1639–1701), begins 'Hears not my Phyllis' and has the refrain 'Phyllis, without frown or smile, | Sat and knotted all the while'. In a letter of 14 May 1941, written immediately after the loss of her flat and its contents, Rose told Daniel George: 'The string bag will nicely hold all I now possess' (ERM 16.107). One wonders whether she recalled that remark when she received Jean's gift for her 62nd birthday.

2 The book was actually to be called *They Went to Portugal*.

3 Philippa of Lancaster, daughter of John of Gaunt, Duke of Lancaster, married John I of Portugal in Oporto in February 1387. She bore him seven children, including five sons who survived to adulthood, and was reputed to be a model wife and mother.

4 The visit of Edward VIII (not described by Rose in either of her Portugal books) was made over three years after his abdication, when he was Duke of Windsor. He and the Duchess spent about three weeks in Portugal in July 1940 before he took up his appointment as Governor of the Bahamas. On 1 August they sailed from Lisbon in the liner *Excalibur* under the names 'Captain and Mrs Wood'.

5 Edward VII made State visits to Portugal in 1876, as Prince of Wales, and in 1903, as King. Rose writes entertainingly about them in *They Went to Portugal* 55–61. In 1903 Edward came in the yacht *Victoria and Albert*, and, although 'a yachting call' suggests something more informal and recreational than a State occasion, it is probably to this that Rose refers. If Edward ever made a third visit to Portugal, information about it has eluded the present editor and his knowledgeable Portuguese contacts.

6 George Edward Alexander Edmund, Duke of Kent, fourth son of George V and Queen Mary, represented Britain at the celebrations of the eight-hundredth anniversary of the foundation of the Portuguese State and the three-hundredth anniversary of the restoration of Portuguese independence. He was in Lisbon from 25 June to 2 July 1940.

7 An independent subscription library founded, on the initiative of Thomas Carlyle, in 1841 and located since 1845 at the north-west corner of St James's Square, SW1. Rose became a member on 4 February 1928 and served on its Committee for several years. After Rose's death Veronica Wedgwood recalled how she often encountered her in the library, especially when she was working on *They Went to Portugal* and *Pleasure*

of Ruins, and describes how Rose, in her search for books and in defiance of warning notices, frequently moved from floor to floor via dangerous ladders rather than via the stairs (Harold Nicolson et al., 'The Pleasures of Knowing Rose Macaulay', *Encounter* 12, 3 (March 1959) 28). It is also recorded that Rose's daring and head for heights on ladders served the library well after it was damaged by a bomb on the night of 28–29 February 1944: of those who assisted with the recovery of books, 'Rose Macaulay was bravest, telling them to hang on to her legs as she leant out into space' (John Wells, *Rude Words: A Discursive History of the London Library* (London, 1991) 179). In the reading room is a rose-coloured leather armchair, donated by Rose's friends in her memory. Above the chair is a plaque and, above that, a framed photograph of her.

8 Mussolini ceased to be Prime Minister of Italy on 25 July 1943. In the last days of the month unrest in northern Portugal was followed by strikes in the Lisbon area. The Salazar government's response to the disturbances included strong police and military measures. The official (government) line was that the strikers' actions were non-political and 'due to the inevitable scarcity of food'.

9 The allied invasion of Sicily ('Operation Husky') began on the night of 9–10 July 1943, and the liberation of the island was completed on 17 August. The slopes of Etna were heavily defended by the enemy.

10 Marshal Pietro Badoglio replaced Mussolini as Prime Minister. The unconditional surrender of Italy to the allies was agreed on 3 September and announced on 8 September. On 13 October the Italian government, based in Brindisi, declared war on Germany.

11 In a statement to the House of Commons on 27 July 1943 Winston Churchill, the Prime Minister, said that the allies 'should let the Italians, to use a homely phrase, stew in their own juice for a bit, and hot up the fire to the utmost, in order to accelerate the process', until, by agreeing to unconditional surrender, they satisfied 'all the indispensable requirements we demand for carrying on the war against our prime and capital foe, which is not Italy but Germany'.

12 Edgar Prestage had occupied the Camoens Chair of Portuguese at King's College, London (1923–1936). His Portuguese first wife committed suicide in 1918. In 1924 he married Victoria Cobb, and it was she who owned the house at 16 Holland Street, Kensington.

83

Hinde
12 August [1943]

Darling Jean

I think from your letter I must have exaggerated my unwellness. Heart not 'collapsing' (which implies getting worse), but merely 'slightly collapsed' – my doctor's expression, and only, I take it, means tired. I didn't use the word collapsed in talking to Jeanie, who worries about health (other people's, I mean). And it will right itself in time, with rest and gastric improvement. I *shall* rest at Romford, whither I go on Monday[1] for a week, till J. goes to Woking. This cursed shortage of nurses means that she won't take more than a week of her 4 weeks' holiday, and spends 3 of them relieving other people in their jobs so that they can get holidays – I don't know why the Woking matron should take a fortnight and J. only a week, to enable her to get a fortnight, it seems all wrong to me.

J. is muscling in on the Quakers' Post-War European Relief Scheme, as a nurse – but whether any of them will ever get anywhere is doubtful, as the Organization itself says;[2] and, if they do, whether even nurses, if in the 60's, will be taken, is more doubtful still. Still, the postal course will be interesting. It deals largely with European conditions, international, psychological and other: but, as the Quakers, bless their hearts, never knew a thing about European psychological or international conditions before the war or during it, it seems improbable they will after it. A more uninformed, head-in-the-air, fantasy-drugged good religious loving body of people, can never have walked this evil earth, I suppose. I saw so much of them between '36–'39; they used to be the admiration and despair of the (quite shrewd) Dick Sheppard,[3] in the days when they went about swearing that Hitler meant no aggression in Europe. A pity they wouldn't listen more to the German radio; but of course they never would, they are like the deaf adder that stoppeth her ears.[4] Still, they will start off in ex-enemy countries, if they ever get there, with the great initial advantage of having opposed the war; that certainly helps, psychologically.

I hope you'll translate that poem:[5] it would be interesting.

My friend David Ley, from the Lisbon British Institute (he who nearly drowned me!) is home, and is being very nice and helpful about my book.[6] Such a nice person: you would like him. He ferrets out all kinds of points for me. He is now going to the Madrid Institute instead, with some distaste for all that régime – which probably is near its end.[7]

My love. Don't think I am worse than I am, will you. It's only fatigue.

R.

---

1 16 August.

2 The Quakers were prompt and energetic in carrying out relief work in Europe (and elsewhere) after the war. They were awarded the Nobel Peace Prize for 1947, half of it going to the Friends Service Council and half to the American Friends Services Committee.

3 Sheppard first became well known to the public during his years as Vicar of St Martin-in-the-Fields, Trafalgar Square (1914–1927). He kept the church open at all hours of the day and night and provided shelter for the homeless. He was Dean of Canterbury in 1929–1931 and a Canon of St Paul's Cathedral in 1934–1937, but was dogged by ill health. In 1927 he declared himself a pacifist, and he was one of the founders of the Peace Pledge Union (*L75* n. 13). He died in 1937.

4 Psalms 58.4, with 'ear', not 'ears'.

5 Unidentified.
6 David Ley, with his excellent knowledge of Portuguese as well as of Spanish language, culture, and history, was well equipped to assist Rose. He and she remained friends until she died. Copies of her letters to him are in the Wren Library of Trinity College, Cambridge (ERM 15.194–241). The swimming incident occurred at Foz do Arelho, north of Lisbon, on the last full day of her visit to Portugal (6 May). Ley described it in a letter to his father: 'She wanted to bathe there which she did, but unfortunately had a heart seizure in the water and was in a dreadful state. However, people were called from the hotel and they fetched all the restoratives they could think of, and telephoned for the doctor from Caldas. Luckily by the time for the train she was completely all right again' (ERM 10.62).
7 In fact, Franco's dictatorship was to last for another 32 years, until his death in 1975.

84

20 H[inde] H[ouse]
17 September 1943

Darling Jean

My love for tomorrow and the coming year. I had your letter a few days back – thank you for it. I am *much* better, and now getting about again and doing things, though rather warily. I was for a time in hospital,[1] having rather collapsed into faints and sicknesses, after a long time of feeling completely under water, fathoms deep, so that at Romford (I had a week there) I could only loll about and was n.g. for a holiday. But now I feel better than all the summer I did; I take iron, and all kinds of things, and also am having a course of massage from a nice Swede (Miss Schannong, who also does Aunt Mary) – v.g. for general system, circulation, heart, head, everything. I was presented with a sample treatment by Dame Una Pope-Hennessy, found my doctor approved, so ordered 5 more; I have now had 3. Apparently Aunt M. is much better for it; they seem to get on well, and like each other. Aunt Mary pressed Sara[2] on me a few weeks ago, but I have now a nice woman who comes in daily and does all my work – but it was a very generous offer.

And now I am lunching at Boulestin's![3] That was yesterday, with Graham Greene back from Africa, and my first lunch out, and no ill effects.[4] I am also going to the Record Office again, but don't go in the mornings yet, which leaves a short time, as it shuts at 3.30.

Enough about me. How are you? Still, I see, at Clent, and I suppose the flat still let. I hope you are feeling fairly good. I like these September days, the pre-autumn loveliness of them.

I have found now a lot about the founding of the Lisbon College – much more than any of its alumni seem to know! Rather good stuff, in Dodd and Tierney[5] – the frantic (and finally successful) squabbles of its founders with the Jesuits, who tried to nobble it for themselves. The letters between Lisbon and Rome on the subject are very amusing. I am deep in State Papers (Elizabethan). Very enthralling reading. The Plots of the Exiles in Madrid and Rome – with Lisbon as jumping-off ground, but the Portuguese king[6] was faithful to his Oldest Ally, and wouldn't further the invasive expeditions – indeed he diverted one of them to Africa with him. There are some good characters slipping in and out of these intrigues and alarms – Stuk<e>ly,[7] and James Fitzmaurice,[8] and the pensioned English and Irish round the Madrid court and at Rome. Material for a better and more detailed study than has (I think) ever been made of it. Someone should do it.

Poor Rome, and poor Italy, with all these tough-guys fighting to the death across her body, when she had hoped to be out of it all! They are fighting among such precious things – Pompeii and Paestum[9] and everything – like bulls in china-shops – no use to hope they are being careful, I am sure they are not. Poor Mr Osborne,[10] who for a few days could get some exercise again walking about Rome, is now more restricted than ever, I suppose, with even St Peter's piazza full of the foe. Things seem slightly better to-day – but what an awful business there is ahead.

I hope Aunt Nannie is well. My love to her, please, and all to yourself. I have nothing to send you but that. You – and Jeanie – are two of the strongest arguments I know for Christianity (that remarkable and insoluble business). Do you mind being this, or my saying so? I hope not – it is so true, and important!
   Rose.

1 King's College Hospital.
2 Sara O'Callaghan, Mary Macaulay's live-in maid.
3 The famous restaurant opened by Marcel Boulestin in Covent Garden in 1927. Boulestin, who died in Paris just three days after Rose wrote the present letter, was well known not only as a restaurateur but also as a writer on cookery. In 1937 he became the first person to give a cookery demonstration on BBC television. Boulestin's closed in 1994, to be replaced by . . . Pizza Hut.
4 For just over a year Greene was based in Freetown, Sierra Leone, working for the British Secret Intelligence Service (MI6). He returned home on 1 March 1943. At the time Rose wrote this letter, he was in charge of the Portuguese desk in the Iberian sub-section of Section V (the counter-espionage unit) of MI6, where his immediate superior was Kim Philby. Given Rose's interest in Portugal and her recent visit to it, it would be surprising if it had not featured in her and Greene's lunchtime conversation. Both he and his wife, Vivien, were on friendly terms with Rose, and his choice of a book to give to Vivien on their nineteenth wedding anniversary was *They Went to Portugal*. (The copy, in the present editor's ownership, is inscribed: 'So much love. Oct. 15. 1927 – Oct. 15. 1946. G. to V.' The inscription is tear-jerking, because Greene was about to embark on his affair with Catherine Walston. He left Vivien in November 1947.) Despite her friendly relations with him, Rose was not exactly an

unqualified admirer of his novels. For example, she criticises *Brighton Rock* for 'the extreme lowness of its characters' (*LF* 140); and she says that *The End of the Affair* 'isn't good', partly because 'the people are all rather low types, and not convincing', partly because of the writer's trivialisation of religion, adding: 'What a mess his mind must be – nothing in it, scarcely, but religion and sex, and these all mixed up together' (*LF* 196).

5 Charles Dodd and M.A. Tierney, *Dodd's Church History of England: From the Commencement of the Sixteenth Century to the Revolution in 1688, with Notes and Additions and a Continuation by the Rev. M.A. Tierney, F.S.A.* (London, 1839–1843). The foundation of the Lisbon College is described in vol. IV (1841) 123–133.

6 Sebastian (1554–1578). See *They Went to Portugal* 340.

7 Thomas Stukely (or Stucly) was a soldier and adventurer who, coming to Lisbon in the hope of persuading Sebastian to support a proposed expedition to Ireland, was persuaded by him to join in attacking the Moors of north Africa. The African venture was a disastrous failure, and both men were killed in the battle of Alcazar on 4 August 1578. Rose writes about Stukely in *They Went to Portugal* 346–358, in part 2 of the chapter on 'Plotters'.

8 James Fitzmaurice Fitzgerald, the subject of part 1 of Rose's chapter on 'Plotters' (*They Went to Portugal* 337–346), was an Irish nobleman, who, like Stukely, wanted to interest Sebastian in the expedition to Ireland, but failed. The king would not even grant him an audience. When, no thanks to the Portuguese, JFF eventually reached Ireland in July 1579, he was unsuccessful in organising an effective rebellion, and was soon killed by one of his own cousins in a skirmish.

9 The Latin name for the Greek colony of Posidonia, south-east of Naples. Established c. 600 BC, it is particularly renowned for its fine Doric temples. Although there was fighting close to Paestum, the temples were not damaged. There was no fighting at Pompeii.

10 Francis Osborne, Britain's wartime ambassador to the Holy See.

85

20 H[inde] H[ouse]
16 December 1943

Darling Jean

I should have written before, to say how glad I am Aunt Nannie is better.[1] Indeed, I meant to write to her for her birthday (to-day? yesterday?) but was heavily submerged and forgot. And now I write to wish you and her (and Aunt Mary if she is with you) a happy Christmas so far as may be. I think it is splendid to have a severe go of bronchitis at 83 and come up smiling – as I hope she has.

I see Aunt M., you said, was to be gone by now, all being well. I'm glad she came – and how *good* you are, how much better than I am or could be! I must write to her.

I shall be at Romford for Xmas day.

I hear from the Pope-Hennessys that Fr. Burdett has been very dangerously ill again – I think he had rallied a little when I last heard news (last Thursday evening,[2] when I was dining there). What nice creatures John and James are – do you know them? About 28 and 26 – and John, most civilly, asked me to his birthday dinner on Thursday.[3] They have the kind of sensitive cleverness and intellectual sensibility that is so charming. I suppose James is probably spoilt – he is so beautiful and attractive – but he survives it very nicely, though some people get annoyed by him. He is a great friend of Philip Toynbee's. P.T. has written a new novel – *The Barricades*[4] – which is clever, but somehow not 1st class. People who drink too much habitually[5] have a boring trick in their novels of describing every drink taken – 'Two more gins and French', etc, all through the chapter, when why can't they save space and say 'They then had 27 gins'? I suppose they enjoy savouring each glass in imagination, but it is boring.

Did you hear G[ilbert] M[urray] on Sunday night, talking of 'classical humanism'?[6] He was so good and moving. I heard him at a meeting of the National Peace Council last week, and we had tea afterwards.[7] Neither he nor anyone else has much hope for the post-war world. He says he is trying to frame a letter to the Press against our bombing methods; I hope he will – the thing is too horrible.

Do you keep well? I take oatmeal still – admirable post-flu tonic. But better not to need it, and I trust you won't.

My love for Christmas. Please give birthday greetings to Aunt Nannie, though belated.

R.

I met Nancy Rodd (Lady Mos<le>y's sister)[8] at the P.H.'s, and got a lot of Mos<le>y news from her! A nice amusing creature – did you ever read her skit on the British Fascists, about 8 years ago – *Wigs on the Green*? It is very funny and good. Unity comes into it, she and Diana Mos<le>y wouldn't speak to Nancy after it, though they have made it up now. But what relations to have![9]

1 Jean's mother was taken ill on 25 November 1943, whereupon Jean, who had spent the autumn working in the Red Cross Library in Oxford, returned home to take charge of the household. On 29 November, Gilbert Murray, not knowing what had happened, wrote to Jean, inviting her to be his secretary again, on a half-time basis, but she was unable to accept the invitation.

2 9 December. Burdett died five days after Rose wrote this letter.

3 John Pope-Hennessy's birthday, his thirtieth, was on 13 December. James was 27.

4 The second of the three sons of Rosalind and Arnold Toynbee (*L*79 n. 16), Philip, who was currently working in the Ministry of Economic Warfare, had published his first novel, *The Savage Days*, in 1937, when he was still in his early twenties. *The Barricades* (London, 1943) was his third. He wrote poetry as well as fiction and was highly regarded as a literary critic for *The Observer*.

5 Patrick Leigh Fermor, writing on Philip Toynbee in *DNB*, remarks: 'drink . . . was

to remain indeed a bane all his life'. Rose's criticism of heavy-drinking writers who make too much mention of drinking in their novels is implied in 'Week-end at the Hoppers', her amusing parody of Ernest Hemingway in Leonard Russell (ed.), *Parody Party* ([London], 1936) 17–35, in which she keeps making the characters have drinks.

6 The talk was broadcast by the BBC Home Service on 12 December, 10.15–10.30 pm.

7 The meeting of the National Peace Council (a co-ordinating body, founded in 1908, for various peace organisations) was held at lunchtime on Friday 10 December, in the Kingsway Hall. Professor C.A.W. Manning spoke on 'Peaceful Change'.

8 Here and twice just below Rose has the misspelling 'Mosely'. Nancy Rodd, better known as Nancy Mitford, was at this stage still unknown to fame. The situation was to change with the publication of her fifth novel, *The Pursuit of Love*, in 1945. Since March 1942 she had been working as an assistant at Heywood Hill's bookshop at 10 Curzon Street, Mayfair.

9 Diana and Unity Mitford were younger sisters of Nancy. In 1932 Diana and Sir Oswald Mosley, leader of the British Union of Fascists (BUF), fell in love and began an affair. In 1933 Diana's marriage to Bryan Guinness ended in divorce and Mosley's first wife, Cynthia, died. On 6 October 1936 the two were secretly married at a ceremony, attended by Hitler, in Goebbels's apartment in Berlin. Unity, who had met Mosley in 1932 and joined the BUF in 1933, was unmistakably the model for Eugenia Malmains, the chief character in *Wigs on the Green* (London, 1935), Nancy's third novel. Peter Rodd, whom Nancy married on 4 December 1933, was briefly a member of the BUF. So was Nancy. That was in the first half of 1934, when they attended several BUF meetings. But after the BUF rally at Olympia on 8 June 1934 erupted into violence, they ceased supporting Fascism and indeed turned against it.

86

20 Hinde House
24 January 1944

Darling Jean[1]

Thank you for a charming and useful letter. I always feel so pleased that you like that book.[2] Your errata list is useful. I had made a list of some of them in my own copy, which was of course destroyed, though I think I had sent a list to Collins before, in case they should ever reprint. I don't know that all yours were in my list, and will note them, tho' I fear the reprint won't be in this world now.[3] More interesting are your other doubts. 'Unconscious' [361][4] is quite wrong; not in *O.D.*[5] till 19th c. (in that sense). It should have been 'stunned', I think. 'Got cramp' [189]. 'Got' is all right, I think; cf *The Tempest*, 'he has got an ague', etc. But I am sure it should be 'the' or 'a cramp'; and possibly 'took' for 'got' might be more frequent. 'Awful' [251] is utterly wrong; I put it (and stuck to it in proof) in some of those moments of abstracted imbecility that beset me. 'Splendid fellows' [269] *sounds* modern, but I suppose could be used then, as 'splendid' (in the sense of 'good' or 'admirable') was, and 'fellows' was. All the same, I don't feel it is very good, and I think might better be 'Excellent fellows' or something. There are other gaffes: the worst is making Dr Conybeare talk of 'scientists', which was pointed out to me by the Regius professor of Divinity at Cambridge.[6] It should of course be 'philosophers'.

'*Quadriennium*' [156]: I fo<r>get if it was the first 4 years of the 7, or the last. *Quadrivium* and *trivium* would be the actual courses, I suppose – one of 4 subjects, the other of 3. But all this is now a little hazy in my mind, though I mugged it all up at the time. '*Egrocum*' [176].[7] I simply can't think what it means. I know I had marked it as a misprint (or a mis-type), and meant sometime to look it up in the play. I don't suppose I can at present, as so many of the 17th c. books (it was never reprinted, I think) have been sent away from the B.M. for the duration, those that aren't destroyed, as too many were. 'All Hallows' [194] is wrong, of course: again I think I had detected and listed it. Is 'fast' [211] always wrong for keep to fish? I don't know. If it is, Kit wouldn't have used it, except speaking quite loosely, as I suppose one might? *O.D.* gives 'fast bread and water', 'fast with bran and water'; not 'fast with fish'! I will take your word on this. 'Terrifying' [212]. I think you are probably right. 'Terrify' was common enough, but I don't know that 'terrifying' was (as adjective, tho' more likely as verb). 'Dreadful' would be better. 'Remains' [235] (meaning corpse) is doubtful. 1st example in *O.D.* is Dryden, 1700; 'relics' was much commoner. Of course 'remains' was used for ruins, literary remains, etc. etc. On the other hand, I'm not *quite* sure that one would have said 'relics' for a bird? But I dare say they did. I like 'reliques' better, and shall we make her[8] say it, in the improbable reprint. No, I think the mare shouldn't 'do' [261], but 'go'.

There are other errors. 'Dinner' (for 'supper') on p. 23. 'Country gentleman' (for 'gentlem*e*n', plural) on p. 78, which I remember noting. And I am sure many more. Thank you so much for your highly intelligent and informed suggestions.

I don't know if you see *The Cath: Herald*; in case not, I cut out <the> enclosed for you when it appeared; – a nice account of him, by the editor.[9] You might be amused by the other, the following week, from old Lord A.D.[10] He has anyhow the courage of his convictions! Every one seems to have loved Fr Burdett. I wish, for you, that he wasn't gone.

I sent Aunt N. that phot. of Father; I hope she likes it. I hope also that she goes on well, and you too. I do, but for a neuritis arm still. I can type, but writing is painful, so my Record Office copyings (pencil, too, wh: is worse) languish a little. But no matter; there is lots of the book to get on with without them.

A noisy night last Friday.[11] It may, they say, be a start of a noisy season – pre-invasion (our invasion, of course). I could wish Romford was less on the route they come in by; it always seems to get bashed. In central London it was only guns, tho' they got a bomb I believe in St John's Wood. I heard none myself.

The new *Cornhill* has appeared. I had to write on Basic English, a boring theme, but P. Quennell would have it.[12] The mag: looks pretty, and has a nice thing or two, but I see no need for it, and I imagine it won't live long.[13] *Horizon*[14] is more interesting, tho' not by any means always so.

The news has become so exciting that one waits for it painfully. All this Rome landing. Surely there must soon be terrific resistance. It can't go on so smoothly as this. It is horrid to think of all that country being bashed to bits – shelling the Appian Way, the Germans in Frascati, soon the attack on Rome. I suppose we have a very bad few months ahead now.[15] As to Russia and Poland . . .! It is really outrageous.[16]

My love to you

R.

1 This letter is typed, Rose explains, because of her 'neuritis arm'. But there was also the convenience that she could keep a carbon copy of her comments on Jean's queries.

2 *They Were Defeated.* The book was published in the autumn of 1932, and it may seem surprising that Jean had only now sent Rose her criticisms of certain words in the book. But, when the book appeared, she was going through a difficult time, both physically and spiritually (*L*73 n. 1), and she was in no state to check up on Rose's use of seventeenth-century English. What has almost certainly prompted her to communicate her comments and queries (all of which are listed at the back of her copy of the book) now is the exchange of letters Rose had just had with John Hayward, the literary scholar and bibliophile, concerning a poem she included in *The Minor Pleasures of Life*, an anthology of poetry and prose published in 1934. Hayward, who was gathering material for an anthology of his own, *Seventeenth Century Poetry*, asked her to identify the source of the 20-line poem 'The Chase', attributed to 'Anon, c. 1675' and printed on p. 211 at the beginning of the section entitled 'Female Pleasures'. In a letter of 14 January 1944 she answered his enquiry with this confession: 'Unfortunately you happened on the only thing in that book which is not quite as it seems. The fact is that I wanted a poem about women hunting and couldn't lay my hands on one at the moment, so I thought I would write one myself, and it amused me to put it into 17th century garb and date it "c. 1675". (After all, how many years may "circa" cover? I thought perhaps 260 years or so, so dated it thus)'. Hayward's response is not preserved, but was evidently very favourable, for Rose wrote to him on 18 January 1944: 'Thank you so much for a very charming and nice letter', adding: 'I think you are right as to the too late dating of my piece; the spirit is earlier; but if I had put it much earlier, I should have made some of the spelling and capital letters a little different'. She went on to query whether her rhyming of 'Girles' with 'Curles' (lines 19–20) was in order. There can be little doubt that Rose told Jean about her exchange with Hayward, and that the queries about one seventeenth-century-style composition of hers ('The Chase') led on to Jean's and her discussion of another (*They Were Defeated*). Rose's present letter to Jean was written only six days after her second letter to Hayward. Both letters to Hayward are in King's College Library, Cambridge, JDH/26/Macaulay.

3 The book was reissued by Collins in 1960 and by Oxford University Press in 1981.

4 The square-bracketed numbers in the text of this letter are those of the relevant pages

of *They Were Defeated* (1934 edition), and have been supplied by the editor, who has also placed inside quotation marks all the words and phrases discussed, whereas Rose sometimes has them in quotation marks, sometimes underlines them, and sometimes does not distinguish them at all.

5 *Oxford English Dictionary*.

6 Charles Raven.

7 Rose quotes the opening two lines of the prologue to Abraham Cowley's Latin comedy *Naufragium Ioculare*, first performed at Trinity College, Cambridge, on 2 February 1638 and published soon afterwards (London, 1638). Her *egrocum* in line 2 is an error for *ego cum*.

8 Elizabeth Herrick.

9 The obituary of Francis Burdett in *The Catholic Herald*, 31 December 1943, 5, was written by 'M.B.'. This was Count Michael de la Bedoyere, the paper's editor from 1934 to 1962. He describes Burdett as an 'eccentric', whose 'hatred for anything smelling of Liberalism or Socialism was fierce', and who held 'an intense and often seemingly unbalanced conviction that God and the Catholic Church alone really counted in the world of 1943'.

10 Lord Alfred Douglas, best known for his association with Oscar Wilde. He had become a Catholic in 1911. In his letter (*The Catholic Herald*, 7 January 1944, 2) he argues that Burdett's attitude to socialism and communism was not that of an 'eccentric' but that of an orthodox Catholic.

11 21 January. On the night of Thursday 20 January the RAF dropped over 2,300 tons of bombs on Berlin, and the following night over 2,000 tons on Magdeburg. In retaliation for the Berlin raid, the Luftwaffe on the night of the 21st attacked London and south-east England in greater force than usual and encountered a heavy barrage of anti-aircraft fire.

12 Peter Quennell, a prolific writer best known as a biographer, edited *The Cornhill Magazine* from 1944 to 1951. Publication of the magazine, founded in 1860, had been suspended in 1940–1943.

13 Other contributors to *The Cornhill Magazine* 961 (January 1944) include Max Beerbohm, John Betjeman, Osbert Lancaster, Elizabeth Bowen, Maurice Bowra, and Raymond Mortimer. Rose's article, 'Against Basic English', occupies pp. 21–25. The magazine was to cease publication in 1975.

14 *Horizon: A Review of Literature and Art*, ed. Cyril Connolly, 9, 49 (January 1944), includes an article by Peter Ustinov on the state of the British theatre and a poem, 'The Libertine', by Louis MacNeice.

15 The prediction was correct. On 22 January 1944, two days before Rose wrote this letter, American and British troops had landed at Anzio, on the coast south of Rome, in an attempt to outflank the Gustav Line established by the Germans north of Naples, but four months of bitter fighting ensued. The allies broke through the Gustav Line in mid-May and entered Rome on 4 June.

16 On 25 April 1943 the USSR had broken off relations with the Polish government in London, claiming that its leader, Wladyslaw Sikorski, had falsely blamed the USSR for the massacre of several thousand Polish officers at Katyn near Smolensk. Now, as Soviet troops prepared to recapture eastern Poland from the Germans, there was much

disagreement and distrust between the Soviet and Polish governments on the question of where Poland's eastern border would run after the war. In the event, Poland ceded about 69,000 square miles of eastern territory to the USSR, while its western border was altered to accommodate 39,000 square miles of territory received from Germany.

87

Boat to Ryde[1]
21 August [1946]

Darling Jean

I had a most entrancing time at Clent, and continued it all the drive home, seeing Sander<s>on Miller's folly at Edgehill (I think the 1st English folly?) on the site of the battlefield–do you know it? A two towered edifice, joined by a bridge; 63 steps up to the top of one tower, with marvellous views for miles round; 4 Gothic windows and 4 Gothic niches, in one of them a steel cuirass used in the battle. A very pleasant pub on ground floor, now the Castle Inn, whose landlord is full of information, and gave me lunch (a sandwich and cider) on the house. Across the road are ruined cottages, built to match the castle.[2] All very pleasing and sublime, and in the most loveable Oxfordshire-Warwickshire country of quiet lanes and fields and woods. Then on to Banbury and Oxford, then Abingdon, Wantage and Farnborough, where I called on the John Betjemans – his library is full of great architectural volumes, which I inspected.[3] Leaving this, I visited Donnington Castle, close to Newbury, very quiet and noble and decayed, lonely among thickets of alders and brambles etc, its solemnity heightened by a voluminous growth of ivy.[4]

So, you see, I have done very well. Better still were Shenstone's landskip,[5] to which you were such an excellent guide, and Hagley ruin,[6] which I'm glad we located, and ·Hales Owen Abbey, which stays in the mind as such beauty and dignity among its farm surround.[7]

Thank you for conducting me to all this, as well as for my visit, and the comfortable room out of which I turned poor Tom,[8] and enabling me to see Clent again. I'm glad I saw Walton House[9] – except for the barn watchdog, nothing could have gone better, as I wasn't certain to see the inside or the occupants.[10] I have not forgotten the garden as seen, and holly is back again in its place, and the gates swing as of old, and the conservatory[11] is still there to throw balls through, and the pigsty roof to sit on.

Thank you much for having me. I'm afraid I was of little use in the house, and played the pampered guest.

I do hope you will persuade Jim to Portugal, and anyhow you will get away for a holiday somewhere.[12] I am so glad to have seen that quite lovely chapel,[13] and that you have it at hand.

I am now en route for Ryde, where J[eanie] is, and from Fanny Haines;[14] I am there for the day only. Dear love. R.

My brooch never turned up: I expect it fell on the gravel path and got buried. It matters little. My love to my aunt, whom I am so glad to have seen again.

1   Isle of Wight.

2   Sanderson (not Sanderton, as Rose calls him) Miller, a wealthy and cultured local landowner, started building the octagonal Radway Tower in 1742, to commemorate the centenary of the indecisive Battle of Edgehill, the first major engagement of the Civil War. The tower, modelled on Guy's Tower at Warwick Castle, stands on the summit of the ridge, about 700 feet (213 metres) above sea level. As Rose indicates, there is also a second tower, a smaller one, linked to the main tower by a high wooden bridge. The opening ceremony was performed on 3 September 1750, the 92nd anniversary of the death of Oliver Cromwell. The building (which became an inn in 1822) and the alterations Miller made to Radway Grange, his Elizabethan house in the nearby village of Radway, aroused considerable interest and admiration: he found himself much in demand as an architect, and he is a significant figure in the early history of the Gothic Revival. One of his major commissions was at Hagley, on which see n. 6 below. In 1949 Rose was to begin work on *Pleasure of Ruins* (1953). Its opening chapter, entitled 'Art, Fantasy and Affectation', includes the Edgehill folly ('though not the first sham Gothic ruin, . . . perhaps the best known'), as well as Hagley and Halesowen, which she visited with Jean (*Pleasure of Ruins* 27–29).

3   Betjeman and his wife, Penelope (who wrote under her maiden name, Penelope Chetwode), lived at the Old Rectory, Farnborough, Hampshire, from 1945 to 1951. On Rose's friendship with Betjeman, see *L*95 n. 8.

4   The castle, just north of Newbury, dates from the late fourteenth century. Its impressive gatehouse survives, but the rest of it was demolished during the Civil War.

5   'Landskip' for 'landscape', because that is the form used by the eighteenth-century poet William Shenstone, one of whose poems is entitled 'The Landskip'. Shenstone lived at Halesowen, now in Worcestershire, then in Shropshire, about seven miles west of Birmingham. In the mid-1740s he started converting the Leasowes, the family estate at Mucklow Hill, into landscaped gardens; and he did this 'with such judgement and such fancy as made his little domain the envy of the great and the admiration of the skilful: a place to be visited by travellers, and copied by designers' (Samuel Johnson, *Lives of the Poets*). The features with which the gardens were embellished included artificial ruins, some of them designed by Sanderson Miller, as well as paths, seats, urns, and water features.

6   A half-ruined castle in the grounds of Hagley Hall, near Stourbridge in Worcestershire. It was commissioned by George Lyttelton (from November 1756 first Baron Lyttelton), politician and man of letters, who converted his estate into a romantic landscape and replaced the old half-timbered house with a Palladian mansion (completed 1760). The architect, both of the castle and of the Hall, was Sanderson Miller. There was a certain amount of rivalry between Lyttelton and Shenstone in respect of their landscape creations, Hagley and Halesowen being only about five miles apart.

7   The Premonstratensian Halesowen Abbey was founded in 1214. The situation of its

remains among (and partly incorporated into) farm-buildings is mentioned by Rose in *Pleasure of Ruins* 335.

8 Jean's brother.

9 Formerly the home of Kenneth Macaulay and, after his death, of Willie Macaulay, Walton House, with its gardens and outbuildings, was a child's paradise. Rose's description of the young Vallons' 'holiday place made for joy' in her fourth novel, *The Valley Captives* (1911), is closely based on her recollections of the place where she and her sisters and brothers spent happy holidays: 'the red-brick house . . . the glimpses between the trees along the holly-hedge of field and sky and blue Shropshire hills beyond . . . the long shadow of the old holly-tree . . . gates that swung . . . the stables and the pigsty and the washhouse, all with climbable roofs . . . the dim twilight barn' (9–10). She returns to Walton House in *Personal Pleasures* (1935), where, as the description of the view shows, its roof is the setting of the children's picnic of oranges, rusks, ginger pop, pear drops, and Woodbines (287–288). Rose was to make another, last visit to Walton House in September 1956. She mentions it in a letter to Dorothea Conybeare: 'I had such a nice drive to Clent the other day; the lady now there let us go over the garden and outhouses, and it was almost too much, the sense of ourselves when young, playing pirates in the barn and climbing the roofs etc. It was full of noisy little ghosts' (ERM 16.195). Her companion on that occasion was Eric Gillett, with whom she was staying at Droitwich (ERM 9.145).

10 Allan and Deborah Tangye, the parents-in-law of Jean's brother Henry.

11 In the context of Walton House, 'conservatory' means 'greenhouse'.

12 Rose's *They Went to Portugal* was about to appear. She gave Jean a copy of it for her birthday on 18 September. No doubt it was largely Rose's Portuguese researches, in which Jean had taken a keen interest from the beginning, that had whetted the latter's appetite for a visit to Portugal. Her wish to go there with Jim was fulfilled in March–April 1947.

13 The Catholic Chapel of Saints Oswald and Wulstan, Clent. Previously a malt-house, thought to be about four hundred years old, the building became a chapel in 1926.

14 *L*67 n. 2. It seems that Fanny was still living at Liss, Hampshire. Anyhow, Rose was using Liss as a base for a driving and walking holiday (GM 151.80–81).

88

20 H[inde] H[ouse]
27 October [1946]

Darling Jean

Mr Fenlon[1] tells me you took most of the silver, and that the valuation he gave you (by weight) was £36.9.4. Between us and your family, shall we make it £30? Would that be all right?

I hope the things will prove to be what are wanted. When I die, you will get some more, and for nothing. It is only Jeanie's disinterested passion for money[2] that prevents such an arrangement this time – but I won't give her a chance on what I leave! That is, I shall leave to her and Eleanor[3] only what they want to keep, not to sell (of your and our family stuff: the Conybeare silver is different, of course).

I was sorry we didn't meet. I spent Friday evening and night[4] at Oxford, which was fun. My paper to the Palatine Club[5] was about 'The Literary Character' – a good theme, and might be further developed. Such a nice audience, mostly returned warriors, though not quite all; I felt them (as Gervase Mathew[6] put it) to be on the right wave-length for me. First we dined (the Committee and me – G.M. is on it) then had the discussion in a room in Christ Church, candle-lit and lovely, and drank mulled claret. David Cecil was there; a very good and lively discusser.[7]

At dinner we discussed Evelyn Waugh: I found that Gervase Mathew and the Club secretary feel almost exactly as I do about him, – an extreme devotion to his earlier books and some distaste for *Brideshead*.[8] I *think* I am right in feeling that he shouldn't write about real life (or what he believes to be this) but should stay within his brilliant circus, where he moves so surely and beautifully. A kind of falseness traps him when he gets outside the ropes. They all who know him (I don't *really*) complain of his rudeness – Cyril Connolly[9] says he insults everyone he meets now.[10] Perhaps it's partly drink?[11] But *so* brilliant and funny.

My love always.

R.

1 John Thomas Fenlon, a London jeweller.
2 See *L*100: 'She [Jeanie] does so value every pound that comes to her for sending abroad to her medical missions, and all her other charitable objects. Unlike me, she never keeps any for herself beyond the barest necessities.'
3 Rose's only surviving siblings after the death of Will in November 1945. The Macaulay silver that has been valued and offered to Jean is likely to have gone to him after Grace's death in May 1925.
4 25 October.
5 Extensive enquiries in Oxford have not revealed any record of the Palatine Club. Writing to Gilbert Murray on 5 March 1946 Rose describes it as 'a group of undergraduates who meet and discuss literature and life, and invite writers to read them papers' (GM 151.65v). She was expecting to address it in June, but the meeting was postponed (GM 151.76r).
6 The Byzantine scholar and Dominican priest Anthony Mathew, who assumed the name Gervase when he became a friar, spent almost all his adult life at Blackfriars in St Giles, Oxford. He was the younger brother of David James Mathew, also a scholar and writer, who in February 1946 had been created Titular Archbishop of Apamea in Bithynia and had gone to Mombasa as Apostolic Delegate to the British colonies in Africa. Jean had got to know both of them – David in London, where from 1938 until 1945 he was Bishop Auxiliary of Westminster, and Gervase at Blackfriars. Rose became very friendly with both brothers. She admired their scholarship, and regarded

them as particularly broadminded and enlightened Catholics (*LLF* 191). David's book *Scotland under Charles I* (London, 1955) carries the dedication: 'For Rose Macaulay in memory of a long friendship'.

7 David Cecil, English literary scholar and biographer, was at this time Fellow and Tutor at New College, Oxford. He remained there until his retirement in 1969, occupying the Goldsmiths' Chair of English Literature from 1949.

8 *Brideshead Revisited. The Sacred and Profane Memories of Captain Charles Ryder: A Novel* (London, 1945). There can be little doubt that it was Rose who broached the subject of Evelyn Waugh and his latest novel, for she had told Gilbert Murray in a letter of 16 October 1946 that she was 'busy finishing' an article on Waugh (GM 151.83v). The piece, entitled 'The Best and the Worst: II – Evelyn Waugh', was published in *Horizon* 14, 84 (December 1946) 360–376. Although Rose acknowledges that *Brideshead Revisited* 'has remarkable qualities', she considers it the least successful of Waugh's books and wishes 'he would sternly root out the sentimentalities and adolescent values which have, so deplorably as it seems to many of us, coiled themselves about the enchanting comic spirit which is his supreme asset as a writer, and return to being the drily ironic narrator of the humours of his world and of his lavish inventive fancy' (376). On 16 December 1946 Waugh wrote: 'This morning *Horizon* arrived with a long article by Rose Macaulay advising me to return to my kennel and not venture into the world of living human beings.' See Michael Davie (ed.), *The Diaries of Evelyn Waugh* (London, 1976) 667.

9 Rose may have first met Connolly through her friend Logan Pearsall Smith, whose secretary he was in the late 1920s, and by whom his literary style was influenced. He co-founded *Horizon* and edited it from 1939 to 1950. He was literary editor of *The Observer* in 1942–1943, and later had a much longer association with *The Sunday Times*, whose chief book reviewer he was. He achieved more fame as a critic than as an author.

10 James Lees-Milne, *Ancestral Voices* (London, 1975) 169, calls Waugh 'the nastiest tempered man in England, Catholic or Protestant'.

11 If any substance Waugh consumed significantly aggravated a personality disorder, it is less likely to have been alcohol than bromide, which he was in the habit of using as a hypnotic and tranquilliser. See Selina Hastings, *Evelyn Waugh: A Biography* (London, 1994) 560–561, 564–569.

89

20 Hinde House
Hinde St. W.1
16 September 1947

Darling Jean

This brings much love for your birthday. I got back last Thursday,[1] and supposed you at Clent; I rang twice, but you weren't at the flat, which confirmed my view. And now I hear you've been up for the last few days, and only left yesterday; J. says you telephoned her about Aunt M. What a pity we couldn't meet; I have a Spanish crock for you – or rather a choice between crocks. But this can wait till you are up again.[2] Your loans I return, with many thanks (except the parasol, which is probably safer transmitted by hand). The par: was v. useful – if you wear a hat you are pointed and giggled at (as Hare[3] says his lady companions were in the 1870's – this pointing and derision must be a chronic Spanish habit – a very bad one, and especially when turned on a solitary foreigner, as it usually is). Also a woman driving is an object of amaze and is greeted by hoots and cat-calls as she passes – it seems Spanish women never drive cars, only donkeys. I think a lot of the old harem spirit about women survives. The children, especially, are, as a woman said to me, 'muy mal educados'[4] about foreigner-baiting; it's a kind of national sport, and very embarrassing. But, apart from this, what a glorious country! Such a pattern of beauty everywhere, all down the *Ora Maritima* from the frontier to Cape St Vincent.[5] Everywhere the excitement of coming on Phoenician, Greek, Carthaginian, Roman, Visigoth, Moor, medieval Spanish – a thrilling palimpsest. And so much digging up still waiting to be done – Ampurias[6] isn't finished yet, and exploration under the Catalan authorities was in full swing till the civil war: nothing now being done about it, but will again if and when they get rid of these Philistines now in power and set Catalonia free to organize its own culture and researches again.

Goodness, what a country! The profusion with which age-old buildings casually lie about, unheralded and unordered, and still mouldering into faster ruin – compare it with the trim, cared-for neatness of *our* few historic ruins. Of course this has drawbacks as well as charms – but to come on a deserted ruin of an abbey in the mountains, or some wonderful Cartuja[7] with the grass and trees and weeds thrusting up through the broken arches, untended and luxuriant in hot sunshine, surrounding a glorious baroque west door of golden stone (like the one near Jerez, which no one looks after) – gives one a breath-taking shock, as of magic, or of a sudden step back into other centuries. But indeed the whole of Spain seems thus. A Spaniard said this to me (*à propos* of women not driving cars, but 'living very quietly'). He said 'We Spanish don't live in the present century at all; we go far back into the past, and seldom change our ways of thought'. Not true, of course, generally speaking; but in some ways it is.

The destruction of the civil war in Catalonia is sad; old Gothic churches burnt down by the anarchists all over the place. Some are empty shells; some are already rebuilt or nearly so – but what is the use of that? Barcelona has suffered very little; it is the churches of the countryside in the days of '36 before protection was organized. 'Vieja costumbre español<a>',[8] alas, like foreigner-baiting, and like (I was told) keeping girl children indoors while their brothers play and ride donkeys in the streets. It would be dull to be a little girl in Spain.

Algarve was so lovely, all the way from the Guadiana[9] to Cape St Vincent. From thence I drove up to Lisbon for a few days, visited the Marques at Estoril,[10] and went to the frontier via Coimbra and Beira Alta, crossing it near Ciudad Rodrigo (what a place!). I had to go to Madrid, for photographs, and I was interested to go through Castile, so different from the south and east. I spent a night in Avila,[11] that magnificent walled town; and struck the coast again at Valencia, where I saw some things I had missed before, including the Porta Coeli Cartuja 20 kilometres or so back in the pine-forests behind it. Such a place – alone among piney mountains. I arrived there at dusk; my wretched Blue Guide had assured me of a hotel (as it had at Sagres).[12] In both places any hotel there may have been closed for years. As I was 10 kilometres or more from the nearest inn, and that over the roughest and narrowest donkey-track through the woods, which I should never have made safely in the dark, (and also I wanted to see the Cartuja by daylight) I bedded on my lilo in the woods, under an immense pine beneath the moon – a most lovely night, but I got bitten by mosquitoes badly – and when day dawned I went and saw the Cartuja, a great blackened pile, surrounded by a few disused farm buildings and a garden of oranges and lemons and olives and figs, and tenanted, it seemed, by a very few monks – the porter whom I rang up at the *porteria* said there were 'muy poco<s>'.[13] I attended mass at 8 o'clock, the porter showed me the cloisters and church, and I drove away along the donkey-track to Serra, a mountain village of the most enchanting kind, where I got coffee and ripe, black figs (7d a kilo) on an inn terrace with blue *azulejos*[14] and a view over mountains and ravines. And so down to the sea at Sagunto, where I had spent an afternoon on my journey down, so didn't linger, as I am afraid of the Saguntines, they are still fierce and chase foreigners about – perhaps they remember the Carthaginians' attack long since.[15] Anyhow, there was the Mediterranean again, blue and entrancing, and I took the sea road that ran, zig-zag[16] beyond belief, like dog-tooth moulding, to Tarragona.

I rather wished I had gone instead from Madrid to the Andalusian coast, and done all that again, it *was* so lovely, but it would have been much longer. Now I feel sick for Denia, Ifach, Peñiscola, Torremolinos, the whole coast. Wasn't I lucky to get there just in time, before the prison gates clanged again, and while there was still petrol here and in France.[17] The roads of Spain are dilapidated to a degree, pot-holed with Roman (or even Iberian) chariot-wheels and never mended since, and my poor old car fell to pieces rather as we bounced along; the bumpers kept falling off, and the exhaust and once the steering axle (rather startling!) and once the tyre suddenly flew off the wheel and the inner tube was cut to pieces before I could stop. As for punctures, what I don't know about changing wheels beneath a Spanish sun on a shadeless road thick in dust, is nobody's business. But passing Spaniards were very kind in stopping to help me. One of them lifted the car right up when it had knocked the jack over and fallen on its side – a terrific exertion, and one of course entirely beyond any female powers. I said he was very strong. He replied, casually, 'Poco. Comemos muy mal'[18] – which moved me so much. It is too true; they simply don't get enough food, the black market is so bad and so wholly unchecked. Franco won't do anything against it, because the army lives on it, and he depends on the army, and so it thrives, and the poor can't get scarcely any meat, butter, milk, or anything. The restaurant and hotel meals are quite good – lots of meat or fish, tho' no butter and very little sugar. But people remain gay, even exuberant (anyhow in Catalonia, Valencia, Andalusia; the Castilians much graver). And how beautiful they are! Most so in the very Moorish parts, and more in the country than in the towns (as in Portugal, but the Portuguese are much less good-looking).

Your Foldex map[19] was very nice to have – so neat and easy to manipulate.

J. and I are going to see Aunt M. to-morrow. J. tells me she has had an attack of coronary thrombosis; so I expect is in bed. I shall ring up in the morning and enquire.

This letter is huge, and seems to have become a travelogue; forgive it. You know the urge to tell travellers' tales. I wish you could have seen it all too, instead of merely Clent, darling. Forgive also this unfairness, and take my love and good wishes for the year. Love to Aunt Nannie, please.

R.

1 11 September. Rose had returned from just under ten weeks of travelling to and through Spain and Portugal. She left England on 5 July, crossing from Newhaven to Dieppe, and picked up 'Elk', her 1934 model 10 h.p. Morris, in Bordeaux, to which it had been shipped. From there she drove to the easternmost Franco-Spanish frontier post, between Cerbère and Portbou. Here she said goodbye to Dermod and Muriel O'Donovan, Gerald's son and daughter-in-law, who had hoped to accompany her in their car at least as far as Barcelona, but had not yet managed to obtain visas. She entered Spain on or about 12 July. The journey, undertaken after the publisher Hamish Hamilton had commissioned her to write a book for a new travel series, was adventurous: Rose, who had her 66th birthday while she was away, was alone; bits of her car kept dropping off on roads that were often in poor condition; the unaccustomed sight of a woman driver attracted much attention, usually unfavourable; and on two occasions, when inns listed in out-of-date guide books turned out to be non-existent, she inflated her air mattress and slept under the open sky. Despite the difficulties of her journey, during which she encountered much kindness as well as much annoyance, she fell in love with the eastern and southern coastal regions of the Iberian peninsula, and her book, *Fabled Shore: From the Pyrenees to Portugal,* makes entertaining, as well as instructive, reading. (It is remarkable that Crawford (19, 139) seems to think that *Fabled Shore* is only about Portugal.) For four letters Rose wrote to Jeanie during her travels, see *LS* 129–136.

2 Jean returned to London on 26 September.

3 Augustus Hare, *Wanderings in Spain* (London, 1873).

4 'Very badly brought up'. Rose quotes the remark also in *Fabled Shore* 86, where she says it was made to her in Sagunto.

5 The coast from the Franco-Spanish border to the south-west, point of Portugal. *Ora Maritima* ('The Sea-coast') is the title of a work by the fourth-century AD Latin poet

Avienus. Most of the surviving part of the poem describes the coast from Marseilles to Cadiz. Rose wanted to use Avienus' title for her book, with the subtitle *From the Costa Brava to Algarve*, but her publisher disapproved.

6 On the north-east coast of Spain. It was originally a Greek trading settlement, founded by colonists from Massilia (Marseilles) in the sixth century BC. Rose describes it in *Fabled Shore* 20–24 and *Pleasure of Ruins* 257.

7 Carthusian monastery.

8 'Old Spanish custom'.

9 River marking the border, on the south coast, between Spain and Portugal.

10 Susan and Luiz Marques. Rose's friendship with them began when she visited Portugal in 1943. She expresses her gratitude to them in *They Went to Portugal* 9, and Susan, writing under her maiden name, Lowndes, contributed the introduction to *They Went to Portugal Too*. She was a daughter of the author Marie Belloc Lowndes, whose diaries and letters she was to edit (1971), and a niece of Hilaire Belloc. Luiz was the Lisbon correspondent of *The Daily Telegraph* (1936–1976) and *The Sunday Telegraph* (1961–1976), as well as editor of *Anglo-Portuguese News* (1937–1976) and its proprietor (1954–1976). Susan's and Luiz's elder daughter, Ana Vicente, has written an excellent account of her parents' lives: *Arcádia: Notícia de uma Família Anglo-Portuguesa* (Lisbon, 2006).

11 West of Madrid.

12 The non-existence of the inn said to be at Sagres, near Cape St Vincent, and her passing of the night 'in the roofless apse of what must once have been a chapel', are described in *Fabled Shore* 197–198. For the night she spent on her air-mattress at Porta Coeli, see *Fabled Shore* 96–97. Her Blue Guide was Findlay Muirhead (ed.), *Southern Spain and Portugal* (London, 1929). Under Sagres it reports 'good *Inn*' (292), and under Cartuja de Portacoeli 'Hotel, good' (38).

13 'Very few'. According to *Fabled Shore* 97, he said 'Tan pocos', but the sense is not affected.

14 'Glazed tiles'. See *Fabled Shore* 98: 'Here there was a pretty fonda, called Luisa, on whose terrace I had coffee, sitting among blue-tiled pillars beneath a vine trellis in front of an enormous mountain view'.

15 Saguntum, an ally of Rome, was besieged and captured by Hannibal in 219 BC. The incident precipitated the Second Punic War (218–201 BC). Rose was mobbed and mocked by the children of Sagunto, as she reports in *Fabled Shore* 86 and in letters to David Ley (ERM 15.212) and Gilbert Murray (GM 151.111v).

16 Rose has drawn 'zig-zag', instead of writing it.

17 When Rose says 'before the prison gates clanged again', she is referring not to restrictions on the Franco-Spanish frontier but to the severe measures that had been announced by the British government in her absence. The measures, that were to come into effect on 1 October 1947, included: no foreign currency for travel outside the sterling area, unless official approval for the journey had been granted; and abolition of the basic petrol ration, meaning not 'no petrol rationing', but 'no petrol for private motoring'. In France the basic petrol ration was withdrawn on 1 September 1947.

18 'Not very. We eat very poorly.' The kind Spaniard almost certainly said 'No mucho' rather than 'Poco'. The incident is described also in *LS* 135.

19 Foldex maps began life in the mid-1930s, with financial support from Shell. Each map had progressively narrower folds; each fold had a number; and there was a key. This patent system allowed the user to find the required section of the map easily and quickly.

90

20, Hinde House,
Hinde Street, W.1.
18 January 1950

Darling Jean

Thank you for your letter and news. I am very sorry Aunt Nannie is now quite non-walking. And glad you have the nurse coming. Being on call in the nights is too much of a strain to go on with. I think Nurse Jurgens[1] finds it so, when Aunt Mary doesn't sleep through the night; but I gather that she usually does that now? But anyhow Nurse J. has to be on call, of course, and alert to the bell. She wants a holiday, and a temporary substitute, but I hear hasn't so far been able to get one from her Home, and will go on till she does. I was there on Sunday: Nurse J. was out, but I saw Sara,[2] who was rather in a mood of strain because she complains the nurse is 'out every day from 3 or 3.30 till after 8', and leaves her to cope, and she doesn't feel up to it. The other day Aunt M. had a fall, and Sara couldn't help her up alone, so had to fetch Mrs Brown (who chars sometimes) from over the way. Sara feels all these ministrations are a nurse's job: but one can't expect the same nurse to be on call night and all day, and she may need someone else for the afternoons. Aunt Mary spoke to me about being left too long without Miss J. in afternoons and evenings. I rang up Dr Pasmore and consulted him;[3] he was going there yesterday, and was going to see what he felt should be done about it. He doesn't *think* she will get appreciably better or more active (you know she had a slight stroke when she had a fall on the stairs last year?); and if not, the problems of perpetual attendance will arise, of course. It may be she will need two part-time nurses. Dr. P. said he would tell me what he thought; but he hasn't rung yet. I suppose it *is* too much to expect Sara to be on duty every afternoon and evening.

Aunt M. was very quiet and tired and gentle on Sunday. But she feels lonely. No one visits her but Miss Turner and I; I wish they would. If ever Dorothy felt she could bear to, or Tom (but I know it is difficult for him), she would be *so* pleased. Or the great-nieces,[4] if ever they had time? Dorothy has said in the past, when I suggested that she should go, 'I never liked her' – but this seems now irrelevant, and she really does like to see the family very much. Jeanie will try and come up sometimes on her free afternoon, instead of my going to Romford – but she is pretty tired after her morning's work, and oughtn't to do it often.

Really Aunt Nannie and Aunt M. sound rather in the same case just now. I am very sorry about it, and for you, having your end to manage. I'm afraid you will be much too tired.

Yes, I took Aunt M. a wireless before Xmas. I don't know how much she uses it, but she likes the services. She can't bear noise, which rather forbids music. It is a pity, as she is short of occupations. And isn't really interested in any talks, such as the one about the Lascaux cave-paintings last night,[5] or Henry James,[6] or Cambodia, or any other topic.

Didn't I ever thank you for your delicious honey-pot? I should have: but have been so occupied and confused that perhaps not. It is delicious none the less. It was dear of you.

I discovered your Tortosa,[7] by the way, on the Syrian coast near Mount Carmel and Acre, Turkish boatmen and all – a lovely picture. I have a very nice book of Syrian and other engravings, with descriptions:[8] I wish I had Conybeare and Howson's *St Paul*:[9] but I lost mine and apparently didn't get one out of Liss.[10] I have it from the Library just now; some of the engravings are beautiful.

I try to keep my brain as clear as may be, for this task of chasing the world's ruins in a hurry, but find it rather a strain. I have to deliver the MS by May, which doesn't leave me long.[11] Meanwhile the . . .[12] Marylebone Liberals nag at me,[13] but I haven't <time>[14] to do much for them, though my heart really is in their cause, if anywhere – (by which I suppose all I mean is that I dislike the other two more).

I encouraged Nurse Jurgens to write to you when Aunt M. has things to say and doesn't feel up to the pen – but she prefers writing her own letters. I will report any fresh developments. Of course if Dr P. decides that more nursing help is necessary at present, it will be for him or one of us to tell the Trustees[15] – always assuming there is another nurse available. But I think he will agree that a Home Help or something in the afternoons would be the best plan if she could be got. Nurse Jurgens might know as to this. They are a very useful institution, J. says.

Much love, and please give some to my Aunt and the Tom.[16]

I wrote a note of goodbye and thanks for Jim before he sailed – I hope he got it?[17]

R.

---

1 Gertrude Jurgens, who lived not far from Mary Macaulay's home (165 Westbourne Grove, W11), had qualified as a mental health nurse in 1915, but seems to have returned to nursing, after a very long interval, only in 1948, when she was in her mid-fifties.

2 *L*84 n. 2.

3 Henry Stephen Pasmore, whose practice was at 21 Edwardes Square, London W8, was a GP with an interest in psychiatry.

4 Dorothy Gillum's two daughters (Anne and Helen) and Tom Smith's three (Evelyn, Cynthia, and Margaret).

5 The Upper Palaeolithic paintings of animals, executed perhaps about 13,000 BC in the Lascaux caves near Montignac in the Dordogne, were discovered by four youths in 1940. The talk, by Glyn Daniel, was on the BBC's Third Programme on 17 January, 10.55–11.15 pm.

6 This talk too was broadcast on the Third Programme on 17 January, 9.00–9.20 pm. The title was 'Henry James and the Theatre', and the speaker was Richard Heron Ward.

7 'Your Tortosa', because in her London flat Jean had a framed engraving entitled 'Island of Tortosa'. The engraving, now in the editor's possession, is a romantic depiction of a harbour with boats and boatmen and a castle behind, with a full moon illuminating the scene.

8 John Carne, *Syria, the Holy Land & Asia Minor Illustrated* etc. (London, 1836–1838). See *Pleasure of Ruins* ix, xii, xiii, 57–58, 60, 81–82. The 'lovely picture' to which Rose refers just above may be the one reproduced in *Pleasure of Ruins* opposite p. 442 – an engraving of 'Tortosa from the Island of Ruad', by W.H. Bartlett, taken from Carne's book.

9 W.J. Conybeare and J.S. Howson, *Life and Epistles of St Paul* (London, 1852).

10 Probably Rose lost her copy when her flat was bombed in May 1941. Liss is where Margaret was living when she died in March 1941.

11 It was actually to take her more than another three years to deliver the manuscript of *Pleasure of Ruins* to the publishers, Weidenfeld and Nicolson, but this was not due to idleness on her part: the original plan, for a work containing a maximum of 40,000 words, was discarded, and the writing of the book, which runs to at least 180,000 words, involved a great deal of research.

12 Most of the word that described the local Liberals has been obliterated by an ink blot. About eight letters long, it may have begun with b or p and ended with -led. 'Blessed' is possible, but probably a bit too short.

13 There was a general election in Britain on 23 February 1950. Labour was returned to power, but with only a narrow majority over the Conservatives. The Liberals won just nine seats. Writing to Gilbert Murray on 7 February, Rose referred to 'our nice but quite impossible-to-get-in Liberal candidate in Marylebone' (GM 151.165v), and, sure enough, he came a very poor third in a three-cornered contest won by the Conservative.

14 The word has been obliterated by another ink blot.

15 The Trustees of R.H. Macaulay's Settlement of 25 June 1918. The Settlement, one of many manifestations of Regi's generosity, was a discretionary Trust. In this case the possible beneficiaries defined by the Settlement were 'the brothers and sisters of R.H. Macaulay and their respective children and remoter issue', and the intention was to spread the income and capital among them not equally, but in accordance with the financial needs of each individual, as well as to minimise the incidence of tax and Estate Duty. Regi's sisters, Mary and Nannie, were among those who received benefits in the form of annuities and distributions of income and capital both during Regi's lifetime and after his death (15 December 1937). So were Rose, Margaret, Jeanie,

and Jean. The Trust remained in existence until 1976, when a settlement was reached with Jean, the only surviving annuitant, and the balance of the capital was distributed equally between five branches of the family.

16 The overweight tabby cat at Cross Bank. He had every reason to feel specially privileged to receive Rose's affectionate message, given that she was the author of an article entitled 'Why I Dislike Cats, Clothes and Visits' (*Daily Mail*, 2 November 1928, 12).

17 Jim returned to his post in Nigeria at the end of November 1949, flying, not sailing.

91

20 H[inde] H[ouse]
7 February [1950]

Darling Jean

Thank you so much for yours. I really am practically well now, though still a trifle of lassitude. I was only in hospital a few days – the best place, of course, if one lives alone.

I woke one morning feeling sick, and proceeded to fainting and vomiting and general collapse, for a good many hours. I couldn't even get to the telephone – not even to answer when it rang – till at last, after 2 o'clock, I succeeded in ringing J., just before she was starting from Romford to visit Aunt Mary. She gave this up and visited me instead, and did all the needful, got the doctor, who got an ambulance and another doctor, and I was carted off to hospital, where I spent the night having saline fluid dripped into my arm, which was supposed to be, and I daresay was, reviving. I recovered enough to go home in a few days, and am now, as I said, nearly myself. A queer attack: probably actually some form of influenza, but a very noxious form. They didn't know at the hospital quite what it was, but seem to have treated it effectively. I could ill afford the interruption, as I am sticking assiduously to this book which must be finished all too soon – and now have to collect and put in order of pagination all my 40 illustrations – and the order isn't easy before I've written the book![1] I expect they will be all over the place, reminding the reader abruptly of Tortosa or Tyre in the middle of a discourse on Palmyra. Not that I actually have one of Tortosa – or rather I have several, but can't afford a place for any.[2] I feel that I have been to all those Syrian places now – Acre, Tyre, Antioch, Caesarea, Ascalon – oh how beautiful and exciting, with their Roman ruins and the crusaders' castles on crags. *How* I wish to see them!

I'm glad you told the family about Aunt Mary; nice of Anne[3] to go and see her. She loves visitors, and doesn't get nearly enough. I shall be going myself again now, about once a week if I can manage it, tho' not too easy to fit it in at the moment, with spending whole afternoons in libraries and what not. But I do feel sorry for her, sitting there all day, unable to get downstairs even. I've not yet seen the substitute nurse, but Jeanie liked her, and I hope Sara does.

I'm glad you have Miss Burke again, and that she is on for the nights. I wish you had someone for the day too; that someone could take your place at it sometimes. Jeanie says the profession most needing recruits in the world is, she believes, 'home helps' – not necessarily nurses, but people to mind the sick and old at home.

I am glad you have Henry back in England. So sorry about his accident with the tractor; I hope he was not much hurt.[4]

I've just been seeing a man who is going to spend a month of the spring at Denia (Las Arenas) – fortunate creature.[5] I always hope I haven't misled these enthusiasts, and that they won't be disillusioned – but so far my *Turismo* agency has always worked out well.

All my love. Don't stay too close at your task – or is this nonsense? What you must do, you must do; I know that, of course.

R.

1 *Pleasure of Ruins* contains 76 illustrations.
2 Rose was able to include two illustrations of Tortosa.
3 Anne Gillum, Jean's niece and god-daughter. During the war she had worked first at the War Office for MI5 (1941–1943), then for the Special Operations Executive in Calcutta (until 1945). After employment in the British Embassy in Paris (until 1949), she returned in 1950 to Lady Margaret Hall, Oxford, where she had studied English in 1940–1941, to read Italian with French. In 1953–1955 she was a translator and interpreter at the Supreme Headquarters, Allied Powers, Europe (SHAPE) in Paris.
4 Jean's youngest brother had retired from the Bombay Company in March 1948. He then took up farming at Kinlet, Shropshire. In running himself over with a Ferguson tractor, he was fortunate not to be killed.
5 'Of all the lovely places down the Iberian seaboard, I believe Denia . . . to be the most attractive, and the one in which I would most gladly spend my days.' So Rose had written in *Fabled Shore* 99. Las Arenas is the seaside inn where she stayed and dined, although, since all its rooms were taken when she visited, she slept on her lilo in one of its bathing-huts. That was in 1947. In 1948 she returned for several weeks in company with Dermod and Muriel O'Donovan: 'We bathe all day, and play with our rubber dinghy', she wrote to Gilbert Murray on 10 August (GM 151.136).

92

20, Hinde House,
Hinde Street, W.1.
19 May [1950]

Darling Jean

I loved your letter.[1] You are always much too generous to me and my books. I think you are probably right about my characters, which should have received more attention. Yes, probably it *is* too short. Is it that (see separately sent review in *Listener* – I don't want it back) the adults are done *horizontally*, Barbary (he says) more in depth? Or is Barbary, perhaps, improbable (as another review says) against a circle of quite plausible and realised adults? As all my reviews contradict each other on most points, I am at sea. *The Listener* reads into it a lot of symbolism, some of which the kind Mr Painter perhaps invents ('Symbolismus bei dem Werke der R.M.').[2] Well, I don't know. One writes a book, and readers all put something of their own into it. Actually, I usually agree with *your* views on books, and expect you are right about this one. I don't myself think it v.g. and feel less kindly towards it than you, with your kind bias, do!

I forgot to tell you when we met (and how nice that was) that I was lunching soon with Fr. Simpson[3] shortly off to Spain. I liked seeing him so much, and lent him S. Sitwell's *Spain*[4] (which is v.g.). As no doubt you know, his centre will be Barcelona this time.

I dined last night with the Burmese ambassador,[5] to meet his Prime Minister,[6] a charming little figure, how pretty they are! He wanted, it seems, to meet English writers. Elizabeth Bowen and I sat on his either side, making pro-Burma conversation, while he sweetly smiled at us.

Why do the modern generation write so denigratingly of Gilbert Murray's translations?[7] Whether they are for them or not, surely they should speak of such a scholar with respect, not a hurting belittlement. I saw him yesterday, so nice, and I don't like him hurt.

I hope things go well with you, so far as may be. Father S. spoke of you with affection (so, I needn't say, did I).

My love,

R.

1 Jean had communicated her comments on *The World My Wilderness*, published on 8 May. Ruins, as well as being the theme of the book that was to occupy much of Rose's time until its completion in 1953, are also central to the new novel, her first for ten years, for it is in the bombed-out area of London around St Paul's Cathedral that Barbary and her half-brother, Raoul, find themselves most at home. In fact, the centrality of that area in the book was to have been made explicit in the title, as she reveals in a letter of 3 July 1949 to Luiz Marques. After mentioning that she is writing a book about the pleasure of looking at ruins, she says: 'I am just finishing a novel, called (which is a tiresome coincidence) *In the Ruins*. People will begin to think I have ruins on the brain.'

2 'Symbolism in the work of Rose Macaulay'. George D. Painter's review is in *The Listener*, 18 May 1950, 889. He certainly finds much symbolism in *The World My Wilderness*, but the German words are Rose's, not his. It is likely that she uses German because Painter's fanciful interpretation of her writing reminds her of the interpretations presented in the published dissertations of Margot Brussow, *Zeitbedingtes in den Werken Rose Macaulays* (Griefswald, 1934), and Irmgard Wahl, *Gesellschaftskritik und Skeptizismus bei Rose Macaulay* (Tübingen, 1936).

3 Stuart Simpson, a Catholic convert (1922) who had been ordained in 1944, when he was 60, was priest at the Church of St Charles Borromeo in Ogle Street, just over half a mile from Rose's flat.

4 Sacheverell Sitwell's *Spain* had just been published by Batsford (London, 1950).

5 Maung Ohn, former Burmese Minister of Commerce, had been his country's Ambassador in London since April 1949. He stayed until the end of 1950, when he became Ambassador in Moscow.

6 U Nu, known at this time (but not for much longer) as Thakin Nu, was Burma's first Prime Minister after the country gained full independence from Britain in January 1948 and became a republic outside the Commonwealth. During his official visit to Britain in May 1950 he met King George VI and Queen Elizabeth, Prime Minister Clement Attlee, and Foreign Secretary Ernest Bevin, and attended a service, in Westminster Abbey, of thanksgiving and remembrance for those who died in the wartime Burma campaign. He was a cultured man, who wrote novels and plays.

7 Murray translated many Greek tragedies and comedies. Radio performances of his translations were often broadcast by the BBC. Criticism of his versions was not something new, but went back many years. One of his strongest critics had been T.S. Eliot, who complained that he made Euripides sound like William Morris and Swinburne. See also *L*71 n. 5.

93

20, Hinde House,
Hinde Street, W.1.
17 September 1950

Darling Jean,

My love for to-morrow and its year. I got home from Italy a fortnight ago,[1] and am still a fine rich orange nearly all over, from bathing and sitting in the sun, particularly on the Amalfi and Positano beaches, where we had really Italian August weather all the time. Varazze too: but Varazze rather went to my heart, it *is* so changed, grown, built about, turned into a resort for *bagnanti*[2] (all Italian, which is something). A huge hotel quite close to our house, that used to stand so alone between its two *orti*, with the sea in front, and the mule-track along the sands, and the mountains behind, and the jut of rocks along the shore. Now the sand has become shingle (owing to a great storm they had some years back)[3] and the mule track has given place to bathing cabins, and a high wall is built between our garden and the shore, and the *orti* are barren spaces, and the jut of rocks forti-fied, with a villa above it and a building of some kind at the end; and all wired off, including our little cove. It is sad. The actual *town* is the same (½ mile down the shore from us), and it was very nostalgic going about the deep streets and into the dark shops with sacks of coloured beans, and vegetables and fruit. Our old flat in the Caratoni palace, where we first lived, on the main piazza,[4] seems shut and deserted; the door opposite ours on the same floor has a hammer and sickle and is the headquarters of the Partida Communista![5] But the people are the same – so dear and friendly and amiable, like none other, as we always found. We spent 4 days there, then drove down the coast, stopping here and there, driving inland and out again: the coast beyond Spezia is terribly smartened and populated, bathing cabins at Portofino hired for fantastic prices (we didn't bathe there); Lerici less spoilt than most places, and Levanto and Porto Venere, and a few more that the railway doesn't reach and that remain old fishing ports only. We stayed on the sea 20 miles from Rome for 3 days, and drove in to Rome from it. Rome too is spoilt a good deal, as I knew before, with its imperial roads running round the Forum, and the houses of the Borgo[6] cleared away, and the approach to St Peter's much dwindled in beauty. It was rather pilgrimized,[7] but the crowds tended to move about in groups, and could be avoided. And my word, Rome was hot. We drove about the Campagna (again, much spoilt), bathed in Lake Nemi,[8] went down to Ostia (much more dug out than when I last saw it, many years ago),[9] then up into the hills and saw hill places, and the enchanting Ninfa[10] (a ruined, deserted medieval place, grown over with gardens), and so to Terracina and Monte Circeo – what a cape! Then down to the Bay of Naples – and Cicero, who found this coast too populated,[11] gets righter every year. We had the greatest trouble in getting in to hotels – but we did in the end get into a charming *albergo* at Positano (260 steps up a mountain from the beach) which we loved. At Salerno (a stupid, towny place now) we were caught by 4 days' holiday for the new Dogma,[12] and couldn't cash our cheques. However, we drove about the bay, saw a nice Assumption procession at a tiny town near Amalfi, with fireworks all night, and a huge Madonna carried down to the sea to watch them; and we also went to Paestum.[13] Then, full of enterprise, we crossed Italy (wonderful Abruzzi drive) and came up the Adriatic coast – sea very green and warm and shallow – we thought we could have walked across to Dalmatia in it, but had no visas (particularly not in our swim-suits). We stayed at Ravenna, Venice, and Verona, and returned by Susa and the Mont Cenis pass.[14] It was all fun, and lovely, and exciting, and I saw a lot of ruins. I hope you and Jim will have a lovely time too – but December is a less perfect month, of course. Jim wrote to me about my book – so nice a letter.

This letter is a shameless travelogue: forgive me; you know the temptation. Now I am working terrifically hard, trying to finish *Ruins*, terribly behindhand. And you?

Aunt Mary seems very weak and quiet, but, it seems, can use her leg much better, and gets out in her chair when the weather allows.

I wish you a better year than recent years have been for you. I wish you could get about 2 months really away – say Italy, and (say) about Easter – April and May. How lovely that would be![15]

Now I must return to Ghostly Streets, the section of my preposterous book I am in at present.[16] Having done Goa, Antigua, Italica,[17] Ampurias,[18] Pompeii, Herculaneum, Ostia, Ninfa, Norba,[19] I find myself to-day in Les Baux[20] – do you know it?

All my love, R.

1   On 29 August. See the letter Rose wrote to Fr Hamilton Johnson on 30 August (*LF* 27). She was writing there in reply to the first letter she received from him – a letter that came out of the blue while she was abroad and started a correspondence that was to have a profound influence on her in the last eight years of her life. Thanks to him, she soon became again, after a lapse of nearly thirty years, a communicant Anglican. She had encountered Johnson before he moved from London to Boston, Massachusetts, in 1916 (*L*27 n. 2), but had had no contact with him since then. During their correspondence, they discovered that they were distant cousins. Rose's companions on the trip to Italy (which Emery 310–311 misplaces in 1952) were Dermod and Muriel O'Donovan.

2   'Bathers'.

3   The washing away of the sand by 'a great sea' was reported by Rose in *L*24, written nearly thirty years earlier.

4   Piazza San Ambrogio. Caratoni is an error for Carattini, the name of the doctor from whom Rose's parents rented the upper floors of a house, described by Grace in her diary as 'palatial', from the autumn of 1887 until the spring of 1891.

5   An error for 'Partito Comunista'.

6   District on the right bank of the Tiber.

7   For Roman Catholics, 1950 was a Holy Year.

8   In the Alban hills, painted by Turner.

9   On Ostia, ancient Rome's port at the mouth of the Tiber, see *Pleasure of Ruins* 297–299.

10 Town in the Pomptine Marshes, abandoned in the seventeenth century because of malaria. See *Pleasure of Ruins* 299–301.

11 There was an explosion of villa building and holidaying on the Bay of Naples in the late Roman Republic (middle of the first century BC). Cicero himself owned no fewer than three villas there – at Cumae, Puteoli, and Pompeii.

12 15 August is the Feast of the Assumption of the Blessed Virgin Mary. In 1950 the long-held Catholic belief in Mary's bodily assumption into heaven became dogma. The bull in which Pope Pius XII promulgated the dogma (not actually issued until All Saints' Day, i.e. 1 November) is entitled *Munificentissimus Deus*.

13 *L*84 n. 9. In *Pleasure of Ruins* 220–222 Rose records the reactions of Goethe and other eighteenth-century visitors to Paestum.

14 Rose had visited Susa and the Mont Cenis pass with Gerald in 1927 (*L*65, 66).

15 On 3 November 1950 Nannie Smith died, a few weeks short of her ninetieth birthday. For the last seven years of her life, when her health had failed and she became increasingly deaf, Jean, the unmarried daughter, was obliged to spend most of her time looking after her. Although it was a labour of love, as well as of duty, it put her under considerable strain. A month after her mother's death, she joined Jim, who had a period of leave from his Nigerian post just beginning, in Rome, where the Holy Year

was drawing to a close. After a fortnight there, they returned to England to begin the task of closing down Cross Bank, which had been the family home since 1905. After that Jean was able to resume her own life.

16 'Ghostly Streets' is the title of chapter III of *Pleasure of Ruins*.
17 Roman city near Seville.
18 See *L89* n. 6.
19 The impressive ruins of Norba, a town founded no later than the fifth century BC, are south-east of Rome, overlooking the Pomptine Marshes and not far from Ninfa.
20 In Provence. See *Pleasure of Ruins* 303–306.

94

20 Hinde House.
18 September [1951]

Darling Jean,

The sight of the date to-day called your birthday to mind – I'm vexed that I didn't think of it earlier; but I think of nothing these days, being too submerged in ruins: I forget engagements, in the most preposterous way – and birthdays, as you see. But I do send my love, all too late; and to-morrow will send some small token of it.

How, and where, are you and what doing? Do let's lunch one day. Did Isadore and Emily get back happily?[1] How good it was to see them – such a radiant pair.

Aunt Mary was very sleepy and quiet on Sunday: but the nurse said she had been having tantrums and throwing books about lately – I suppose this must happen sometimes, as she is, after all, still herself. With *us*, now, always so gentle and kind.

Let me know if we can meet, and when. I suppose Tom[2] will be over soon. I am a hermit, a mole, a book-worm, grubbing my way through reams of paper. But I go down to the Serpentine[3] at 9, and it is now what people call 'fresh'. I would like it to be 'close' instead. All my love for your new decade.[4] I didn't enjoy that decade myself very much, so many adverse events occurred;[5] it is better now.

R.

1 Jean's American sister-in-law and teenage niece had spent part of the summer in England before and after Emily's stay with a family in France. Rose was Emily's god-mother and in a letter of 22 June 1951 to Hamilton Johnson mentions that she and Jean 'share taking her about', adding that Jean, a Catholic, 'very properly asked my leave before taking her to Westminster Cathedral to hear Gregorian chants' (*LF* 149).
2 The elder son of Bill and Isadore. After graduating from Harvard, he continued his History studies at King's College, Cambridge, in 1951–1953. On his return to the USA, he served in the Marine Corps before entering the diplomatic service as a specialist in economic affairs. He was Ambassador in Ghana (1979–1983) and Nigeria

(1984–1985). In 1985 he learned that he had an incurable cancer, but carried on working, as Deputy Assistant Secretary in the Office of Policy and Program Review in Washington, until shortly before his death, at the age of 57, in 1987.

3 Lake in Hyde Park, about one mile from Rose's flat.

4 Jean's birthday was her sixtieth.

5 By 'that decade' Rose means 1941–1950. 'Adverse events' included the deaths of Margaret, Gerald, and Will, and the bombing of Luxborough House.

95

20 Hinde House
Hinde St. W.1
9 April 1952[1]

Darling Jean

I have been some time answering your letter of March 27th because for the last nearly 3 weeks I have been laid up with a most tedious disease called undulant fever:[2] I think I really had it earlier, when I thought it was flue [*sic*]; after a fortnight's interval I went down with it again, which is its nature, and why called undulant. Symptoms – your temperature goes up to 101 or so for a while, then right down, then up again. Then you devour chloro-mycetin,[3] which costs the earth, and is supposed to kill the germs. Mine weren't killed for some time, but I *hope* now are (anyhow for the time) and to-day I am up for the first time – you stay in bed because you feel unlike moving, liable to faintness etc (at least I did). You get it from milk – 'that lousy stuff' as my doctor calls it, and lousy is right. I can't think why we force it down the throats of children.[4] Actually it is usually milk from Mediterranean goats or cattle. Cattle have it continually, and from time to time it breaks through from the cattle kind into the human. Well, I mustn't be a bore about it. But it has slightly deferred my Italian plan, which I think now won't be till June (incidentally, this foul disease has crashed my book, and I now *certainly* can't finish before end of May). David Ley,[5] whom I saw when he was here, almost certainly can't come; he could in July, but I can't go then, for many reasons. And you and Jim go to Germany at end of May, which doesn't look as if it could fit. (Though of course if it could be made to, and you could join me in the S. of Italy when you had done with Germany, with whatever money you had left (!), that would be lovely.) *I* hope to screw quite a bit out of the Treasury, for literary purposes; that is an excellent racket. So, they tell me, is to be an invalid (which might occur to me), when your country allows you £10 a week I think.[6] This is all very vague and uncertain, and I'm sure you can't work it; what fun if you could!

I am now just beginning to work again, and am really on the way out of this mess.[7] Kind Fr. Whiteman (of Liddon House and Grosvenor Chapel),[8] who has been more than good to me, is bringing me the Reserved Sacrament to-morrow (Maundy Thursday); I shan't get to church for a little while, I suppose. But it's lovely to feel better. To-day is baking: the 1st warm day since the snow and blizzards.

I'm glad you are having a nice time – your account of the New Englanders does sound delightful, and the sort of thing one has always heard of them. Those 3 – Tom, Jim, Emily – are certainly fine flowers of their species. Tom I found delightful when he and Helen lunched with me.[9] I hoped to see him again while he was in London, but illness prevented. He is a great friend of the son of George Barnes, a friend of mine and the head of Television; he has stayed there, and G.B. thought him charming.[10] There seems (I gather both from Tom and others) to be rather a movement towards religion in King's and Cambridge just now (perhaps Oxford too). Partly under the influence of T.S. Eliot,[11] partly some very effective priests – chaplains of colleges. Just Anglicanism – not that rather unattractive Students' Christian Movement evangelicanism that has sometimes got going in Cambridge. Rather High Anglicanism, but not the aesthetic, sometimes rather silly, extreme ritualism that the young so often affect – at least, there is probably some of that, there always is, but not wide-spread. What kind of Anglicanism obtains in New England? I much like the American P[rayer] B[ook]. Would they, e.g. distribute palms on Palm Sunday, as so many churches do here? The only religious centre I know much about is the Cowley Fathers, of Cambridge,[12] who of course carry on much as here.

Don't feel you must answer this, as you won't know your plans yet (even if I do). Just keep it in mind, in case. Meanwhile, my love to you and to Isadore, bless her. And, of course, Emily, if she is home from school.

R.

1 An air letter, postmarked 11 April 1952 and addressed to Jean c/o A.W. Smith Esq., 7, Gracie Square, New York 28, USA. For most of their married life Bill and Isadore had their home in Ipswich, Massachusetts, but from 1946 to 1953 Bill worked in New York City for the Conservation Foundation and, later, for the Children's Medical Center.

2 Brucellosis.

3 An antibiotic, first marketed in 1949.

4 Rose makes the same remark, and reports the same remark of her doctor, to Hamilton Johnson in a letter of 29 March 1952 (*LF* 296). Several years earlier, she had condemned 'the unwholesome draughts of milk which [British children] are made to imbibe in the middle of the morning', and even suggested that they may lay the foundation of British drunkenness! (*Fabled Shore* 103).

5 *L*83 n. 6. Rose originally planned to visit Cyprus in May, but, after investigating travel options and the cost, decided instead to drive to Italy and make a tour of the Campagna and Calabria (ERM 15.229–231). But, because of illness, she did not get abroad in 1952.

6 The Conservative government's Chancellor of the Exchequer, R.A. Butler, reduced the basic foreign travel allowance, with effect from 30 January 1952, to £25 for each adult and £15 for each child, with an additional £15 for a car.

7 Rose was mistaken. Two days later her fever returned, and many months were to pass before she recovered her health.

8 Liddon House, an Anglican centre for young men of education, started its life at 15 Thurloe Street, South Kensington in 1907, but in 1916 was attached to Grosvenor Chapel in South Audley Street, Mayfair, about three-quarters of a mile from Rose's flat. Grosvenor Chapel, built in 1730, was her favourite place of worship from late February 1951, when she again became a regular Anglican church goer after a lapse of almost thirty years. The chapel pleased her aesthetically, but above all spiritually. Her customary seat was at the back on the left as one enters (Fig. 15). From here she had a good view of the chapel, including the altar; from here too she could make an easy exit and head straight off to the nearby Serpentine for a swim. Among other regular worshippers there were Susanna Lister and John Betjeman. Susanna, or Susan as she was known to her friends and family, had been educated at the Godolphin School, Salisbury, and had worked in India for the Cambridge Mission to Delhi in 1929–1933. In 1946, when she was aged 46, she had enrolled for a BD Honours course at King's College, London, and, after obtaining a first class degree in Theology in 1951, stayed on as a part-time teacher of female students, to whom she insisted on donating her salary. A good friendship soon developed between her and Rose. She checked the proofs of *Pleasure of Ruins* (1953) and is the dedicatee of *The Towers of Trebizond* (1956). In 1959, the year after Rose died, she married the Right Rev. Mark Hodson, Bishop of Taunton, later (1961–1973) Bishop of Hereford. Writing under her married name, she affectionately recalls Rose's attendance at Grosvenor Chapel in 'Rose Macaulay in the Courts of God', in Ann Callender (ed.), *Godly Mayfair* (London, 1980) 37–38. John Betjeman and Rose already knew one another before she joined the Grosvenor Chapel congregation (*L*87), but after that became good friends. In the Introduction to *Godly Mayfair* Betjeman recalls not only his friendship with Rose but also her love for Fr Harry Whiteman, who had been the priest in charge of the Chapel since 1947. In *L*99 Rose regrets his recent departure. A memorandum, dated 13 August 1956, from her to Jeanie reveals that she wanted him to have her set of the *Oxford English Dictionary* after her death (ERM 9.213), and in her Will she left him £2,000, twice as much as she bequeathed to anyone else apart from Jeanie.

9 The lunch was on 18 March 1952. Helen Gillum was the younger daughter of Jean's sister Dorothy. She was employed at the Foreign Office from 1944 until about 1950. Later, until her marriage to David Huntingford in October 1956, she was secretary to Lord Jowitt, Lord Chancellor in the post war Labour government (1945–1951) and Leader of the Opposition in the House of Lords from 1952 to November 1955.

10 George Barnes, who had joined the BBC in 1935 and contributed much to radio, especially, as its first Controller, to the development of the Third Programme, established in 1946, was appointed Director of Television in October 1950. From 1956 until his death in 1960 he was Principal of the University College of North Staffordshire, which in 1962 became the University of Keele. His son, Anthony, read English at King's College, Cambridge (1951–1954). Much of his career was spent

with Schweppes and Imperial Chemical Industries, but in between these jobs in industry he was Administrative Manager of the Royal Opera House, and he went on from ICI to become Director of the Redundant Churches Fund.

11 Eliot was baptised into the Church of England in June 1927, when he was 38. Thereafter much of his work, both in poetry and in prose, had a religious and/or moral dimension. He described himself as an Anglo-Catholic.

12 Cambridge, Massachusetts.

96

Limassol
Cyprus.
5 June 1953

Darling Jean

I am just about to leave this enchanting island for Lebanon, Syria, and Jordan, and then Israel.[1] The Beirouth packet sails in a few hours – a night passage, it is. I have had a wonderful 3 weeks here. Kyrenia, my last abode, is a very charming little sea-port town, backed by great mountains, and all along the coast little coves and beaches where I went and bathed, sometimes alone, sometimes with friends, of whom I have acquired a miscellaneous assortment; the ones I saw most of in Kyrenia were a slightly tarnished nosegay of British pansies with whom I fell in (this seems my natural fate) who spend their time sitting and drinking outside a small wine shop in Herodotus street, and collecting Cypriote bags. Also Lawrence Durrell (not a pansy), a poet whom I like much; he brings up and dotes on a 2-year-old daughter, Sappho.[2] We all went out together on Coronation night[3] and saw the fireworks bursting and blooming over the harbour – very lovely, in the deep blue night and smooth sea. Next day I drove up into the Olympus range, and saw a number of the little medieval Byzantine churches that hide in remote spots and are built to look like houses, to elude the persecuting Latin Church authorities, who burnt Orthodox bishops and priests for heretics. So these small churches have the air of steep-roofed little houses; but inside (if you can find the Papas, climb the path above the village, and get the door unlocked) they are painted all over, ceiling, walls, apses, arches, pendentives, the haloes gleaming gold in the gloom; elongated Byzantine saints and Bible characters, lions (do you know St Mamas, patron of tax-payers? he rides a lion always), sea and land scenes. Lovely colours, some much faded, some scarcely at all; those wretched Turks often spoilt them, and put out the eyes of the figures; but the general effect is *so* attractive, I wished I had time to visit many more.

One doesn't feel Cyprus a particularly religious island; the Greek churches function, but not many services; the Roman ones I suppose have something, but I never yet found one open. Even on Corpus Christi, they were adamantly shut, and no processions. The Anglican ones usually share a chaplain with some other town, so don't produce anything regular. I have a feeling that Cyprus really belongs to the pagan gods, and that anything else laid on it through the centuries has lain rather lightly.

Still, they must have cared enough for their own church not to have been intimidated out of it by the ferocious crusaders and Turks: instead, they started hermitages and monasteries in the mountains. St Mamas lived in a cave, and refused to pay taxes as he used no public services. Sent for by the Governor, he leaped on to a lion and thus rode into Nicosia to the Governor's palace. Startled, the Governor hastily remitted all taxes for him. So he is the patron of those who wish to refuse income-tax.

I wonder what you did on the 2nd. I hear the streets and crowds were shocking. I'm sorry it was wet – all those unfortunates camping on pavements for 2 days and nights. The Abbey ceremony came over quite well here, and was very impressive, I thought. I hope now the papers will consent to forget about royalty till Prince Charles gets married. But I'm afraid they won't.

This time to-morrow I shall be in Beirouth, possibly calling on the Presidentess,[4] possibly on someone at our embassy. I have introductions to both, and both can be of service. If I play my cards well, one of them may think to drive me the 70 miles to Balbek. Or, anyhow, to Aleppo. I shall miss my hired car badly.[5] But they say there are efficient buses. The real hurdle is getting into Israel and out again; but, with expert advice, I hope to surmount it.[6]

Now I must pack my things again, those that have got out of their cases, and prepare for the packet.

Limassol is an attractive harbour town, with a long sea front, rather for business than for pleasure – one has to go outside the town to bathe. But here come in the ships, both great and small, and here the merchants peddle their freights, and oranges spill and float in the sea.

My love always.

Rose

St Hilarion[7] and Bellapais,[8] both up in the Kyrenia mountains, were wonderful.

---

1 Rose made this trip alone, flying London to Nicosia, via Rome, on 16 May and returning by the same route on 1 July. She had promised to deliver *Pleasure of Ruins* to Weidenfeld and Nicolson, the publishers, before her departure. She had a terrible rush to fulfil her promise: she had the work parcelled up ready for collection from her flat at 4.30 p.m. on 15 May. When she returned from her travels, during which she saw some of the places about which she had written, including Baalbek, Palmyra, Tyre, Tortosa, and Jerash, she was able to make some additions to the book. This task and the task of reading the galley proofs were not made easier by an incident that occurred the morning after her return home. Her wireless 'got spontaneous combustion' (*LLF* 102), and the fire spread through her sitting room and did considerable

damage. *Pleasure of Ruins* was published on 7 December 1953, and Rose gave Jean a copy of it for Christmas.

2 Lawrence Durrell lived in Cyprus from 1953 to 1956. When Rose met him, he was indeed best known as a poet, but later he achieved fame as a novelist and travel writer. In *Bitter Lemons* (London, 1957), an account of his years in Cyprus, he mentions Rose in the chapter entitled 'The Swallows Gather', the swallows in this context being the human 'visitants from other worlds, bringing with them the conversations of the great capitals, refreshing the quotidian life in small places by breaths of air which make one live once more, for a moment in the airs of Paris or London' (96). The swallows include Freya Stark and Patrick Leigh Fermor as well as Rose. Durrell mentions how enjoyable it is 'to see the Lion Mount, as if for the first time, through the cool rare eyes of Rose Macaulay, herself bound for ruins stretching still farther back into time than this Gothic castle in the shadow of which I lived. ('Have you ever wondered how it is that the utilitarian objects of one period become objects of aesthetic value to succeeding ones? . . . Does time itself confer something on relics and ruins which isn't inherent in the design of the builder? . . .') The thoughts of a fellow-writer which tease the mind long after she has gone.' 'The attractive' and 'beautiful' Sappho, as Rose calls her in a letter to Durrell of 13 April 1954 (among the Lawrence Durrell Papers at Southern Illinois University, Carbondale), was the daughter he had with Yvette ('Eve') Cohen, the second of his four wives. Rose attended the celebration of her second birthday on 30 May 1953. Sappho's life was to be a disturbed and unhappy one. Whether the allegation, which she made after Durrell's death, that he committed incest with her is true or not (Ian S. MacNiven, in *Lawrence Durrell: A Biography* (London, 1998) 553–554, and in his *ODNB* article on the writer, is inclined to reject it 'on the basis of present evidence'), he was not exactly an ideal father to her, and the relationship between the two was unsatisfactory. She committed suicide by hanging on 1 February 1985, at the age of 33.

3 The coronation of Elizabeth II in Westminster Abbey took place on 2 June 1953. Rose recalls the occasion in the aforementioned letter to Durrell: 'I think our last meeting was on Coronation night, celebrating beneath all the flags which said "Enosis."' In a letter of 20 January 1953, she tells Luiz Marques that she timed her trip to Cyprus not only to coincide with the best season, but also 'to miss the coronation, that hectic blight'. It was not the first time that she had avoided a royal event. In his diary for 27 February 1922 Edward Conybeare notes: 'Rose Macaulay here [in Cambridge] to escape Royal Wedding ructions', the wedding being that of Princess Mary to Viscount Lascelles.

4 Zalfa Chamoun, wife of the President of Lebanon, Camille Chamoun (Kamil Sham'un).

5 The self-drive car she hired in Cyprus.

6 The hurdle was surmounted by the possession of a second passport (*LLF* 93, 101).

7 Castle built in the eleventh century.

8 An abbey, whose main building dates from the second half of the thirteenth century. Lawrence Durrell lived in the village of the same name.

97

20 Hinde House
Hinde St, W.1
18 January 195<4>[1]

Darling Jean

Lovely to have your Villa Medici[2] card. What a pity you had the cold spell when in Rome. It seems, for the moment, over here, and I hope Abroad too; if so, it will be heavenly in Malta, which must be an entrancing island (I hope just now not too much embroiled in wrecked-Comet business).[3] It is full of objects to see, of the most lovely kind: one day I shall go there, I hope. After Malta you will be all among almond blossom and February sunshine – you could even do a spot of bathing? Wish I was there! I hope Helen[4] is all right again, and that you are too, and will be so. Try to get to Paestum if you can, en route from Sicily back to Rome. It is of incredible magnificence and delight.

London, now that Christmas and the vile weather are subsided (both only pro tem, of course), is blandly, lightly cold, no wind now, no snow or real frost. A lot going on – parties for the 25th birthday of *The Listener*,[5] the 1st number of *The London Magazine* (John Lehmann's venture,[6] rather a scrannel pipe[7] so far, but will, I hope, improve), besides a rash of private parties – and a great 80th birthday party for Somerset Maugham[8] – scarcely, in fact, a dull moment. My *least* dull, just now, are those I employ in reading the 17th century Cambridge Platonists, *à propos* a book on them that I am reviewing.[9] I always feel that really they represent the stream of reasonable Renaissance liberal humanism that Colet[10] and More[11] and Erasmus[12] were in earlier, and that has never dried up. Such light and liberty and reasoning speculation, such belief in the Light that has lighted every man, such repudiation of fundamentalism (whether puritan or Catholic), Augustinianism, Lutheranism, and all irrational theology. I never read them but I feel, here is my spiritual home. Do you know Whichcote's sermons and letters?[13] They *are* so good. I think if I had to instruct anyone in Christianity, it would be by way of the Christian Platonists. For the rest, I try and answer Christmas letters, do an odd review or two, and prepare my side of the case of 'Moral Changes', which I have now induced the BBC to change from a talk by me to a discussion with John Betjeman. *He* (probably) thinks morals have declined, I (certainly) that they have improved. I suppose the main thing will be human kindness and justice: here one must set against the abolition of torture, slavery, cruel work for children, grinding poverty – the devilish weapons of war we have now thought up: but, as to that, people in earlier stages of mechanical invention did the worst they could think up, and few holds were barred. I expect John will get the best of the argument, because he is such a good and witty talker: but I, in my plodding, less spectacular way, shall be RIGHT. I don't fancy John knows very much history: I know much more; but he will entertain, and is delightful on the air (or, indeed, off it). He has theories; I delve about for facts, like a beetle, and trundle them up in a dull way.[14]

Shall you see the lately excavated Villa in Sicily?[15] And shall you have time in Rome to get out to Palestrina and see what's doing at the Temple of Fortuna?[16] You ought to have at least one good Campagna expedition, I suppose. Even now that it's so spoilt. Rather nice to show Helen Rome for the 1st time – and Sicily. Next summer I shall, I hope, be showing Venice to my godchild Mary Anne,[17] aged 12, as I have engaged to take her out by train to join her parents and sister in the Yugoslav villa we are all to spend August in D.V. Rather fun introducing a 12 year old – no, just 13 she'll then be – to Venice. I was 10 when I saw it.[18] Tho' I had dreamt of marble halls and blue water, I fell at once for brick palaces and green water. In those days it was all gondolas, and they were *cheap*. Now it's *vaporetti*,[19] and gondolas cost the earth.

Give my love to Helen, and all to yourself. Have a lovely time, both of you. Rose.[20]

1 Rose has dated the letter 1953, but the coronation commemorative air letter she has used is postmarked 18 January 1954. Jean's address is Tigne Court Hotel, Sliema, Malta.

2 Palace in a magnificent situation at the top of the Spanish Steps in Rome, built about 1540.

3 On 10 January 1954 a British Comet jet airliner crashed near Elba. 35 people were killed. Three months later (9 April 1954) another Comet was to crash north of Messina, with the loss of 21 lives.

4 *L*95 n. 9. For Jean's niece, the visit to Malta turned out to be unexpectedly significant, for during it she met her future husband.

5 The first issue of *The Listener*, a weekly established by the BBC, appeared on 16 January 1929. The magazine continued publication until January 1991.

6 John Lehmann, writer and publisher, was the brother of Rose's friend the novelist Rosamond Lehmann. He was with Virginia and Leonard Woolf's Hogarth Press in 1931–1932 and rejoined it in 1938, buying out Virginia's financial interest. In 1946 he sold his interest and founded his own publishing company, John Lehmann Ltd, with Rosamond as co-director. He edited *The London Magazine*, an old title (the original magazine started life in 1732) resurrected for a new publication, until 1961. Vol. 1 no. 1, dated February 1954, but published in January, includes contributions by Elizabeth Bowen, T.S. Eliot, Thom Gunn, Elizabeth Jennings, Louis MacNeice, and William Plomer.

7 Milton, *Lycidas* 123–124: 'Their lean and flashy songs | Grate on their scrannel pipes of wretched straw.'

8 Maugham was born on 25 January 1874. The party Rose was to attend was probably the private view of an exhibition of manuscripts and first editions of his works. The event, attended by the author, was held at The Times Bookshop, Wigmore Street, in the evening of 26 January.

9 Ernst Cassirer, *The Platonic Renaissance in England* (London, 1953), a translation

of his *Die platonische Renaissance in England und die Schule von Cambridge* (Leipzig, 1932). Rose's review is in *The New Statesman and Nation*, 29 May 1954, 708. She calls it a 'learned little book', but criticises the quality of J.P. Pettegrove's translation.

10 John Colet, English theologian and humanist.

11 Thomas More, English lawyer, scholar, statesman, and saint.

12 Dutch humanist and scholar.

13 Benjamin Whichcote, Provost of King's College, Cambridge, from 1664 to 1660. Although none of his works was published in his lifetime, he was the father of Cambridge Platonism.

14 The programme, entitled 'Talking of Changes in Morals: Conversation Between Rose Macaulay and John Betjeman' was broadcast by the BBC Home Service on 15 June 1954, 10.20–10.45 pm. Rose makes brief references to it in *LS* 157, 162–163.

15 The large and luxuriously appointed fourth-century AD Roman villa near Piazza Armerina. It is particularly famous for its magnificent mosaic floors. Excavations, interrupted by the Second World War, had been resumed in 1950.

16 Palestrina, the ancient Praeneste, is a hill-town east-south-east of Rome. The famous temple of Fortuna is huge. Its exposure was assisted by the 1944 bombing that destroyed houses built on top of the ancient ruins. A famous mosaic of the Nile was discovered early in the seventeenth century, and it is probably the thought of this that prompts Rose to mention Palestrina immediately after Piazza Armerina. In *Pleasure of Ruins* she writes: 'Of all the Campagna pre-Roman cities, Praeneste is, in history and imagination and present ruin, the grandest and most imposing' (204).

17 The elder daughter of Dermod and Muriel O'Donovan. The plan for the summer of 1954 did not materialise, but in the late summer of 1955 Rose took Mary Anne and her sister, Jane Caroline Rose, for a week's holiday at Butlin's Holiday Camp, Skegness – a destination less exotic and architecturally magnificent than Venice, but not unadventurous.

18 This visit was in the spring of 1892, soon after Rose's youngest sibling, Gertrude, had died of meningitis. Rose's grandmother Eliza Conybeare took her, Margaret, Jeanie, and their mother to Venice, evidently in the hope of easing the pain of bereavement.

19 Motor-launches.

20 A few weeks after she wrote this letter, on 27 February, Rose had an unpleasant experience. Returning to her flat in the afternoon, she interrupted two burglars, who had emptied all the drawers, scattered the contents over the floor, and made a heap of silver and other valuables to take away. When she asked 'What are you doing here? Who let you in?', they replied that they were CID inspectors, pushed her into her bedroom, and knocked her to the floor before escaping down the stairs. They were unable to take much of their loot, and Rose was not hurt ('They had no cosh, luckily'), but, understandably, she was angry. She describes the incident in letters to Hamilton Johnson (*LLF* 147–148), David Ley (ERM 15.238), and Dorothea Conybeare (ERM 16.192).

98

Darling Jean

I forget if I sent you a p.c. from my ship or not, but I am writing this from Trebizond,[1] romantic ghost of Byzantine glory, once Queen of the Euxine,[2] and now an all-Turk town, all the Greek churches mosqued, all Greeks expelled. It must have been superb in its Byzantine hey-day, its palace and great keep towering on a hill-top, its churches all over the city, its steep ravines grown with figs and vines and oaks, and the wide view over the sea from the palace windows. I was taken over the palace and walls this afternoon by a kind young Turk;[3] we climbed about the broken walls and windows, and the banqueting hall full of greenery and wild flowers – very beautiful. He showed me the Byz: churches too – the best is Aya Sophia, a lovely group of roofs and gables, in which (tho' a mosque) a little wall painting is still to be seen.

Turkish women in remote places like this one are still heavily hooded and muffled in black (sometimes in striped colours). They also do nearly all the work, in the fields etc., the men sitting all day in cafés or squares, talking, playing dominoes, or sleeping. The women are never to be seen eating out: in the restaurant of this ancient hotel[4] last night, I was the only woman dining, in a room packed with men. If a woman ever protests against her lot, and says why shouldn't the men do the work too, both men and other women soon get her down. It is Allah's arrangement that women should be the slaves of men. The consul's wife told me that when they had a Turkish lunch party at the Consulate, no wives could be asked, and she herself can't eat with them.[5] All this has a bad effect on male manners: in Istanbul (where women do get about) they scramble for the seats in trams and leave women standing, shove them about in queues for boats, buses etc. In Istanbul they are quite westernized in dress and customs, but the old tradition remains that women are under-dogs. I don't really much *like* Turks, as a race: they are stupid, indifferent to antiquity, and, when not too apathetic, destructive. And of course cruel – but then all nations have been that.

The Black Sea is *beautiful.* On Thursday[6] I leave Trebizond for Samsun, from whence, on Friday or Sat. I get a train for Antioch, changing at Kaiseri (Caesarea Philippi),[7] where I wait 2 days for the train on to Alexandretta,[8] unfortunately. Finally I get to Alexandretta, and somehow make my way to Antioch. It makes it difficult, having no Turkish, and few Turks except the educated ones know anything else. I was lucky in Istanbul in having introductions to several helpful people. Here too there is the Consul and wife, very nice. On this long trek to Antioch I shall be left to my own (very poor) wits and the mercy of Allah. But I suppose somehow I shall make it. Then to Smyrna, to see Priene, Miletus, Pergamum, etc. Then (if it's allowed) to Troy, but this is doubtful.[9]

I hope Emily is having a good time. When does she begin her studies?[10]

I am followed about by hooting mobs of children and boys, being dressed European. Rather disconcerting. The Consul's wife says one just has to try and ignore them, but it does rather spoil one's pleasure. The idea of *bathing* is out of the question: one would probably be stoned.[11] But the Black Sea is worth it. Every prospect pleases, and only man is vile.[12]

I have written to Mr Ayling[13] at Duchess of Bedford House, Campden Hill, and hope he may get it. I don't know their number at the D. of B. House, nor if it's Campden Hill, or Square, or Road, or what.

I wish the Greeks were back in their own Pontus,[14] it's too bad.

Very much love, R.

1 Rose flew London to Istanbul on 2 June (ERM 15.237) and returned home at 4 am. on 6 July (*LLF* 159). Although she suffered at times from the heat and from illness, and did not get to all the places she had planned to visit (n. 9), Turkey made a deep impression on her, and no place in it a deeper one than Trebizond (Trabzon). Greek colonists established the settlement of Trapezos on the north coast of Asia Minor, towards the south-east corner of the Black Sea, perhaps c. 700 BC. It was well placed for trade, but was unable to take full advantage of its location until harbour improvements were carried out in Roman Imperial times. It flourished under Hadrian and his successors, but attained the peak of its prosperity and power when it was the capital of the Comnenian Empire (1204–1461), the last Byzantine empire, founded in the year Constantinople was sacked by the Fourth-Crusaders and destined to continue for eight years after the capture of Constantinople by Mehmet the Conqueror in 1453. Its territory was not large (about 7,000 square miles), but its wealth and influence were out of all proportion to its size, partly because of skilful diplomacy and management, partly because of trade. It is to the towers of Trebizond's magnificent buildings in this Byzantine period that the title of Rose's last and best known novel refers.

2 The Black Sea. The Greeks gave it the euphemistic name Euxeinos, 'Hospitable', in the hope of placating a sea they regarded as thoroughly inhospitable.

3 Rose's Turkish guide was Cumhur Odabaşıoğlu, a 30-year-old businessman, who had been Mayor in 1950–1952. He cared passionately about Trabzon and its history. He wrote about it, and was always generous in putting his knowledge, advice, and courteous attention at the disposal of visitors who showed an interest in it. He appears in *The Towers of Trebizond*, ch. 14, as Odobasiogli. Anthony Bryer, Emeritus Professor of Byzantine Studies at the University of Birmingham, who knew Odabaşıoğlu extremely well and became his blood-brother in 1959, wrote his obituary, published in *The Independent* on 3 February 1993. The piece begins with *The Towers of Trebizond* and Odabaşıoğlu's appearance in it.

4 Yeşilyurt Oteli, the best hotel in Trabzon at that time, and the only one judged to be suitable for European visitors. Aunt Dot and her party and the BBC group stay there in *The Towers of Trebizond*, with Aunt Dot's camel stabled nearby. According to Laurie, 'it was a nice hotel, old and cleanish, and all the rooms opened out of a circular hall on the first floor, and the dining-room was beyond' (78, near the end

of ch. 8). The hotel, on the north side of Trabzon's *meydan* or central square, survives. In the last decades of the twentieth century it underwent a sad decline, and in
the 1990s became much frequented by 'Natashas' – prostitutes from former Soviet
republics. In 1998 Anthony Bryer dissuaded a party of clerics, including the Bishop
of London, from entering to enquire about Rose–an understandable but regrettable
intervention! (Latest reports are that the hotel is seeing better days again.) Even the
nearby stables are not fictional. As Rose may well have been informed by Odabaşıoğlu
or the Consul, there had been pack-horse and pack-camel stables just off the *meydan*
until they were swept away to make room for (appropriately enough) the Ulusoy Bus
Company.

5 The British Consul in Trabzon, the last holder of the post, was Vorley Harris. He
was not a career diplomat, but a former RAF officer, who during the Second World
War had spent two years as Chief Instructor at the Turkish War Academy. His wife,
Mary, acted as his office assistant. Their son, Christopher Harris, has edited *The
Reports of the Last British Consul in Trabzon, 1949–1956: A Foreigner's Perspective
on a Region in Transformation* (Istanbul, 2005). 'The civilized Consul' and his wife
('pure Birmingham – and pure gold') are described by Patrick Balfour (Lord Kinross),
Within the Taurus: A Journey in Asiatic Turkey (New York, 1954) 8–10. The British
Consul and his wife are unnamed characters in *The Towers of Trebizond*, as is a wholly
fictional Turkish Cypriot Vice-Consul.

6 17 June. It seems that Rose had just two full days in Trabzon.

7 A mistake: Kayseri is not Caesarea Philippi, which is in Palestine, but Caesarea
Mazaca, the chief city of Cappadocia. Rose gets this right in *The Towers of Trebizond*
ch. 14 (169).

8 Iskenderun.

9 Troy is situated close to the southern mouth of the Dardanelles and at this time was
inside a military zone. But Rose did manage to visit it, from Istanbul, on her last day in
Turkey. From Smyrna (Izmir) she got to Ephesus (which she had visited on a Hellenic
cruise in 1912), but not to Priene, Miletus, or Pergamum. She was not feeling well
at that stage of the journey. It did not help that she took rooms in bad hotels, even
though she had other options: she could easily have afforded better ones, and Patrick
Balfour had given her an introduction to friends in Smyrna, who would gladly have
had her to stay.

10 Rose's god-daughter, having just completed her freshman year at Radcliffe College,
Harvard University, was expected to attend a summer-school course on Shakespeare
in Stratford-upon-Avon. The course turned out to be less than scintillating, and she
did not complete it.

11 In *The Towers of Trebizond* (ch. 9, p. 89) Aunt Dot and (the female) Dr Halide swim
at Trebizond. The consul's wife admired their courage in doing what she did not dare
to do herself. Whenever they swam, great crowds assembled to watch and boys threw
apples and tomatoes at Aunt Dot.

12 Rose is quoting from Reginald Heber's hymn 'From Greenland's Icy Mountains'.
Heber, who became Bishop of Calcutta, was a brother of the first wife of Rose's and
Jean's grandfather Samuel Herrick Macaulay. Mary Cholmondeley was a widow
with four sons. She and Samuel did not have any children, and she died in 1846. He

remarried in 1851 and had seven children, including Rose's father and Jean's mother. (Babington Smith (*LF* 143 n. 1) is mistaken in making Mary a daughter of Bishop Heber, and LeFanu (254) is wrong to call the Bishop Rose's great-great-uncle.)

13 *L*100 n. 12.

14 A region of north-east Asia Minor adjoining the Black Sea and including Trebizond. In her poem 'Dirge for Trebizond', printed in *TLS*, 24 June 1955, 342, Rose laments the departure of the Greeks from Trebizond and its occupation by 'barbarians'. The piece provoked a strong but polite and well-argued protest from M[ehmet] A[li] Pamir, Press Attaché at the Turkish Embassy in London (*TLS*, 12 August 1955, 461). His letter is followed by a note in which Rose unconvincingly claims that the views expressed are not hers, but those of 'the imagined ghosts of the defeated Byzantines of Trebizond', and that 'barbarians' simply means 'non-Greeks'.

99

Springfield St Mary
Banbury Rd
Oxford.
17 September 1954

Darling Jean,

One isn't, I believe, supposed to write letters while on retreat,[1] but I can't let the 18th approach without sending my love for it. I wonder if you will be in London, and what you'll do with your Feast. I hope you will be comparatively (but not more so than you like) free from nieces – nice creatures, but troublesome. All the same, I could do with a few (and nephews to match) myself.[2]

I am liking it here – though rather *cold*. It's good to have Fr Whiteman again, and his addresses (on the Mass) are v. good and interesting. He talked partly this morning about the Liturgical Movement.[3] How good to have a priest of his solid *learning*, as well as all the other things. We shall miss it in our (quite nice) Mr Derry from Lancing.[4] He seems pleasant, amiable, has a sense of humour. Fr W. says he is a very good person. On the walls of Liddon House now hang pictures that suggest the Christmas supplements of illustrated magazines, and devotional scenes. But he is musical, sings in tune, is a friend of Benjamin Britten's,[5] and likes insects (or some of them),[6] and, I am sure, people. So there we are, and I'm sure he will be v.g. with boys and young men, which is, after all, the original purpose of Liddon House. Intellect would, of course, be desirable too; but one mustn't make a fetish of this; probably I do, too much.

Staying here too, for a time, is Fr Victor, C.R., the original Company founder, a very pleasant elderly priest, who, of course, being from those parts, knows Reggie well.[7] He is v. fond of Reggie, naturally: he thinks however that, now he grows older, he won't for much longer be up to all the trekking about that he now does, and likes so much. I suppose, if they take him off that, that he will be stationary somewhere. But I imagine that so long as he *feels* fit for mobility, they won't stop him. After all, Reggie is no age at all, by *my* senile standards.[8]

I'm glad to have had the last news of dear Dorothea from you.[9] Oh I do *hope* the right arm, and both legs, will gradually mobilize. I think of her a lot here. Any use? Who knows? I mean, physically speaking. Spiritually I'm sure it is. About the effects of prayer on people's *bodies*, I keep an open (I hope) mind. But I do have a feeling that one may in some way affect the intelligence and care of the doctors who are looking after people, and help them to get good ideas. And, I'm sure, nervous and half mental ailments. Broken or bruised bones and sinews are another matter. One prays, but rather into a questionable country of doubts and institutions, and even negations – (anyhow *subjective* negations, for no one knows the truth).

Anyhow, I pray without inhibitions for you on your feast day.

I *might* drive up to Yatscombe one afternoon, but don't know. I didn't tell G[ilbert] M[urray] I was coming to Oxford. In his last letter he had been 'only moderately well, but treasuring the little gleams of sunshine' that occasionally came.[10] What a shame it is they are so few, and so chilly.

Dear love,

Rose

1 Springfield St Mary was a convent run by the Anglican Community of St Mary the Virgin. Sister Benedicta Ward of the Convent of the Incarnation, Fairacres, Oxford, was a student-helper at Springfield St Mary during a retreat attended by Rose. She remembers 'going along to make [Rose's] bed and finding the room festooned with galley-proofs'. She also remembers her being 'very friendly and kind' (e-mail to the editor, 24 June 2005). The date of this encounter is most likely to have been September 1953, when *The Pleasure of Ruins* was in the press. If writing letters during retreats is discouraged, one wonders if proof-reading is not discouraged also.

2 None of Rose's siblings married.

3 Presumably Whiteman focused most attention on the Anglican (mainly Anglo-Catholic) Liturgical Movement; and if, as is likely, he was concerned more with twentieth-century developments than with nineteenth-century ones, he may have given some attention to Dom Gregory Dix's *The Shape of Liturgy* (Westminster, 1945), a book whose 'breadth of insight decisively altered the scope and the course of liturgical reform both within and beyond the Church of England' (*ODNB*).

4 The Rev. Wilfred Derry, Whiteman's successor as priest-in-charge at Grosvenor Chapel and Warden of Liddon House (*L*95 n. 8), was chaplain at Lancing College in Sussex from 1938 to 1954, when he left after a disagreement with the new headmaster, John Dancy. He was to remain in his new posts until 1967. After that (1968–1980) he was Provost of the Midland division of the Woodard Corporation, a body by which some Church of England schools (including Lancing College) are owned, and to which others are affiliated. Rose seems to have warmed to him somewhat as time went on, without ever becoming an ardent fan. Writing to Jeanie on 25 September 1958, just over a month before her death, she says: 'Fr Derry, though he has some

faults of articulation, is educated, intelligent, and (when I hear him) preaches well' (ERM 9.203). When a Requiem Mass for Rose was celebrated at Grosvenor Chapel on 6 November 1958, it was he who officiated, assisted by Gerard Irvine (*L*101 n. 14).

5 Derry had a good tenor voice. One result of his friendship with Benjamin Britten and Britten's partner, the tenor Peter Pears, was the commissioning of Britten's *St Nicholas* cantata to celebrate the centenary of Lancing College (formerly College of St Mary and St Nicholas) in 1948.

6 No record of Derry's entomological interests has been located, but he is said to have been an expert gardener and forester.

7 Reggie, or Regie as he and his family spelt the name, is Jean's brother. Like Fr Osmund Victor, he belonged to the Anglican Community of the Resurrection and served for a long period in Africa. From 1934 to 1962 he was working at and from the Community's mission station at Penhalonga in what was then Southern Rhodesia and is now Zimbabwe. Fr Victor, after being Provincial of the Community in southern Africa, including Rhodesia, from 1919 to 1935, had spent the years 1939–1954 in Salisbury (now Harare) as Dean of the Cathedral. The Company of which Victor became known as 'Father Founder' is described by Doris Thompson, *Priest and Pioneer: A Memoir of Osmund Victor, C.R. of South Africa* (Westminster, 1958) 97–112. It arose out of his pastoral links, both in South Africa and in England, with the Girls' Diocesan Association, and membership was confined to females. The Mother Company was formed in 1919, when 'a group of eight members met and bound themselves into a closer fellowship in response to a call each felt to offer herself for more consecrated Christian living. . . . Thus began the first of several Companies or "cells" of people who, while living in the world and pursuing ordinary social duties and occupations, yet were being moulded in their spiritual lives by discipline in prayer and service. . . . Each member of the Company bound herself to a certain minimum of prayer each day; to attendance at Communion at such frequent intervals as the circumstances of life shall make possible and desirable; and to service of some sort for the Kingdom of God' (Thompson 100–101). Whether Rose was actually a Company member is not clear. In 1957 she was a patron of the Community of the Resurrection's Penhalonga Appeal in support of university education for Africans.

8 Regie was 58 at this time – 15 years younger than Rose.

9 Dorothea Conybeare had been partly paralysed as a result of an accident. A letter from Rose to Jeanie, written two years later (ERM 9.145), reveals that her condition had not much improved. Nevertheless she lived until 1973, attaining the age of 92.

10 Murray's exact words are: 'I have been only moderately well, but have treasured the little bits of sunshine that are still spared to us' (Letter of 13 September 1954, GM 151.224v).

100

20 Hinde House
Hinde Street W.1
[postmarked 22 September 1954]

My dear Jim[1]

How very nice to get a letter from you! As to the money that came to us when Aunt Mary died,[2] it seemed ridiculous that I and Jeanie should get most simply because of a chance of birth, so I thought I should prefer to be on the same footing as the rest of the nephews and nieces, many of whom have much less money than I have.[3] This was the merest common sense. I didn't mention it to Jeanie, in case she had felt constrained to the same decision, and she does so value every pound that comes to her for sending abroad to her medical missions, and all her other charitable objects. Unlike me, she never keeps any for herself beyond the barest necessities. I feel this is a splendid ideal, which however I simply can't attempt to follow myself.[4]

Yes, how strange it seems that you are really about to retire! It doesn't seem so long ago that you came to see us at Beaconsfield, nor even since you stayed with us at Great Shelford and read our old *Strands*[5] in the attic. I think you were about 12.[6] And now you are still not very old, but all the same about to become a retired gentleman of leisure. I hope they give you a nice fat pension, enough anyhow to be comfortable on. I wonder what you will do. There are so many things that want doing, and many others that it would be fun to do. My own favourite thing is going places and seeing things; unfortunately it is rather expensive. But this summer I had a wonderful time in Turkey; the Turks are immensely stupid, don't give tuppence for their antiquities (or rather, not theirs, but those they have inherited from the Greeks and Romans) and despise and maltreat women – it would be dreadful to be a Turkish woman – but their country is most exciting. I went down the Black Sea as far as Trebizond, a most romantic place for its past history, but now an all-Turkish town with only the ruins of a ghostly Byzantine p<a>lace[7] on a hill. I couldn't bathe anywhere; the Consul's wife at Trebizond said I might well get stoned by shocked onlookers if I did. Going down the Black Sea one saw faintly, at the Sea's narrowest point, the Crimea on the other side.[8] The Turks hate and dread Russia; they spit if you mention the Russian Ballet, even. They are getting ready to fight if opportunity offers; fighting is the one thing they are good at. I went to Constantinople, Ankara, Alexandretta, Antioch, Smyrna, Ephesus (splendid ruins; but the great temple of Diana is sunk in a green swamp, and the Turks scarcely know what it is and wouldn't care if they did.) Now I am writing a novel,[9] but am much hampered by too many other jobs and too little time.

It was fun seeing Emily when she was over here, though I saw too little of her, owing to Turkey. She is such an attractive, clever child. I had a cheerful letter from Anne the other day. She sounds very happy; I gather she hasn't so far changed her Church; I wonder if she will.[10]

I went to the baptism of John's son Benedict; a very intelligent looking infant, who didn't take very kindly to the water. Then we all went to a tea party in John's and Mary Rose's flat.[11] Those nice Aylings[12] were, of course, there. Mr Ayling was so kind in giving me an introduction to the Shell Co. in Turkey, who were very kind to me. I got about Turkey largely floated by Shell, as I got about the Levant last year on Petroleum.[13] I like these oils, they are most helpful. I had no car in Turkey, of course.

It will be very nice to see you next summer when you are back, and I hope it will be a better one than this has been.

Love from Rose

1 Jean's brother. The letter, typed on an air-letter form, is addressed to 'J.S. Smith Esq, The Residency, Umatria, Nigeria'. Umatria is an error for Umahia or Umuahia. Jim was Senior Resident of Owerri province, a position from which he was to retire in March 1955. In his retirement he wrote a memoir of his life and career, entitled *The Last Time*. He gave typescript copies to family and friends, but the book was not published. Some reminiscences of him are recorded by Malcolm Milne, *No Telephone to Heaven: From Apex to Nadir—Colonial Service in Nigeria, Aden, the Cameroons and the Gold Coast, 1938–61* (Longstock, Hants, 1999) 49–51, 164–166. Milne, a junior colleague, describes him as 'confident, humorous, firm and kindly'. He recalls his passion for cricket, his penchant for quoting Latin in his reports (especially, Milne suspects, in those to senior colleagues whom he disliked), and his nickname, 'Hyena', which he was given, on account of his explosive and infectious laugh, to distinguish him from two other Smiths in the Nigerian service.

2 Mary Macaulay died intestate on 29 January 1953, aged 85. Her estate had a net value of just under £4,000.

3 Rose's wealth at her death was £89,547 15s 7d. The 'chance of birth' to which she refers is that she and Jeanie were daughters of Mary's *brother* George, while Jim, Jean, and the other nephews and nieces were children of Mary's *sister* Nannie.

4 For Jeanie's generosity to charities and meanness to herself, see also *L88* and *LLF* 244. But when she died in 1973, she was well-off, leaving £138,038 1d. She had been the chief beneficiary of Rose's will. The chief beneficiary of her own was the United Society for the Propagation of the Gospel.

5 Issues of *The Strand Magazine*, which began its life in 1891 and published serialisations and short stories by writers who included Arthur Conan Doyle.

6 If Rose has remembered correctly, the year would be 1912 or 1913.

7 Rose has erroneously typed 'place'.

8 Rose will have been aware that this observation would be of particular interest to Jim, given that he was born in Odessa and spent his early years there. As British Consul-General in the city, his father was responsible for many of the consular districts on the north side of the Black Sea, including the Crimea. But what she describes having seen was an illusion. The shortest distance between the Turkish and Crimean coasts

is about 260 kilometres (just over 160 miles). If one assumes that the deck of Rose's ship, just off the Turkish coast, was 20 metres above sea level, the horizon would have been about 16 kilometres distant, and the mountains of the Crimea could not have been visible, even 'faintly', unless they were about 4,500 metres high. In fact they rise to only just over 1,500 metres. The Greek geographer Strabo, born about 64 BC in Amaseia (modern Amasya), inland from the Black Sea coast of Turkey, reports (7.4.3) that many who have sailed through the Black Sea at its narrowest point claim to have seen land on both sides simultaneously. Charles King, *The Black Sea: A History* (Oxford, 2004) 15, disputes even that claim ('surely an old salt's tale'), and yet it is far less extravagant than Rose's, which is made also in *The Towers of Trebizond*: 'And, when the weather was clear, a faint shadow loomed on the Euxine's northern side, which was the shadow of the Crimea' (ch. 6, p. 62).

9   *The Towers of Trebizond.*

10 Jim's and Jean's niece Anne Gillum (*L*91 n. 3) had married a Frenchman, Robert Saint Pierre, on 8 May 1954 and was living in France. She did join the Roman Catholic Church.

11 John Gillum, brother of Anne, and his wife. John, educated at Winchester and King's College, Cambridge, had been an officer in the Buffs, with whom he served in Hong Kong and Sudan, but had left the army in 1951 and was destined for a distinguished career in the City of London. The baptism, at Holy Trinity Church, Brompton, on 26 August 1954, was of the Gillums' first child. (Mary Rose gave birth to twins, but the daughter, Alexandra Katharine, did not survive.) The flat was at 47 Princes Gardens. Rose's visit must have brought memories of the early 1920s flooding back, because it was at 44 Princes Gardens that she had had a room in Naomi Royde-Smith's flat.

12 Mary Rose's parents, Alan and Katharine Ayling. His career was in Shell, abroad before the 1939–1945 war, thereafter in the London office.

13 In *Pleasure of Ruins* xiv Rose thanks 'those members of the Irak Petroleum Company who so kindly gave me hospitality and transport in Syria'.

101

20, Hinde House.
Hinde Street, W.1.
17 November 1954

Darling Jean

I thought you would like me to unload on you a little from the best Commentaries on those three women in the Gospels, who weren't identified with one another till Gregory the Great.[1] Even after that, the Greek Fathers didn't accept the identification, and I think no modern critics do? Westcott said 'The identity of Mary (Bethany) with Mary Magdalene is a mere conjecture, supported by no direct evidence'.[2] St John says that Mary of Bethany anointed Christ's feet;[3] St Luke says his head.[4] But this was obviously another occasion from the supper at the Pharisee's house at Nain (?).[5] (The place seems unnamed.)

Different remarks were made on the two occasions; at Bethany they complained of the waste of ointment, but said of the woman who was a sinner, 'if he were a prophet he would have known what manner of woman this is that toucheth him',[6] and a quite different conversation followed. And, had the 'woman in the city which was a sinner'[7] been a known friend of His like one of the well-known Bethany family, whom he used to visit, the Pharisee wouldn't have said that. And there is no indication that Mary of Magdala was a harlot; she had been 'healed of evil spirits and infirmities', and 7 devils were cast out of her,[8] which is thought usually to refer to some kind of madness or epilepsy, certainly not to prostitution. She is always called by her name, being well known, not 'a certain woman'. Gore's Commentary, contributed to by a large and learned panel of scholars, says 'In no case is there the least ground for accepting Gregory the Great's identification of the woman who was a sinner, or Mary of Bethany, with Mary of Magdala. Plainly Luke does not identify them. They appear to be three distinct women. Gregory's view has been rejected by many later Roman Catholic scholars, especially in France.'[9]

Of course it would be interesting to identify them, and one would like to: it would make them all more interesting and dramatic; but I can't see the slightest evidence for it, can you? (*The Catholic Encyclopedia* is quite illogical about it.)[10]

Even the rather jejune Mr Jackman last night doesn't do it;[11] he makes Mary of Bethany go out to get flowers and meet Him on the road; she doesn't go to the tomb, or she would have said so. Mary Magdalene, who did, went back to tell Peter and John, not to Martha. I once asked a Catholic (*your* kind) priest what he thought about this question; he said on the whole the identification was unlikely. This priest wasn't a Mathew,[12] but one I met somewhere, I forget his name.

Forgive this screed; the subject has always seemed to me interesting. I feel somehow that you are too scholarly to accept such an unverified tradition! But perhaps you feel that it is verified; if so, I think your belief is the more interesting and attractive.

Well, it was fun last night, and fun to have you. I don't think the plays can be called good – I didn't like that sneering angel much, did you – but they were interesting, and on the whole well acted. I think he left it a little too unanswered a question *why* poor Lazarus had been called back in that partial way; the angel ought to have supplied some explanation, he was such a know-all. The minister[13] was good, I thought.

I'm glad you have made friends with nice Gerard.[14] I gather he was dropping in on you one day; I fancy he would rather like to talk about the two branches of the Church.[15] By the way, don't, if you don't mind, talk about the family to him; I mean, of course, my bit of it, not yours; and particularly not about me; I suppose I have a morbid dislike to that.[16] But don't tell him this; and anyhow he's not a person likely to talk about people, his interests are church, literature, building<s,>[17] travel, all kinds of things, as you will have discovered by now. I am going down to luncheon there[18] on the 27th. Do you know Patrick Mc<L>a<ug>hlin? He is amusing, but erratic.[19]

Now I must embark on a more difficult and sad letter; perhaps this excursion into Biblical Criticism has been an excuse for deferring it. I have had to-day rather a body-blow, metaphorically speaking, and feel slightly dazed. But it's all rather private.[20] Bless you always, and my love.

R.

1 The matter of the Marys is one about which Rose felt strongly. She raises it also in *LF* 161–162, *LLF* 34, 38–39, and *LS* 234–235, 264–265. Writing to her Catholic cousin, Rose refrains from repeating what she said when opening the subject with Hamilton Johnson: 'How *very* disingenuous the R.C. church is about many things, including St Mary Magdalene' (*LLF* 34).

2 B.F. Westcott, *The Gospel According to St. John: The Greek Text with Introduction and Notes* (London, 1908) II 80, on John 11.1. His exact words are: 'It may also be added that the identification of Mary with Mary Magdalene is a mere conjecture supported by no direct evidence, and opposed to the general tenor of the Gospels'.

3 John 12.3.

4 A mistake: according to Luke (7.38, 46), the woman anointed Christ's feet. The anointing of his head is reported in Matthew 26.7 and Mark 14.3.

5 The query is Rose's. The only mention of Nain in the New Testament is at Luke 7.11. It was there that Jesus brought a dead man, a widow's only son, back to life.

6 Luke 7.39.

7 Luke 7.37.

8 Luke 8.2.

9 C. Gore, H.L. Goudge, and A. Guillaume (eds), *A New Commentary on Holy Scripture* (London, 1928) 220.

10 Rose refers to Hugh Pope's article 'Mary Magdalen' in vol. 9 (New York, 1913) 761–762.

11 Stuart Jackman wrote the two plays Rose and Jean had seen the previous evening – *The Prototype*, based on the story of Lazarus, and *The Blind Man*, based on the story of the healing of the blind man of Capernaum. They were presented under the general title *But They Won't Lie Down*, which is also the title of the book containing them and a nativity play by the same author (SCM Press, London, 1955). The venue was St Thomas's Church, Regent Street, whose Vicar, Patrick McLaughlin, was much interested in drama and promoted it both in his church and at St Anne's House, Soho, of which he was Warden. Among those who contributed to the literary and dramatic life of St Anne's House were T.S. Eliot and Dorothy L. Sayers. When the latter died in December 1957, her ashes were deposited in the chapel there, and Rose was one of the eight persons present at the ceremony. Sayers was a Churchwarden of St Thomas's, as was Rose in the last months of her life (*ERM* 4.241). The director of the plays on which Rose comments was James Brabazon, who had worked at St Anne's House and went on to a varied career as, among many other things, a writer and producer. His books include biographies of Sayers (1981) and Albert Schweitzer (1976). Jackman

was a Congregational minister. At this time his pastoral work was in Pretoria, where his anti-apartheid stance was unwelcome to the authorities.

12 Rose means that the priest was not David Mathew or his brother Gervase (*L*88 n. 6).

13 The minister (unnamed) and the angel (Karis) are characters in *The Prototype*.

14 The Rev. Gerard Irvine, who had ministered at St Thomas's and been involved with St Anne's House in 1951–1953, was now priest-in-charge at the Church of St Dunstan with Holy Angels, Cranford, Middlesex. He and Rose saw much of one another in her last years. He and Patrick McLaughlin were to assist 'Jock' Henderson, the Bishop of Tewkesbury, in conducting her funeral on 3 November 1958, and he was to give the address at the Requiem Mass for her in Grosvenor Chapel three days later. It is likely that Jean first met him at a sherry party Rose gave in October 1954 (*LLF* 172).

15 Irvine later had good reason to be grateful to the Catholic Church. In 1977 St Matthew's Church, Westminster, of which he was Vicar, was almost destroyed by fire, and was not reopened after rebuilding until 1984. During the period of closure, temporary hospitality for him and his congregation was provided not only by other Anglican churches but also by Westminster Cathedral: he was on friendly terms with the Archbishop, Cardinal Basil Hume, and was permitted to take services in the Cathedral's Crypt Chapel of St Peter.

16 Rose's dislike of having her private life, and that of her family, discussed has already been mentioned (*L*5 n. 5). It is not clear what prompted her to make the present plea to Jean, whose discretion, tested over a period of many years, was well known to her, but one suspects that the bad news which she mentions in the next paragraph had intensified her touchiness.

17 Here and in one or two other places in this letter Rose's typing has run off the right edge of the page.

18 St Anne's House, Soho.

19 So 'erratic' was McLaughlin (whom Rose misspells 'McClachlin') that he resigned his Anglican orders in 1962 and became a Roman Catholic. Dorothy Reynolds suggests that he and Gerard Irvine contributed something to Rose's portrayal of Fr Chantry-Pigg in *The Towers of Trebizond*. She also argues that Aunt Dot 'is an affectionate take-off of Dorothy Sayers'. See 'Take away the Camel, and All Is Revealed', *The Church Times*, 8 September 2000, 14–15.

20 What was this 'body-blow'? When the original edition of this book was in preparation, the answer to the question was not available, but I drew attention to a passage in Rose's letter of 3 December 1954 to Hamilton Johnson, in which she mentions some recent difficulties: 'You must try and forgive my over-long pause between letters: it's not that I forgot, but that life has been, with one thing and another, rather harassing, and I waited till things cleared a little before writing, since you aren't one of the people I can write to about other things while my mind is full of things I don't refer to …'. I conjectured that the upsetting news concerned the marriage of Dermod and Muriel O'Donovan. The full version of Rose's letter, available since 12 June 2012, reveals that, while she had indeed received bad news of Muriel, the real 'body-blow' was Father Harry Whiteman's decision to leave the priesthood and the Church. (See also 'Editor's preface to the paperback edition', pp. xii–xiv.)

102

21 Ashley Court
London S.W.1.
17 January 1955

Darling Rose,[1]

You wrote to me two months ago, about the identification of S. Mary Magdalene with Mary of Bethany, and either or both with the unnamed woman of *S. Luke* VII (the sinner). Thank you for the quotations from Westcott and Gore's commentary, and your own. There is, of course, no direct evidence of any such identity in the Gospels; but the case is not quite so simple as you say, nor as you say.

All four evangelists relate an anointing:
1. S. Luke:

place, Galilee; time, fairly early in the gospel; a woman *in civitate peccatrix*,[2] who anointed Xt's feet and wiped them with her hair, having washed them with her tears.[3]

The host's comment[4] shows that he knew her reputation, but knew nothing of any previous contact between her and Xt., and knew little of Xt. ('The well-known Bethany family' have not yet entered the story.)

From the dialogue it is clear that it was usual to anoint a guest's head with oil, and suggested that it was unusual to anoint his feet with ointment.

2a. SS. Matt. and Mk:

place, Bethany, the house of Simon the Leper; time, two days before the Passover (after the Palm Sunday entry); 'a woman' broke an *alabastron* and anointed Xt's head; was criticised for waste, and defended: 'she did it for my burial . . . the poor have you always . . .' and 'wheresoever this gospel . . .'[5]

2b. S. John:

place, Bethany; time, six days before the Passover (the day before the Palm Sunday entry v. 12); Mary (by context Mary of Bethany) anointed Xt's feet and wiped them with her hair; was criticised for waste and defended, 'the poor have you always'., and the reference to his burial.[6]

2a and 2b must be the same incident (1 of course different)? in spite of the discrepancy of date between 2a and 2b. S Augustine says here that when two accounts of the same thing are different but compatible you assume that both are true, i.e. that at Bethany both head and feet were anointed (*de Consensu Evang*[*elistarum*][7] <book 2> c. 79). What St John chooses to record is a repetition of the act in *S Luke* VII; having in the previous chapter identified Mary as 'the one who anointed the Lord with ointment and wiped his feet with her hair' – *ēn de Mariam hē aleipsasa ton Kyrion . . .*[8] That construction reads most *naturally* as a reference to a past action – past at the time of the narrative, the one recorded by St Luke and assumed by St John to be known to his readers? It can also be read as an aside from the narrative, a reference to something which was past at the time of writing; and so many people read it. But Garrigou-Lagrange,[9] who strongly opposed the identification of Mary of Bethany with the woman in *St Luke*, felt the difficulty of the tense so much that he suggested *aleipsousa* the future participle for *aleipsasa* the aorist.[10] The text however (Westcott and Hort is the one I have here)[11] gives no sign of a doubtful reading here.

S. Augustine held it a matter of opinion that 'the same Mary did this deed on two separate occasions'; quoting *S. John* XI.2, 'by this statement John attests what Luke has told us' (*de Consensu Ev.* <2>.79): *Nihil itaque aliud intelligendum arbitror nisi non quidem aliam <fuisse> tunc mulierem, quae peccatrix accessit ad pedes Jesu . . . sed eandem Mariam bis hoc fecisse.*[12] A good many (twenty?) years later in *The Tractates on S. John* he says: *Ecce ipsa soror Lazari (si tamen ipsa est quae pedes Domini unxit unguento et tersit capillis suis quod laverat lacrimis) melius suscitata est quam frater eius . . . erat enim famosa peccatrix, et de illa dictum est: Dimittuntur ei peccata multa quoniam dilexit multum.*[13]

S. Jerome and S. Ambrose left this identification open; as did S. Albert the Great and S. Thomas Aquinas; later Salmeron (for instance) and Casaubon 'strenuously asserted' that there were three distinct women.

S. Gregory certainly supported both identifications – of S. Mary Magd. with the sinner in *Luke* VII (25 *Homily in Evang.*)[14] and of Mary of Bethany with both ('*credimus*',[15] he says): *Hanc vero quam Lucas peccatricem mulierem, Iohannes Mariam nominat, illam esse Mariam credimus, de qua Marcus septem daemonia eiecta fuisse testatur* (33 *Hom. in Evang.*).[16]

S. Chrysostom and S. Irenaeus 'nowhere distinguish the Penitent and Magdalen', but S. Chrysostom did not identify her with Mary of Bethany. Clement of Alexandria thought the Penitent was S. Mary Magd.

As regards the liturgy: Alban Butler (1711–1773) says: 'In the Roman Breviary the Penitent is honoured on this day (July 22) under the name of Mary Magdalene, and for our edification the history of all these examples of virtue is placed in one point of view as if they belonged to one person . . . but the offices are distinct in the Breviaries of Paris, Orleans, Vienna, Cluni and some others'.[17]

On the other hand, in the East there are three separate feasts (the Uniates agreeing with the schismatics). It is nothing to do with *faith*, of course; has always been open.

In sum, I can't find anyone who thinks it is *proved* out of the Bible! And in the Commentary which I have here (1953) of course the commentators on all four Gospels agree about that.[18] The commentator on *St John*, however, finds the account in *S John* XII.3 (of the surely unusual gesture of wiping Christ's feet with her hair) 'readily intelligible only on the assumption of the identity of this Mary with the sinner' of *Luke* VII. The article in *The Catholic Encyclopedia* is by the late Fr Hugh Pope O.P., who was a considerable biblical scholar; I find it rather telescoped and summary, but not illogical if you allow for that.

I don't find it insurmountable that St Luke does not name the Penitent, and in the next chapter introduces Mary Magdalene by name. It is like his calling S. Matthew Levi in the account of his call, and immediately afterwards Matthew in the list of the Apostles;[19] thus (also S. Luke) Simon and Peter, Saul and Paul.

You say that S. Mary Magd. is 'always called by her name, being well known' – meaning that you accept only the references where she is so called? but actually S. John at XX.11 calls her 'Mary', and S. Luke XXIII 49 and 55 says 'the women who followed <him> from Galilee' and we know that she was there, from the other gospels.

As to Magdala and Bethany, is that a difficulty? it has been suggested that Mary Magd. married or inherited property at Magdala; or made her career there? then 'followed from Galilee'; and later came home to her family. It was not necessarily a poor household; (indeed Mary's pound of ointment represented a year's wages for a workman, someone says; anyhow would sell 'for much'.) Mary Magd. is twice mentioned with Joanna,[20] whose husband was Herod's steward [21] (one of Herod's palaces was near Magdala). All this assuming that 'Magdalene' means 'of Magdala' – there are other derivations.

I feel it is less than scholarly to deny any possibility to these speculations.[22] I feel strongly that the actions of S. Mary Magdalene (standing by the Cross, being first at the tomb and staying there) have an affinity with the actions of the Penitent, and with the Mary of *St John* XII.3. Further one cannot go. I have never heard it taught, one way or the other, that I can remember; except Fr Cary, long ago, recording someone's theory (without asserting it of course) that Martha was the wife of Simon the leper, and Mary = S. Mary Magdalene.

(I have overheard an instruction to the Westminster[23] children, on the story in *Luke* VII: 'she was a *bad lady*, but she was *sorry*', which anyhow gets the point.

The Mass for S. Mary Magdalene's day in the Roman Missal has a collect which goes all the way: *Beatae Mariae Magdalenae, quaesumus, Domine, suffragiis adjuvemur: cujus precibus exoratus, quatriduanum fratrem Lazarum vivum ab inferis resuscitasti: Qui vivis . . .*[24] The Gospel is from *S. Luke* VII;[25] which certainly suggests that the identification with the Penitent is intended: perhaps not necessarily, though; for till 1950 the Gospel for the Assumption was *Luke* X.38–42,[26] without any idea of identifying Mary of Bethany with Our Lady.

I have not been able to discover the origin of the Collect; have asked Stanbrook, but no answer so far. (I asked them in Advent, and they do not write letters in Advent – a good idea for us all.)[27]

All my love,

Jean.[28]

1 Like 107, the only other surviving letter from Jean to Rose, this letter is preserved because she typed it and kept a carbon copy.

2 '. . . in the city, which was a sinner.'

3 Luke 7.37–38.

4 'This man, if he were a prophet, would have known who and what manner of woman this is that toucheth him: for she is a sinner' (Luke 7.39).

5 Matthew 26.6–13; Mark 14.3–9.

6 John 12.3–8.

7 *The Agreement of the Evangelists.*

8 John 11.2 in Greek: 'It was that Mary which anointed the Lord . . .'

9 Réginald Garrigou-Lagrange was a prolific scholar, and the present editor has not found the place where he proposes the textual emendation mentioned here.

10 That is, 'who was to anoint' for 'who anointed'.

11 B.F. Westcott and F.J.A. Hort (eds), *The New Testament in the Original Greek* (Cambridge, 1881; several later editions).

12 'So I do not think that anything else is meant than that there was at that time no other woman, who came as a sinner to the feet of Jesus . . ., but that the same Mary did this twice.'

13 *Tractatus in Iohannis evangelium* (*Sermons on the Gospel of John*) 49.3: 'See how the sister of Lazarus herself (*if indeed* it was she who anointed the Lord's feet with ointment and wiped with her hair what she had washed with her tears) had a better resurrection than her brother . . . For she was a notorious sinner, and it was said of her: "Her sins, which are many, are forgiven; for she loved much."'

14 *Homiliae in evangelia* (*Homilies on the Gospels*) 25.1.10 = Migne *PL* 76 col. 1239.

15 'We believe'.

16 'Indeed, this woman, whom Luke calls a sinner and John names Mary, we believe to be that Mary concerning whom Mark declares that seven devils had been cast out' (*Homiliae in evangelia* 33.1 = Migne *PL* 76 col. 1239). The passage of Mark is 16.9.

17 The quotation is from Alban Butler's *The Lives of the Fathers, Martyrs, and Other Principal Saints* III (London, 1757) 251 (note), but several minor variations in Jean's version indicate that she is using a later edition, while at the same time not being entirely accurate in her use of that. Moreover, '(July 22)' is her own addition.

18 B. Orchard and others, *A Catholic Commentary on Holy Scripture* (London, 1953) 1002. The commentator on John is W. Leonard.

19 Luke 5.27–29; 6.15.

20 Luke 8.2–3; 24.10.

21 Chuza (Luke 8.3).

22 This is a pointed response to Rose's comment: 'I feel somehow that you are too scholarly to accept such an unverified tradition.'

23 Westminster Cathedral.

24 'May the prayers of blessed Mary Magdalen help us, O lord: for it was in answer to them that thou didst call her brother Lazarus, four days after his death, back from the grave to life. Who live . . .' In the *Missale Romanum* from which Jean quotes, 22 July is called the day of 'St Mary Magdalen, penitent'. But in the revised Missal of 1969 the Church accepted the view that Mary Magdalene is not to be identified with the

sinning woman and/or Mary of Bethany. The Collect was replaced. So (n. 26) was the Gospel.

25 Luke 7.36–50. In the 1969 Missal the passage was replaced with John 20.1–2, 11–18.

26 The replacement Gospel was first Luke 1.41–50 and is now, since 1972, Luke 1.39–56 for the day Mass and Luke 11.27–28 for the vigil Mass.

27 Stanbrook Abbey, at Callow End near Worcester, became the home of a community of Benedictine nuns in 1838. It gained a fine reputation for its scholarship and music, and for its printing press. In the last century three of its nuns, Abbess Laurentia McLachlan, Dame Felicitas Corrigan (*L*103 n. 6), and Dame Hildelith Cumming became particularly well known. In May 2009 the community moved to new, eco-friendly buildings at Crief Farm, Wass, North Yorkshire, but the name 'Stanbrook Abbey' has been retained. The nuns continue to refrain from writing letters during Advent and Lent. As for the Collect for St Mary Magdalene's Day quoted by Jean, the earliest surviving manuscripts in which it is found are the Sacramentarium Udalricianum and Sacramentarium Rossianum, both missals of the eleventh century. The former, written for Udalrico II, Bishop of Trent(o) in 1022–1055, may well be the original source of the Collect.

28 In a postscript, omitted here, Jean starts to make a point to do with the Greek words used by Luke and John for 'ointment', but then retracts it ('No, I see that goes nowhere . . .').

103

20, Hinde House,
Hinde Street, W.1.
28 August [1956]

Darling Jean

You'll get *The Towers of Trebizond*[1] (which I hope sounds like a Cornish manor house)[2] to-morrow, I hope. I don't know if you'll like it, or how much of it, but I hope some. It has some levity on serious subjects, I'm afraid – I do *hope* no one will mind, neither my Anglican nor my dear Popish friends, nor Moslems, nor American Baptists, nor Greek Orthodox. I don't mind levity myself, and one sometimes forgets that some people are jarred by it. I don't mean that there's much of that: the theme is fundamentally very serious and religious, as seen through the eyes and commented by the tongue of a rather haphazard character.[3] Of course that's only an underlying theme, there are others, and I hope you'll like the Turkey and Black Sea parts of it, as I liked writing them.

I had a good letter from Emily, on the ocean, with a drawing of her candle-sticks. She seems really to want these objects, so I suppose it's all right.[4] You must now (I hope) be enjoying a relaxed peace, having sped an inexperienced brother and an erratic niece so efficiently across the seas. What *would* they all do without you?[5]

The small bits I have seen of the anonymous narrative part of *In a Great Tradition* make me wish *you* had written it indeed, on facts supplied. Surely it is rather flattish and cliché? But I haven't seen enough to judge, perhaps. What a fine person. And what an old silly Shaw was in many ways, and *how* untruthful.[6] I really do rather dislike him.

Are you in London, I wonder.

My love always

R.

1 Rose's last novel is a remarkable mixture of the comic and the serious, reflecting her view that human life is a similar mixture. It exhibits much variety in other ways too, including geographically, culturally, spiritually, and emotionally. Its reception by critics and the public was generally, though not universally, very favourable, and it is the book for which Rose is best known. Some readers only noticed the comedy and missed the main message, which, she insisted, is a serious one. Writing to Hamilton Johnson just before the novel went to press, she explains: 'Trebizond stands for not merely the actual city . . . but for the ideal and romantic and nostalgic vision of the Church which haunts the person who narrates the story' (*LLF* 219). Among the most ardent fans of the book were members of the British Royal Family, especially Princess Margaret. Between 21 September and 25 October 1956 the Princess made an official tour of East Africa. She flew out and back, but during the tour used the royal yacht *Britannia* for visits to Mauritius and Zanzibar, and Rose learned that, while aboard, 'she was absorbed in *The Towers of Trebizond* . . ., and kept reading bits of it aloud to her companions; especially she liked the bits about adultery' (ERM 9.147). On 15 November Mark Bonham Carter, Rose's editor at Collins, gave a dinner party to enable the Princess and Rose to talk. The two ladies, who had met briefly at his wedding reception on 30 June 1955, much enjoyed the evening, and the party did not break up until nearly 4 am (ERM 16.171). Rose reports her enjoyment of the occasion in *LLF* 245–246; and the Princess does the same in a letter of 29 October 1999, written to the present editor on her behalf by Annabel Whitehead, Lady-in-Waiting. The same letter also conveys the Princess's remark 'that everybody in The Royal Family at the time was most enthusiastic about *The Towers of Trebizond*'. According to Rose's report of the dinner-party conversation, the Princess 'first read the *Towers* at Balmoral, and laughed so much, alone in a room, that the Queen her sister came down to know what was the matter. Then the Queen read it, and also laughed' (*LLF* 246). On 18 February 1958, a week after Rose had been invested as DBE in a ceremony at Buckingham Palace, she was a guest of The Queen and Duke of Edinburgh at dinner (*LS* 255). Some copies of *The Towers of Trebizond*, destined for selected friends of Rose, carried the following imprimatur:

> *Nihil Obstat*
>
> ✤ Raymond Long Crichel
>
> *Imprimatur*
>
> Johannes Betjeman, *Decanus*

But the copy Rose gave Jean does not contain this notice, presumably for fear that the joke might not be appreciated. For Raymond Mortimer's country home, Long Crichel, see *L*108 n. 6.

2 Tre- ('settlement') is very common in Cornish place names. Conflate Trebartha with Marazion, and the result is quite close to Trebizond.

3 Laurie, who, although not Rose, contains much of her. *The Towers of Trebizond* is the only one of her novels told in the first person by a single narrator.

4 The candlesticks, a pair made by Matthew Boulton (1728–1809) of Birmingham, were bought by Emily with money that Rose gave her for her 21st birthday. What little of the money that remained was used to buy a history of the Quakers. 'Memorably', writes Emily, '[Rose] didn't understand either purchase' (e-mail to the editor, 19 November 2004).

5 The 'inexperienced brother' is Regie, the only one of Jean's brothers who was still a bachelor, and the 'erratic niece' is Emily.

6 *In a Great Tradition: Tribute to Dame Laurentia McLachlan, Abbess of Stanbrook* (London, 1956), by the Benedictines of Stanbrook. Dame Laurentia, Abbess of Stanbrook Abbey from 1931 until her death in 1953, was a scholar and leading authority on plainsong. Among her friends were Sydney Cockerell and George Bernard Shaw. Shaw described her as 'an enclosed nun with an unenclosed mind'. The story of her long friendships with him and Cockerell is told in *In a Great Tradition*. Although unnamed, the book's chief author was Dame Felicitas Corrigan, who later produced a revised version, entitled *The Nun, the Infidel and the Superman: The Remarkable Friendship of Dame Laurentia McLachlan with Sydney Cockerell, Bernard Shaw and Others* (London, 1985), reprinted as *Friends of a Lifetime* (London, 1990). Dame Felicitas's book inspired Hugh Whitemore's play *The Best of Friends*, first staged in London in 1988, with John Gielgud, in his farewell stage performance, playing Cockerell, and revived in 2006. The play was also presented on television. (On Whitemore's dramatisation of *The Towers of Trebizond*, see L20 n. 13.)

104

20, Hinde House,
Hinde Street, W.1.
3 September [1956]

Darling Jean[1]

Having been out since my party left, I am now in again, and thought I would write to you about one or two things in my book that are a little on my mind. I put into people's mouths and thoughts various comments on your Church – and I should hate it if the members of it whom I love – you and Jim, e.g. – were to be hurt by them. I remember one thing in particular, about how R.C.s in C. of E. churches for baptisms and funerals etc. refrain from joining in the prayers. I know they have to, and that it isn't their own initiative. But it is a thing that I feel does cause some resentment among Anglicans – I dare say among nonconformists too, but I don't know how much that arises – and therefore makes cordial relations between the churches less easy, and I do feel that is a pity. So I didn't refer to it by accident, but because I think every one who does so may possibly help to start a new habit in such matters, so that perhaps it is worth while that a lot of people should; I mean it may not have occurred to those who decide such things that it seems discourteous and puts friendly relations back a little. Just as your Church may and does complain that some tourists and visitors pass the altars without respect etc. But when I saw you and Jim and Rosemary[2] (how nice she is) today, my heart rather smote me that I had written these things and that you would read them, and perhaps be hurt, and that I should hate. You are always so generous and tolerant to me in what you must feel are my perversities. I hope you'll understand and forgive me. Charity between the different branches of the Church is so vital, and both branches go wrong about it so often. I greatly hope I haven't gone wrong about it in this book, in saying the things I feel strongly about. To me the Christian Church is so much one body (in all its various divisions) that I feel we should be able to pray together and worship together, in one another's churches or anywhere else, and that this is what was meant for us. So it annoys me when Anglicans take an exclusive line about nonconformist clergy etc, and the fuss some of them make about South India.[3]

Well, perhaps there is no need to write all this to you, but I thought I would like to clear things up, in case.

I enjoyed our Cozenage;[4] I like Mary too;[5] but Rosemary in particular. And Jim always a dear; and you I needn't say.

Much love,
Rose

1 This typed letter was written on the day *The Towers of Trebizond* was published. Although Jean's reply is not preserved, Rose describes it in a letter of 5 September 1956 to Dorothea Conybeare: 'I apologised to Jean (Smith) for anything I had said in the book which might hurt her as an R.C., as I thought I had better warn her. She wrote back very generously, and I hope won't mind. I was thinking especially of a bit about R.C.s at Anglican baptisms etc standing with closed lips during the prayers and creed, which I really got from her and Jim at baptisms and at Aunt Mary's Requiem Mass. She says the directive is "take no part", but that this <is> interpreted in different ways, and Fr Pilkington says it need only mean "don't read the lessons", which is easy, but he is a very broad-minded priest. I hope he is influencing Jean' (ERM 16.180). The relevant passage in *The Towers of Trebizond* is in ch. 21 (243). Ronald Pilkington came to Westminster Cathedral, beside which Jean lived, at the end of the Second World War, after many years as a chaplain in Florence. According to his obituary in *The Times*, 28 January 1975, 17, 'His scholarship made him famous as a liturgist, an authority on the Eastern Church, while his continuing devotion to the Church of England combined to make him an ecumenist before the word came into general use.'

2 Throughout more than thirty years' service in the colonial administration of Nigeria, Jim Smith had led the life of a confirmed bachelor. So it came as a considerable surprise to his family and friends, when, just six months after his retirement, he got married. The wedding took place on 24 September 1955, with Rose among the

guests (Fig. 16). Jim's bride, Rosemary Hughes, was a musical scholar, writer, and broadcaster, best known for her book *Haydn* (London, 1950). She later wrote *Haydn String Quartets* (London, 1966) for the BBC Music Guides series. Haydn was her chief interest, but by no means her only one: she edited the 1829 travel diaries of Vincent and Mary Novello under the title *A Mozart Pilgrimage* (London, 1955) and wrote *Beethoven: A Biography with a Survey of Books, Editions and Recordings* (London, 1970). Although Jim was not musical, the marriage was a completely happy one. Like him, she was a Catholic convert.

3 The Church of South India had been formed in September 1947 as a union of several different denominations, including Anglicans, Methodists, Congregationalists, and Presbyterians. Inside the Church of England there was much discussion, and not a little disagreement, about how it should be treated. Some, seeing it as a shining example of ecumenicalism, wanted the Church of England to enter into full communion with it. Others, pointing out that the Church of South India combined episcopal and non-episcopal traditions, were hostile to such a relationship, arguing that it would compromise the Catholic principles of the Church of England.

4 Playful use of an old form, for 'cousinage'.

5 Mary Chance, wife of Rose's and Jean's cousin Roger Chance (*L*110 n. 13).

105

La Calcina
780 Zattere
Venice[1]
22 May [1957]

Darling Jean

Thank you so much for your letter, which slightly softened the shock of reading this morning in yesterday's *Times* the news of dear and beloved G.M.'s death.[2] Of course it shouldn't really be saddening, at his age and with that magnificent life behind him; but of course it is, not only to those who loved him, and to whom he was so kind a friend, but to all the world, which one feels has lost perhaps its most fine, civilized and noble representative, both intellectually and in all the human wisdoms and generosities. *What* a record his is! Has anyone else been at once so great a scholar and so splendid a worker for civilization and for people everywhere, and for the whole precarious future of the world? With such vision, and such concentration of purpose, and such deep *minding* of people's troubles everywhere. And at the same time such individual care for people – family, friends etc. I shall personally miss him a great deal, and those elegantly typed letters about his work, about things I had written, about nothing much except a kind impulse to exchange a friendly word.

I'm glad the memorial service is after my return – but will the University Church contain all who will want to be there?[3]

Well, a great tree has fallen. I have written to Rosalind,[4] hoping she wouldn't mind one letter more among the thousands. I liked the *Times* account; and Masefield's lines.[5]

I'm afraid I shall just miss you, as I shan't be back till 30th now, having decided to stay on for the 1st night of the Biennale[6] *Titus Andronicus* – such a bad play, but I would like to see how Venice takes it and Olivier.[7] Victor Cunard,[8] and one or two other friends are here; he inhabits in a beautiful *palazzo*[9] in the Carmini – or rather in 3 large saloons of it. Tomorrow we go together to Asolo to see Freya Stark.[10] Venice is really about as sociable as London. This is *such* a nice place to stay, near the Salute[11] end of the Zattere,[12] with the Giudecca to look at, and San Giorgio,[13] and the ships coming in and out, and a nice *terrazzo* outside to sit in and breakfast in, and a charming staff.[14] It is quite close to the Gesuati church, which has a daily vespertine mass at 7.15, but unfortunately preceded by a longish address, so I haven't time, when I go, to finish mass before dinner.

We are mostly English in the Calcina, and sometimes someone pleasing turns up, such as the nice old Howarths[15] (who know all the King's people – he went up in 1897) and an occasional charming young couple on a honeymoon. Jock Henderson and his wife[16] are also in Venice for a very few days – he as an incog: *vescovo*[17] in lay clothes; I had a nice morning with them and their two friends yesterday – all innocents abroad, with no knowledge of the scene or tongue.

Your family news is interesting – Jim's Pershore House,[18] the Spanish travel, and young Jim,[19] whom I am more than sorry to be missing; I would have much liked to meet him. What charming young those three[20] are. Shall I miss you also? I shall ring up when I get back and find out.

Meanwhile, all my love.

R.

1 Rose went to Venice after the cancellation of a Hellenic cruise she was to have joined with David and Gervase Mathew and other friends (letter of 5 April 1957 to Luiz Marques). She travelled by train, leaving England on 6 May and returning on the 30th. During her three weeks there she gave some thought to, and made some notes for, her next novel, provisionally entitled *Venice Besieged*. But she managed to complete only the first chapter before she died. That chapter and Rose's notes are presented by Constance Babington Smith in an Appendix to *LS* (299–327). Rose was to return to Venice in August 1958, to spend a few days there before the start of a Hellenic cruise (*L*110).

2 Gilbert Murray died on 20 May 1957 at the age of 91.

3 The memorial service was held in the University Church of St Mary the Virgin, High Street, Oxford, on 5 June 1957. *The Times* (6 June 1957, 12) reports that Rose was among 'the large congregation'.

4 Rosalind Toynbee, Murray's daughter.

5 John Masefield, poet laureate, was a friend and neighbour of Murray. His lines, printed in *The Times*, 21 May 1957, 11, under the title 'On the Death of Professor

Gilbert Murray, Scholar and Humanist', are: 'Surely, in some great quietude afar, | Above man's madness and the greed of night, | Wisdom will crown this spirit with her star | In conquerors' peace, in her undying light.'

6   Venice's biennial international art exhibition, established in 1895.

7   Laurence Olivier took the title role in Peter Brook's production, which had been first presented in Stratford-upon-Avon in August 1955. Vivien Leigh appeared as Lavinia, and Anthony Quayle as Aaron the Moor. The production came to Venice from Paris, and went on to Belgrade, Zagreb, Vienna, and Warsaw, before starting a five-week run at the Stoll Theatre, London, on 1 July. The drama critic of *The Times* called Olivier's performance 'one of the great things in his career', adding: 'The total impression is of an actor whose reserves are so great that he can wring beauty out of a poor art without appearing to be engaged in a feat of virtuosity' (2 July 1957, 11).

8   Cunard, foreign correspondent of *The Times* in Rome (1922–1927) and Paris (1927–1933), had an outstanding knowledge of Italy and France and their languages and literature. That knowledge was much valued when he served in the Political Intelligence Department of the British Foreign Office (1941–1946). He was a first cousin of Nancy Cunard (*L*20 n. 6), and a supportive and affectionate friend of hers from childhood until his death in Venice on 28 August 1960.

9   Casa Foscali.

10 Freya Stark had invited Rose and Cunard, a neighbour of hers in Asolo before the war, to lunch at her house, known as the Villa Freia. If lunch was served in the garden, the scene of it can be viewed in the photograph captioned 'Lunch in the garden of the Villa Freia, mid-1950s' in Molly Izzard, *Freya Stark: A Biography* (London, 1993), between pp. 230 and 231. Freya, celebrated for her travels in Arabia, Turkey, and elsewhere, and for the books she wrote about them, is likely to have been admired by Rose both for her spirit of adventure and for the quality of her writing. But Freya was a less than ardent admirer of Rose, whom she had known since at least 1934 (Freya Stark, *Letters* II (Tisbury, 1975) 179). On 15 May 1949 both were guests of Harold Nicolson and Vita Sackville-West at Sissinghurst, and the following day Freya wrote to her husband, Stewart Perowne: 'The visit was rather spoilt by Rose Macaulay being there. She is rather old, virginal, and embittered, until she smiles, very sweetly. She has strange goat's eyes and pale suffering lips, and I was quite surprised to see how self-centred authors can be for she kept the whole party discussing her review for about twenty minutes till Harold came and asked me if I was an egotist' (*Letters* VI (Wilton, 1981) 95). As for *The Towers of Trebizond*, she comments to Jock Murray: 'I thought it fun but not enough to bear a second reading: is that the test of a book?' (*Letters* VII (Wilton, 1982) 202). It was to Rose that Ivy Compton-Burnett remarked about Stewart Perowne's marriage to Freya in 1947: 'Of course he had to get married. He's homosexual' (Izzard 274). Unsurprisingly, the marriage was not a success, and was dissolved in 1952. On Perowne, see *L*110 n. 5.

11 Santa Maria della Salute. The church overlooks the mouth of the Grand Canal.

12 Series of quays lining the Canale della Giudecca.

13 The church of San Giorgio Maggiore stands on an islet.

14 La Calcina is one of Venice's oldest-established *pensioni*. John Ruskin once stayed in it, although not, as is often claimed, while he was writing *The Stones of Venice*. When

Rose was a guest, and for thirty years afterwards, it was managed by Agnes Steiner, multilingual and reputed never to have forgotten a name or a face. Its 'nice *terrazzo*' floats on the canal.

15 Walter and Esther Howarth. He had retired from a distinguished career as an ENT surgeon. Although he was indeed 'old', his wife was only in her mid-sixties – much younger than him and Rose.

16 The Rt Rev. Edward Barry Henderson and his wife, Hester. He had been Vicar of St Paul's, Knightsbridge, one of the churches in which Rose liked to worship. He was consecrated Suffragan Bishop of Tewkesbury in 1955. Later he was Bishop of Bath and Wells (1960–1975). Assisted by Patrick McLaughlin and Gerard Irvine, he was to conduct Rose's funeral service.

17 A bishop incognito.

18 Jim and Rosemary, who had been living in London since their marriage in 1955, had bought Wyre House in the village of Wyre Piddle near Pershore, Worcestershire.

19 Jean's nephew, the younger son of Bill and Isadore, who, after representing the USA in the free rifle (300 metres) shooting competition in the Olympic Games in Melbourne in November–December 1956 and travelling in India and USSR, had spent a fortnight in England before returning home. He and Rose had met when he visited England in 1948.

20 Jim, his brother Tom, and sister Emily.

106

20, Hinde House,
Hinde Street, W.1.
N[ew] Y[ear's] Eve 1957

Darling Jean

Thank you for that adorable nice letter. I'm glad you like the Spanish pitcher; and glad you are considering and preparing to write about your Yatscombe past;[1] and gladdest that you feel affection for me, which warms the heart; and you know it to be a two-way love. I hope, in writing of Yatscombe, that you'll feel free to relate the nice stories of G.M. and Lady Mary, so characteristic of both, including her occasional turbulence, and his undefeated patience and gentleness.[2] But I see it is perhaps a little difficult, with their children at hand. I hope Mrs <He>nderson[3] persuaded you also to consider the job of editing the whole *Life*, and that the family approved this. I think they couldn't do better; but it would be a tremendous job to undertake, perhaps too demanding and worrying.

You say you wish it was in your power to do a thing for me ever. That is absurd, because you do all the time, in all ways, but partly by your charity and courtesy to what *The Catholic Herald* calls 'the denominations' (it can't use the name churches for them) to one of which I belong, and most of which I respect as enshrining each some valuable aspect of the Christian faith and life. And what you and your fellows can do for us is, I think, by influence and speech to resist the outspoken contempt and self-righteousness, the almost crowing note, which some R.C. writers often use. It does seem so shockingly discourteous and unChristian; and surely would have got very short shrift in the Gospels. In *The Cath. Her.* e.g., there is a report on Catholic Progress in 1957, by various priests.[4] It says 'And alongside all this' (the progress) 'the Sunday morning streets empty but for the milkman and the Catholics'. How can this reporter know the religion, if any, of the non-milkmen in the streets, unless they are all seen to enter some church? It is the kind of silly, empty boast which is partly, of course, wishful thinking, partly malicious propaganda, partly genuine ignorance. He goes on, about how 'the decline of the denominations makes the issue clear. It is the Catholic Church, or irreligion.' And much more in the same strain, the whole article being headed 'The issue to-day is the Church v. Irreligion'[5] – so improbable, and, in a way, contemptuous. This matter of self-righteousness is discussed in an interesting book I am reading by Dr Daniel Jenkins,[6] a very nice and learned Congregationalist minister (of the King's Weigh House)[7] who took tea with me yesterday. He is deeply in the Ecumenical Movement, and the book is partly about that. He writes,

'The ecumenical movement . . . enables members of a particular church to see other churches as they are "in Christ", and to see Christ manifested in the other churches. It carries with it a compulsion to draw nearer to other churches because it teaches us that we cannot properly follow Christ Himself without doing so. The compulsion remains even if the differences between other churches and one's own may seem, for the present, insuperable. The ecumenical vision reveals a unity lying behind all the differences, which it is the duty of those who see it to bring out and express in the midst of the contradictions and confusions of authority and liturgy and teaching and organizations which arise both because of the sinfulness of men and because of the incalculable movement of the Spirit amidst the changes of history. The external unity of all believers in one organization may never reach perfect and final expression on this earth. But the compulsion remains upon all who have seen this vision to be ministers of Christ's reconciling grace among the churches and to bring them to that unity of heart and mind and wholeness of purpose which is His will for all His people. . . . Yet it is clearly unreal to suppose that a church can enter into deep communion with another church without itself undergoing a painful inner transformation. . . . A church must look at itself not only defensively in relation to other churches, but also positively as a church of which God may be requiring some new departure. . . . All organizations are exposed to the sin of self-righteousness. This has often enough been pointed out in the cases of states or nations, which will perpetrate deeds in their corporate capacity which most of their individual members would never dream of committing to further their own personal interest. It is not always so clearly seen, especially by churchmen, that churches receive no exemption from the same temptation. Protestants constantly complain against those churches which call themselves Catholic, and especially the Roman Catholic Church, that, so far from being conscious of the dangers of this corporate self-righteousness, and trying to safeguard themselves against it, they make a virtue of it, and so organize themselves as to buttress and justify it. Protestants also have need to remember that they have no automatic freedom from this danger. It is too deep rooted in the nature of society for that to be likely. . . . It is the belief of those who lead the ecumenical movement that the movement is sufficiently blessed by the Holy Spirit to enable churches to resist this temptation, but they will do so only if they frankly recognise it as a temptation and take steps to overcome it. . . . All churches like to claim that they are more faithful to the New Testament conception of a church than others, but it is precisely such efforts at self-justification which this fresh understanding calls into question. The N.T. does not present us with the model church whose external characteristics we should strive to copy in every detail. . . . It confronts us with the presence of the living Christ in the Spirit, who reconciles men to God, and thro' that reconciliation gives them a new relationship of unity and peace with each other and guides them thro' their lives. It forces them to listen to the voice of Christ concerning his church in a new and more radical way. It becomes a call to repentance, not merely for having failed to live up to the church's own ideal of itself, but for having possessed an inadequate and misleading ideal. Its basis is called into question by the One who has the right to do so, Christ who is Himself the wholeness of the Church, and who ever and anew reasserts His lordship over the churches. In the light of this renewed vision, of the divine purpose of the Church and of the consequent realisation of its own failures, each church must humbly seek from other churches ways of making up that which is lacking in its own life and of working with them more adequately to realise the divine purpose. This is far removed from the common attitude of seeking to justify the claims of one's own church in the face of the counter-claims of other churches. Like us, they have their failures, and need our help as we need theirs, yet they will have seen some aspect of His will denied to us, and they hold in trust treasures of grace which we would do well to covet.'

And so on; all very good. And a long way from the *C.H.* boasting and arrogance and certainty of having the Truth and desiring to annihilate all other Xian bodies and sweep triumphantly over them leaving them dead in the road, or rather, sweeping them all up into their own chariot, ignoring their especial gifts to the Church. This attitude profoundly shocks outsiders, and, I know, some insiders too. The denying to other churches, e.g., of Orders, so that they can't think what to call other bishops, priests and deacons; it seems so childishly rude! Of course they would say that, after *Apostolicae Curae*[8] there is no way round this; but then that encyclical was all wrong and the Holy Spirit should be asked to utter on the matter. It seems really a question of courtesy, not (to me) of 'validity', a word which carries no meaning to me in such connections. But even if it is thought that we have no Orders, and that our priests are just laymen, they should be given the courtesy titles that they are generally known by, not called 'bogus', which Fr Whiteman once, as he passed by the Farm Street church, heard a priest saying to a woman he was with – 'there goes one of those bogus priests'.[9] I think this goes much deeper than mere manners, and that the Church really is depriving itself of a great deal of richness that it might have by a wider understanding and tolerance. Anyhow, I believe that a great many potential converts are repelled by this 'corporate self-righteousness', even when they might accept the doctrines intellectually and the general ecclesiastical set-up without much demur. I, for one (tho' I couldn't belong on other grounds), should always feel I couldn't possibly join a Church which despised other churches and claimed so much exclusive Truth with so loud a voice.

This is all so much the opposite of the line taken by you, by Jim and Rosemary, by Renée Haynes,[10] by many other individual R.C.s that I know, and no doubt by many thousands more that I don't, that I do feel that pressure might be exerted to make those who speak for the Church aware of the disastrous effects they have on outsiders. I don't quite know how it could be done; but you might have a try! You might ask Dr Pilkington what he thinks about it; because I am sure he too is shocked by this arrogance. Fr Agnellus Andrew seems to think he has got the BBC well into his hands;[11] he gets leave to have the R.C. Midnight Mass every Xmas, instead of turn and turn about with the Anglican one. But I believe this question has been raised, and next year it may be the Anglican turn. After all, tho' we may be a minority, as they say, we are a very deserving one, and those who can't go out would like their own Mass in their own language at Xmas sometimes. Fr Agnellus might reply that it's not a Mass, and would do us no good; but we think it is, and that it would. Alas, what a sad battling it all leads to. Darling, forgive this immense screed; but you say you would like to do something for me, and religious tolerance and respect is what I want to see before I die. So, since every one loves and respects you, do join in this campaign. Of course I know you and I think differently about the Church, and the possibility of any Church having very much of Truth, but that's not really the point; the point is human respect, and of this you have so much.

I am now going to a New Year's Eve party.[12] What ails my church that it doesn't have watch night services? Only the very Low do, and the Free Churches I think. That seems to me a thing we might well adopt from them. However, as I am going to a party . . .

I rather dread this Dame nonsense, it's so foolish. I shall feel in a pantomime.[13] And I know people will waste my valuable time writing congratulations. *The Sunday Times* rang up wanting to photograph me and make me a Portrait Gallery on Sunday, but this is going too far and I won't have it. Leonard Russell[14] said what a good journalist Constance was, and I agree, don't you.[15] Of course she has had a lot of practice in it. I wonder if she'll go on with it. She has had offers of various kinds. I was much struck by her grasp of all that technical stuff, though in some ways her brain doesn't seem very strong or well-furnished.

All my love for 1958. I do hope you won't mind anything I've said in this letter about the Church. But it *is* so important, a greater comprehension between the churches. I feel this so strongly that I sometimes now go to the Weigh House for a service – I quite like its liturgy, though very little ritual, of course. But all very quiet and nice.

My love to Jim and Rosemary, please. Has Jim caught any fish yet???[16]
Rose.

1 After the death of Gilbert Murray in May 1957 Jean returned to his house, Yatscombe, where she had been his secretary in 1919–1922, to sort his papers in readiness for their transfer to the Bodleian Library. She also co-edited with Arnold Toynbee *Gilbert Murray: An Unfinished Autobiography*. One of her two chapters in the book is entitled '1889–1957: Some Personal and Chronological Notes', but there is no mention of *her* 'Yatscombe past'.

2 The Murrays' marriage lasted almost 67 years, until Lady Mary's death in September 1956, but was not without its difficulties. From a quite early stage she experienced feelings of insecurity and jealousy, and suffered from nervous strain. A major drawback was that, in contrast to her husband, she possessed little or no sense of humour (*L*18 n. 2).

3 Rose has written 'Anderson', but Murray's literary executor was Isobel Henderson, Fellow of Somerville College, Oxford, an authority on Roman history and Greek music, and a friend of his for thirty years. An affectionate friendship between her and Jean developed during the work on his papers.

4 The *Catholic Herald* report that upset Rose is in the issue of 27 December 1957, 1, 5. Under the heading 'The Church in England: "C.H." Survey of 1957', it records the opinions of four 'distinguished priests'. (The title Rose gives it is hers, not the *CH*'s.)

5 This is the article's second heading.

6 The book Rose was reading is *Congregationalism: A Restatement* (London, 1954). In her next paragraph she quotes parts of pp. 11–17. The omissions are more numerous than those she indicates. Moreover, she sometimes adapts, as well as abbreviates, the original. Daniel Jenkins, the son of a South Wales bricklayer, was a prominent theologian in the Reformed tradition. Between 1950 and 1962 he combined pastoral work in or near London with a part-time professorship of Theology at the University of Chicago. From 1963 to 1973 he was Chaplain of the new University of Sussex and also Reader in Religious Studies there. One of his five children is the distinguished journalist, editor, and writer Simon Jenkins, who remembers Rose 'often coming round to our flat' and says: 'Both my parents were fascinated by her writing' (e-mail to the editor, 30 June 2010).

7 King's Weigh House Chapel, Duke Street, was just round the corner from Rose's flat in Hinde Street. It opened in 1891 (after a long life elsewhere) and closed, as a Congregational church, in 1966. Since 1968 it has been the cathedral of the Ukrainian Greek Catholic Church in Great Britain.

8 Encyclical (September 1896) in which Pope Leo XIII pronounced the orders of the Anglican Church invalid. Rose's complaints in the present paragraph echo comments in *The Towers of Trebizond* ch. 21, p. 243.

9 The Jesuit Church of the Immaculate Conception in Farm Street is close to Grosvenor Chapel and Liddon House, of which Fr Whiteman had charge from 1946 to 1954.

10 A writer married to a writer, the novelist Jerrard Tickell, Haynes became a Catholic in 1942. Her early books include *Neapolitan Ice* (London, 1928) and *Pan, Caesar, and God. Who Spake by the Prophets* (London, 1938). From 1946 until her death in 1992 she was a member of the Society for Psychical Research, whose journal she edited from 1970 to 1981. The books in which she explores her interest in the paranormal include *The Hidden Springs: An Enquiry into Extra-sensory Perception* (London, 1961) and *Philosopher King: The Humanist Pope Benedict XIV* (London, 1970).

11 Agnellus Matthew Andrew, OFM, one of the four priests interviewed by *The Catholic Herald*, had been assistant to the head of religious broadcasting at the BBC since 1955. Rose's comments about an RC monopoly of midnight services broadcast by the BBC at Christmas are inaccurate. So far as radio is concerned, the midnight service on the Light Programme was Roman Catholic in 1952, 1953, and 1956, but Church of England in 1954, 1955, and 1957. In 1958 it was to be Roman Catholic. When midnight services were introduced on television, they alternated between Roman Catholic (1955, 1957) and Church of England (1956, 1958).

12 The party was given by Rosamond Lehmann at 70 Eaton Square, SW1. The postcard, of 1 January 1958, conveying Rose's thanks, is in King's College Library, Cambridge.

13 In the New Year Honours List, published the following day, it was announced that Rose had been appointed Ordinary Dame Commander of the Civil Division of the Order of the British Empire (DBE). She was somewhat hesitant about accepting the award – not surprisingly, for in 1937, when she declined a request to support the nomination of the suffragette Emmeline Pethick-Lawrence for an Honour, she explained: 'I could not ask that any one should be in the Honours List – it does not seem to me a good list to be in' (ERM 15.168); and, also in the 1930s, she had declined a CBE for herself (*LS* 22–23). The joke about the title 'Dame' making her sound as though she were in a pantomime is one she made to many other people, including John Hayward (*L86* n. 2): 'How pleased I was to get your greetings . . . on my strange translation into pantomime, (or is it into a muttering crone mixing a devil's brew of herbs and nettles in her cottage garden? I would rather it was into Zenobia the Dame of Antioch . . .)' (Letter dated Twelfth Night 1958 in King's College Library, Cambridge, JDH/26/Macaulay).

14 Literary editor of *The Sunday Times* from 1945 to 1954. He then left the paper briefly before returning to edit a succession of serials.

15 Constance Babington Smith. After the Second World War, during which she did important work as an interpreter of air reconnaissance photographs, she spent six years in the USA – two at the Pentagon, where her expertise in the analysis of aerial photographs was again invaluable, and four as a researcher for *Life* magazine. On her return to Britain in 1951, she embarked on a writing career. Her first book, *Evidence in Camera: The Story of Photographic Intelligence in World War II* (London, 1958), was about to appear when Rose wrote the present letter.

16 Jim and Rosemary's house, in which Jean was staying, is very close to the River Avon.

107

[No address]
4 February 1958[1]

Darling Rose

Your long letter of New Year's Eve. I haven't, you may believe, been without thought of this; have followed your letters, and to some extent the answers, in the little C[atholic] H[erald],[2] and send love and thanks for your courtesy to us all. Much much love and more thanks in particular for your love to me.

You have made a timely complaint of some execrable bad manners and ignorance; 'bogus' of course was terrible – meaningless in the context. The bad manners make us 'feel quite ill' as Fr Pilkington says.

Is it worth reminding you that a very large proportion of converts are from nothing (no religion at all or virtually none), and from a generation with little or no diffused religious culture or habit of respect for religion? (You realise that it is to these that the efforts to convert – some of which wouldn't appeal to you or me either – are directed in the first place.) It means that it is not only Irish conditioning, or faults blameable on earlier generations of RCs, that make so many of them lamentably ignorant of the Church of England.

A lot of them are, too, very puzzled by its variety and changes. Converts of my own tradition have better sea-legs here. As likely as not the Anglicans they know have never called their service the Mass, would be scandalised to hear it so called, or to see a High Mass televised as an Anglican service – surely this is so? They can't know which parish to judge it by, as to these details of rite and nomenclature; all of which is very well understood, by me as by you. And remember how local are the contacts of so many of us in the scattered parishes, how isolated the individual can be.

Conversions are sometimes supposed to be matters of preference or enchantment; of impatience perhaps. So I suppose on one level they can be (God making use of the weak things . . .?). Much deeper than this, one finds, is the strong pull of the religion that has taken flesh in one's own culture, language, landscape. Beyond that again you may come to see the Catholic unity, and in it the greater diversity (of race, language, rite, custom, outlook), acknowledged and accepted, making the greater width and freedom. But, it is the other that is in your blood; and in order to leave it you must, surely (?)[3] have found something, seen something you didn't see before, something corresponding to, say, a new dimension (metaphors all no good) after which nothing matters compared with what you found. What then?

There is a lot of confusion on all sides, don't you think, between 'invalid' and 'inefficacious', and I think the pronouncements deal with validity? As to that, I can't see that any one can say that other people's sacraments are inefficacious. Or, on the other hand, that any person or power except a Church can define what that

Church thinks necessary for validity. It was when I got some realisation of the idea of *jurisdiction* and so forth that my focus altered, with the cutting away of some exhausting uncertainties. I would put it now that there has to be the actuality of a visible body living by its own laws, if the spiritual thing is to come to grips with our mortal condition and the power of the world, is in fact to be engaged in history, to spiritualise the whole as history goes on (it hasn't gone on very long yet). In the Church this full incarnation has been risked; and is surely a process of *la bienheureuse mainmise du Christ sur son univers*;[4] and maintained at its peril – *une Église livrée au monde pour le sauver et qui risque à chaque pas de devenir sa proie?*[5] And without a reality in this mode surely there *is* a vital thing missing, and you are left with something disembodied, queer or impermanent; or that loses itself in the natural; or disengaged from history? One can think of examples –

Intercommunion. The so far insuperable thing here seems to be that the condition for communion for us is the acceptance of the teaching power of the Church; like all the Sacraments it has (and this one outstandingly has) relation to the *caritas*, the Unity. May it come soon, however. I read your passage from Dr Jenkins with interest – a noble statement; how many mansions in the Church are waiting to be filled, and how deeply we all need it. But for the Church itself you know what is claimed; and that we know the faults and miseries of its members, but believe it to be in essence indefectible. What is waited for is the full articulation of its life when we are all together.

I do greatly hope you are better. You know how I love you.

Jean

I think the plea for better manners *has* been about recently; I heard something of the kind in two of the few sermons I listened to during the Unity Octave,[6] notably by Fr Henry St John,[7] the Dominican in the Cathedral (very strong on the sanctity of a man's conscience); did you read him in the January *Blackfriars*[8] too? It is terribly terribly important; and I never hear it[9] without the deepest distaste and sense of the damage done.

1 This letter (a carbon-copy typescript) is Jean's reply to *L*106. At the top of the first page she has written the following manuscript note: 'RM had found herself involved in a correspondence in the *Catholic Herald*, calling down a plague of brash and wounding letters, in the *C.H.* and in her own post. She was also having flu.' Rose had four letters published in the *CH* in January–February 1958. They are in the issues of 3 January, 2; 17 January, 2; 31 January, 2; 7 February, 2. The correspondence was concluded in the issue of 14 February. By no means all the letters were hostile to her.
2 By 'little' Jean presumably means 'small-minded'.
3 The query is Jean's.
4 'Christ's blessed control over his world'. The quotation is of Pierre Teilhard de Chardin, *Le milieu divin: Essai de vie intérieure* (Paris, 1957) 52, except that he writes 'l'Univers', not 'son univers'.

5 'A Church delivered to the world in order to save it, and that risks at every step becoming its prey'. Jean is quoting René Schwob, *Rome ou la mort* (Paris, 1938) 236.
6 The eight days from 18 to 25 January, during which prayers are offered for Church unity.
7 Fr St John of Westminster Cathedral was the author of *Essays in Christian Unity, 1928–1954* (London, 1955).
8 'Towards Ecumenical Understanding', *Blackfriars* 39 (1958) 31–35. The article reviews three books – two by Catholics, one by an Anglican – on the subject of Christian unity.
9 A display of bad manners.

108

20, Hinde House,
Hinde Street, W.1.
6 February 1958

Darling Jean

It was good to get your letter. Bless you for writing so, and for being as you are. It is a great comfort to me, amid the assaults and snarls I am getting by post from Catholics who seem to hate us to think we have the Real Presence.[1] Such a strange thing to resent other people having; they ought to be glad we think so. Someone asked me, in a long, angry letter, what grounds I had for such a belief. I indicated the B[ook of] C[ommon] P[rayer] communion service, in which it is explicitly declared and taught throughout; not least in the Prayer of Humble Access, composed mostly by Cranmer, on the basis of older liturgies. Nothing could be more explicit: 'Grant us so to eat the flesh . . . and to drink his blood . . . etc' – nothing subjective or 'receptionist' here. I have wondered lately if perhaps the *BCP* is on the Index, as so many of those who write to me about it never seem to have looked inside it. One person told me that Cranmer had 'eliminated all references to Communion'; another that she had heard it had been completely rewritten some time in the nineteenth century. Very strange, making such assertions about a book it is so easy to look at. But I expect you are right. Some of the writers say they are 'converts' – but not from what; sometimes they say from Anglicanism, but perhaps they weren't very church-going or informed Anglicans. And many were dissenters, I imagine.

I think (I have lately learnt, in fact) that there is a real confusion in people's minds between the Real Presence and Transubstantiation. The latter is to them synonymous with the former; they know no other mode. Article 28, which defines the distinction, is not known to them, mostly. Both modes are mysteries; I should find Trans[ubstantiation] the more difficult, they the spiritual Presence only.[2] One can't help that, and it doesn't matter. What does matter is that they get so annoyed about it, and let fly at unknown people like me, as if we had done them some personal injury by assuming for our Church something they are sure we haven't got. Dom Bede Camm O.S.B. wrote over 50 years ago, 'If only Catholics could realise the harm they do by rash and unkind judgments of those outside the fold!'[3] I think it may well decide potential converts against joining the Church. I like all you say about conversion, and the sound reasons for it. As you probably know, I myself am too incurably Broad Church to consider jurisdiction, or rule of the Church, or validity. It doesn't come into my latitudinarian purview. What I see is the expression of God through whatever mode or way or structure is available between him and us (different ways and structures, I feel, with different people). The thing is to find him, or let him find us, somehow; I suppose I shall never get to the stage so many people get to, of recognising one Church, or one mode of communication, as the thing he necessarily has ordained for us. So I don't discuss such things with the same premises as many Anglicans, and presumably all Catholics, must. Between many Anglicans and Catholics, I mean, there could be a fruitful (if contentious) argument; but not with me, because my premises seem quite different. 'The spiritual thing that has to come to grips with our mortal condition and the power of the world . . .' yes. If the Church can incarnate this spiritual thing, good luck to it. But I so often feel that Churches are somehow askew, not quite aiming right. I do see what you mean about being left with something disembodied and vague. That is indeed the danger. That is where the focus of Communion comes in, to anchor and root us. And, of course, prayer. And Church, in so far as it seems to keep on the lines that seem to one right and not irrelevant.

I have written my last letter to the *C.H.* This kind of discussion seems to engender heat, not light, and I don't like it. Thank you for all you have written; stuff to keep. Let us all try to live peaceably with all men.

I had Constance in yesterday. I rather wish she would simmer down a little. She goes about with her scrap-book of reviews in hand, showing them and all the photographs of that party,[4] and when in London tours the bookshops to make sure they are displaying the book in the windows. I was never enterprising like that about my first book – or indeed about any. She calls it 'promotion', and is beginning to think Chatto aren't pushing it enough. I hope she will soon come down to earth. She is *such* a darling; but has this odd side; and doesn't inhibit it *quite* enough.

I'm *much* better. I am going to Dorset on Tuesday afternoon[5] for the rest of the week, to do nothing, with Raymond, who is alone there.[6] No, I will of course do some work, but restfully.

I still feel M.and B.-ish.[7] But the lung is quite healed. Now I must write to two widows,[8] poor dears. Bless you,

    R.

1 The doctrine of the true and substantial presence of the body and blood of Christ in the elements of the sacrament.

2 The 39 Articles of Religion of the Church of England, based on Thomas Cranmer's 42 Articles of 1553, were adopted in 1563. Article 28, headed 'Of the Lord's Supper', accepts the Real Presence, but asserts: 'Transubstantiation (or the change of the substance of Bread and Wine) in the Supper of the Lord, cannot be proved by Holy Writ; but is repugnant to the plain words of Scripture, overthroweth the nature of a Sacrament, and hath given occasion to many superstitions.' So Rose's belief is in line with orthodox Anglican teaching.

3 Bede Camm, son of an Anglican clergyman, was educated at Westminster School and Keble College, Oxford. He served a curacy in the Church of England before being received into the Roman Catholic Church at the age of 25 and going on to become a Benedictine monk. He is best known as the author of historical studies of Roman Catholicism in England, with a particular focus on that Church's martyrs, pilgrims, and shrines, and on notable recusant families and their houses.

4 Presumably a party given by Chatto & Windus, Constance Babington Smith's publishers, to mark the publication of *Evidence in Camera*.

5 The afternoon of 11 February. In the morning Rose was to attend an investiture at Buckingham Palace and receive her DBE insignia from The Queen.

6 Raymond Mortimer shared Long Crichel House at Wimborne in Dorset with the painter Eardley Knollys, the novelist and music critic Eddy Sackville-West, and the music critic Desmond Shawe-Taylor. Rose had been a guest at Long Crichel before – most recently on 10–12 January, when all four men were in residence. On 14 February she told Jeanie that she has 'been living such a lethargic life in this comfortable house, lying in bed till lunch time nearly, then lunch, then a short stroll of ¼ mile, then back to more lethargy'. She adds that she and her host 'talk and read, and it is all very nice' (*LS* 257). Who would have guessed that such a warm friendship would develop between her and the 'bumptious and offensive youth' who savaged *Told by an Idiot* in 1923? A brief but vivid account of the atmosphere at Long Crichel is given by Alan Pryce-Jones, *The Bonus of Laughter* (London, 1987) 168. He describes it as one 'of books, music, and talk'.

7 M & B: the trade mark of the pharmaceutical company May & Baker Ltd., often used in reference to anti-bacterial drugs prepared by that company and, sometimes, by other companies. Rose was still not feeling well on the day of the investiture (*LLF* 263). From 20 March until late April 1958 she was hospitalised, first in Charing Cross Hospital, then in University College Hospital – not because of illness, but because of an accident. The accident occurred on 20 March at St Anne's House, Soho, where after lunch with Patrick McLaughlin and Denis Marsh (*L*109 n. 12) she fell down the steps to the street, fracturing her right wrist and femur. CBS 215 reports Marsh's 'vivid memories of the incident': 'There was an uproar among the passers-by and Patrick McLaughlin exclaimed "My God, we've killed her!" "Don't be ridiculous", came Rose's voice. "Call an ambulance."' However, after the publication of Constance Babington Smith's biography, McLaughlin wrote to give her a very different version: he was not present when Rose fell, for he was upstairs clearing up after the lunch; there was no 'uproar among passers-by', although there were offers of help; he did not say

the words attributed to him; and Rose did not utter the words attributed to her, for she was unconscious (ERM 4.241).

8 One of the widows may well have been Florence Margaret Tomlinson, wife of the journalist, travel writer, and novelist Henry Major Tomlinson. He died on 5 February 1958, and his obituary was printed in *The Times* on 6 February, the date of the present letter.

109

20, Hinde House,
Hinde Street, W.1.
22 July [1958]

Darling Jean

I met last night a young man who looks after the cruises in the Fairways office,[1] and he says he doesn't think you, or Jim, are on the passenger list. Didn't you book? He is checking it again today, but seemed sure. This is disappointing, if true.[2] It would be fun to see Odessa with you.[3] Did it prove too costly?[4] I feel pretty mean, going for practically nothing. It seems now certain that we *shall* go, unless something sudden flares up. Last week it seemed less certain, but now the Middle East is settling down.[5] Dorothy Nicholson,[6] who went with a party for a fortnight and is just back, says the Russians were charming to them. She particularly enjoyed Kieff and the Ukrainians. How I wish we were visiting there. And it will be maddening to pass the coast of Bulgaria and the Byzantine domes of Imbria without landing.[7] Steven Runciman says they are wonderful. But it can't be helped. One thing we are doing is a bus expedition into the Caucasus, returning to the coast to join our ship at a place 100 miles south of where we left it.[8] That will be very exciting. I hope to buy a Circassian slave in the mountains. Oh why aren't you and Jim and Rosemary coming too? I wish you were.

Did you chance to hear me Frankly Speaking[9] on Sunday night at 9.15? I had nice civilized interrogators, who didn't ask me what was my favourite pudding or book, but on the whole intelligent questions which could be discussed. Rather intimidating having to answer on the spur of the moment such questions as how I regarded the Christian Church, and I expect it all sounded pretty foolish, but some people have fared worse in that series, and it was quite enjoyable. We talked for about an hour, then the producer got to work on the transcript and cut it about, cutting out about half, so I had no notion of what I should hear when I listened a week later.

I wonder how you are. I do hope better than when you were doing all that train-work between London and Oxford. And how are things going. I hear you won't be back in your flat till the end of Sept. Shall I see you before that? I hope so.

But I still have a hope that the young man was wrong and that you may be on the *Hermes*.

I have been living among bishops, priests and deacons; as you know, there is a great pride of bishops about, all colours and shapes. I went to the Lambeth garden party, and there they all were, the great beards from the East looking very benign, but hot.[10] I also went to parts of the Eucharistic Congress, for the first time in my life; it was really very impressive; and the opening address from Ebor really splendid; I didn't know he was so good.[11] Fr Denis Marsh, that charming Franciscan (worldly, I think, but fun), wound it up very well at the final High Mass.[12] I think the Church Union, which organised it all, worth supporting, so I have for the 1st time joined it, tho' heaven knows I don't share half of its cherished beliefs. But it is going the right way (i.e. the way for me, with all my doubts and disagreements), and it grows less narrow and rigid, and really is trying for inter-communion, in its own much too episcopacy-bound fashion.

As you see, no more space. Let me have a word sometime, about how you are etc.

V. much love,

Rose

1 Fairways & Swinford (Travel) Ltd. Although Rose was not one of the guest-lecturers, she had been invited to accompany an Aegean and Black Sea cruise, starting in Venice on 27 August and returning there on 12 September. The arrangement, which involved her paying something, but not much, suited the company as well as herself, because it was able to mention 'Dame Rose Macaulay' in its advertisements and obtained publicity when she wrote about the cruise afterwards. One of the places on the itinerary was 'her' Trebizond. Others included Delphi, Athens, Skyros, Odessa, the Crimea, the Caucasus, Istanbul, Lemnos, and Aigina.

2 What the young man thought was true. One would like to think that the disappointment expressed by Rose was true also. Probably it was, but, writing to her sister Jeanie on 12 March 1958, Rose indulged in the following dyspeptic outburst: 'As to Jean, she seems just to meet R.C.s, with a few exceptions. I have great anticipations that J. may bore me on this cruise. She is so very long-winded and didactic, like Aunt N[annie]. The other day she was telling at immense length what Reggie [Jean's brother] had said to her about homosexuals, and how they often make good schoolmasters when they sublimate their inclinations because of their natural interest in boys. I knew all that long ago, and anyhow would have guessed it, but J. imparted it with such gravity and length, and was *so* like aunt N. with her "Reggie says, and Reggie certainly knows . . ." etc. And if one speaks out of turn, she gets cross and says "I was in the middle of saying something, if I may finish". Oh dear. Perhaps after all I won't go. But it would be a pity, when so interesting and so (for me) cheap, and seeing the Crimea and all. She is so good and aff[ection]ate, too. I wonder if anyone has ever told her the effect (which isn't only on me) of her didactic ways. And all the long stories about their childhood, which she laughs about so much and one has to laugh a lot too, and they aren't really funny' (ERM 9.185). It is true that Jean could be didactic and even pedantic at times,

but it is probably significant that Rose's opening shot in this barrage of criticisms is her complaint that Jean for the most part meets only Roman Catholics. The likelihood is that any irritation that Jean's conversation might have caused Rose in other circumstances had been greatly magnified in the context of the latter's displeasure at the attitude of the Catholic Church to non-Catholics, and at what she undoubtedly saw as her Catholic cousin's own narrow-mindedness. Jean was well aware that Rose was irritated with her about her religion (*L*111 n. 7), and probably found Rose's criticisms of Roman Catholicism considerably more trying than Rose found her stories of her childhood. At least one non-Catholic friend of Rose found those criticisms excessive: Raymond Mortimer, in a letter of 18 October 1961 to Constance Babington Smith, writes: 'I thought Rose had rather a bee in her bonnet on that subject, and used to try to change the conversation' (ERM 13.109).

3 On Odessa as the home of Jean's family, see Introd. II.1. In the early 1970s Jim, accompanied by Rosemary, revisited the city of his birth during a cruise, but Jean never returned.

4 It is not known why Jean, Jim, and Rosemary did not book the cruise, but the cost, a minimum of 93 guineas per person, will not have been the reason. The possibility that Rose's critical attitude to Jean was a factor cannot be ruled out, but it is more likely that Jean, who was busy with Gilbert Murray's papers and struggling with depression, did not feel up to the trip.

5 On 14 July 1958 Abdul Karim Kassem led a military coup in Iraq. The monarchy was overthrown, and King Faisal II and the prime minister Nuri es-Said were killed. After the coup, the USA sent forces to Lebanon (15 July), and Britain paratroops to Jordan, at the request of the respective Arab governments.

6 Formerly Dorothy Brooke.

7 Imbria is a mistake. Rose means Mesembria, called Nesebur by the Bulgarians. The town, built on a peninsula, contains many late Byzantine churches. Runciman, knighted at the same investiture at which Rose received her DBE, was an eminent Byzantine historian.

8 The passengers left the ship at Sochi and rejoined it at Sukhumi after visiting Lake Ritsa.

9 The title of a series of 30-minute radio programmes broadcast by the BBC Home Service. In each programme a distinguished person faced three interrogators. On 20 July Rose answered questions put by William D. Clark, Nicholas Fenn, and Alec Robertson. Fenn, who was to have a distinguished diplomatic career, being British Ambassador in Rangoon, then in Dublin, before becoming High Commissioner in India, was at that time a student at Cambridge, aged only 22. He reports that the BBC 'wanted a bright young Christian who would ask the great lady 'penetrating questions from the standpoint of innocence" (letter to the editor, 10 February 2007).

10 The Lambeth Conference of Anglican Bishops began with a service at Canterbury Cathedral on 3 July and ended with a service at Westminster Abbey on 11 August. The garden party, hosted by the Archbishop of Canterbury, Geoffrey Fisher, and his wife, Rosamond, was held at Lambeth Palace on 5 July. It was attended not only by the bishops but also by leading lay members of the Anglican Church and representatives of civic life.

11 The Church Union Eucharistic Congress opened with a service in Westminster Abbey on 1 July. The opening address, by the Archbishop of York, Michael Ramsey, was delivered in the Albert Hall on 2 July. Ramsey was to become the hundredth Archbishop of Canterbury in 1961.

12 Marsh had entered the Anglican Society of St Francis in 1939. At this time he was Guardian of Hilfield Friary at Cerne Abbas in Dorset. He was noted for his powerful preaching and for his gaiety and sense of humour. Although Rose calls him 'charming', the two did not get on well together on the first occasion they met socially. This was at the lunch to which Patrick McLaughlin invited them at St Anne's House, Soho, on 20 March 1958 (*L*108 n. 7). According to McLaughlin (ERM 4.241), 'Rose "needled" Denis on many points; Denis replied flippantly'. They were still 'bickering' when she tried to leave, but succeeded only in falling down the outside steps.

110

20, Hinde House,
Hinde Street, W.1.
10 August 1958

Darling Jean

Thank you so much for yours of 2nd, which I had meant to answer earlier, before you leave Wyre Piddle,[1] but you may have left it already, for the de Bunsen wedding. They kindly asked me to that, but I can't go, tho' would have liked to for many reasons. I like the de Bunsens, both her and him.[2] Now you will be in Rome before I am in Venice, <for> which I start on 21st by train, being collected by S.S. *Hermes* on 27th from the Zattere. We shall be like a lot of pictures of parties embarking from Venice to the east (for crusade purposes or others) with porters running on board with bales and corded trunks (but Marco P. seems to have embarked from the Molo, according to that pleasant card you send).[3] I think several of the ship's party are going for a few days 1st in Venice; I rather hope none of them will stay at my *pensione* (the Accademia)[4] or I shall have to chatter with them, and how I love Venice alone. Of course it never is alone, as so many people one knows live or stay there, and are so hospitable; already Stewart Perowne[5] has arranged that I dine at the *palazzo* of one of his smart *contessa* friends with whom he will be staying, and there is always Victor Cunard, and often Nancy Mitford,[6] and no doubt this time several stray argonauts bound for the *Hermes*.[7] I wish you were one of them, and Jim and Rosemary two of them. I will tell you all the Odessa news, and the Colchis news, and the Caucasus news. I met a doctor of part-Armenian provenance, I mean his grandfather was, who wants me to look up some Vart<a>ns[8] in Armenia, for it seems that that is what many of them, including him, are called, and give them his regards. But I think our Caucasus bus won't stop long enough for that.

I do hope you are feeling strong enough for all this Murraying and hard work.

Don't overdo. Rome will be hottish now, I expect; and, goodness, how hot Rome can be. Venice less so. Istanbul hotter, but nice bathing, if time. Skyros and Lemnos most exciting.⁹ Crimea humid, Caucasus frosty I presume. I shall be home after you, somewhere about last week of Sept.

Just returned from the send-off service for the Bishops at St Paul's.¹⁰ I sat next the black and comely wife of the Bp of Lagos, all in scarlet. I'm glad they know how well that suits their colouring.¹¹

Teresa Symons and her man,¹² the Chances,¹³ and Grace Usher¹⁴ lunch with me on Wednesday. Any chance you could join us (Lansdowne Club,¹⁵ 1)? It would be lovely if you could.

Much love to Jim and Rosemary if you are there, and all to yourself.

Rose

1 The village in which Jim and Rosemary lived.

2 Margaret and Charles de Bunsen. Margaret, an elder sister of Constance Babington Smith, was Jean's first cousin. The wedding was that of Margaret's and Charles's daughter, Bridget, and John Joseph Buxton. It took place on 11 August 1958 at St Joseph's Roman Catholic Church, Sheringham, Norfolk.

3 The Molo ('Wharf') is where gondolas and other boats tie up close to Piazza di San Marco. It is indicative of its importance and picturesqueness that it is the subject of more than thirty paintings by Canaletto. Rose's words to Jean about the anticipated embarkation are echoed in the article she wrote about the voyage (n. 7 below): 'Like Marco Polo and many more, we took ship from the Venice quays for our eastward voyage. . . . It was like some embarkation in a Poussin picture, where men run about the quays with bales and corded boxes'. The departure of Marco Polo from Venice is the subject of the illuminated frontispiece of a manuscript (no. 264) in the Bodleian Library. The portrayal is well known and, given that Jean was working in Oxford at the time she wrote to Rose, it is more than likely to have been the one reproduced on her card.

4 At Ponte delle Maravegie.

5 Married briefly and unsuccessfully to Freya Stark (*L*105 n. 10), Perowne, both son and grandson of a Bishop of Worcester, had held various diplomatic and administrative posts, mainly in Arab countries, including Palestine and Iraq. In 1952, the year of his divorce, he returned to Palestine and devoted himself to the welfare of Arab refugees. During a lengthy 'retirement' he wrote books on ancient historical and archaeological themes and was much in demand as a guest-lecturer on Mediterranean cruises. Rose met him in Jerusalem in June 1953. Her mention of him in *The Towers of Trebizond* ch. 12 (p. 129) made him 'very pleased' (*LS* 199).

6 From 1956 to 1971 Nancy Mitford visited Venice each summer. Next to Paris, where she had lived since just after the end of the Second World War, it was the city in which she felt most at home. One of her friends there was Victor Cunard.

7 When, after the end of the cruise, Rose wrote an account of it, published in *The Queen*, 30 September 1958, 40–43, she entitled it 'The New Argonauts'. Like Jason's ship *Argo*, Rose's *Hermes* was to sail, on a voyage of adventure, through the Hellespont

into and around the Black Sea. Jason and his company went to fetch the Golden Fleece from Colchis, and in *The Queen* Rose writes that she and her companions too 'returned with a golden fleece', one 'woven of beauty, interest, good company, and good fun'. Rose will not have forgotten that the Macaulay children's canoe at Varazze was called *Argo*.

8 Rose's spelling is 'Vartons', but the name of the doctor she met was Charles Keith Vartan, a consultant obstetrician and gynaecologist.

9 When Rose mentions Skyros in 'The New Argonauts', it is only to record that they 'abandoned culture . . . to swim in a sea of translucent rippled jade' (40). But the visit to the island must have brought back memories of her friend Rupert Brooke, who was buried there on 23 April 1915. No doubt the whole cruise evoked many memories of the one Rose and her father joined in 1912. Organised by the Hellenic Travellers' Club, it began in Marseilles on 4 April and ended there on the 22nd. It took them to Kalamata (for Messene and Ithome), Corinth, Athens, Marathon, Thermopylae, Volos (for Tempe), Mount Athos, Smyrna (for Ephesus), and several Aegean islands, including Delos. During it, Rose developed a friendship with a young man called Ronald Ross, and after it she wrote 'The Empty Berth' (Bibliog. I.7), a short story whose setting is a Hellenic cruise that starts from Marseilles on the same day as the April 1912 one ('the Thursday before Easter Day') and follows the same itinerary. In their experience of Greece, Shipley, a young schoolmaster, and Nancy Brown, aged about 18, independently benefit from the illuminating and liberating influence of the ghost of H. Cottar, who was to have been a passenger, but died three days before the cruise began. 'Cottar' was clearly suggested by the name of the vessel used for the 1912 cruise, the RMS *Dunottar Castle*, which in the story becomes the *Cruising Castle*. Details of the historical cruise can be found in *The Proceedings of the Hellenic Travellers' Club: 1912* (London, 1912).

10 Rose has slipped up here. The bishops had attended a service in St Paul's Cathedral on 6 July, but the service with which the Lambeth Conference closed on 11 August was in Westminster Abbey.

11 *The Times*, 10 July 1958, 6, has a photograph of 'the wife of the Bishop of Lagos adjusting her "gele"'. Her name was Aduke-Daniel Howells. Her husband, Adelakun Williamson Howells, was Bishop of Lagos from 1955 until his death in 1963.

12 Teresa, daughter of Madeleine Symons (Robinson after her marriage in 1940), who had died on 21 March 1957, was now aged 31. Her fiancé was Gerald Maurice Stephen Corbett, a divorcee eleven years older than her. Rose died just four days before their marriage, which took place at Fulham Register Office on 3 November 1958. They were to have two children. Teresa died on 2 May 1972, at the age of 45.

13 Sir Roger Chance, cousin of Rose and Jean, and his wife Mary (*L*104) were very friendly with Rose and friends also of the Symonses and Ushers. Educated at Eton and Trinity College, Cambridge, he served with distinction as an army officer in the First World War, gaining the Military Cross, but losing a leg, and was a Squadron Leader in the RAF Volunteer Reserve in the Second World War. Between the wars he obtained a PhD at London University, had his doctoral thesis and two other books published, worked in publishing and journalism, and briefly, in 1938, was Press Attaché in the British Embassy in Berlin. After the Second World War he combined farming and writing.

14 *L*23 n. 5.
15 In Fitzmaurice Place, just off Berkeley Square. The Club, established in 1935, was conveniently close to Rose's flat. But there are probably at least two other reasons why she favoured it. One is that it was unique among London clubs in, from its inception, giving women equal standing with men. The other is that it has a 25-metre indoor swimming pool. Rosamond Lehmann, in a tribute to Rose first published in *Encounter* 12, 3 (March 1959) 24–25 and reprinted by CBS 224–226, gives a detailed description of a post-prandial dip in the pool with Rose and Mark Bonham Carter, their publisher. Rose, always happy in water, was ecstatic when Rosamond towed her up and down on an inflated rubber mattress: 'Oh, Rosamond dear, this is extraordinarily pleasant! I feel like Cleopatra in her barge'.

111

20, Hinde House,
Hinde Street, W.1.
21 October 1958

Darling Jean
 Scrummaging about my old writing cases, where I stuffed a lot of miscellaneous letters as they came, I have collected these from G.M., between 1942–57.[1] I have put them in date order, and each year in a separate packet. No doubt there are more elsewhere, and some will turn up; I seem, for instance, rather short on '52 and '53 and '51, as compared with other years. Some, no doubt, I threw away. There were, I imagine, some in '42, besides the two I have kept. I think I probably threw away nearly all letters I got in '42, being somewhat dejected then. But I have found (in at last opening my own letters to him) two early ones from him, (when my flat was bombed – how kind he was about books!), in the days when he called me Miss Macaulay and dictated his letters and filed the carbons. What method he had: or I suppose his secretaries had. But of course with a correspondence on the scale of his, without method one would suffer total shipwreck. How good he was. He came up to see me in a room I took in Manchester St for a time, and loaded me with books.[2] But how good *every one* was; and not least you.[3]
 I find that looking thro' one's old letters is like sitting by a warm fire; affection and friendship leap out and envelop[4] one with their lovely warmth – 'and a deluge of love drowns all'.[5] It makes one ashamed not to have deserved it more. Friends, relations, even acquaintances, sometimes even strangers. It grieves me to think how soon one must leave it, and how little time there is to repay it.[6] But I am getting morbid and soppy: so much for resurrecting the past.
 How nice it was to see you and talk.[7] I am concerned about your tenants, though. When someone one doesn't know well begins not paying a debt, it is nearly always a sign that he means to go on in the same course, and lacks

integrity. I gather there is no dispute between you as to the amount, even though it wasn't in writing, so at least *that* trouble won't arise. But don't let him wait and put it off indefinitely; tell him you really do need the money, and need it now, not in small instalments. If he hasn't told his wife, I think you should. Of course it would be much friendlier if you could get it out of them personally, without recourse to a lawyer. Let me know sometime how it goes on. Meanwhile I send the packet, and do use any of them you like. Perhaps none of them will come in easily, but I should quite like it if they could. I was (as we all were) so fond of him. I'm glad the book seems going well.

All love,

R.

1 Gilbert Murray's letters were the only private letters to Rose that were preserved by her wish. In a memorandum, addressed to Jeanie and dated 13 August 1956, she wrote: 'Please ask the executors, or else do it yourself, to destroy all papers unread and in bulk, except those essential for business papers. I do not want letters and papers sorted and gone through. Please do not let any relations or friends go to the flat to help' (ERM 9.213). But, when Murray's executors wrote to ask Rose if she would be willing to add his letters to her to the collection of his papers in the Bodleian Library, she responded positively (letter of 9 March 1958 to Isobel Henderson: GM adds. 12.149). LeFanu 283 mentions a suggestion, emanating from Constance Babington Smith and Jeanie, that 'the reason that Rose had asked for all the papers in her flat to be destroyed was to ensure that one particular cousin, a convert to Roman Catholicism, should not be able to go through them'. The cousin who became a Catholic is of course Jean, but why should Rose or anyone else imagine that Jean would have wanted to go looking through Rose's private papers? What possible motive could Jean have had? In any case, she was not that kind of person: for over thirty years she had faithfully kept the secret of Rose's affair with Gerald O'Donovan, and she was to continue to keep it after Rose's death. The relations who, contrary to Rose's wishes, went through her letters and papers and made her private life public were Constance and Jeanie.

2 See *L*78 n. 1. As soon as Murray and his wife heard of the loss of Rose's library, he wrote to offer books from theirs (30 May 1941: GM 151.7). In her reply, Rose said that she would particularly welcome copies of his own translations of Greek plays (31 May 1941: GM 151.8).

3 *L*78 n. 2.

4 Rose has typed 'envelope'.

5 G.K. Chesterton, *Gloria in profundis* 12.

6 On 22 March 1955 Rose wrote to Jeanie: 'I have an intuition that I shall die in three years, i.e. in 1958' (*LS* 174). Her intuition was correct: she died at home of a heart attack in the morning of 30 October 1958, nine days after writing the present letter.

7 The last meeting between Rose and Jean, at Rose's flat, was very important to Jean. She recalled it in a letter of 11 March 1966 to her brother Henry: 'We had not seen *much* of each other for some time before her death – my rendering of the RC position, probably done stupidly, irritated her. But I came up to London for a weekend, ten

days before her death (from Oxford, where I was at the Gilbert Murray work), and went to tea with her on the Sunday Oct. <1>9 (1958). Unusually, she seemed to have unlimited time, and eventually drove me to my destination when I left: the best time I had had with her for years, of which I couldn't be more glad.'

Appendix 1
Rose Macaulay's birth and first weeks
INTRODUCTION

CBS 21 laments the loss of Grace Macaulay's diaries for 1881 and 1882, so that 'we know hardly anything of the first year of Rose's life'. However, among family papers in the present editor's custody are several letters written by Grace and/or George Macaulay in 1881. Three of them are of particular interest. The first was written on the day Rose was born (1 August 1881), the second a week after her birth, and the third when she was just over three weeks old. All three were written to Rose's paternal (Jean's maternal) grandmother, Anne Georgiana Macaulay, *née* Ferguson.

For comparison and contrast with Grace's and George's account of, and reactions to, Rose in the first hours, days, and weeks of her life, it is worthwhile to start by quoting some entries Grace made in her diary for 1880 after the birth of her first child, Margaret.

23 March
   '*Baby born at 2 a.m.* George not allowed to see it till morning because ugly – telegraphed to mother,[1] Mrs. Macaulay, and Edward.[2] Baby's features are swollen and shapeless, she is rather tall for her age and has a *thick* head of hair (dark).
   . . .
   Mother arrived (much longed for) at 2.30 and thought the baby much maligned.'

24 March
   'Baby showed much vigour and some selfwill.'

25 March
   '. . . Baby very obstinate and perverse – a most troublesome time all night.'

26 March
   'A very tiring day again with Baby who yells unceasingly and will do nothing she is told – the naughtiest and strongest child Mrs. Blyth[3] has ever had to do with. . . . Baby became submissive in the evening. Dr Dukes[4] orders not to put a foot to the ground for 4 weeks.'

5 April
'Got on the sofa.'

6 April
'Baby *is* improving. I feel quite proud of her now.'

13 April
'Baby three weeks old.

George got me a wicker work bath chair and took me out in the garden. He and cook (Sarah Wonder, who came when baby was 2 days old) carry me downstairs to sofa in diningroom daily now and up again at night, sedan-chair-wise'.

. . . .

14 April
'Mother went to Rothley Temple.

Baby is growing so pretty, her mouth and chin lovely now – and such nice downy dark hair.'

1 Eliza Conybeare.
2 Grace's brother, Edward Conybeare.
3 Mary Blyth, the nurse, was in her early 30s.
4 Clement Dukes, an able and versatile doctor, well qualified in obstetric medicine, was the physician to Rugby School, in which George was teaching at this time. Dukes held the post for 37 years (1871–1908) and had a formidable reputation with the boys on account of his abrupt manner and no-nonsense approach. His publications were to include several books on children's health, with particular reference to diet and hygiene.

LETTER I

1 August [1881]

My dearest mother

Nothing could have gone better than our affairs today, except that Grace has not got the boy she wished for, and was a good deal depressed by her disappointment, but she is pretty cheerful now and wonderfully well. The whole affair was very short. She only began to feel ill about half past seven this morning and the child was born before half past eight, while I was gone for the doctor. It is a better-looking baby than Margaret at her age, and different altogether, as Grace and I think, though others think her very like. She is also much quieter than Margaret, and has been lying like a lamb all the afternoon with Grace, though it must by this time be ravenously hungry. It has hair like Margaret, but a much less swollen face, and consequently not quite such slits of eyes. Complexion not good, but better than when first born – much larger than Margaret was at first (weighing over 9lb.)[1] – Grace wishes me to go away soon for a short time, and Kenneth[2] and I shall probably go to the Isle of Man for a few days. I do not think we should care for staying at any one place. I was over at the Glass Works[3] on Thursday and Kenneth came here (as you know) on Saturday and returned last night.[4]

My love to Nannie.[5] I wonder when we shall see you or her next. Is Aunt Fanny at Shenfield now?[6] We were intending to send her Margaret's photographs when she was at home again. I suppose you do not exactly know what your plans are to be.

Your affectionate son
G.C. Macaulay
Rugby.

1 When Rose was 70, she weighed only 7 stone, despite being 5 feet 8 inches tall (*LF* 313). Who would have guessed that she had such a high birth weight?
2 George's brother.
3 Chance Brothers of Smethwick, Birmingham, the company in which Kenneth made his career.
4 Sunday.
5 George's sister and Jean's mother. Aged twenty and not yet married, she was living at home with her widowed mother in Hodnet, Shropshire.
6 Frances Ferguson was an elder, unmarried sister of George's mother. She lived with her widowed brother Thomas Ferguson, Rector of Shenfield in Essex.

LETTER 2

Rugby
8 August [18]81

My dear Mother[1] – I will write just a line to tell you myself how well we are getting on and what a darling our new little one is. She is the sweetest quietest most contented and pretty baby I ever saw. It is impossible for even me to regret the boy that I wanted in her place. I think she will be like George as she grows older.[2] I study the dear little face for hours. I do so hope you will see the likeness as I do. She has lovely little features, and Miss Bowden Smith[3] who is very sincere said she thought her far the prettiest child of under a month old she had ever seen. 'Such a perfect little *lady*', is Mother's comment on her. You will come and see her and all of us will you not, next week? We do so want you dear Mother. George would be very much disappointed if you did not come. I have a telegram from him today in good spirits from Castletown just starting to walk to Port Erin. They go on to Peel if all is well. I am so very glad he got K. as a companion. I would not have got him to go alone for a change, and indeed it would not have done him half the good. Kenneth is such a delightful companion. – You ask baby's name. We think of calling her Emilie Rose after my dear friend and cousin.[4] I should rather like as you suggest to *call* her Rose but G. likes Emilie best, however that can be settled later.[5]

Mother says I must stop – your loving child
Grace Macaulay
Nannie's letter was very welcome to us.

1 Grace is actually writing to her mother-in-law.
2 Writing to Hamilton Johnson on 16 May 1952, Rose says: 'I believe I take entirely after my father's family, and look very like him, and still more (I was always told) like his mother . . .' (*LF* 314).
3 Emily, the eldest daughter, and the second eldest of the 12 children, of the Rev. Philip Bowden Smith, assistant master at Rugby School 1852–1895, and his wife, Emily. She was aged 25 at this time.
4 Emilie Rose, who died of cancer on 21 July 1880, five days after her 29th birthday, was Grace's first cousin. Her father, Henry Rose, was a brother of Grace's mother.
5 As ERM grew up, the preferred name was at times 'Emilie' or 'Emily' rather than 'Rose' or 'Rosie'. During her adult life she was 'Rose', but her first Christian name proved useful whenever she wanted to conceal her real identity, most notably when she appeared in court in 1939 after a car crash (*L*78 n. 1).

LETTER 3

Rugby
23 August 1881[1]

The first paragraph is written by Grace. George then takes over and signs off, but Grace returns to give more news.

My dear Mother –

We are so very sorry to think of your being knocked up by the long day of travelling. I trust you are really better now and resting comfortably at Durley.[2] It is such a nice peaceful place to rest in, and I think drives are good for you too are they not? I shall not soon forget the pleasant days we spent there last year. – All is going very well with us. I write this lying on the drawing room sofa fully dressed again at last and feeling so well. Dear baby flourishes and grows prettier and more intelligent looking daily. I have got just enough for her, but she has such a good appetite that it was thought best to give her one bottle in the 24 hours. It seems not to make the least difference to her health and makes the difference between my having only just enough and *plenty*.

Grace is obliged to break off by baby's entrance so I am going to finish the letter. We have had Edward and his eldest boy here for a night and this morning we all went down to the station to see Frances and the rest of her children on their way to the North.[3] Grace was wheeled down in the bathchair in which she goes out regularly now, and she is certainly remarkably strong and well. I do hope that you are feeling better now. We are intending to go to Margate I think – probably on Monday next[4] but perhaps on Saturday.[5] We shall probably stay at the Cliftonville Hotel, at any rate at first. It would be very pleasant to see something of you, but I do not know whether this move would suit you. The reason we go there is because it is good sea air and not much out of the way. My love to all.

Your affect[ionate] G.C.M.

I have still a few minutes before post time now baby has left again. The bathchair of which G. speaks is a delightful plan by which I get fresh air without draughts, and George wheels me and Margaret together in it into the school close generally where I sit well bundled up in wraps while he and she run races after the lambs and have all sorts of fun together. We get on well without the monthly nurse for my mother quite takes the place, dressing and undressing me and forcing me to be prudent, tho' indeed I am willing enough to be so. The nursery maid came on Saturday and seems to do very well. Baby is so good and sweet tempered that she passed into Bessie's hands without any fretting. Mother says she never knew so good an infant. It would be delightful to meet you by the sea if you are only well enough to move there safely before we leave.[6] We hope to go to Weybridge[7] on the 12th. Love to Nannie and thanks for her letter. I will write soon – your loving child G.M.M.

1 The letter is not dated, but the envelope is franked 'RUGBY AU 23 81'.
2 A village in Hampshire, on the Southampton side of Bishop's Waltham. George's mother was staying with her brother Richard Ferguson and his wife, Louisa. Richard was Rector of Durley.
3 Edward and Frances Conybeare had three sons followed by two daughters. The eldest son was James, aged nine at this time. Edward records his and James's visit to Rugby in his diary for 22–23 August. He mentions that he 'found Grace wondrous well, and *Emily Rose* very like me'. His diary reveals that Frances had been 'to see new Rugby babe' on 11 August, and that his and his family's destination on 23 August was Ellergreen, near Kendal, in the Lake District, where the Croppers, his wife's family, had – and still have – a paper-making business and owned Tolson Hall.
4 29 August.
5 27 August.
6 George's mother never made it to the seaside and never set eyes on her second grand-daughter, for she died at Durley on 7 September 1881, just 15 days after this letter was written.
7 The home of Grace's mother.

Appendix 2
'Ash Wednesday 1941'

Among the Rose Macaulay papers in Trinity College, Cambridge, is the type-script of a 40-line poem entitled 'Ash Wednesday 1941' (ERM 8.74). On the back of the sheet of paper Jeanie has written: 'I don't know what this is.' Although the authorship of the piece is not indicated, Alice Crawford assigns it to Rose. She prints the whole poem in her book *Paradise Pursued*, Appendix B (162–163), and comments on it in the body of the book (140). Here is what she says:

> 'Ash Wednesday 1941' incorporates familiar Macaulayan ideas and images. Souls in the Platonic cave read the play of shadows from the world above; the wholeness of deity subsumes the partiality of humanity; the subject strives towards union with God. Perhaps inspired by her sister's death in March 1941, this piece is striking for its specifically religious overtones.

This is unfortunate, for the author of the poem is not Rose, but Jean. It is not known where, or even if, she published it, but among her papers are her manu-script, dated 1941, and two typescript versions with manuscript notes and altera-tions, including one alteration made as late as 1975; also preserved are two pages of notes relating to the poem – one mainly in typescript, the other entirely in manuscript. In a letter she wrote to Gilbert Murray on 21 September 1952 and must have retrieved from his papers after his death, she says: 'You said I might send you the fragment (which I call *skias onar*).[1] The theme is the morning rite for Ash Wednesday, coming as it did in 1941 among such a lot of dust and ashes.' He sent her his comments in a letter of 28 September. The first sentence reads: 'I have kept the poem to read and re-read, and I think it is a beauty though part of the thought is rather beyond me.' Perhaps Jean sent the poem to Rose around the same time.

---

1 'A shadow's dream'. This is how the fifth-century BC Greek poet Pindar describes a human being (*Pythian* 8.95). Jean's poem contains the phrase in both Greek and English.

Bibliography

WORKS BY ROSE MACAULAY

All references to Rose's books in the present work are to the first English editions. The first American editions, with any variations of title or date, are recorded here in parentheses. The works in each section are listed in chronological order.

1 Novels

Abbots Verney: A Novel. London: John Murray, 1906.

The Furnace. London: John Murray, 1907.

The Secret River. London: John Murray, 1909.

The Valley Captives. London: John Murray, 1911. (New York: Henry Holt.)

Views and Vagabonds. London: John Murray, 1912. (New York: Henry Holt.)

The Lee Shore. London: Hodder & Stoughton, 1912. (New York: Doran.)

The Making of a Bigot. London: Hodder & Stoughton, 1914.

Non-Combatants and Others. London: Hodder & Stoughton, 1916.

What Not: A Prophetic Comedy. London: Constable, 1918 (so dated, but not published until March 1919).

Potterism: A Tragi-farcical Tract. London: W. Collins, 1920. (New York: Boni & Liveright.)

Dangerous Ages. London: W. Collins, 1921. (New York: Boni & Liveright.)

Mystery at Geneva: An Improbable Tale of Singular Happenings. London: W. Collins, 1922. (New York: Boni & Liveright, 1923.)

Told by an Idiot. London: W. Collins, 1923. (New York: Boni & Liveright, 1924.)

Orphan Island. London: W. Collins, 1924. (New York: Boni & Liveright, 1925.)

Crewe Train. London: W. Collins, 1926. (New York: Boni & Liveright.)

Keeping up Appearances. London: W. Collins, 1928. (*Daisy and Daphne.* New York: Boni & Liveright.)

Staying with Relations. London: W. Collins, 1930. (New York: Horace Liveright.)

They Were Defeated. London: Collins, 1932. (*The Shadow Flies.* New York: Harper.)

Going Abroad: A Novel. London: Collins, 1934. (New York: Harper.)

I Would Be Private. London: Collins, 1937. (New York: Harper.)

And No Man's Wit. London: Collins, 1940. (Boston: Little, Brown.)

The World My Wilderness. London: Collins, 1950. (Boston: Little, Brown.)

The Towers of Trebizond. London: Collins, 1956. (New York: Farrar, Straus & Cudahy, 1957.)

Venice Besieged. Fragments in *Letters to a Sister* (Bibliog. I.6) 299–327.

2 History and Travel

Life Among the English. London: William Collins, 1942.

They Went to Portugal. London: Jonathan Cape, 1946

Fabled Shore: From the Pyrenees to Portugal. London: Hamish Hamilton, 1949. (New York: Farrar, Straus.)

Pleasure of Ruins. London: Weidenfeld and Nicolson, 1953. (New York: Walker, 1966.)

They Went to Portugal Too (introd. Susan Lowndes; ed. L.C. Taylor). Manchester: Carcanet Press, 1990.

3 Essays and Literary Criticism

A Casual Commentary. London: Methuen, 1925. (New York: Boni & Liveright, 1926.)

Catchwords and Claptrap. London: Hogarth Press, 1926.

Some Religious Elements in English Literature. London: Hogarth Press, 1931. (New York: Harcourt, Brace.)

Milton. London: Duckworth. 1934. (New York: Harper, 1935.)

Personal Pleasures. London: Victor Gollancz, 1935. (New York: Macmillan, 1936.)

An Open Letter to a Non-Pacifist. W. Collins for the Peace Pledge Union, 1937. Reprinted from *Time and Tide*, 5 December 1936, pp. 1695–1697.

The Writings of E.M. Forster. London: Hogarth Press, 1938. (New York: Harcourt, Brace.)

4 Collected Poetry

The Two Blind Countries. London: Sidgwick & Jackson, 1914.

Three Days. London: Constable, 1919.

The Augustan Books of English Poetry 2nd series no. 6: *Rose Macaulay*, ed. Humbert Wolfe. London: Ernest Benn, [1927]. A selection of 21 poems, 19 of them contained in the two collections just listed.

5 Anthologies

The Minor Pleasures of Life. London: Victor Gollancz, 1934. (New York: Harper, 1935.)

All in a Maze: A Collection of Prose and Verse Chronologically Arranged by Daniel George *with Some Assistance from* Rose Macaulay. London: Collins, 1938.

6 Letters

Letters to a Friend from Rose Macaulay 1950–1952, ed. Constance Babington Smith. London: Collins, 1961. (New York: Atheneum, 1962.)

Last Letters to a Friend from Rose Macaulay 1952–1958, ed. Constance Babington Smith. London: Collins, 1962. (New York: Atheneum, 1963.)

Letters to a Sister from Rose Macaulay, ed. Constance Babington Smith. London: Collins, 1964. (New York: Atheneum.)

7 Selected Articles

'The Empty Berth', *The Cornhill Magazine* new series 35 (July–December 1913) 186–196.

'Miss Anstruther's Letters', in Storm Jameson (ed.), *London Calling: A Salute to America*

(New York, 1942) 299–308. (Reprinted: *The Times*, 23 September 1972, 'Saturday Review' 8; CBS 161–170.)

'Coming to London – XIII', *The London Magazine* 4, 3 (March 1957) 30–36. (Reprinted: W. Plomer et al., *Coming to London* (London, 1957) 155–166.)

II Books about Rose Macaulay

Babington Smith, Constance. *Rose Macaulay*. London: Collins, 1972.

Bensen, Alice R. *Rose Macaulay*. New York: Twayne, 1969.

Benton, Jill. *Avenging Muse: Naomi Royde-Smith, 1875–1945*. Xlibris, 2015.

Crawford, Alice. *Paradise Pursued: The Novels of Rose Macaulay*. Madison, NJ/London: Fairleigh Dickinson University Press/Associated University Presses, 1995.

Emery, Jane. *Rose Macaulay: A Writer's Life*. London: John Murray, 1991.

Feigel, Lara. *The Love-charm of Bombs: Restless Lives in the Second World War*. London, Bloomsbury, 2013.

LeFanu, Sarah. *Dreaming of Rose: A Biographer's Journal*. Bristol: SilverWood, 2013.

LeFanu, Sarah. *Rose Macaulay*. London: Virago, 2003.

Passty, Jeanette N. *Eros and Androgyny: The Legacy of Rose Macaulay*. Rutherford [NJ]/London: Fairleigh Dickinson University Press/Associated University Presses, 1988.

Key to first names

BILL: A.W. Smith, *brother of Jean*
CHARLIE, UNCLE: C.S. Smith, *husband of Nannie; father of Jean*
DOROTHY (1): D. Brooke *née* Lamb, later Nicholson, *wife of Reeve*
DOROTHY (2): D. Gillum *née* Smith, *sister of Jean*
ELEANOR: E.G. Macaulay, *sister of Rose*
EMILY: E.J.M. Smith, later Cain, *daughter of Bill and Isadore; god-daughter of Rose*
GERALD: G. O'Donovan, *Rose's lover*
HENRY: H.F. Smith, *brother of Jean*
ISADORE: I.L. Smith *née* Luce, *wife of Bill*
JEANIE: J.B. Macaulay, *sister of Rose*
JIM (1): J.S. Smith, *brother of Jean*
JIM (2): J.M. Smith, *younger son of Bill and Isadore*
KENNETH, UNCLE: K.A. Macaulay, *brother of Rose's father and of Jean's mother*
MADELEINE: M.J. Symons, later Robinson, *friend of Jean and Rose*
MARGARET: M.C. Macaulay, *sister of Rose*
MARY, AUNT: M.F. Macaulay, *sister of Rose's father and of Jean's mother*
NANNIE, AUNT: A.G. Smith, *sister of Rose's father; mother of Jean*
NAOMI: N.G. Royde-Smith, *literary editor and writer; friend of Rose*
PRUE: P.M. Smith *née* Martin, *wife of Tom (1)*
REEVE: J.R. Brooke, *first husband of Dorothy Brooke*
REGI(E), UNCLE: R.H. Macaulay, *brother of Rose's father and of Jean's mother*
REG(G)IE: C.R. Smith, *brother of Jean*
ROSEMARY: R.S.M. Smith *née* Hughes, *wife of Jim (1)*
TERESA: T.M. Symons, later Corbett, *daughter of Madeleine*
TOM (1): T.M. Smith, *brother of Jean*
TOM (2): T.W.M. Smith, *elder son of Bill and Isadore*
WILL: W.J.C. Macaulay, *brother of Rose*
WILLIE, UNCLE: W.H. Macaulay, *brother of Rose's father and of Jean's mother*

FAMILY TREES

I   THE FAMILY OF ROSE MACAULAY

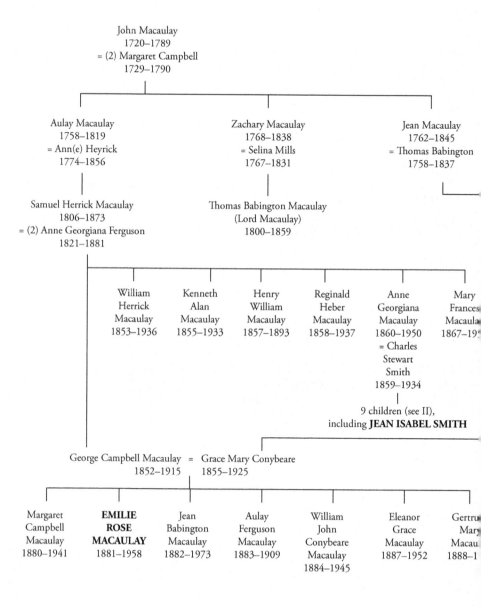

John Macaulay
1720–1789
= (2) Margaret Campbell
1729–1790

Aulay Macaulay
1758–1819
= Ann(e) Heyrick
1774–1856

Zachary Macaulay
1768–1838
= Selina Mills
1767–1831

Jean Macaulay
1762–1845
= Thomas Babington
1758–1837

Samuel Herrick Macaulay
1806–1873
= (2) Anne Georgiana Ferguson
1821–1881

Thomas Babington Macaulay
(Lord Macaulay)
1800–1859

William
Herrick
Macaulay
1853–1936

Kenneth
Alan
Macaulay
1855–1933

Henry
William
Macaulay
1857–1893

Reginald
Heber
Macaulay
1858–1937

Anne
Georgiana
Macaulay
1860–1950
= Charles
Stewart
Smith
1859–1934

Mary
Frances
Macaula
1867–19

9 children (see II),
including **JEAN ISABEL SMITH**

George Campbell Macaulay = Grace Mary Conybeare
1852–1915   1855–1925

Margaret
Campbell
Macaulay
1880–1941

**EMILIE
ROSE
MACAULAY**
1881–1958

Jean
Babington
Macaulay
1882–1973

Aulay
Ferguson
Macaulay
1883–1909

William
John
Conybeare
Macaulay
1884–1945

Eleanor
Grace
Macaulay
1887–1952

Gertru
Mary
Macau
1888–1

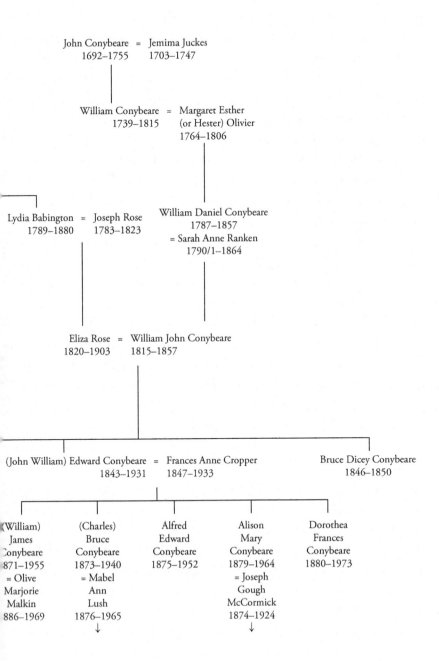

John Conybeare = Jemima Juckes
1692–1755   1703–1747

William Conybeare = Margaret Esther
1739–1815   (or Hester) Olivier
1764–1806

Lydia Babington = Joseph Rose   William Daniel Conybeare
1789–1880   1783–1823   1787–1857
= Sarah Anne Ranken
1790/1–1864

Eliza Rose = William John Conybeare
1820–1903   1815–1857

(John William) Edward Conybeare = Frances Anne Cropper   Bruce Dicey Conybeare
1843–1931   1847–1933   1846–1850

(William)   (Charles)   Alfred   Alison   Dorothea
James   Bruce   Edward   Mary   Frances
Conybeare   Conybeare   Conybeare   Conybeare   Conybeare
1871–1955   1873–1940   1875–1952   1879–1964   1880–1973
= Olive   = Mabel   = Joseph
Marjorie   Ann   Gough
Malkin   Lush   McCormick
1886–1969   1876–1965   1874–1924
↓   ↓

THE FAMILY OF JEAN SMITH

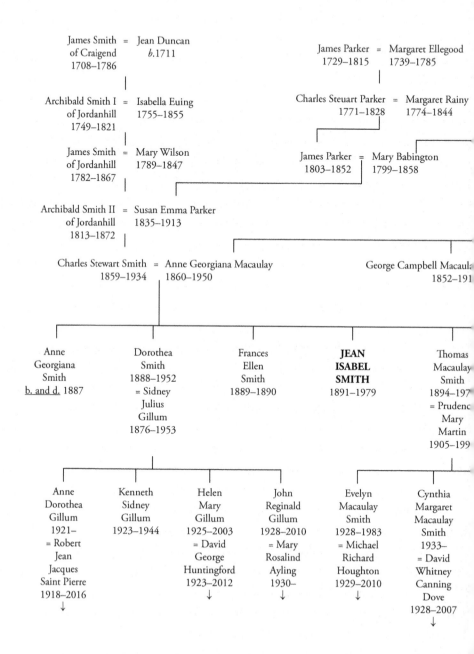

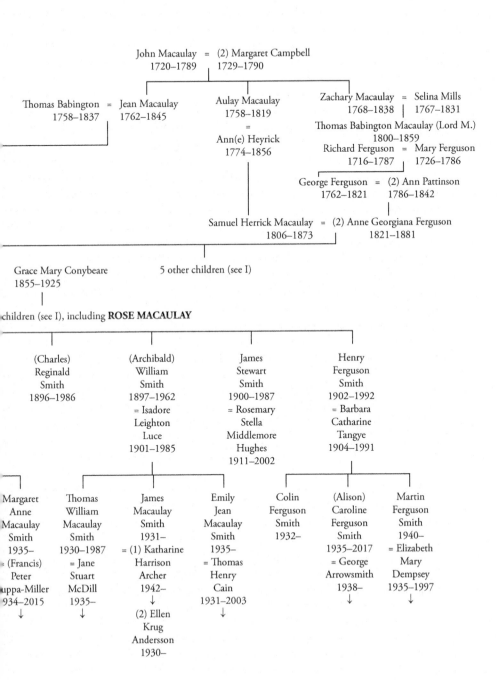

Index

Note: 'n.' after a page reference indicates the number of a note on that page. Numbers in **bold** refer to illustrations.

Lightning Source UK Ltd.
Milton Keynes UK
UKOW01f1312101017
310734UK00004B/490/P